kare kano

his and her circumstances

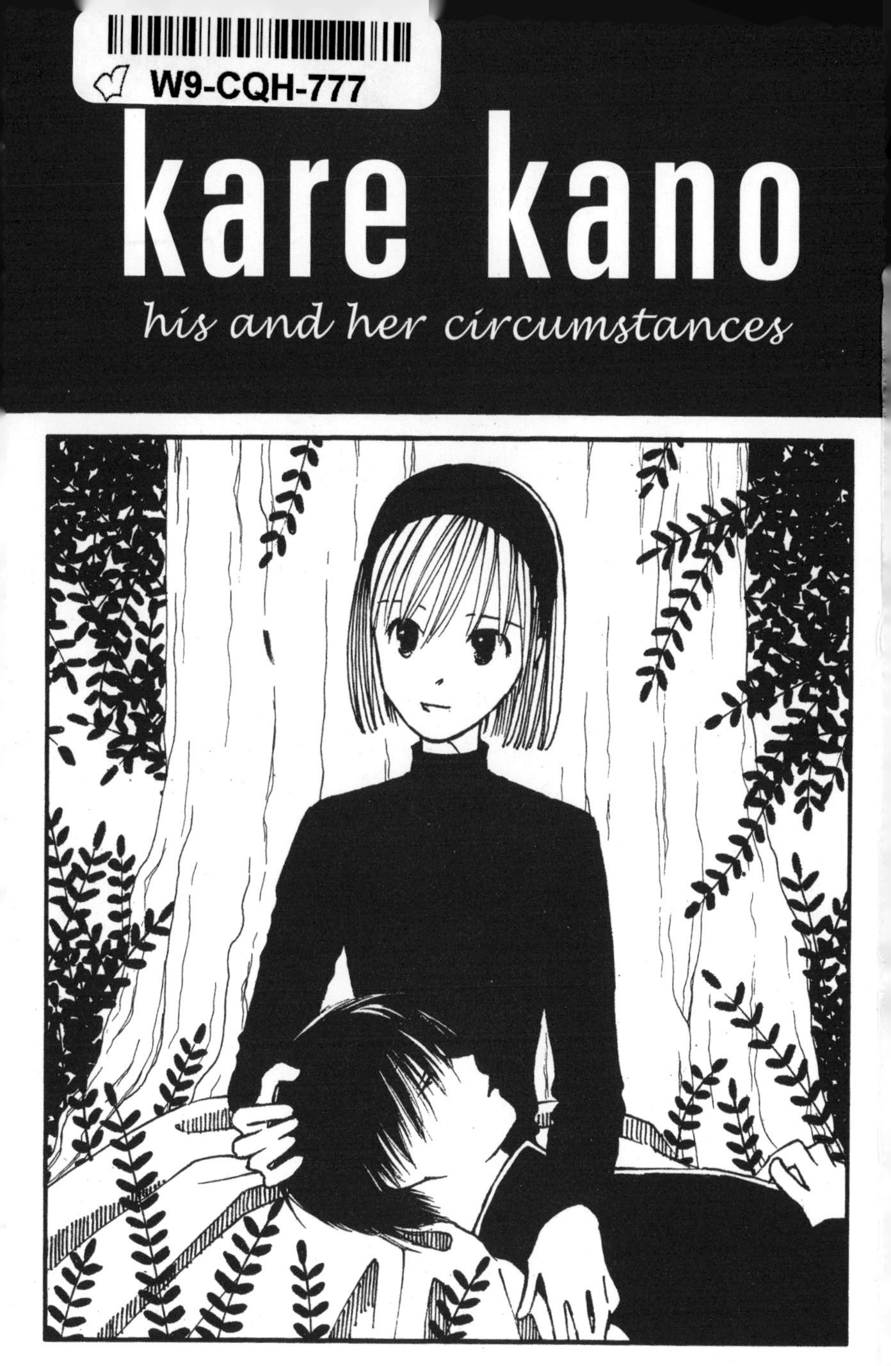

ALSO AVAILABLE FROM TOKYOPOP®

For more
information visit
www.TOKYOPOP.com

03.03.04T

ALSO AVAILABLE FROM ☺TOKYOPOP®

MANGA

.HACK//LEGEND OF THE TWILIGHT
@LARGE
ABENOBASHI: MAGICAL SHOPPING ARCADE
A.I. LOVE YOU
AI YORI AOSHI
ANGELIC LAYER
ARM OF KANNON
BABY BIRTH
BATTLE ROYALE
BATTLE VIXENS
BRAIN POWERED
BRIGADOON
B'TX
CANDIDATE FOR GODDESS, THE
CARDCAPTOR SAKURA
CARDCAPTOR SAKURA - MASTER OF THE CLOW
CHOBITS
CHRONICLES OF THE CURSED SWORD
CLAMP SCHOOL DETECTIVES
CLOVER
COMIC PARTY
CONFIDENTIAL CONFESSIONS
CORRECTOR YUI
COWBOY BEBOP
COWBOY BEBOP: SHOOTING STAR
CRAZY LOVE STORY
CRESCENT MOON
CULDCEPT
CYBORG 009
D•N•ANGEL
DEMON DIARY
DEMON ORORON, THE
DEUS VITAE
DIGIMON
DIGIMON TAMERS
DIGIMON ZERO TWO
DOLL
DRAGON HUNTER
DRAGON KNIGHTS
DRAGON VOICE
DREAM SAGA
DUKLYON: CLAMP SCHOOL DEFENDERS
EERIE QUEERIE!
END, THE
ERICA SAKURAZAWA: COLLECTED WORKS
ET CETERA
ETERNITY
EVIL'S RETURN
FAERIES' LANDING
FAKE
FLCL
FORBIDDEN DANCE
FRUITS BASKET
G GUNDAM
GATEKEEPERS

GETBACKERS
GIRL GOT GAME
GRAVITATION
GTO
GUNDAM BLUE DESTINY
GUNDAM SEED ASTRAY
GUNDAM WING
GUNDAM WING: BATTLEFIELD OF PACIFISTS
GUNDAM WING: ENDLESS WALTZ
GUNDAM WING: THE LAST OUTPOST (G-UNIT)
GUYS' GUIDE TO GIRLS
HANDS OFF!
HAPPY MANIA
HARLEM BEAT
I.N.V.U.
IMMORTAL RAIN
INITIAL D
INSTANT TEEN: JUST ADD NUTS
ISLAND
JING: KING OF BANDITS
JING: KING OF BANDITS - TWILIGHT TALES
JULINE
KARE KANO
KILL ME, KISS ME
KINDAICHI CASE FILES, THE
KING OF HELL
KODOCHA: SANA'S STAGE
LAMENT OF THE LAMB
LEGAL DRUG
LEGEND OF CHUN HYANG, THE
LES BIJOUX
LOVE HINA
LUPIN III
LUPIN III: WORLD'S MOST WANTED
MAGIC KNIGHT RAYEARTH I
MAGIC KNIGHT RAYEARTH II
MAHOROMATIC: AUTOMATIC MAIDEN
MAN OF MANY FACES
MARMALADE BOY
MARS
MARS: HORSE WITH NO NAME
METROID
MINK
MIRACLE GIRLS
MIYUKI-CHAN IN WONDERLAND
MODEL
ONE
ONE I LOVE, THE
PARADISE KISS
PARASYTE
PASSION FRUIT
PEACH GIRL
PEACH GIRL: CHANGE OF HEART
PET SHOP OF HORRORS
PITA-TEN
PLANET LADDER

03.03.04T

Translator - Michelle Kobayashi
English Adaptation - Darcy Lockman
Retouch and Lettering - Keiko Okabe
Cover Layout - Gary Shum
Graphic Designer - Yoohae Yang

Editor - Julie Taylor
Digital Imaging Manager - Chris Buford
Pre-Press Manager - Antonio DePietro
Production Managers - Jennifer Miller, Mutsumi Miyazaki
Art Director - Matt Alford
Managing Editor - Jill Freshney
VP of Production - Ron Klamert
President & C.O.O. - John Parker
Publisher & C.E.O. - Stuart Levy

E-mail: info@TOKYOPOP.com

Come visit us online at www.TOKYOPOP.com

A  Manga

TOKYOPOP Inc.
5900 Wilshire Blvd. Suite 2000
Los Angeles, CA 90036

Kare Kano Vol. 9
KARESHI KANOJO NO JIJOU by Masami Tsuda © 1999 Masami Tsuda.
All rights reserved. First published in Japan in 2000 by HAKUSENSHA, INC., Tokyo
English language translation rights in the United States of America
and Canada arranged with HAKUSENSHA, INC., Tokyo
through Tuttle-Mori Agency Inc., Tokyo

English text copyright ©2004 TOKYOPOP Inc.

ISBN: 1-59182-474-5

First TOKYOPOP® printing: May 2004

10 9 8 7 6 5 4 3 2 1

Printed in the USA

kare kano

his and her circumstances

volume nine
by Masami Tsuda

LOS ANGELES • TOKYO • LONDON

kare kano
volume nine

TABLE OF CONTENTS

KARE KANO: THE STORY SO FAR

Yukino Miyazawa is the perfect student: kind, athletic and smart. But she's not all she seems. She is really the self-professed "queen of vanity," and her only goal in life is winning the praise and admiration of everyone around her. Therefore, she makes it her business to always look and act perfect during school hours. At home, however, she lets her guard down and lets her true self show.

When Yukino enters high school, she finally meets her match: Soichiro Arima, a handsome, popular, ultra-intelligent guy. Once he steals the top seat in class away from her, Yukino sees him as a bitter rival. Over time, her anger turns to amazement, when she discovers she and Soichiro have more in common than she ever imagined. As their love blossoms, they promise to stop pretending to be perfect and just be true to themselves.

But they have plenty of obstacles in their way. First, Hideaki, the school's token pretty boy, tries to come between them. Then, Yukino and Soichiro's grades drop because they've been spending so much time together, and their teacher pressures them to break up. Once that's resolved, two more speed bumps are encountered on their road to romance. Maho, a jealous classmate, is convinced that Yukino is deceiving everyone and vows to turn everyone against her. Then, an old friend of Soichiro's from junior high tries to steal Soichiro's affections. Somehow, Yukino and Soichiro's love manages to persevere...even after Soichiro spends the summer away at a kendo tournament. In fact, it makes their romance that much stronger, although Soichiro is trying to deal with some personal issues. When Tonami, a transfer student who's been away for three years, returns to school, sparks start to fly between he and Tsubaki. There's also a major rivalry going on between Tonami and Soichiro. But all that takes a backseat to the upcoming culture festival. Everybody's totally psyched, especially Aya, who's written a new play, just for the occasion!

DAISY = YOUTH

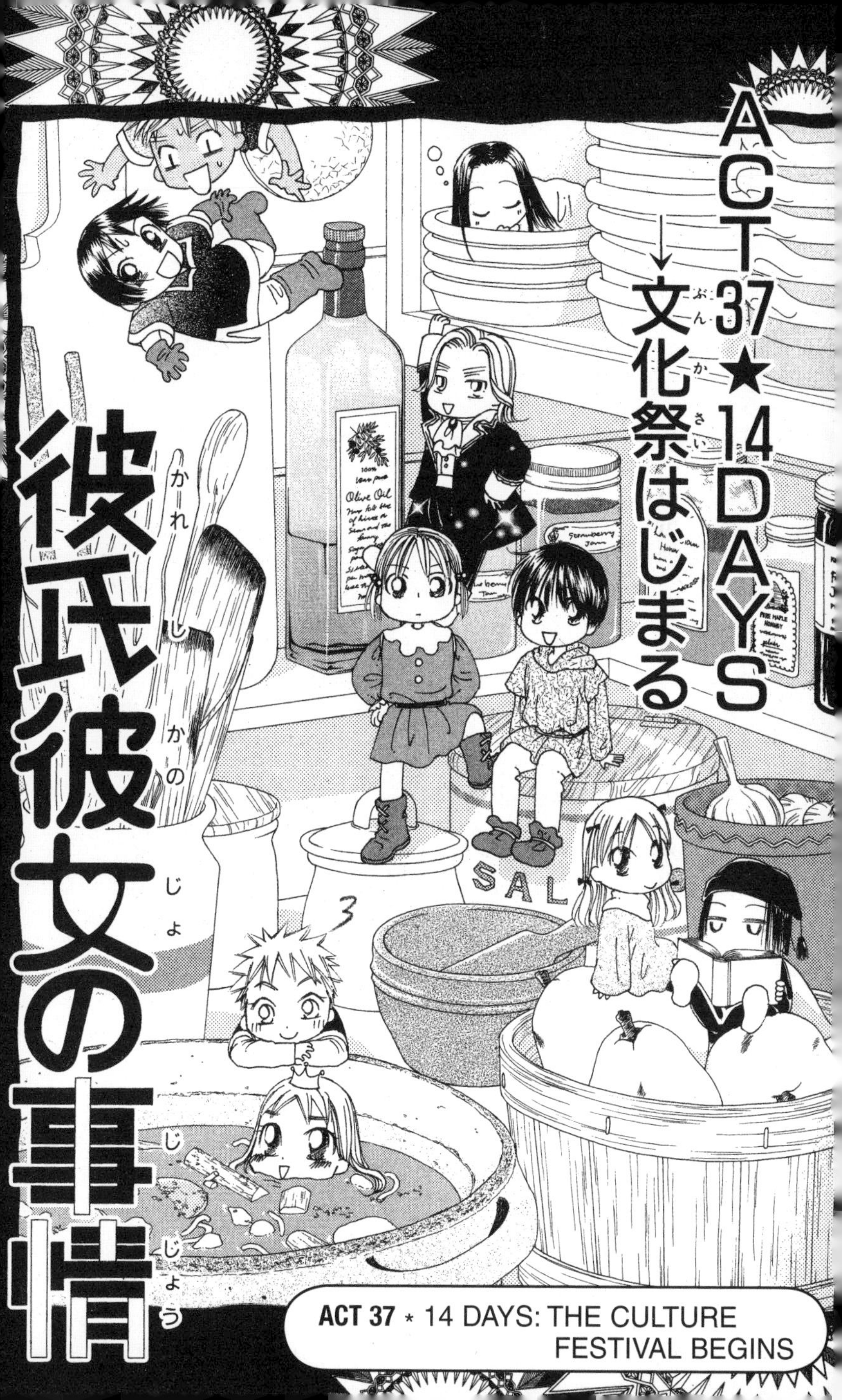
ACT 37★14 DAYS
文化祭はじまる
彼氏彼女の事情
Olive Oil
SAL
ACT 37 ⋆ 14 DAYS: THE CULTURE FESTIVAL BEGINS

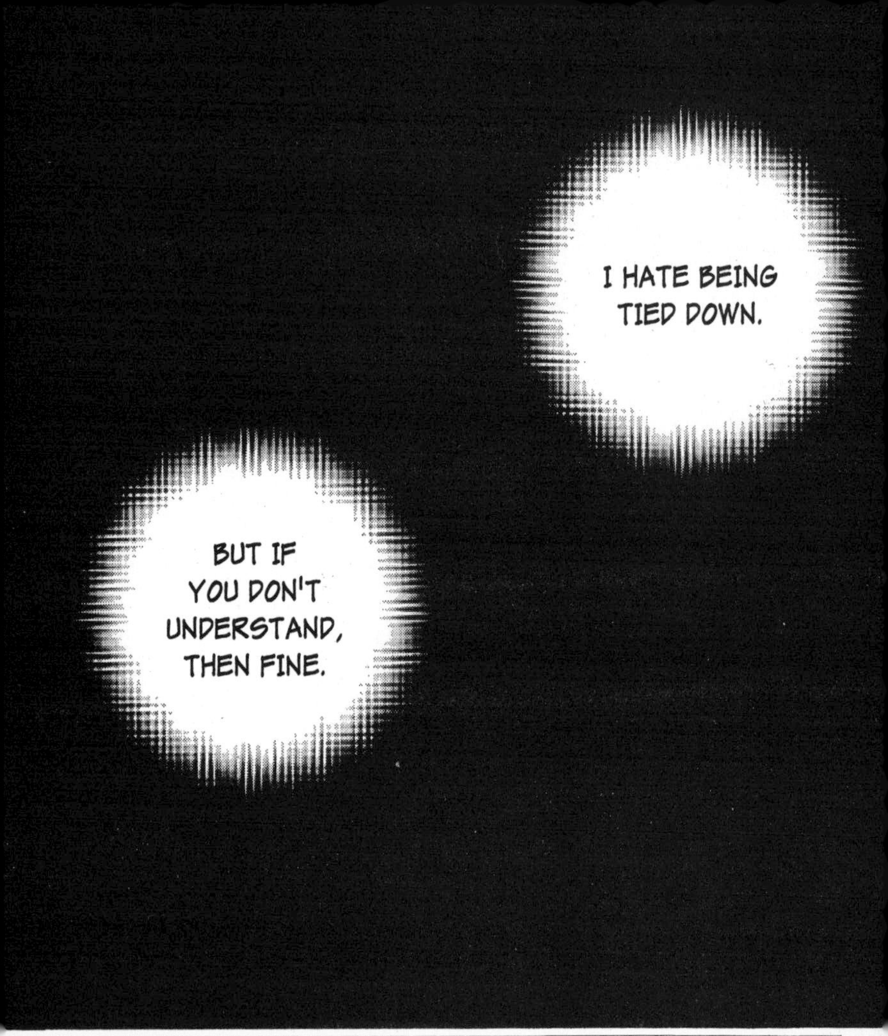
I HATE BEING TIED DOWN.
BUT IF YOU DON'T UNDERSTAND, THEN FINE.

Hi everybody!

Yours truly is in the middle of a "tea craze" right now. I'm gulping down all kinds of different teas, like Japanese green tea, roasted green tea, and coarse leaf tea (it's so aromatic and tasty!).

Next, I want to try brown rice tea.

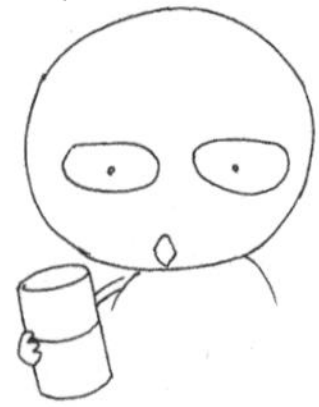

Drinking lots of Japanese teas is good for you! I highly recommend it!

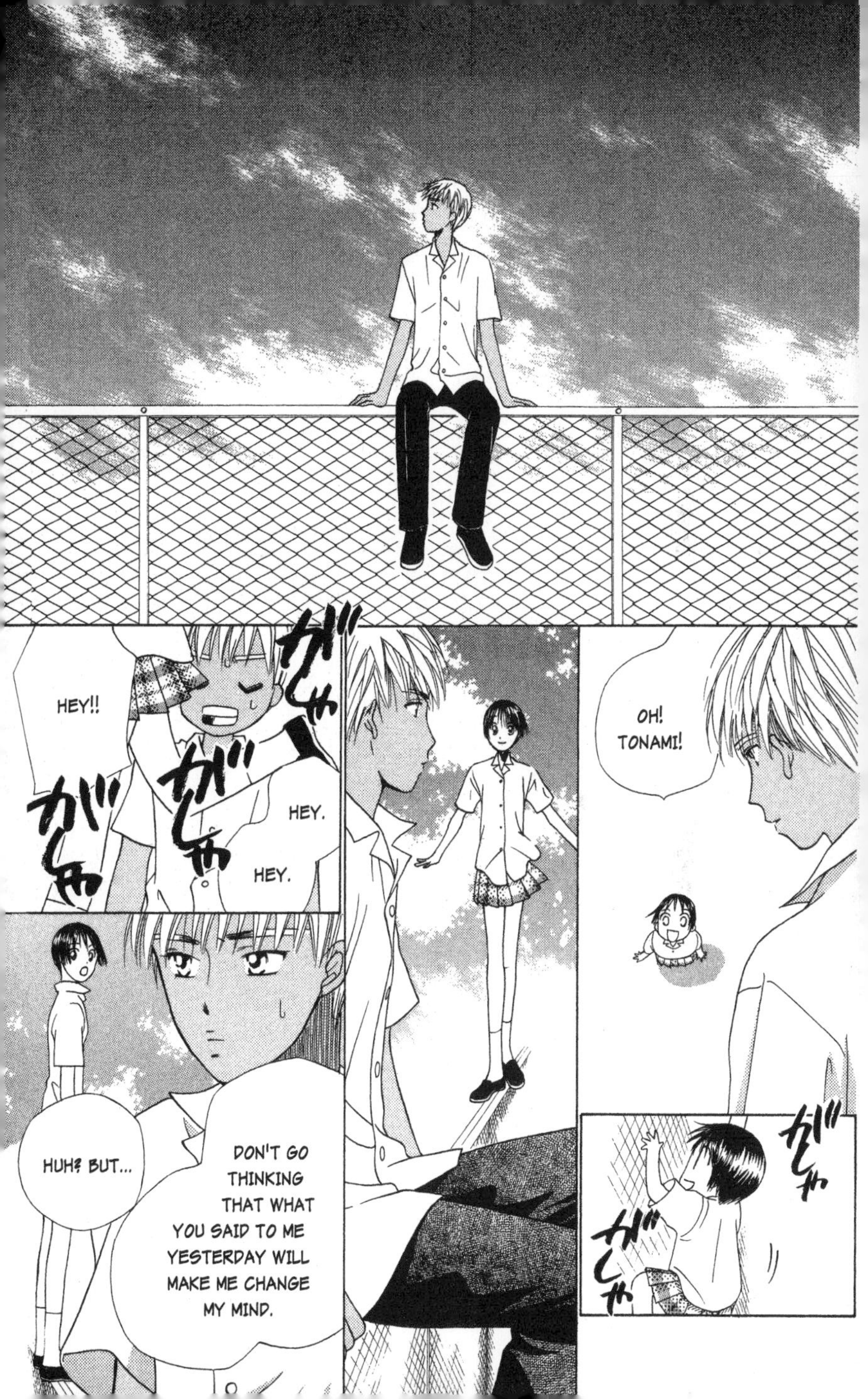
OH! TONAMI!
HEY!!
HEY.
HEY.
DON'T GO THINKING THAT WHAT YOU SAID TO ME YESTERDAY WILL MAKE ME CHANGE MY MIND.
HUH? BUT...

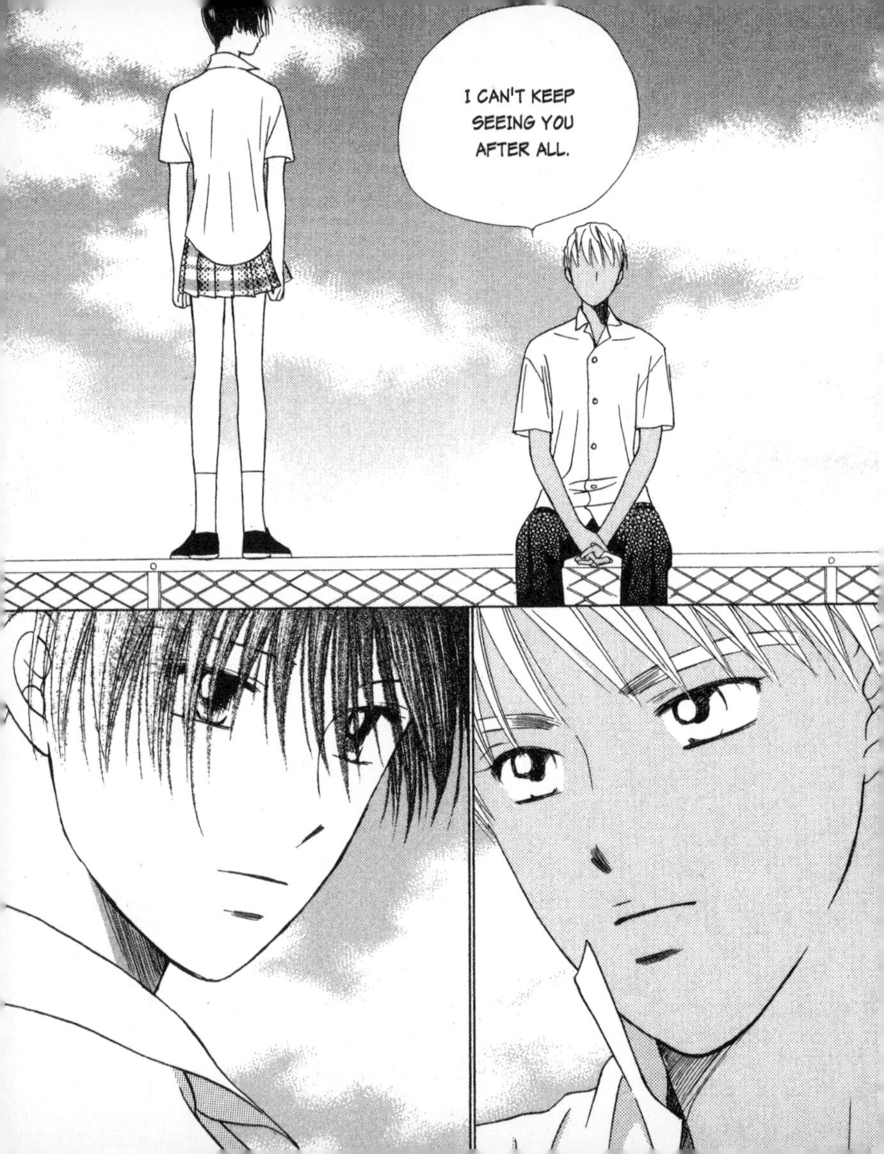
I CAN'T KEEP SEEING YOU AFTER ALL.

1

This is it!

Kare Kano volume 9!!

I'm writing this little piece during a one month vacation (It's November, 1999). We're heading for the year 2000.

I'm spending my time getting massages, going to the dentist (to get my wisdom teeth pulled), and going to the gym (for the first time in 6 months!) to build some muscles.

And I think I need to get new glasses too...

My wisdom teeth were starting to come in.

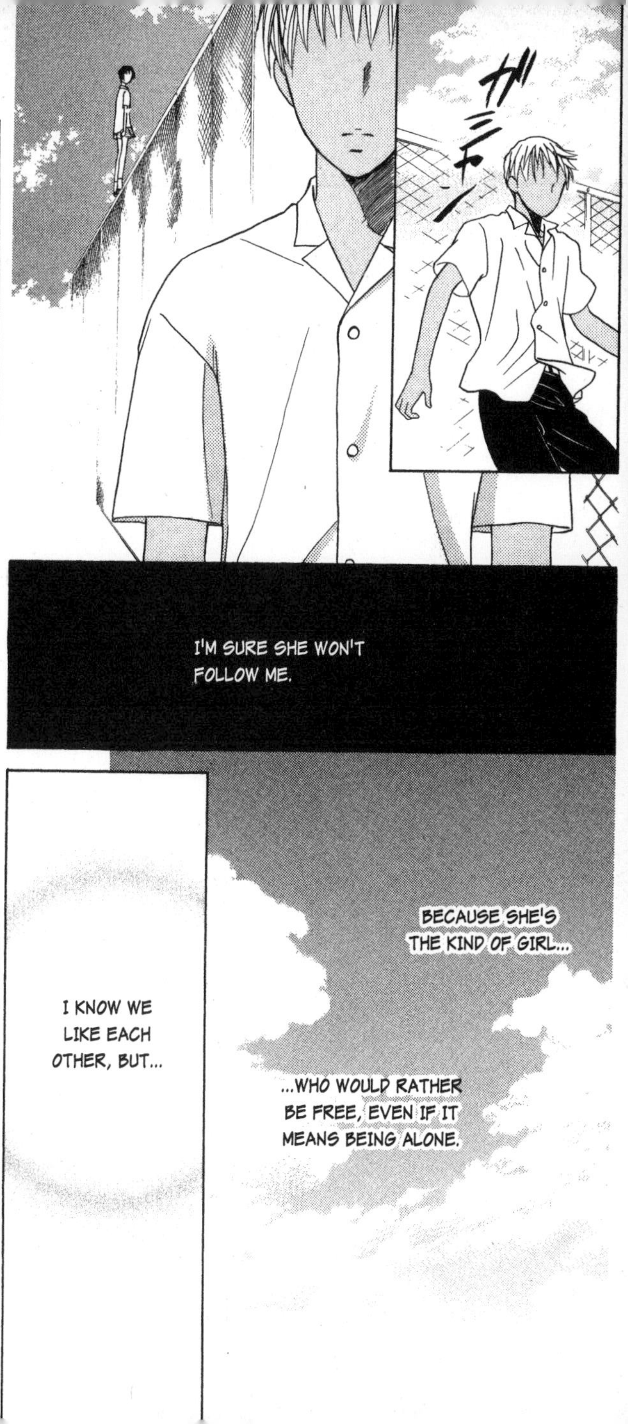
I'M SURE SHE WON'T FOLLOW ME.
BECAUSE SHE'S THE KIND OF GIRL...
...WHO WOULD RATHER BE FREE, EVEN IF IT MEANS BEING ALONE.
I KNOW WE LIKE EACH OTHER, BUT...

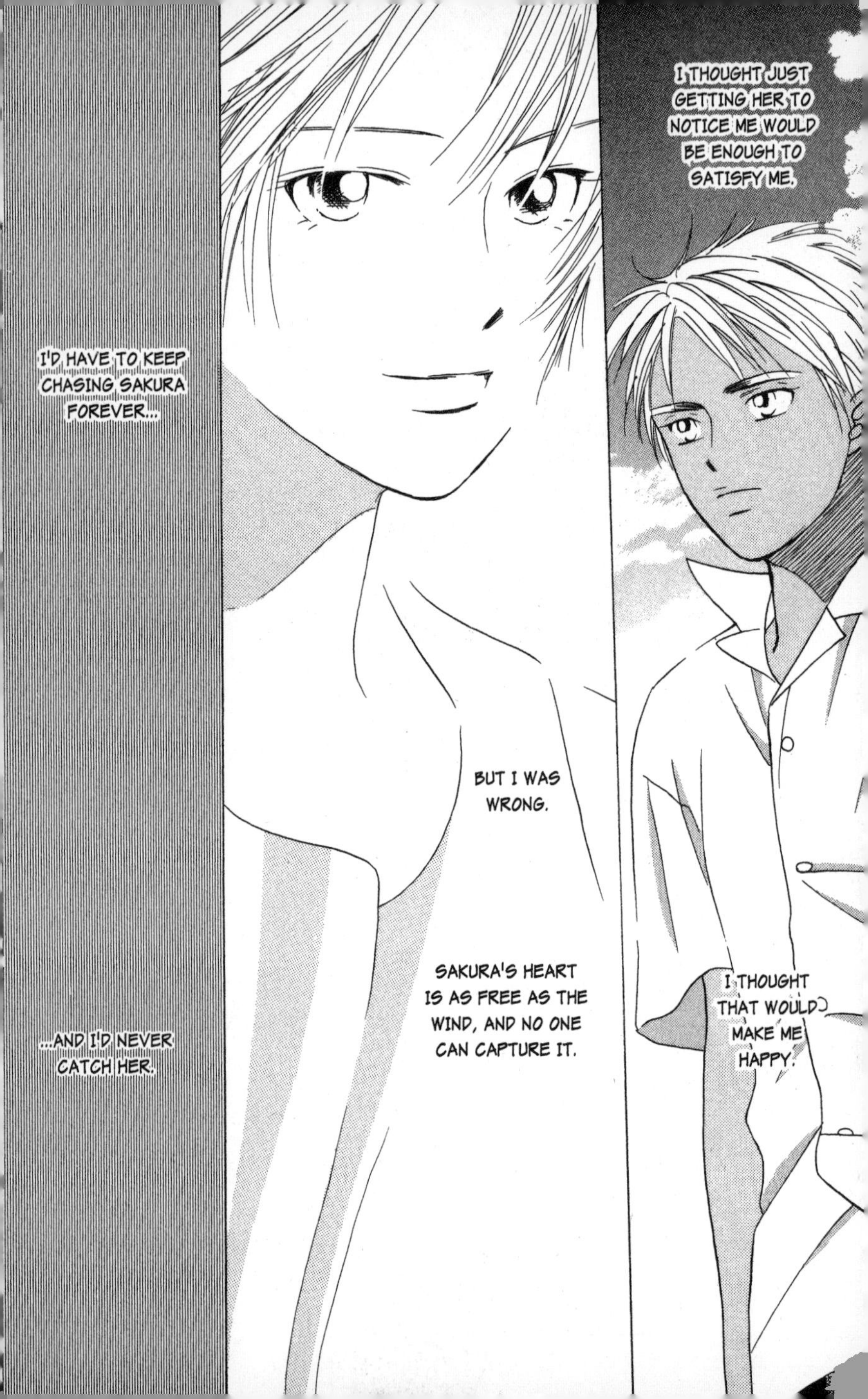
I THOUGHT JUST GETTING HER TO NOTICE ME WOULD BE ENOUGH TO SATISFY ME.
I THOUGHT THAT WOULD MAKE ME HAPPY.
BUT I WAS WRONG.
SAKURA'S HEART IS AS FREE AS THE WIND, AND NO ONE CAN CAPTURE IT.
I'D HAVE TO KEEP CHASING SAKURA FOREVER...
...AND I'D NEVER CATCH HER.

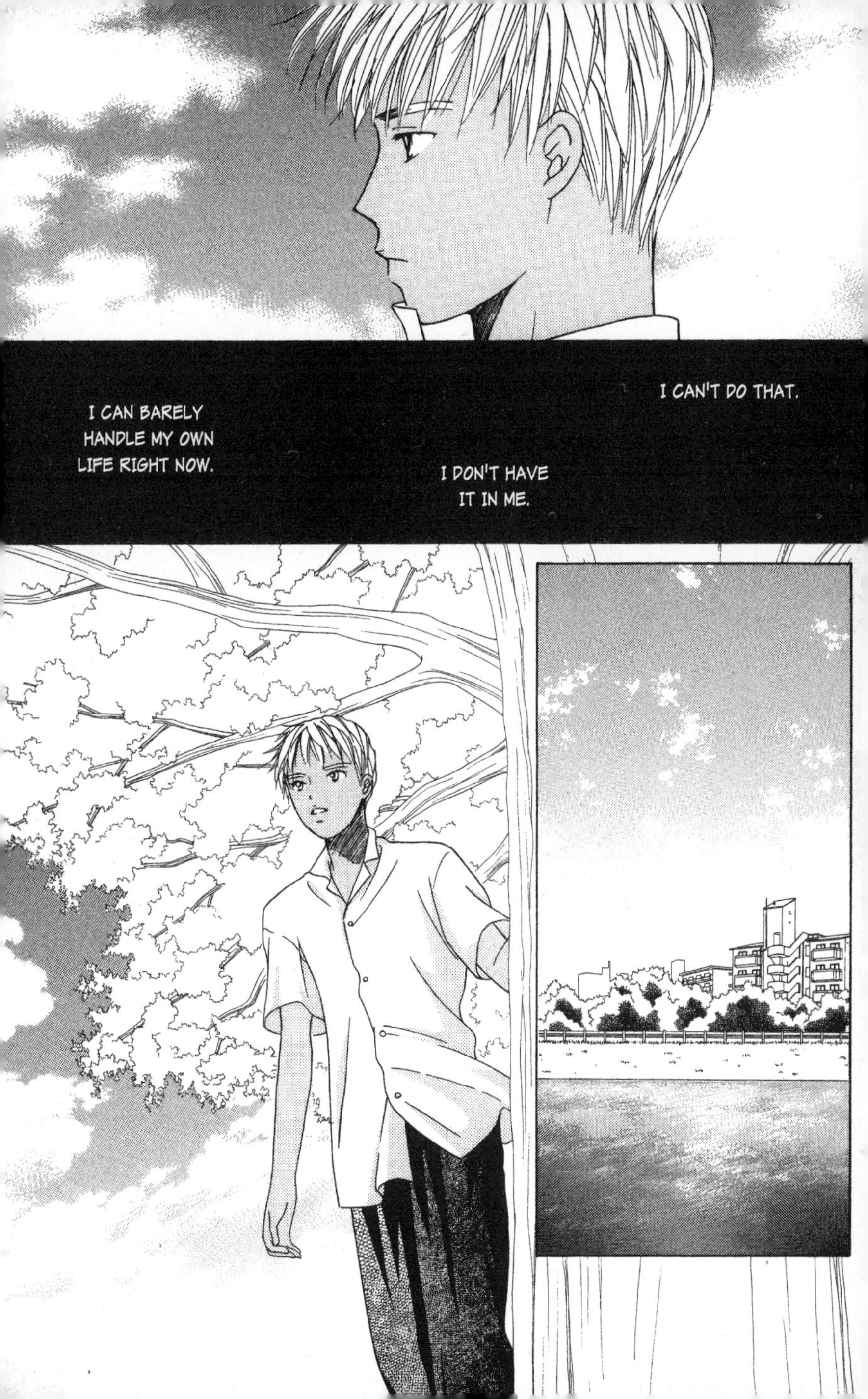
I CAN'T DO THAT.
I DON'T HAVE IT IN ME.
I CAN BARELY HANDLE MY OWN LIFE RIGHT NOW.

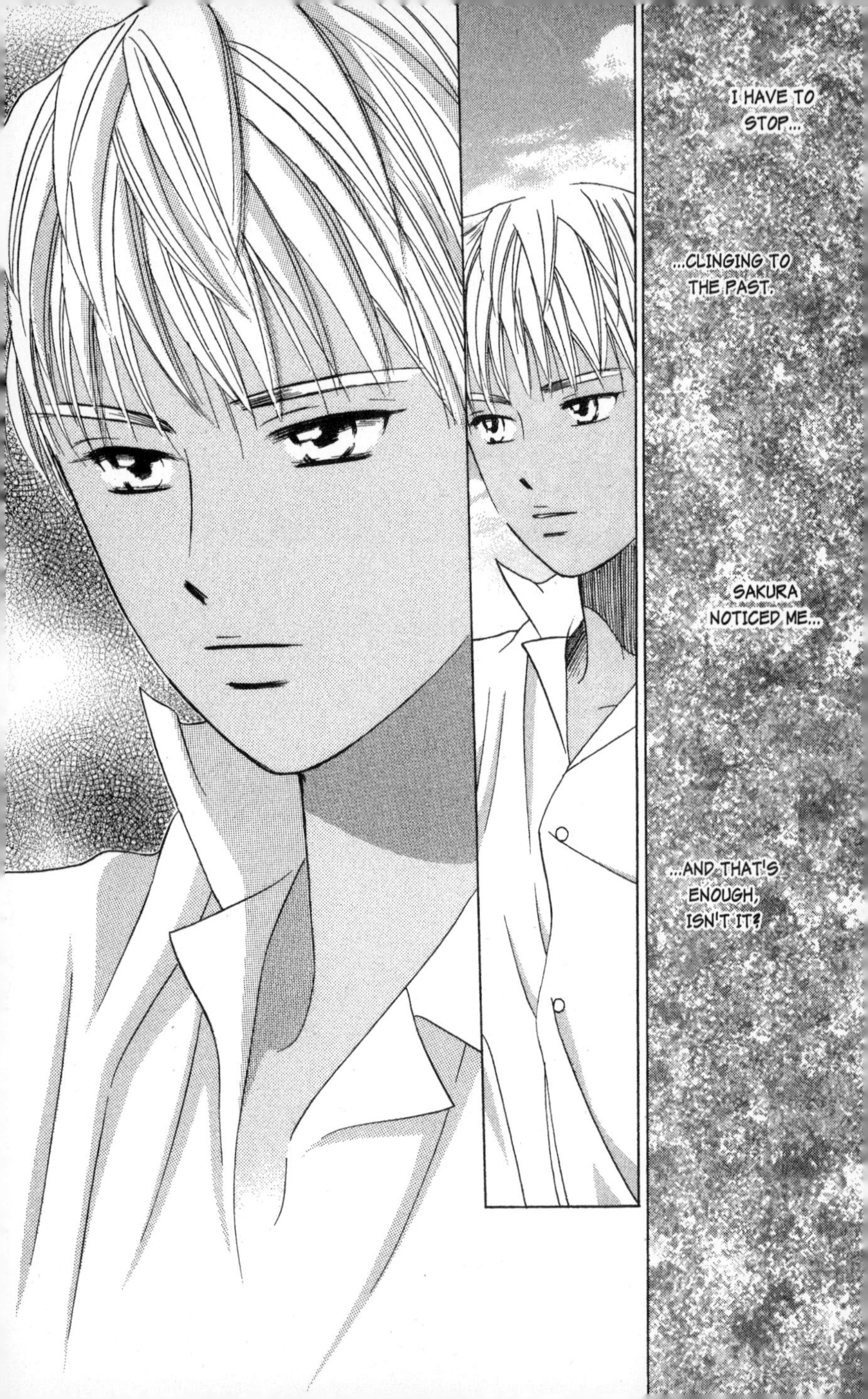
I HAVE TO STOP...
...CLINGING TO THE PAST.
SAKURA NOTICED ME...
...AND THAT'S ENOUGH, ISN'T IT?

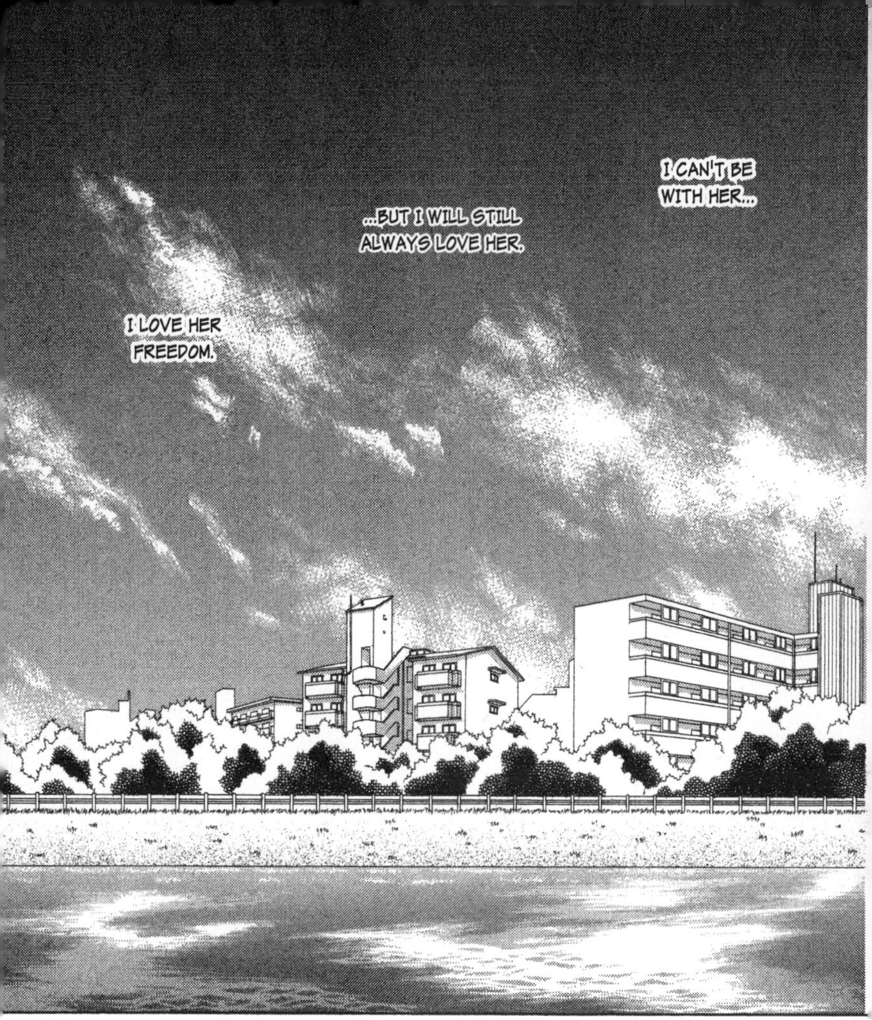
I CAN'T BE WITH HER...
...BUT I WILL STILL ALWAYS LOVE HER.
I LOVE HER FREEDOM.

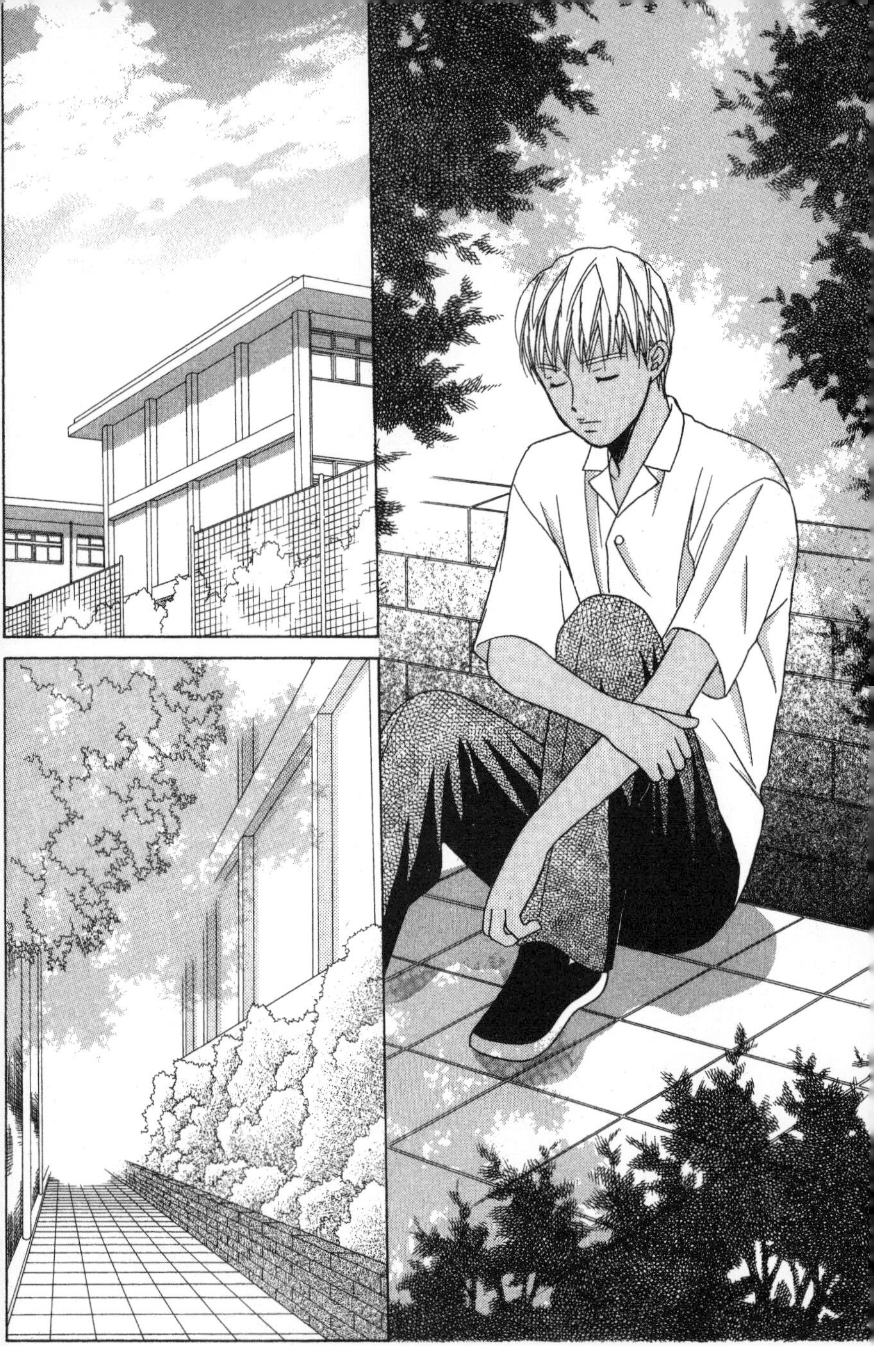

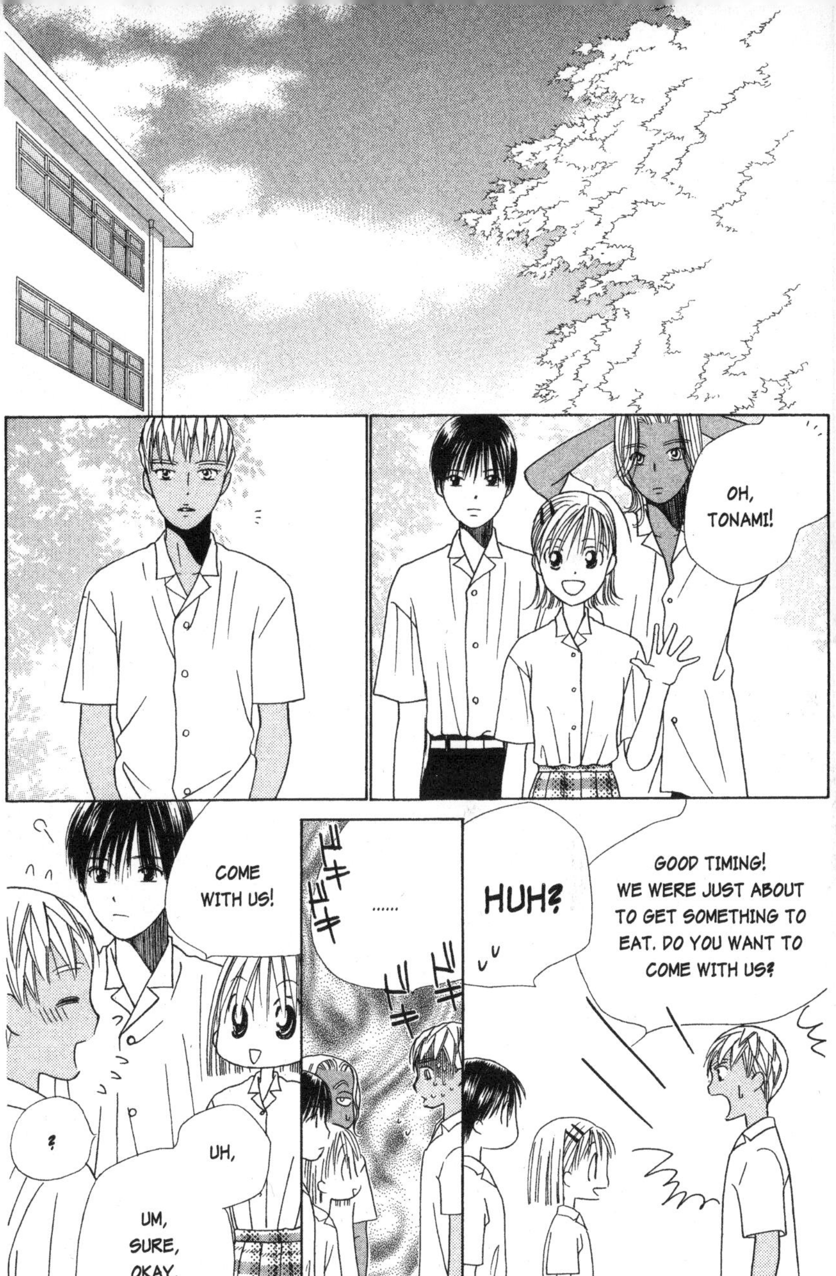
OH, TONAMI!
GOOD TIMING! WE WERE JUST ABOUT TO GET SOMETHING TO EAT. DO YOU WANT TO COME WITH US?
HUH?
......
COME WITH US!
?
UH,
UM, SURE, OKAY.

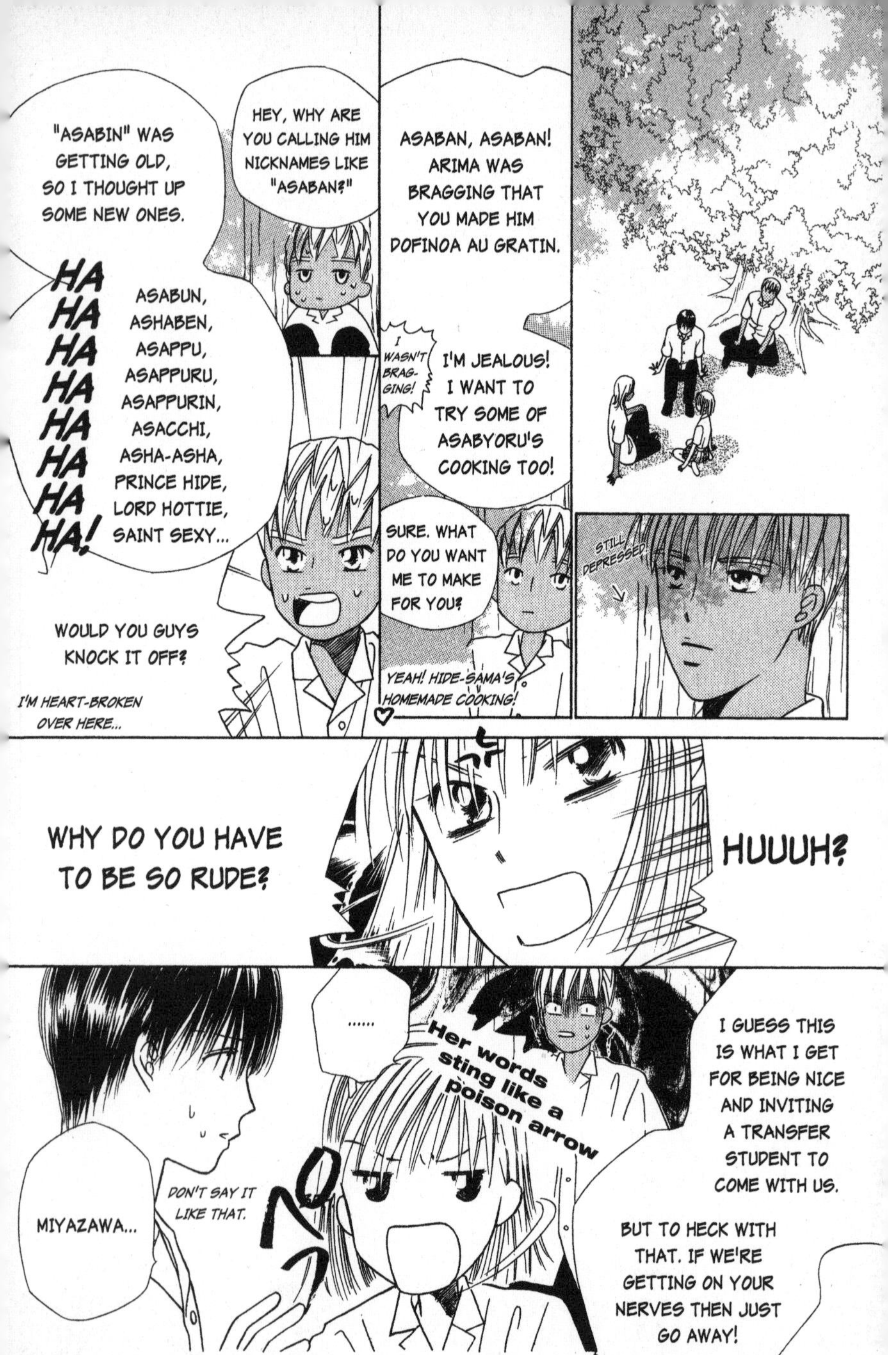

STILL DEPRESSED
ASABAN, ASABAN! ARIMA WAS BRAGGING THAT YOU MADE HIM DOFINOA AU GRATIN.
I WASN'T BRAG-GING!
I'M JEALOUS! I WANT TO TRY SOME OF ASABYORU'S COOKING TOO!
SURE. WHAT DO YOU WANT ME TO MAKE FOR YOU?
YEAH! HIDE-SAMA'S HOMEMADE COOKING! ♡
HEY, WHY ARE YOU CALLING HIM NICKNAMES LIKE "ASABAN?"
"ASABIN" WAS GETTING OLD, SO I THOUGHT UP SOME NEW ONES.
HA HA HA HA HA HA HA HA!
ASABUN, ASHABEN, ASAPPU, ASAPPURU, ASAPPURIN, ASACCHI, ASHA-ASHA, PRINCE HIDE, LORD HOTTIE, SAINT SEXY...
WOULD YOU GUYS KNOCK IT OFF?
I'M HEART-BROKEN OVER HERE...
HUUUH?
WHY DO YOU HAVE TO BE SO RUDE?
I GUESS THIS IS WHAT I GET FOR BEING NICE AND INVITING A TRANSFER STUDENT TO COME WITH US.
BUT TO HECK WITH THAT. IF WE'RE GETTING ON YOUR NERVES THEN JUST GO AWAY!
Her words sting like a poison arrow
......
DON'T SAY IT LIKE THAT.
MIYAZAWA...

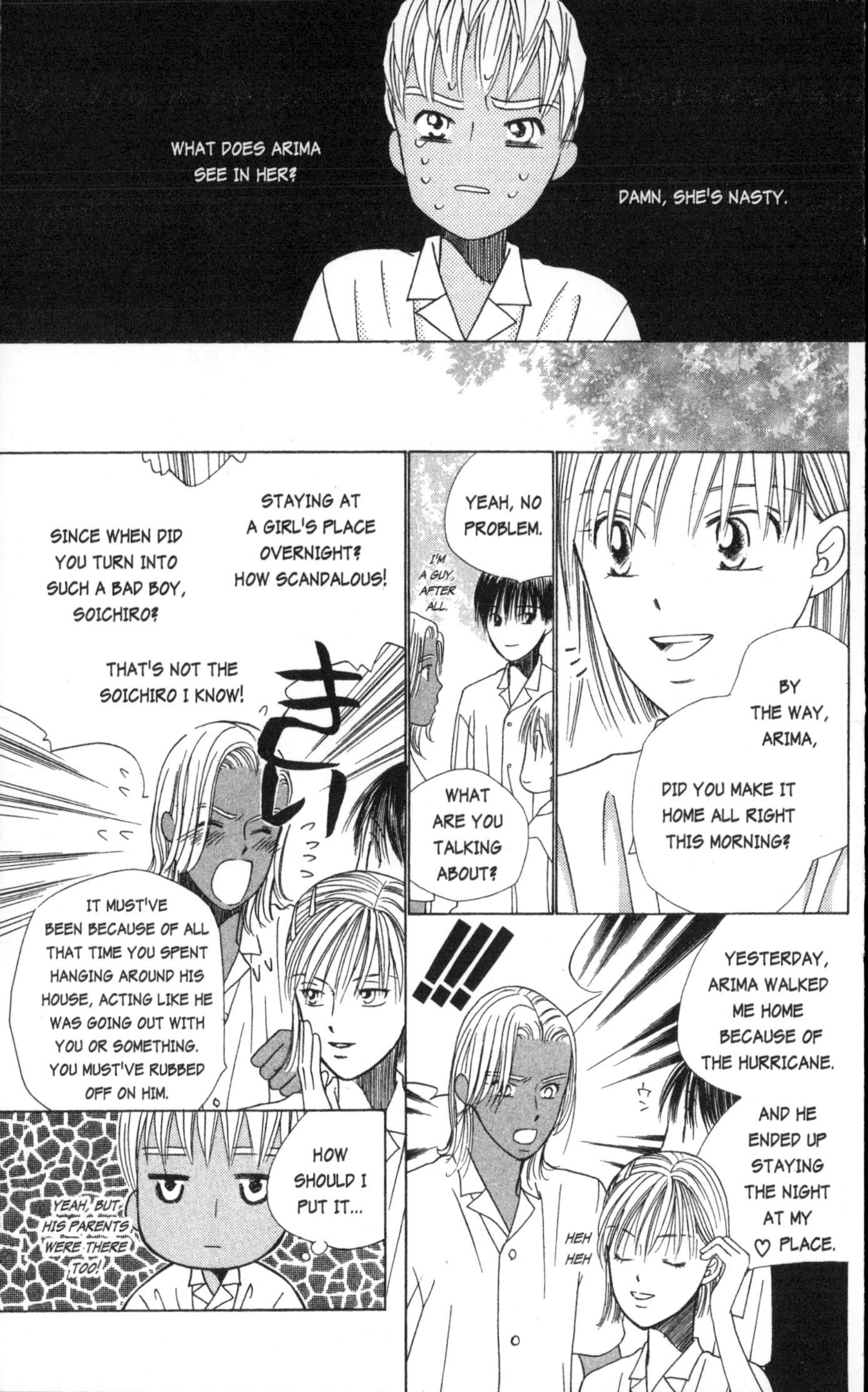
DAMN, SHE'S NASTY.
WHAT DOES ARIMA SEE IN HER?
BY THE WAY, ARIMA,
DID YOU MAKE IT HOME ALL RIGHT THIS MORNING?
YEAH, NO PROBLEM.
I'M A GUY, AFTER ALL.
WHAT ARE YOU TALKING ABOUT?
YESTERDAY, ARIMA WALKED ME HOME BECAUSE OF THE HURRICANE.
AND HE ENDED UP STAYING THE NIGHT AT MY ♡ PLACE.
HEH HEH
!!!
STAYING AT A GIRL'S PLACE OVERNIGHT? HOW SCANDALOUS!
SINCE WHEN DID YOU TURN INTO SUCH A BAD BOY, SOICHIRO?
THAT'S NOT THE SOICHIRO I KNOW!
きー
IT MUST'VE BEEN BECAUSE OF ALL THAT TIME YOU SPENT HANGING AROUND HIS HOUSE, ACTING LIKE HE WAS GOING OUT WITH YOU OR SOMETHING. YOU MUST'VE RUBBED OFF ON HIM.
HOW SHOULD I PUT IT...
YEAH, BUT HIS PARENTS WERE THERE TOO!

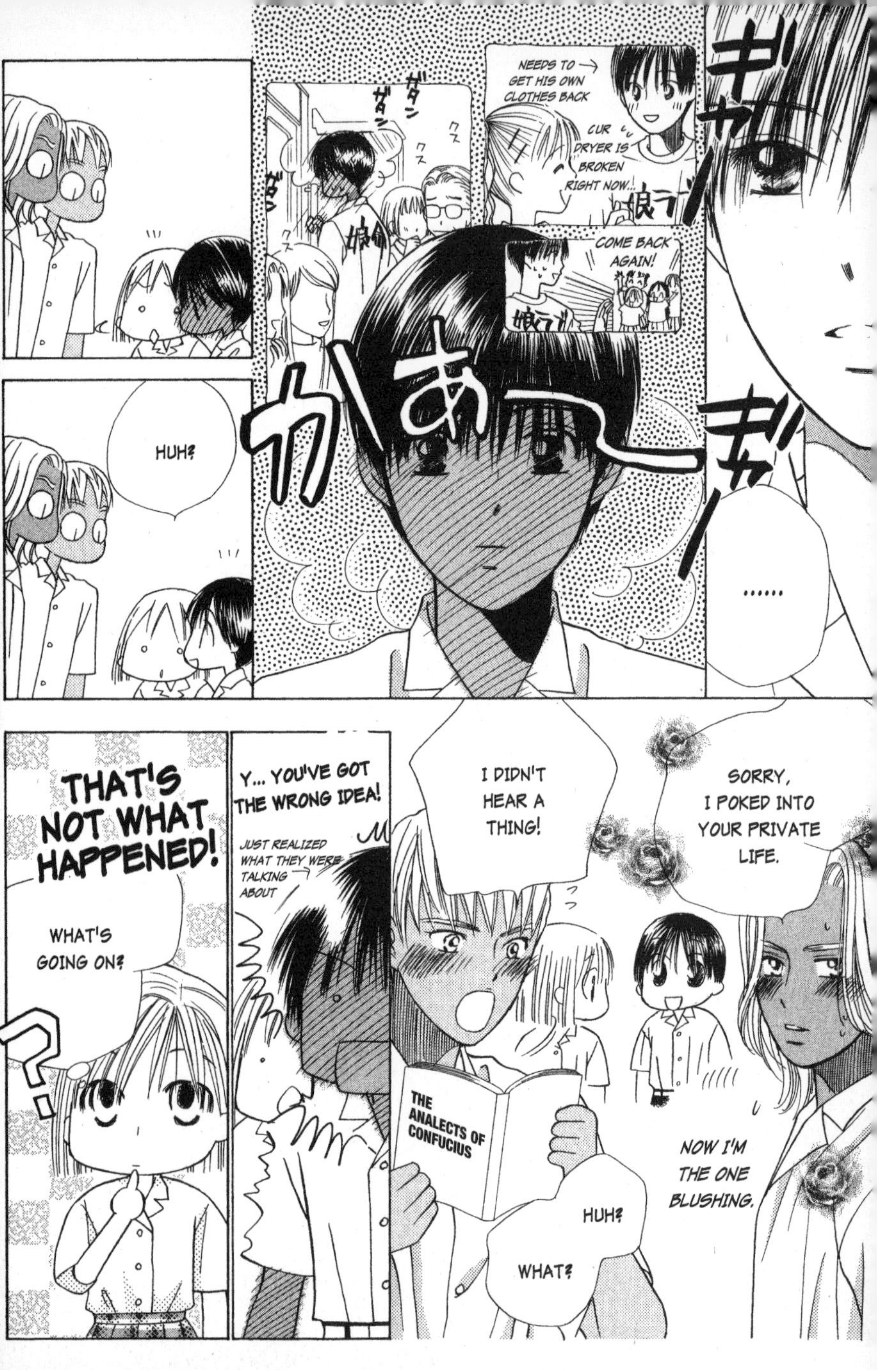

......
NEEDS TO GET HIS OWN CLOTHES BACK
OUR DRYER IS BROKEN RIGHT NOW...
COME BACK AGAIN!
HUH?
SORRY, I POKED INTO YOUR PRIVATE LIFE.
NOW I'M THE ONE BLUSHING.
I DIDN'T HEAR A THING!
HUH?
WHAT?
THE ANALECTS OF CONFUCIUS
Y... YOU'VE GOT THE WRONG IDEA!
JUST REALIZED WHAT THEY WERE TALKING ABOUT
THAT'S NOT WHAT HAPPENED!
WHAT'S GOING ON?

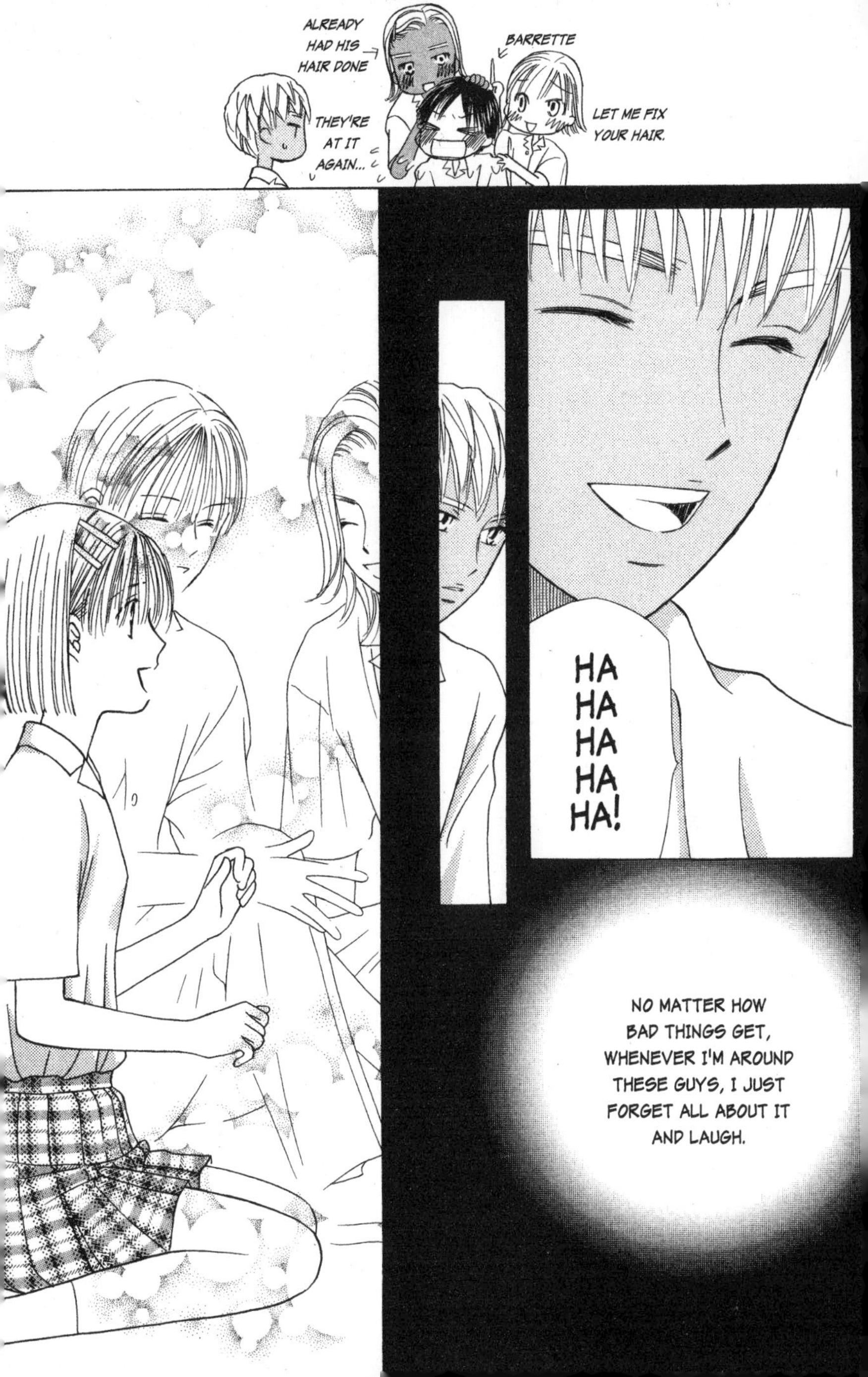
LET ME FIX YOUR HAIR.
BARRETTE
ALREADY HAD HIS HAIR DONE
THEY'RE AT IT AGAIN...
HA HA HA HA HA!
NO MATTER HOW BAD THINGS GET, WHENEVER I'M AROUND THESE GUYS, I JUST FORGET ALL ABOUT IT AND LAUGH.

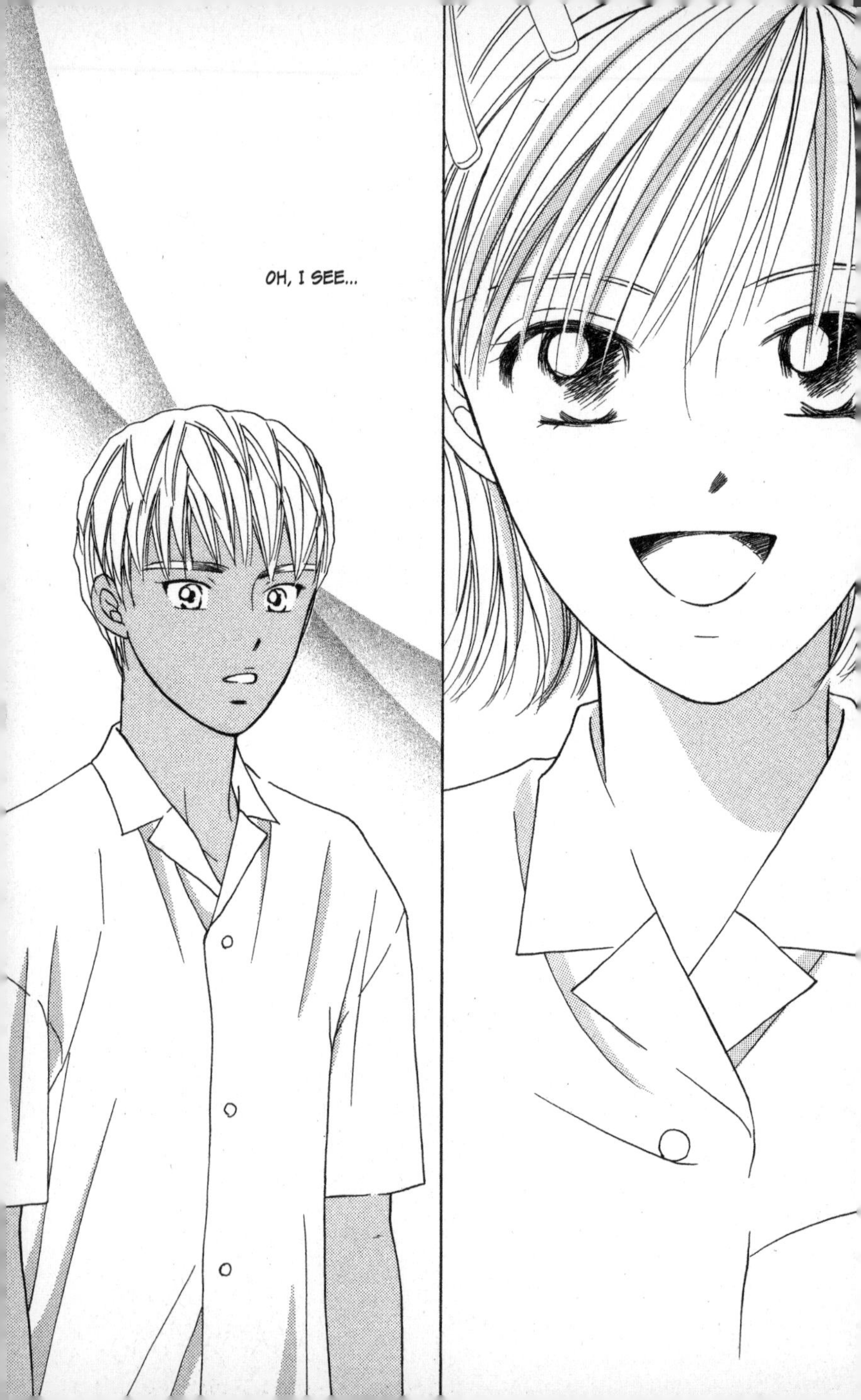
OH, I SEE...

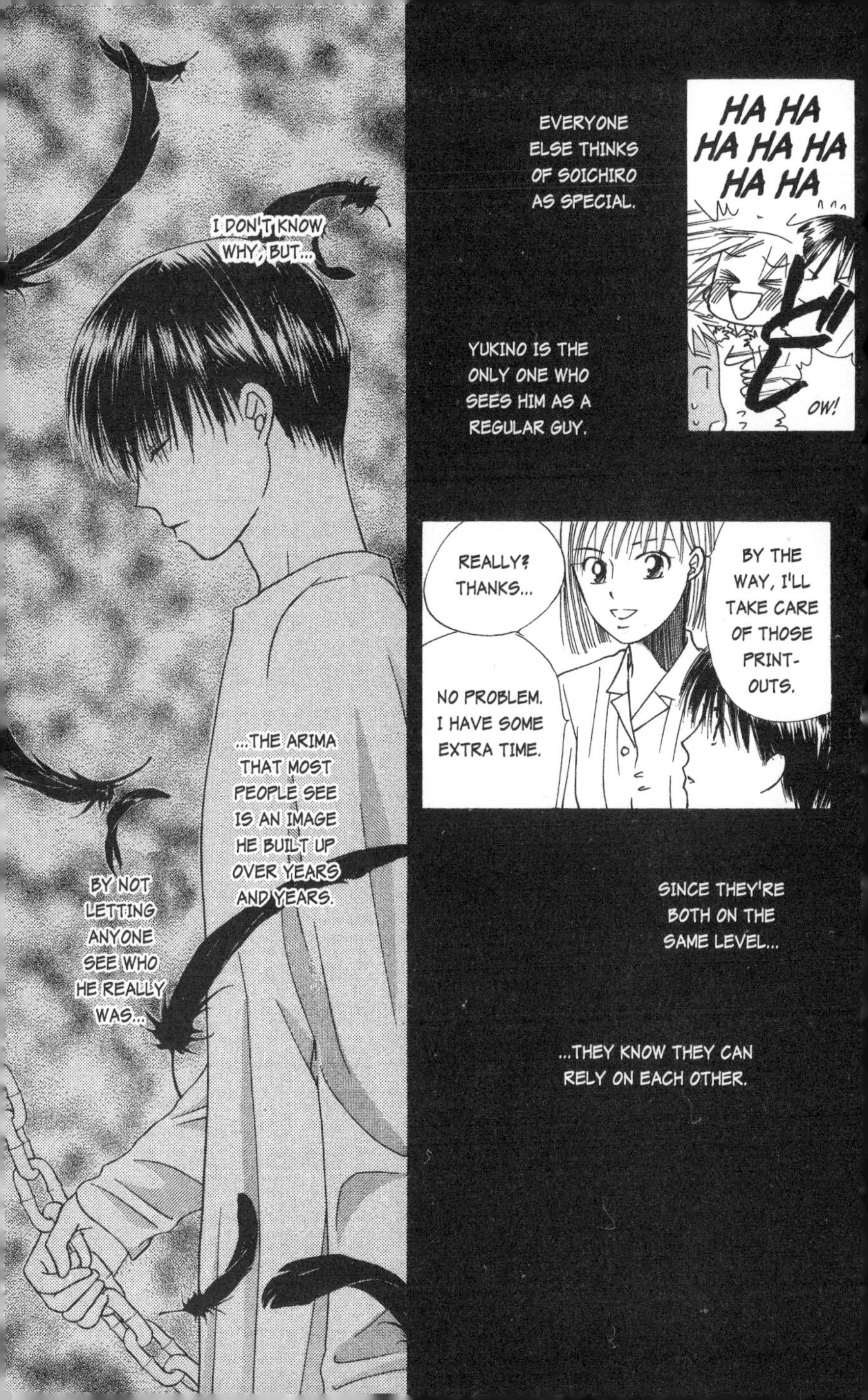
HA HA HA HA HA HA HA
OW!
EVERYONE ELSE THINKS OF SOICHIRO AS SPECIAL.
YUKINO IS THE ONLY ONE WHO SEES HIM AS A REGULAR GUY.
BY THE WAY, I'LL TAKE CARE OF THOSE PRINT-OUTS.
REALLY? THANKS...
NO PROBLEM. I HAVE SOME EXTRA TIME.
SINCE THEY'RE BOTH ON THE SAME LEVEL...
...THEY KNOW THEY CAN RELY ON EACH OTHER.
I DON'T KNOW WHY, BUT...
...THE ARIMA THAT MOST PEOPLE SEE IS AN IMAGE HE BUILT UP OVER YEARS AND YEARS.
BY NOT LETTING ANYONE SEE WHO HE REALLY WAS...

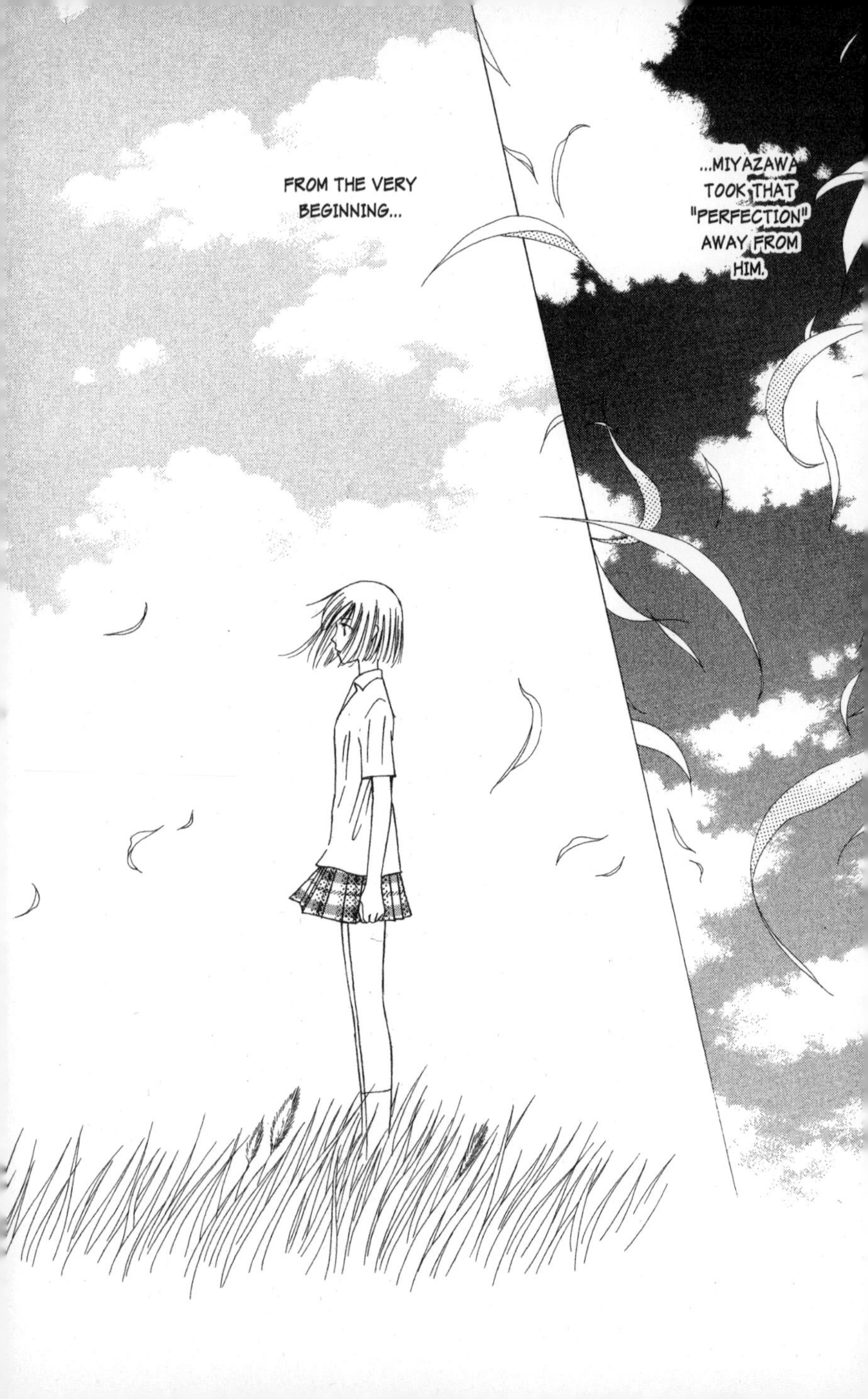
...MIYAZAWA TOOK THAT "PERFECTION" AWAY FROM HIM.
FROM THE VERY BEGINNING...

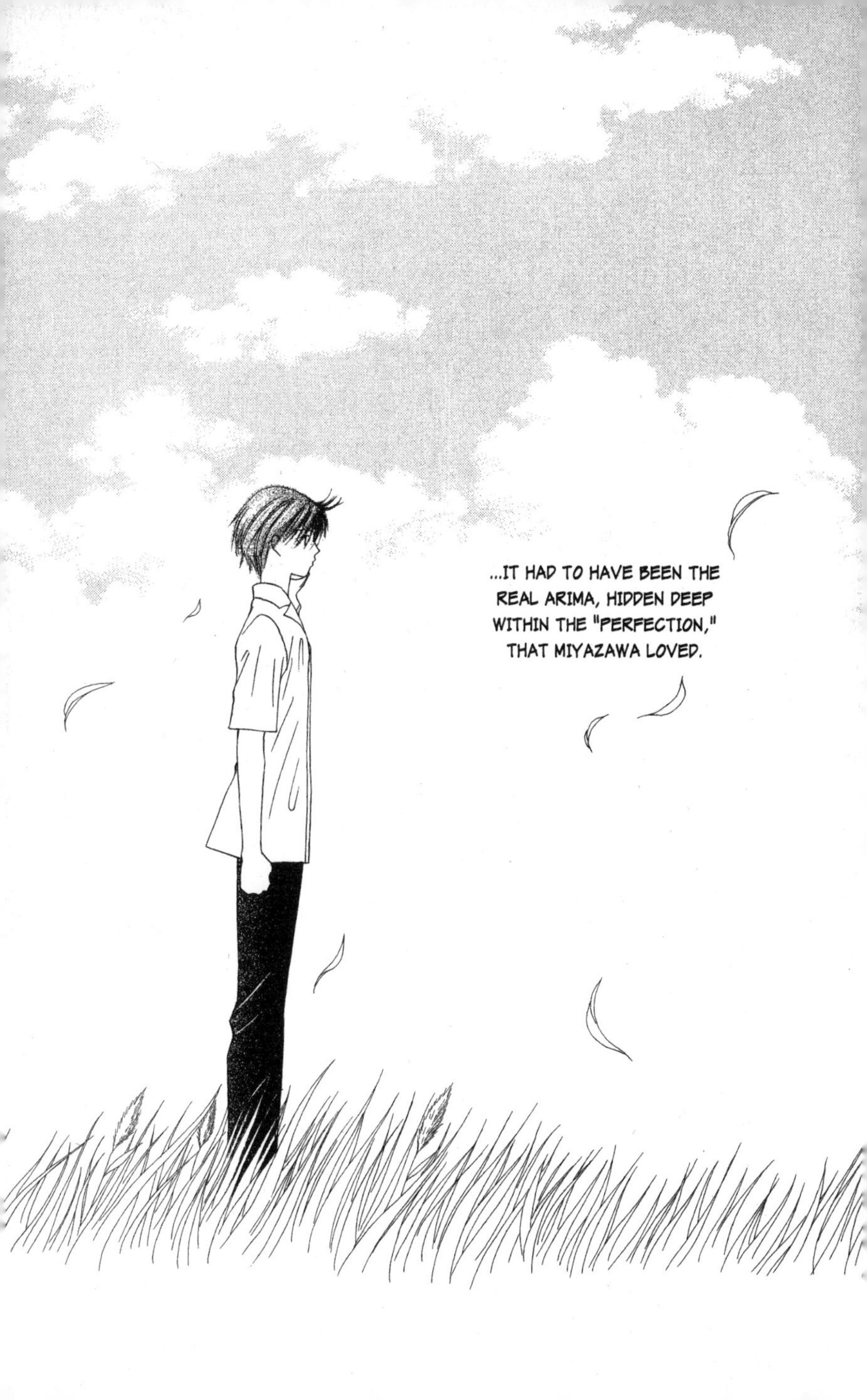
...IT HAD TO HAVE BEEN THE REAL ARIMA, HIDDEN DEEP WITHIN THE "PERFECTION," THAT MIYAZAWA LOVED.

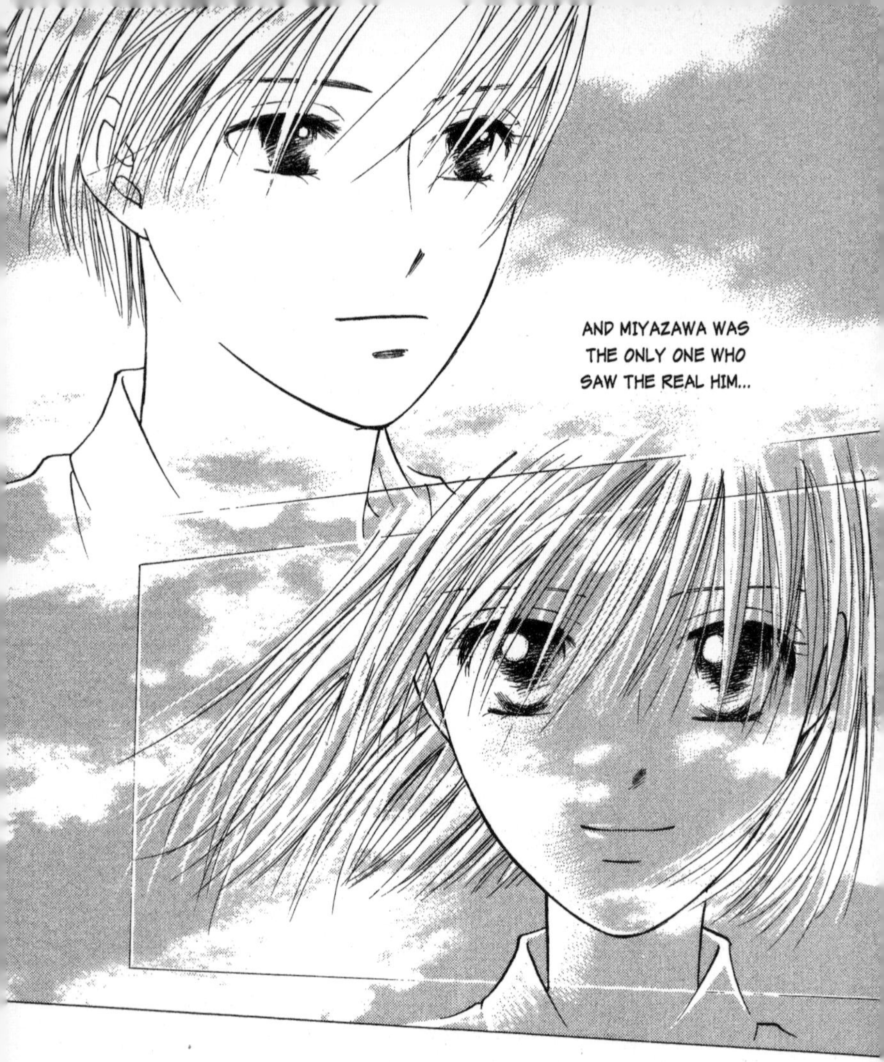
AND MIYAZAWA WAS THE ONLY ONE WHO SAW THE REAL HIM...

THAT'S WHY SHE'S SO PRECIOUS TO HIM.

THAT'S WHY SHE'S SO SPECIAL.

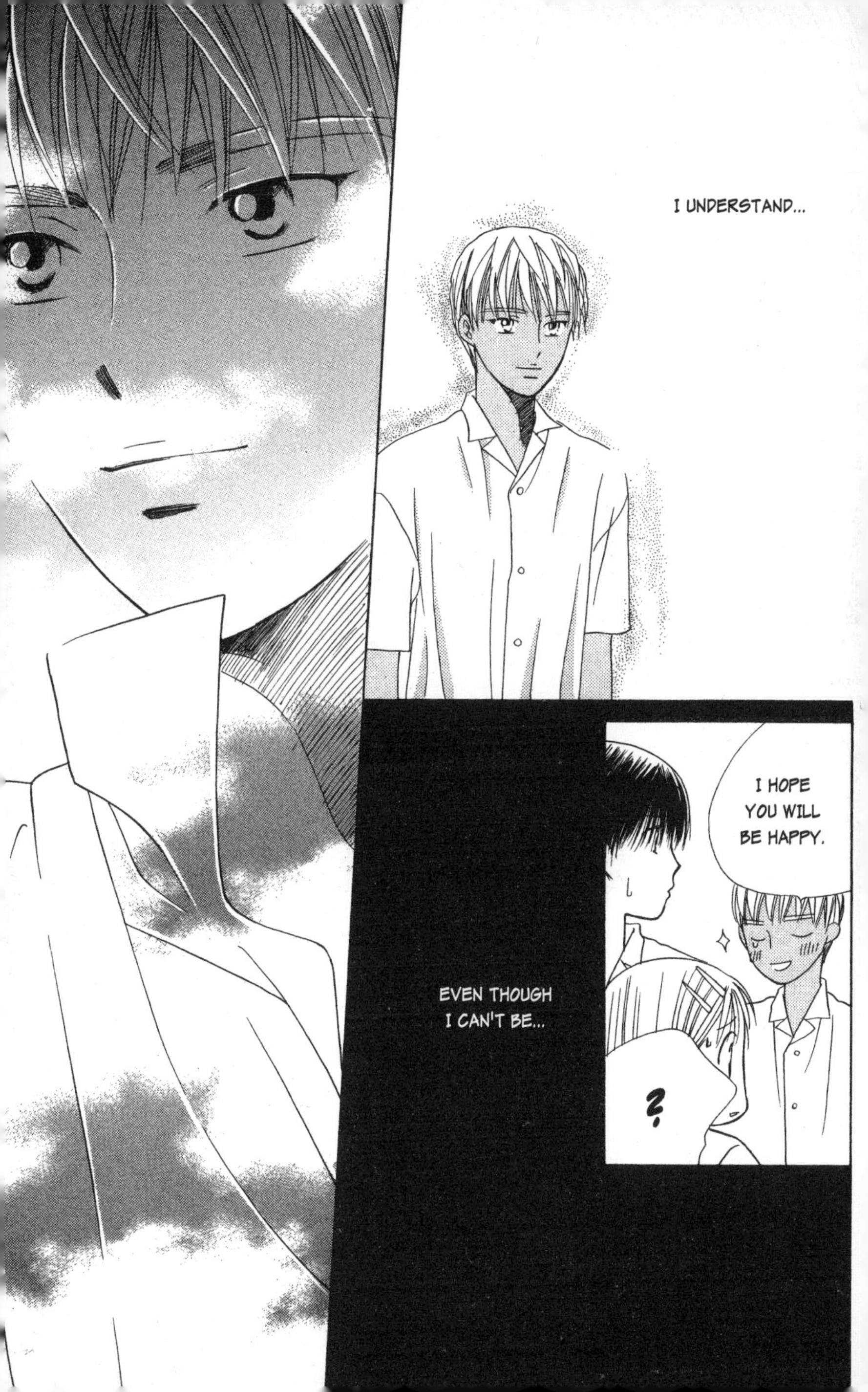
I UNDERSTAND...
I HOPE YOU WILL BE HAPPY.
?
EVEN THOUGH I CAN'T BE...

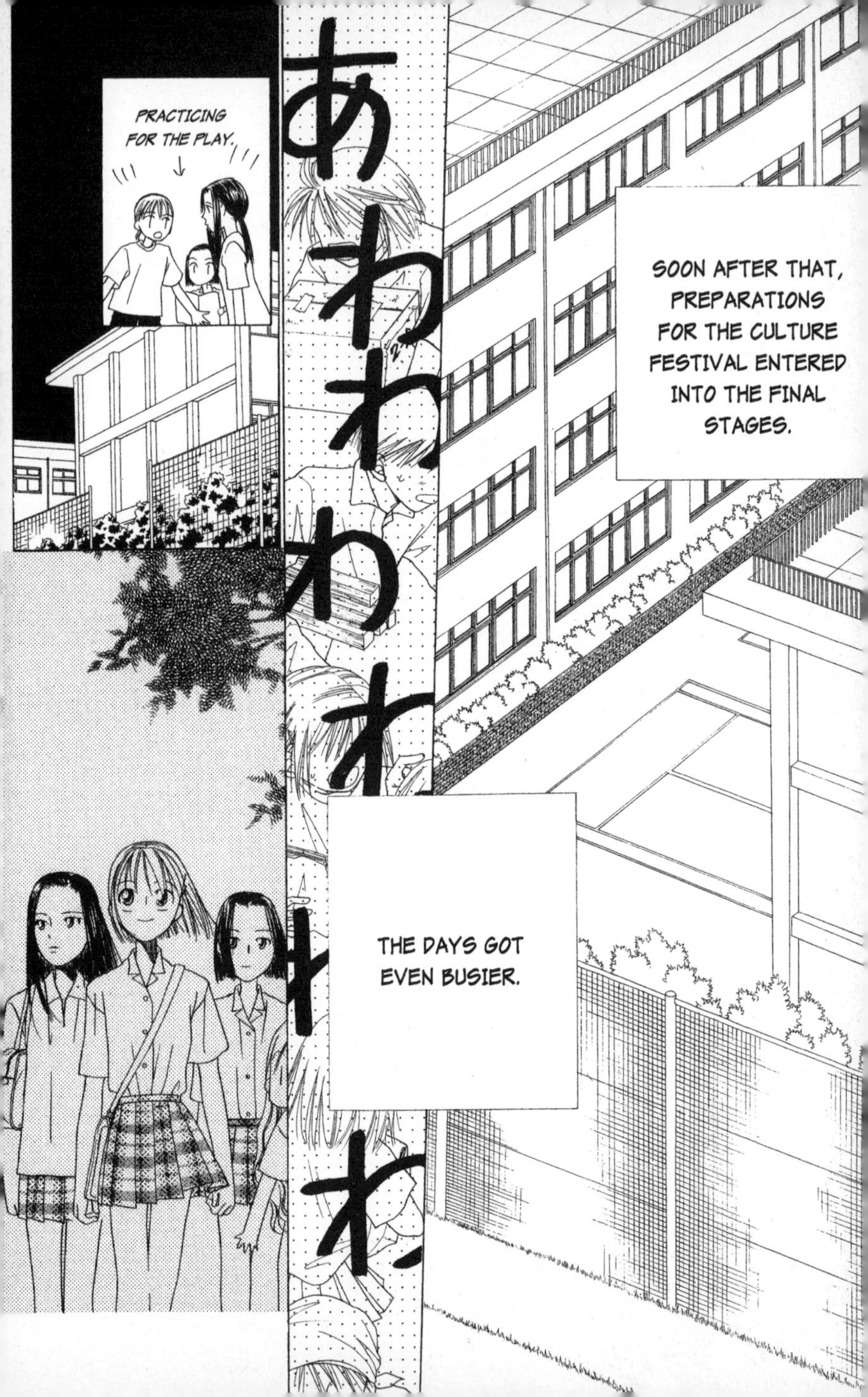
SOON AFTER THAT, PREPARATIONS FOR THE CULTURE FESTIVAL ENTERED INTO THE FINAL STAGES.
THE DAYS GOT EVEN BUSIER.
PRACTICING FOR THE PLAY.

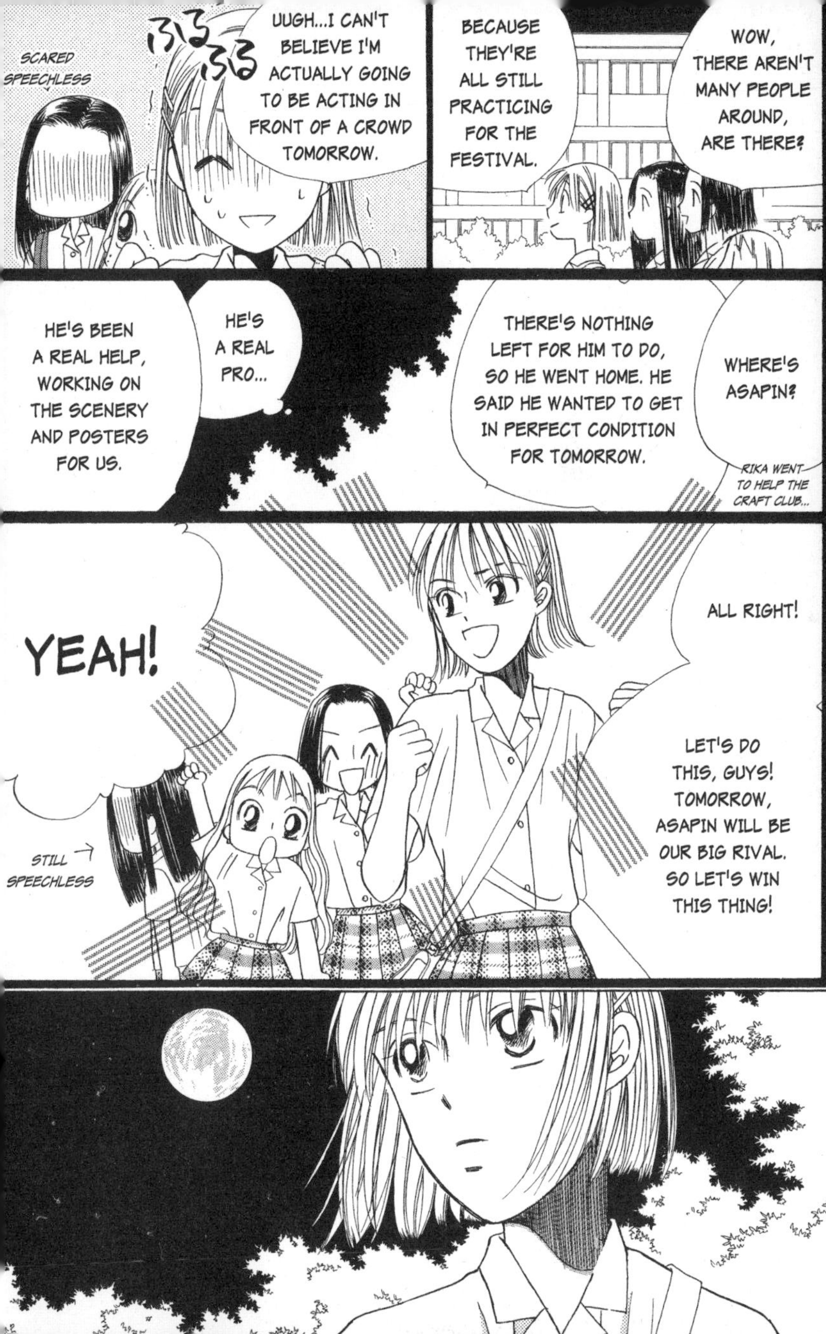
WOW, THERE AREN'T MANY PEOPLE AROUND, ARE THERE?
BECAUSE THEY'RE ALL STILL PRACTICING FOR THE FESTIVAL.
ふるふる
UUGH...I CAN'T BELIEVE I'M ACTUALLY GOING TO BE ACTING IN FRONT OF A CROWD TOMORROW.
SCARED SPEECHLESS
WHERE'S ASAPIN?
RIKA WENT TO HELP THE CRAFT CLUB...
THERE'S NOTHING LEFT FOR HIM TO DO, SO HE WENT HOME. HE SAID HE WANTED TO GET IN PERFECT CONDITION FOR TOMORROW.
HE'S A REAL PRO...
HE'S BEEN A REAL HELP, WORKING ON THE SCENERY AND POSTERS FOR US.
ALL RIGHT!
LET'S DO THIS, GUYS! TOMORROW, ASAPIN WILL BE OUR BIG RIVAL. SO LET'S WIN THIS THING!
YEAH!
STILL SPEECHLESS

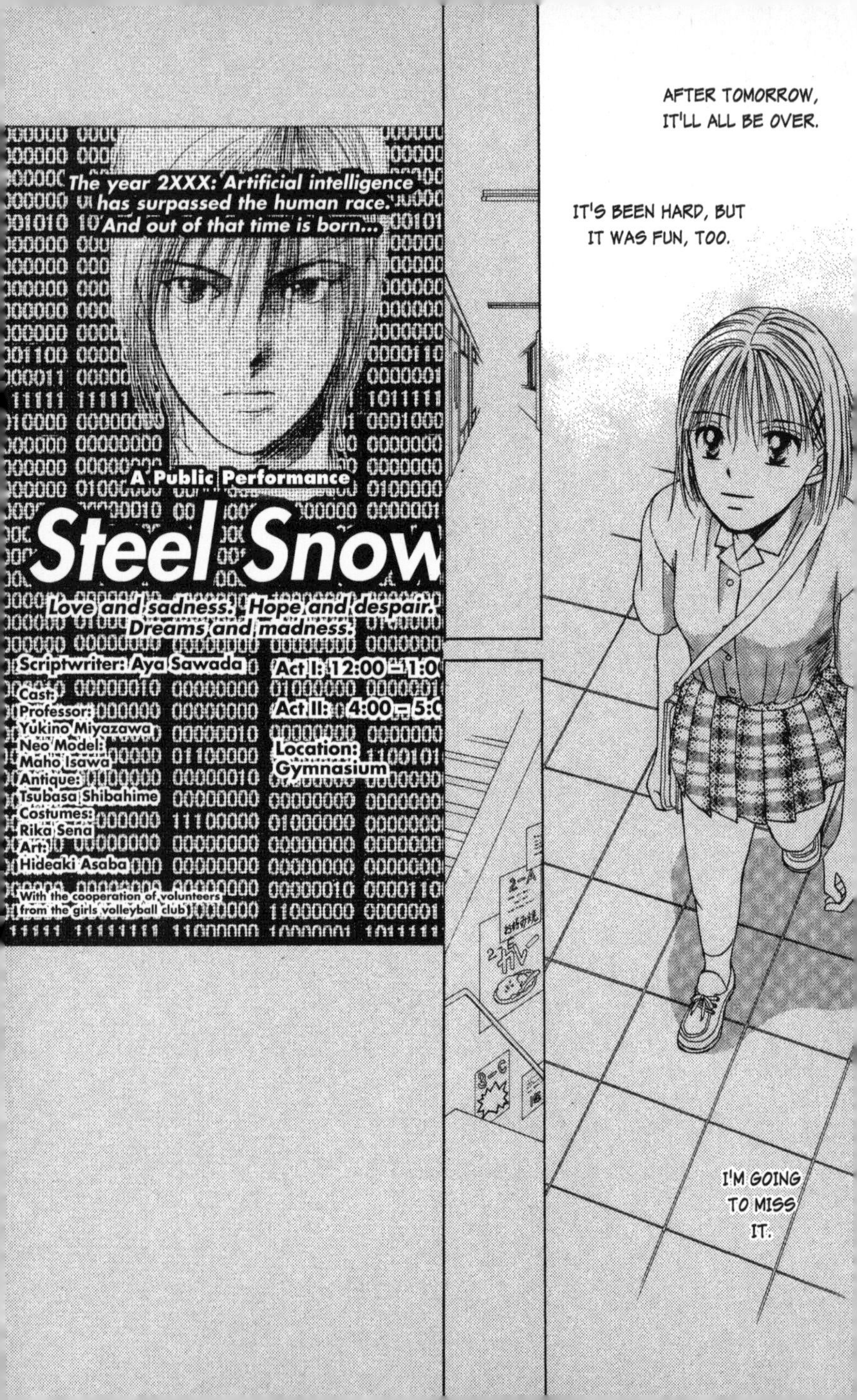
AFTER TOMORROW, IT'LL ALL BE OVER.
IT'S BEEN HARD, BUT IT WAS FUN, TOO.
I'M GOING TO MISS IT.
The year 2XXX: Artificial intelligence has surpassed the human race. And out of that time is born...
A Public Performance
Steel Snow
Love and sadness. Hope and despair. Dreams and madness.
Scriptwriter: Aya Sawada
Act I: 12:00 – 1:0
Act II: 4:00 – 5:0
Location: Gymnasium
Cast:
Professor: Yukino Miyazawa
Neo Model: Maho Isawa
Antique: Tsubasa Shibahime
Costumes: Rika Sena
Art: Hideaki Asaba
With the cooperation of volunteers from the girls volleyball club

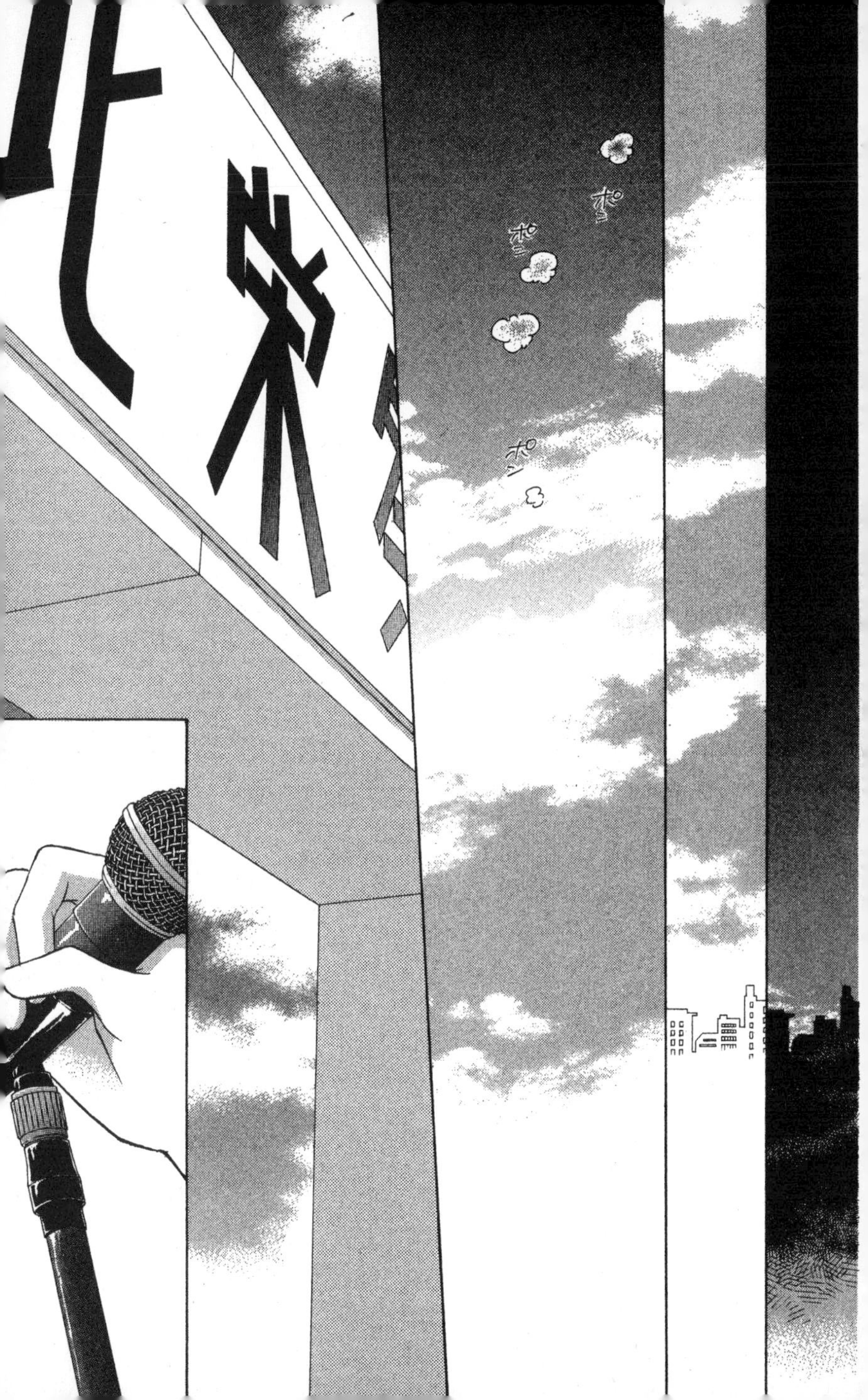
ポョ
ポョ
ポン

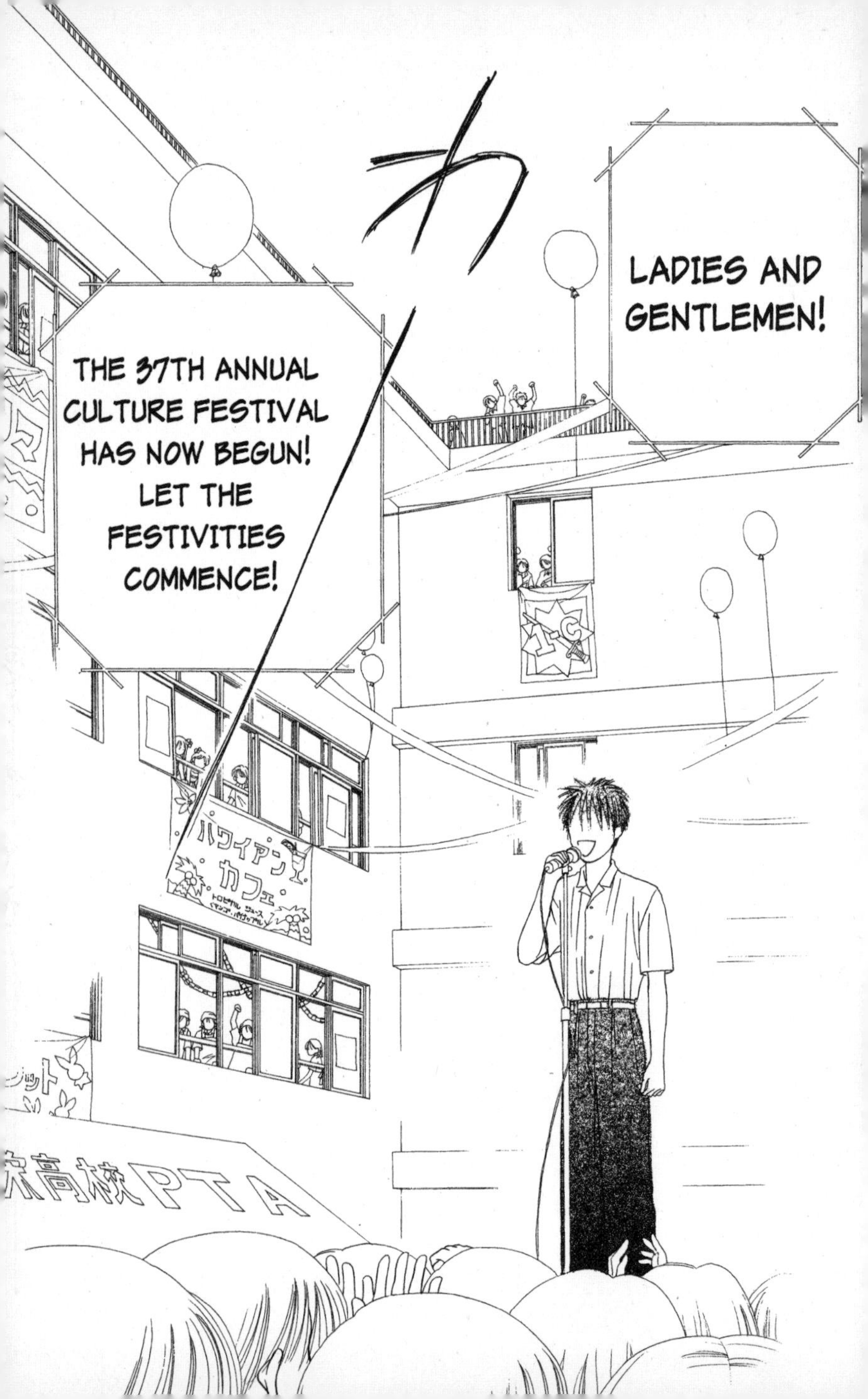
LADIES AND GENTLEMEN!
わ
THE 37TH ANNUAL CULTURE FESTIVAL HAS NOW BEGUN! LET THE FESTIVITIES COMMENCE!
1-C
ハワイアン カフェ
高校PTA

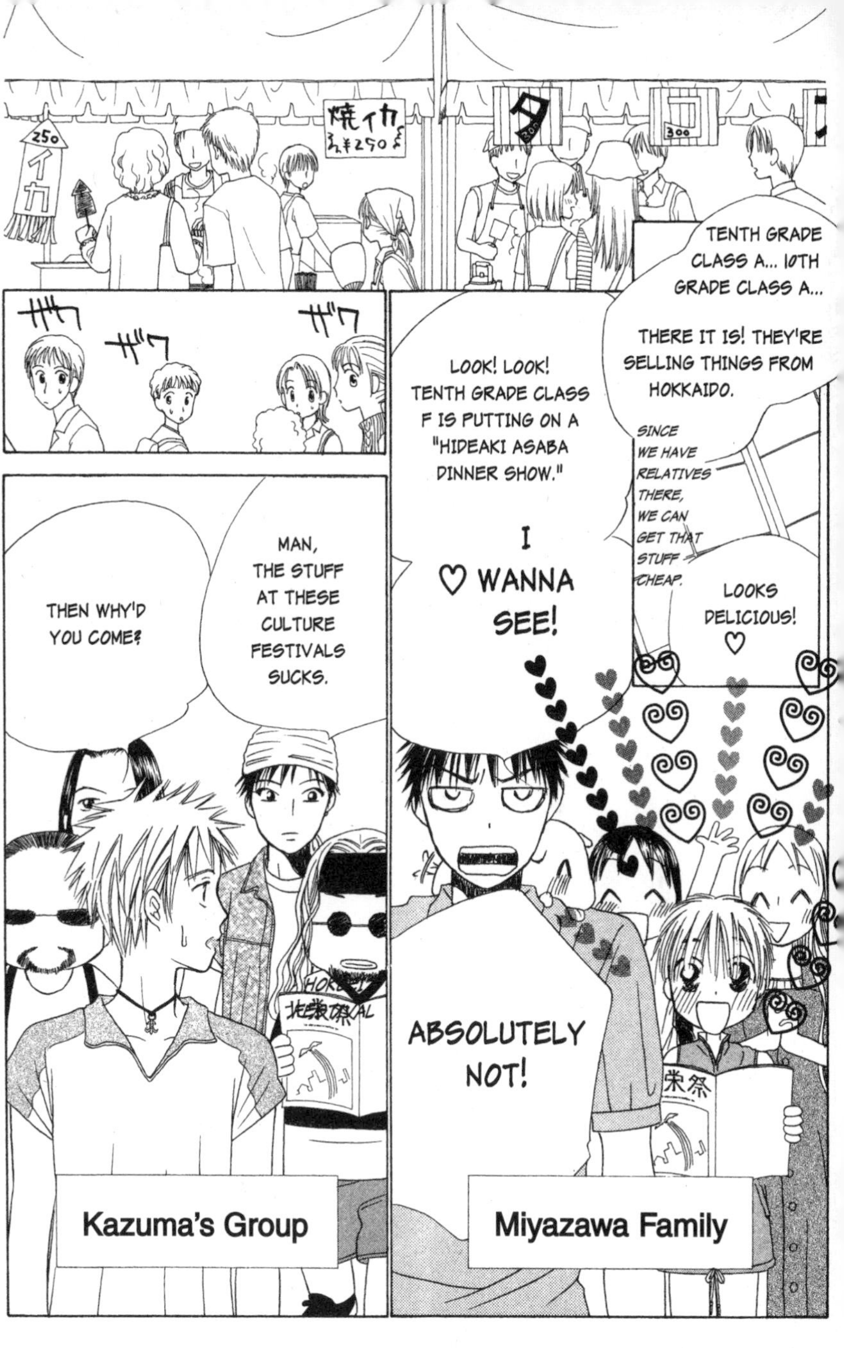

焼イカ
250
イカ
TENTH GRADE CLASS A... 10TH GRADE CLASS A...
THERE IT IS! THEY'RE SELLING THINGS FROM HOKKAIDO.
SINCE WE HAVE RELATIVES THERE, WE CAN GET THAT STUFF CHEAP.
LOOKS DELICIOUS! ♡
LOOK! LOOK! TENTH GRADE CLASS F IS PUTTING ON A "HIDEAKI ASABA DINNER SHOW."
I ♡ WANNA SEE!
ザワ
ザワ
ザワ
ABSOLUTELY NOT!
Miyazawa Family
MAN, THE STUFF AT THESE CULTURE FESTIVALS SUCKS.
THEN WHY'D YOU COME?
Kazuma's Group

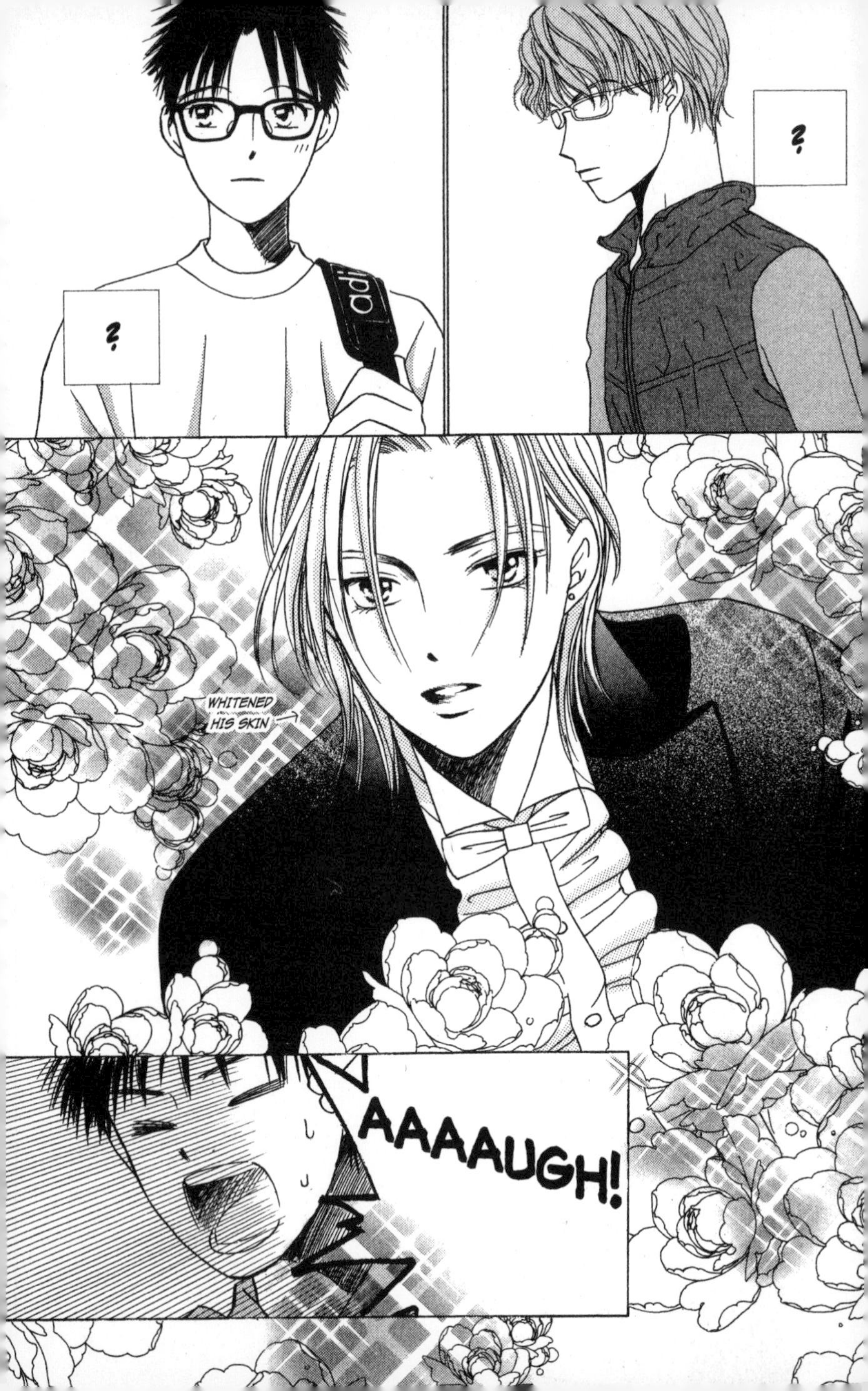
?
?
WHITENED HIS SKIN
AAAAUGH!

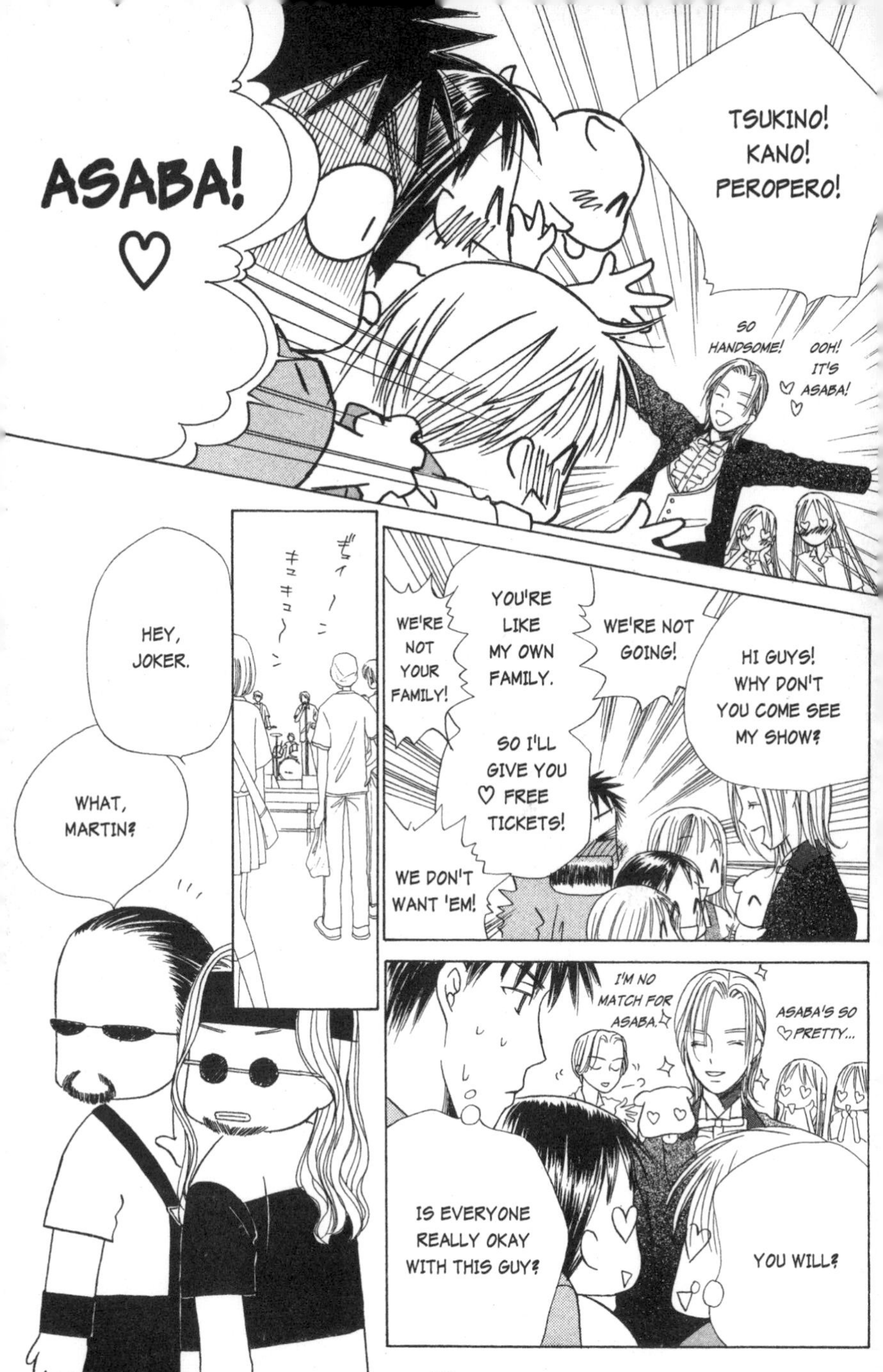
TSUKINO! KANO! PEROPERO!
ASABA! ♡
OOH! IT'S ASABA! ♡
SO HANDSOME! ♡
HI GUYS! WHY DON'T YOU COME SEE MY SHOW?
WE'RE NOT GOING!
YOU'RE LIKE MY OWN FAMILY.
WE'RE NOT YOUR FAMILY!
SO I'LL GIVE YOU ♡ FREE TICKETS!
WE DON'T WANT 'EM!
HEY, JOKER.
WHAT, MARTIN?
ASABA'S SO ♡ PRETTY...
I'M NO MATCH FOR ASABA. ♡
YOU WILL?
IS EVERYONE REALLY OKAY WITH THIS GUY?

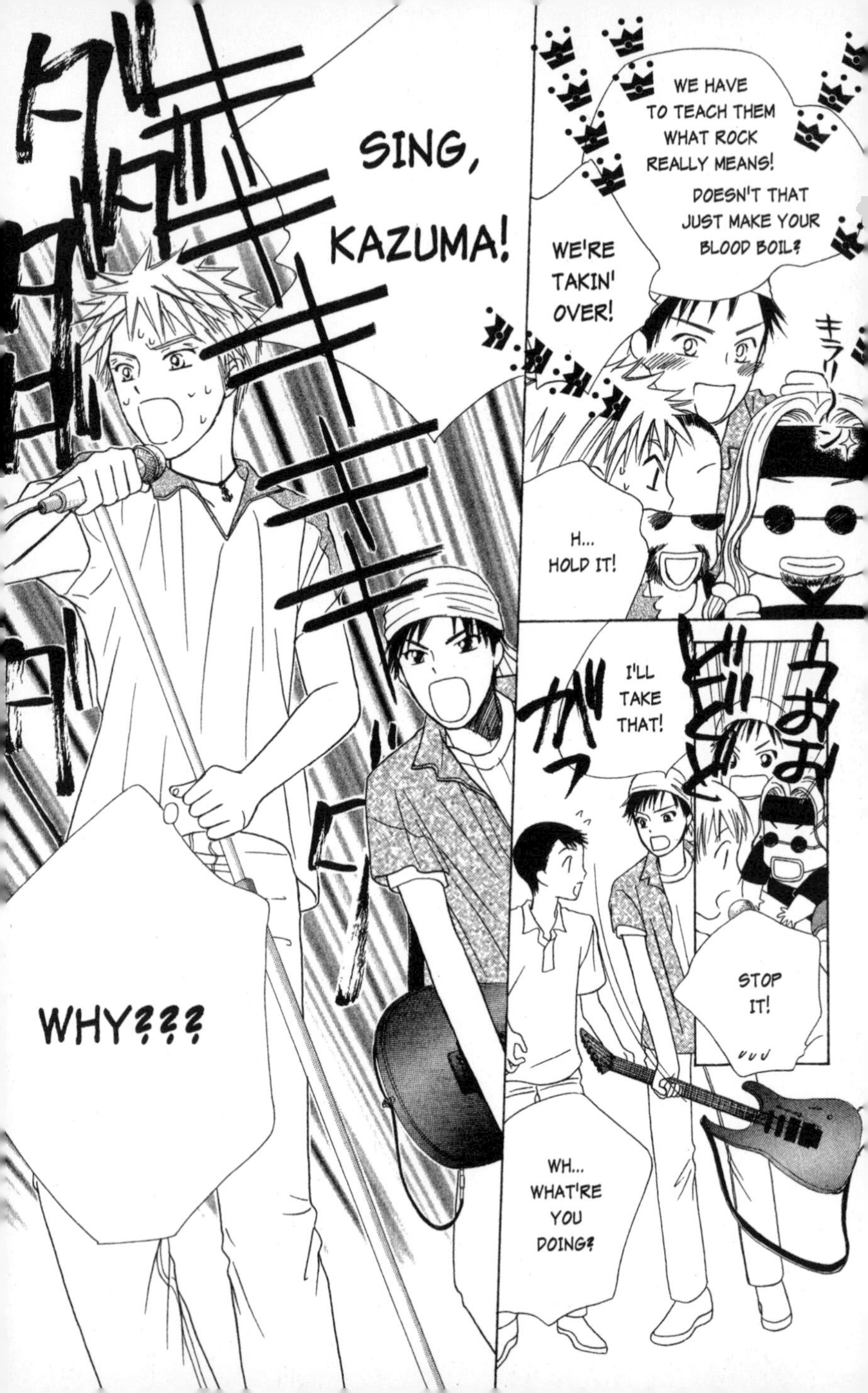
WE HAVE TO TEACH THEM WHAT ROCK REALLY MEANS!
DOESN'T THAT JUST MAKE YOUR BLOOD BOIL?
WE'RE TAKIN' OVER!
H... HOLD IT!
I'LL TAKE THAT!
STOP IT!
WH... WHAT'RE YOU DOING?
SING, KAZUMA!
WHY???

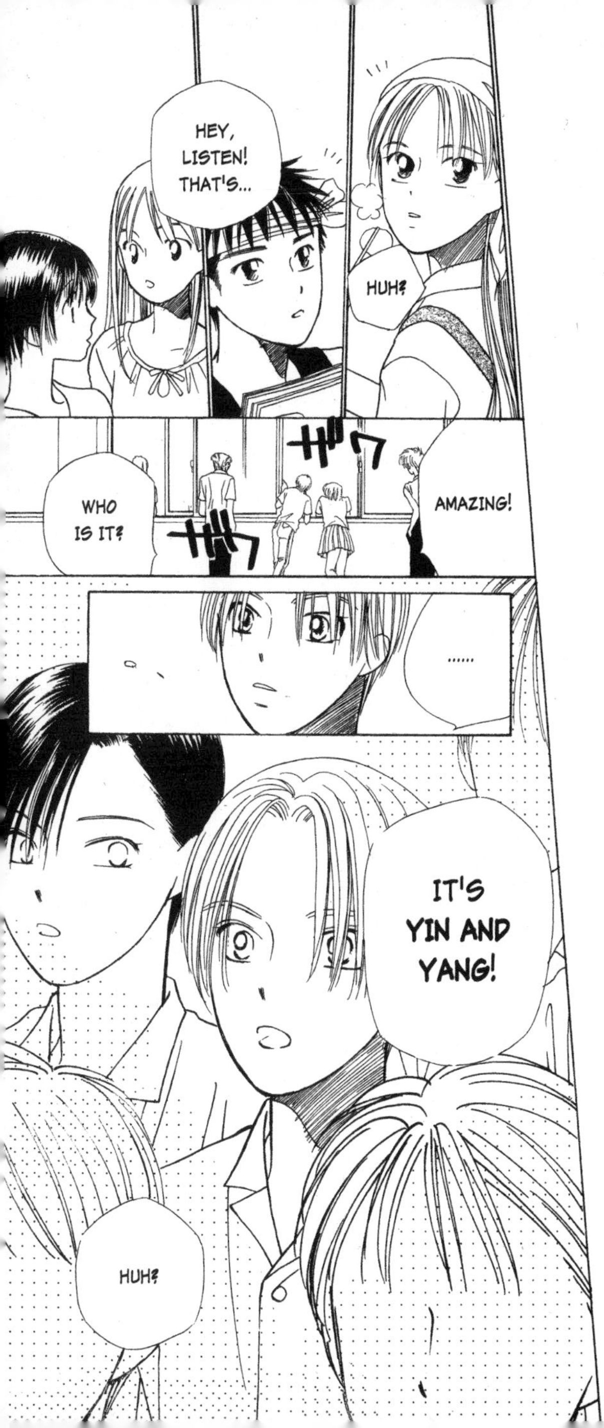
HEY, LISTEN! THAT'S...
HUH?
AMAZING!
ザワ
WHO IS IT?
ザワ
......
IT'S YIN AND YANG!
HUH?

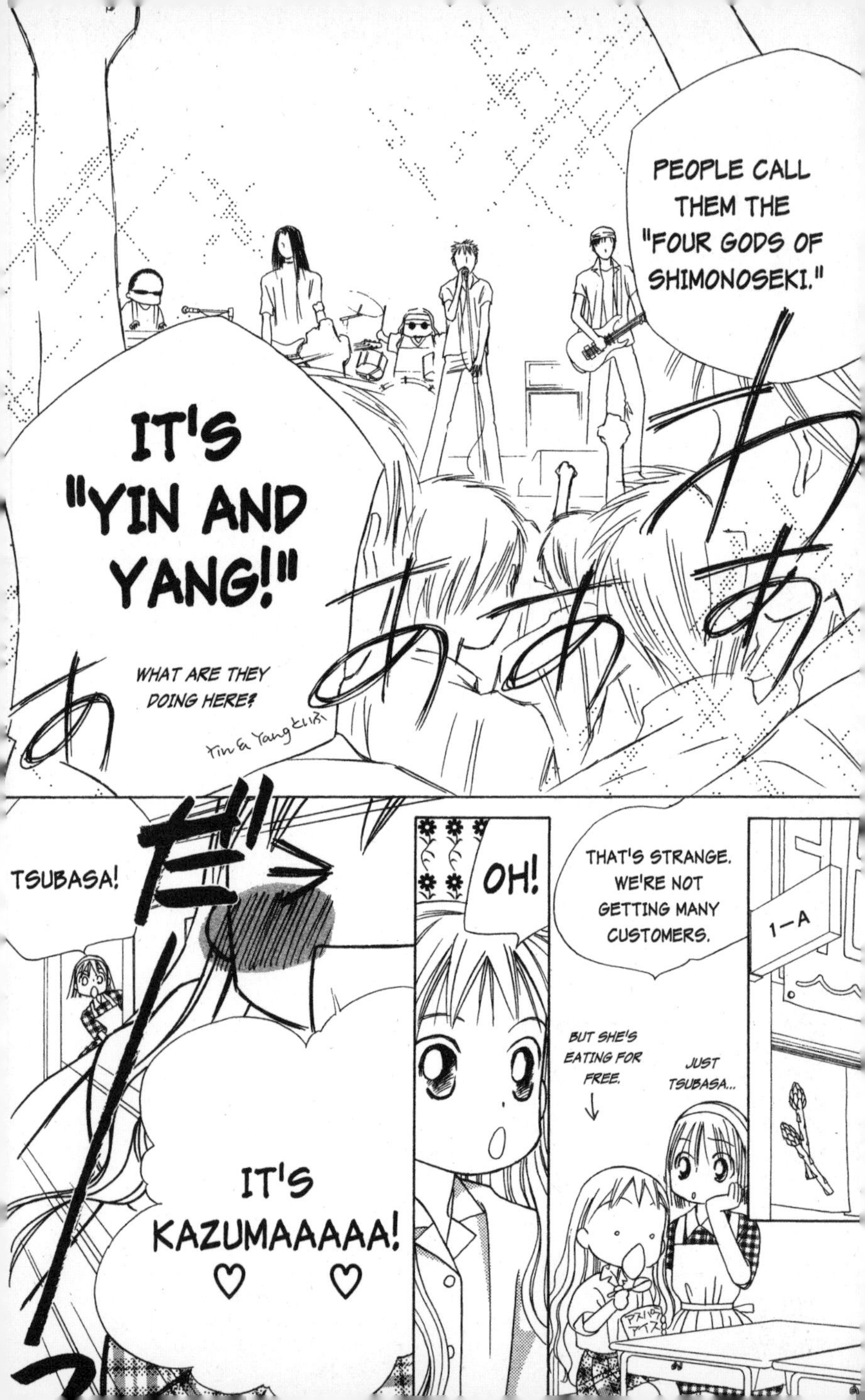
PEOPLE CALL THEM THE "FOUR GODS OF SHIMONOSEKI."
あああああ
IT'S "YIN AND YANG!"
WHAT ARE THEY DOING HERE?
1—A
THAT'S STRANGE. WE'RE NOT GETTING MANY CUSTOMERS.
JUST TSUBASA...
BUT SHE'S EATING FOR FREE.
OH!
TSUBASA!
だっ
IT'S KAZUMAAAAA! ♡ ♡

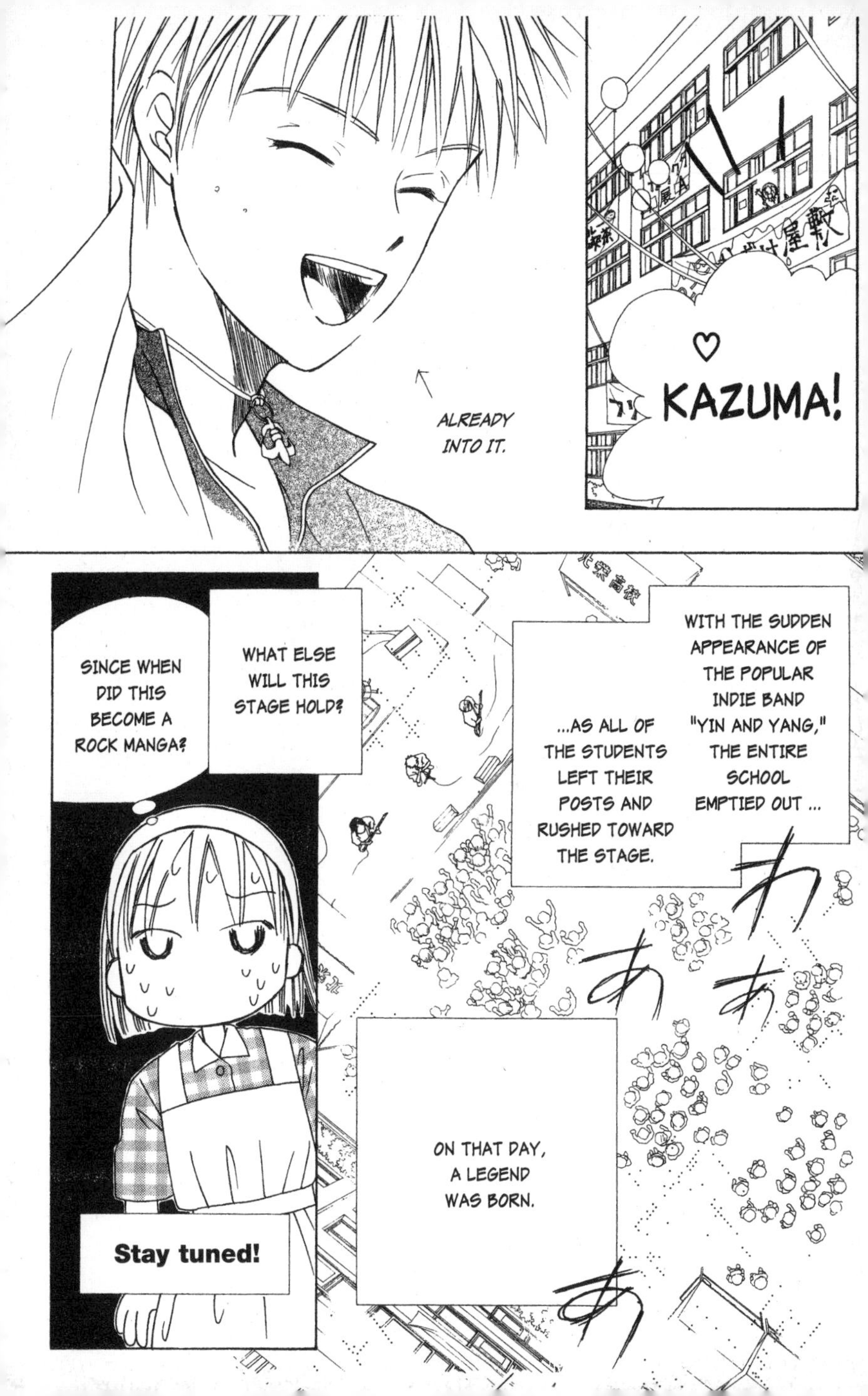
♡ KAZUMA!
ALREADY INTO IT.
WITH THE SUDDEN APPEARANCE OF THE POPULAR INDIE BAND "YIN AND YANG," THE ENTIRE SCHOOL EMPTIED OUT ...
...AS ALL OF THE STUDENTS LEFT THEIR POSTS AND RUSHED TOWARD THE STAGE.
わあああ
ON THAT DAY, A LEGEND WAS BORN.
WHAT ELSE WILL THIS STAGE HOLD?
SINCE WHEN DID THIS BECOME A ROCK MANGA?
Stay tuned!

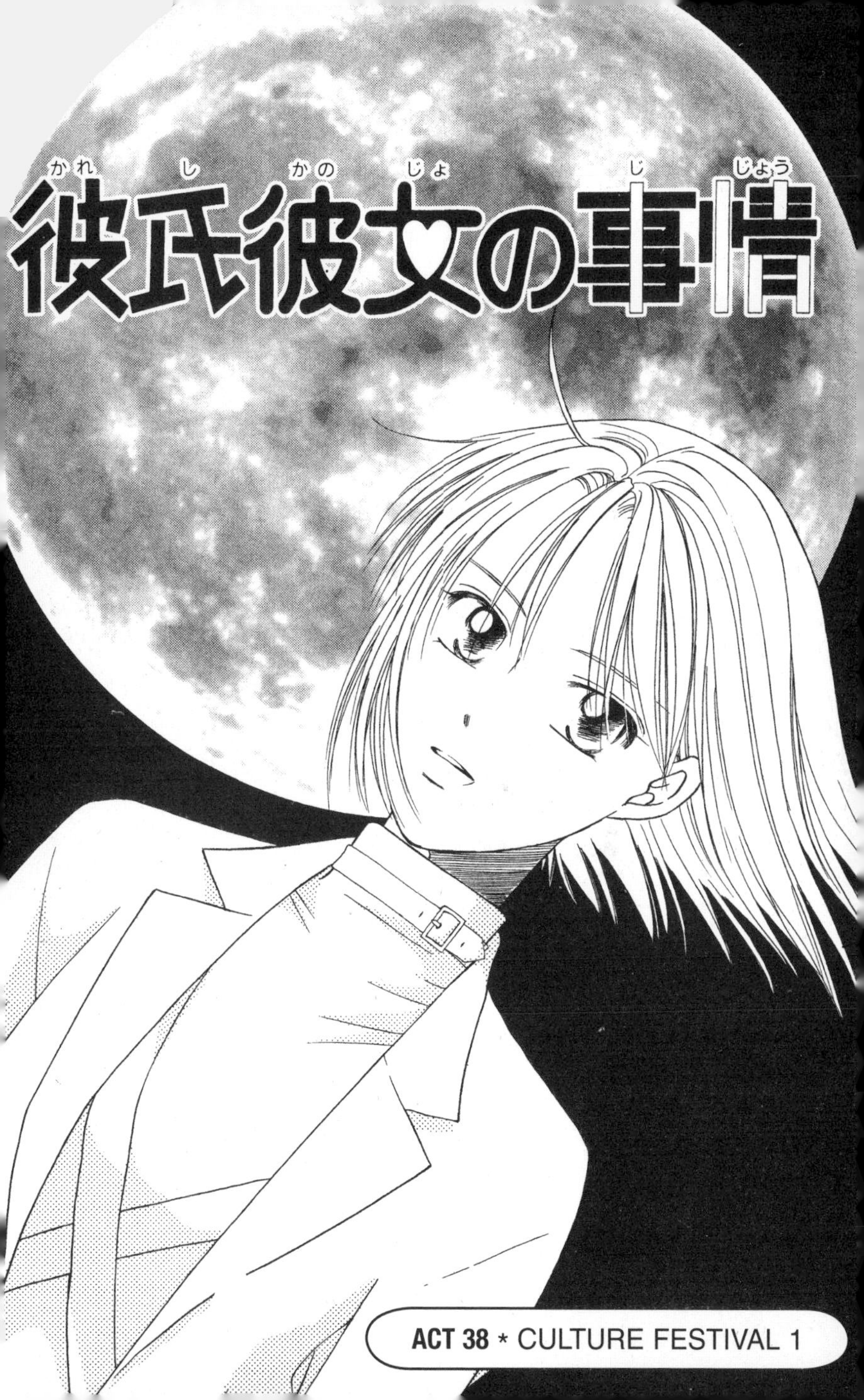
彼氏彼女の事情
ACT 38 * CULTURE FESTIVAL 1

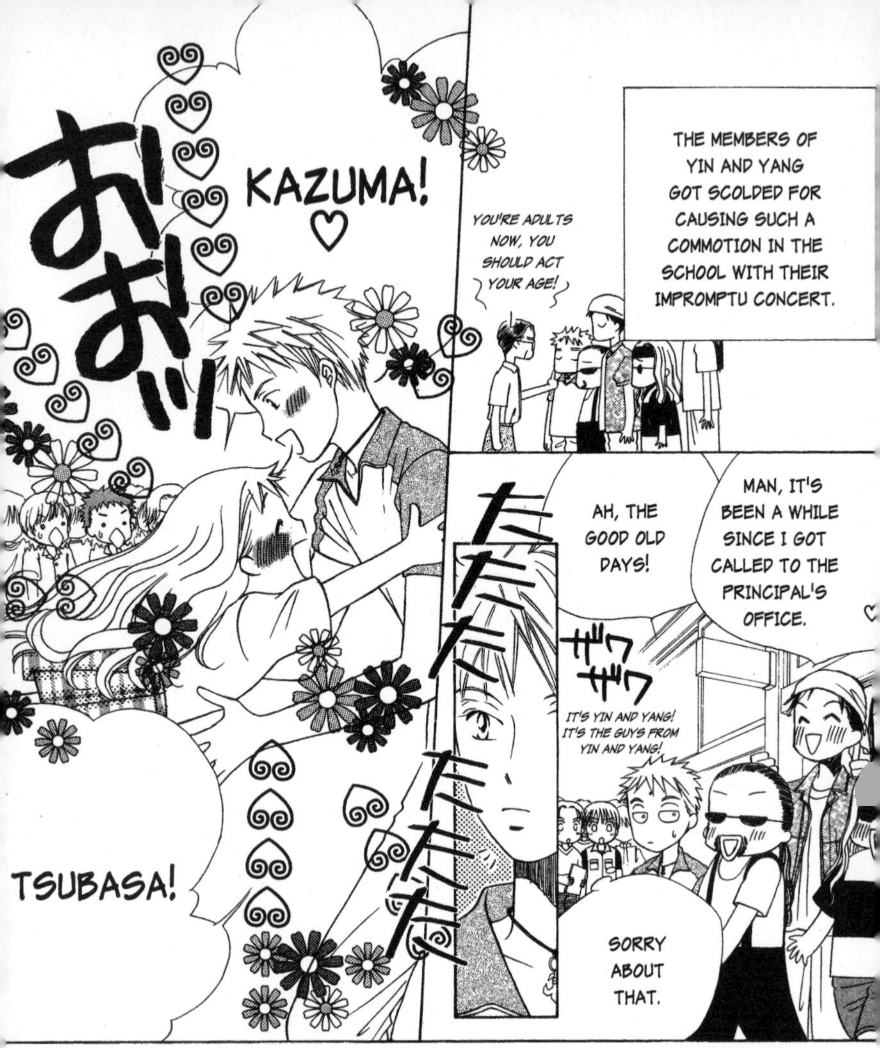
THE MEMBERS OF YIN AND YANG GOT SCOLDED FOR CAUSING SUCH A COMMOTION IN THE SCHOOL WITH THEIR IMPROMPTU CONCERT.
YOU'RE ADULTS NOW, YOU SHOULD ACT YOUR AGE!
MAN, IT'S BEEN A WHILE SINCE I GOT CALLED TO THE PRINCIPAL'S OFFICE.
AH, THE GOOD OLD DAYS!
ザワザワ
IT'S YIN AND YANG! IT'S THE GUYS FROM YIN AND YANG!
SORRY ABOUT THAT.
たたたたたた
おおッ
KAZUMA!
TSUBASA!

I eventually want to get better at making it.

Reasonably done.

Japanese sweets go with green tea or toasted tea.

Wedgewood

My editor gave me this.

European snacks go with tea with milk.

I've started to buy black teas. Although so far I only drink it with milk. I finished with the "Fauchon" tea, so now I'm drinking "Ridgeway." After that, I'm going to try "Marriage."

Ms. "N" told me about this.

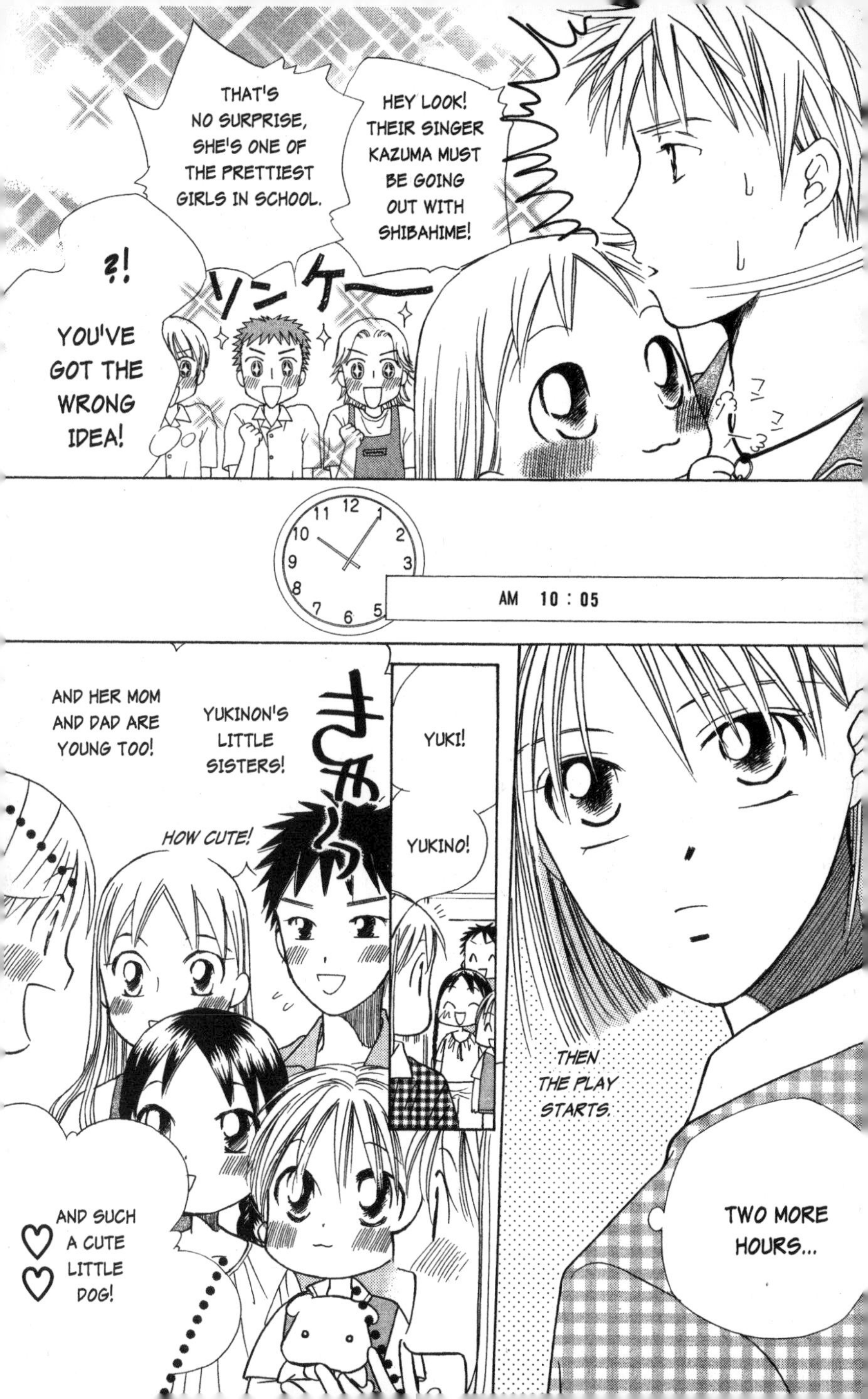
HEY LOOK! THEIR SINGER KAZUMA MUST BE GOING OUT WITH SHIBAHIME!
THAT'S NO SURPRISE, SHE'S ONE OF THE PRETTIEST GIRLS IN SCHOOL.
ソンケー
?!
YOU'VE GOT THE WRONG IDEA!
AM 10 : 05
TWO MORE HOURS...
THEN THE PLAY STARTS.
YUKI!
YUKINO!
YUKINON'S LITTLE SISTERS!
AND HER MOM AND DAD ARE YOUNG TOO!
HOW CUTE!
AND SUCH A CUTE LITTLE DOG!

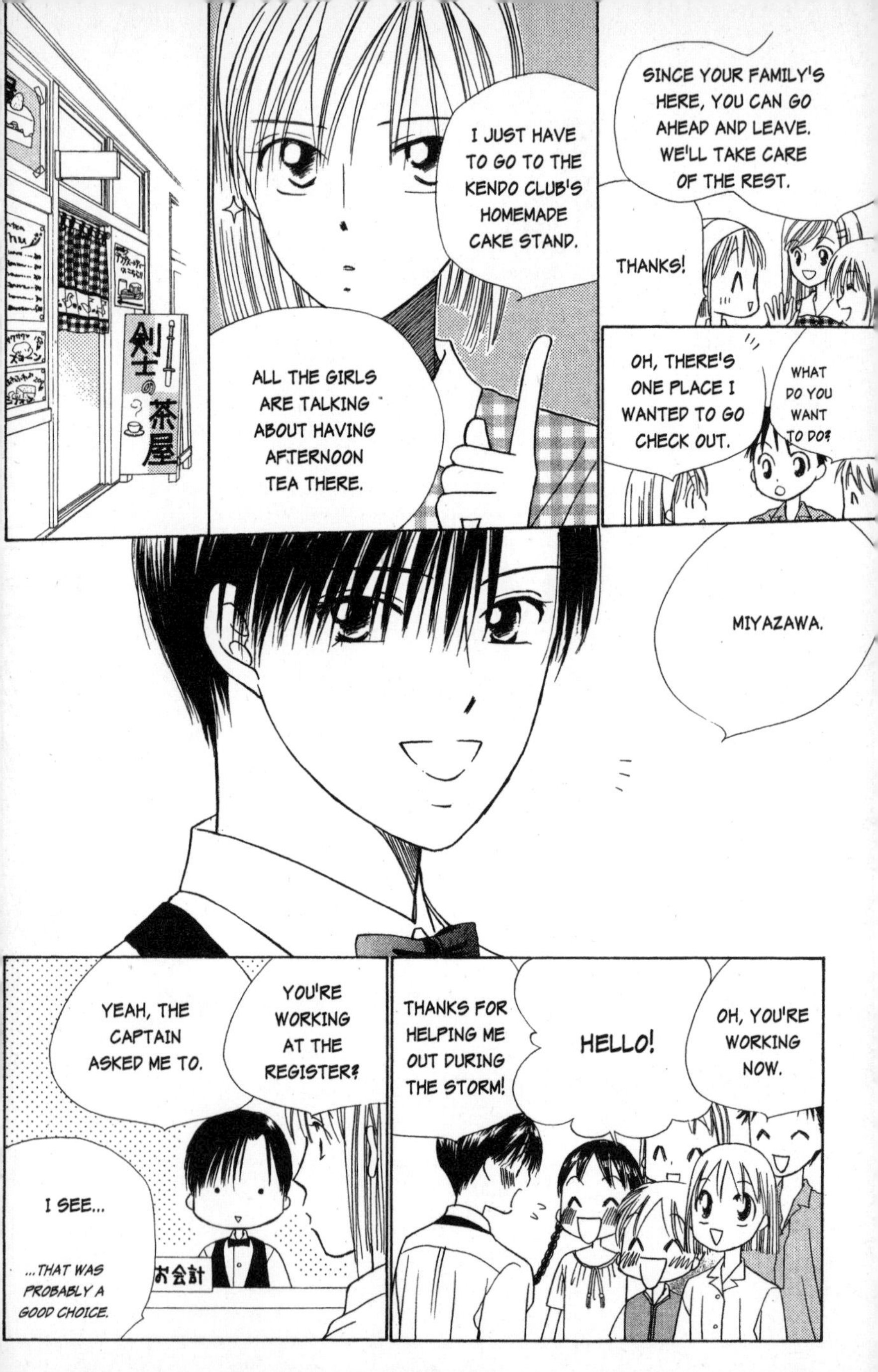

SINCE YOUR FAMILY'S HERE, YOU CAN GO AHEAD AND LEAVE. WE'LL TAKE CARE OF THE REST.
THANKS!
WHAT DO YOU WANT TO DO?
OH, THERE'S ONE PLACE I WANTED TO GO CHECK OUT.
I JUST HAVE TO GO TO THE KENDO CLUB'S HOMEMADE CAKE STAND.
ALL THE GIRLS ARE TALKING ABOUT HAVING AFTERNOON TEA THERE.
剣士の茶屋
MIYAZAWA.
OH, YOU'RE WORKING NOW.
HELLO!
THANKS FOR HELPING ME OUT DURING THE STORM!
YOU'RE WORKING AT THE REGISTER?
YEAH, THE CAPTAIN ASKED ME TO.
I SEE...
...THAT WAS PROBABLY A GOOD CHOICE.
お会計

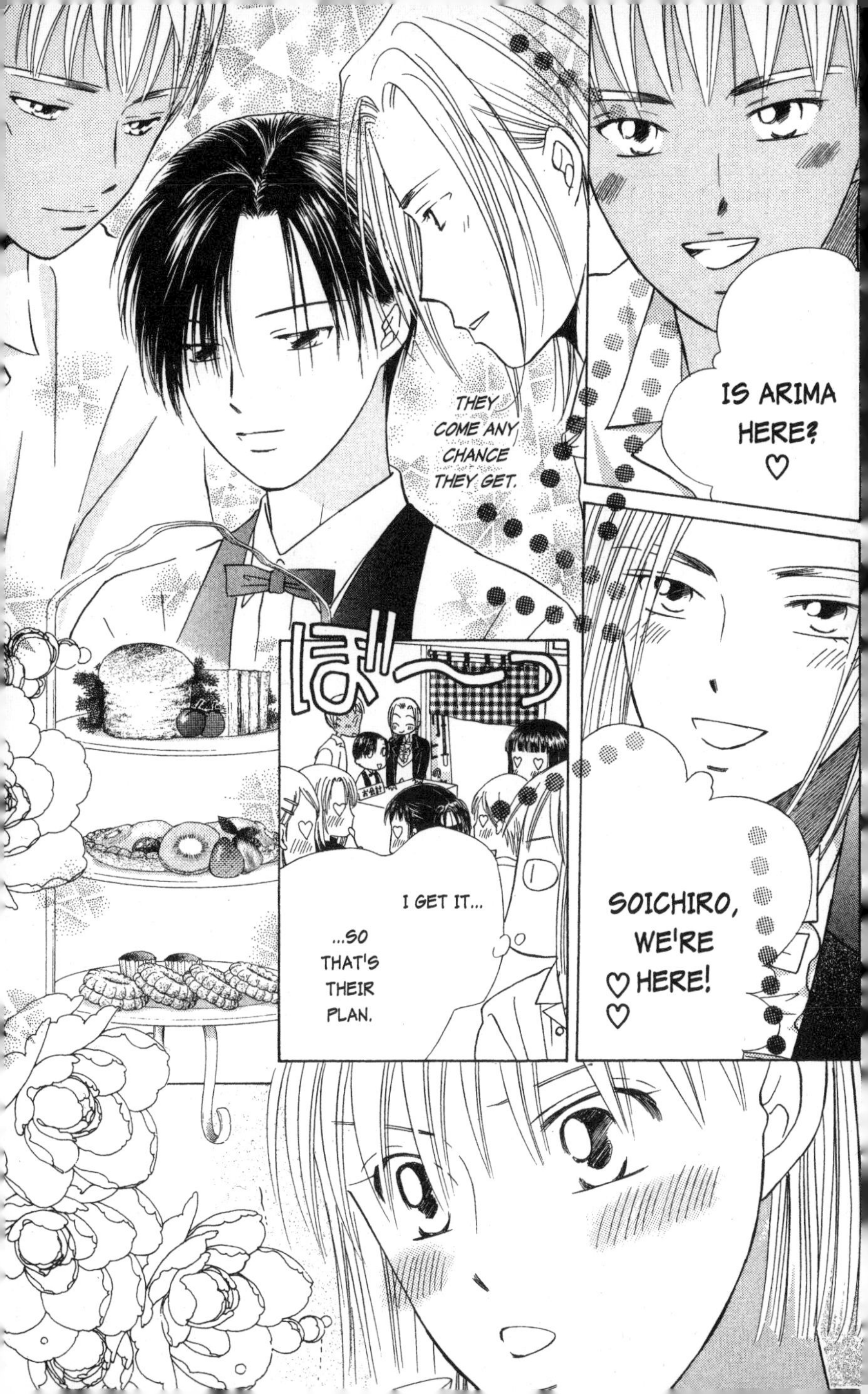
IS ARIMA HERE? ♡
THEY COME ANY CHANCE THEY GET.
SOICHIRO, WE'RE HERE! ♡ ♡
ほーっ
I GET IT...
...SO THAT'S THEIR PLAN.

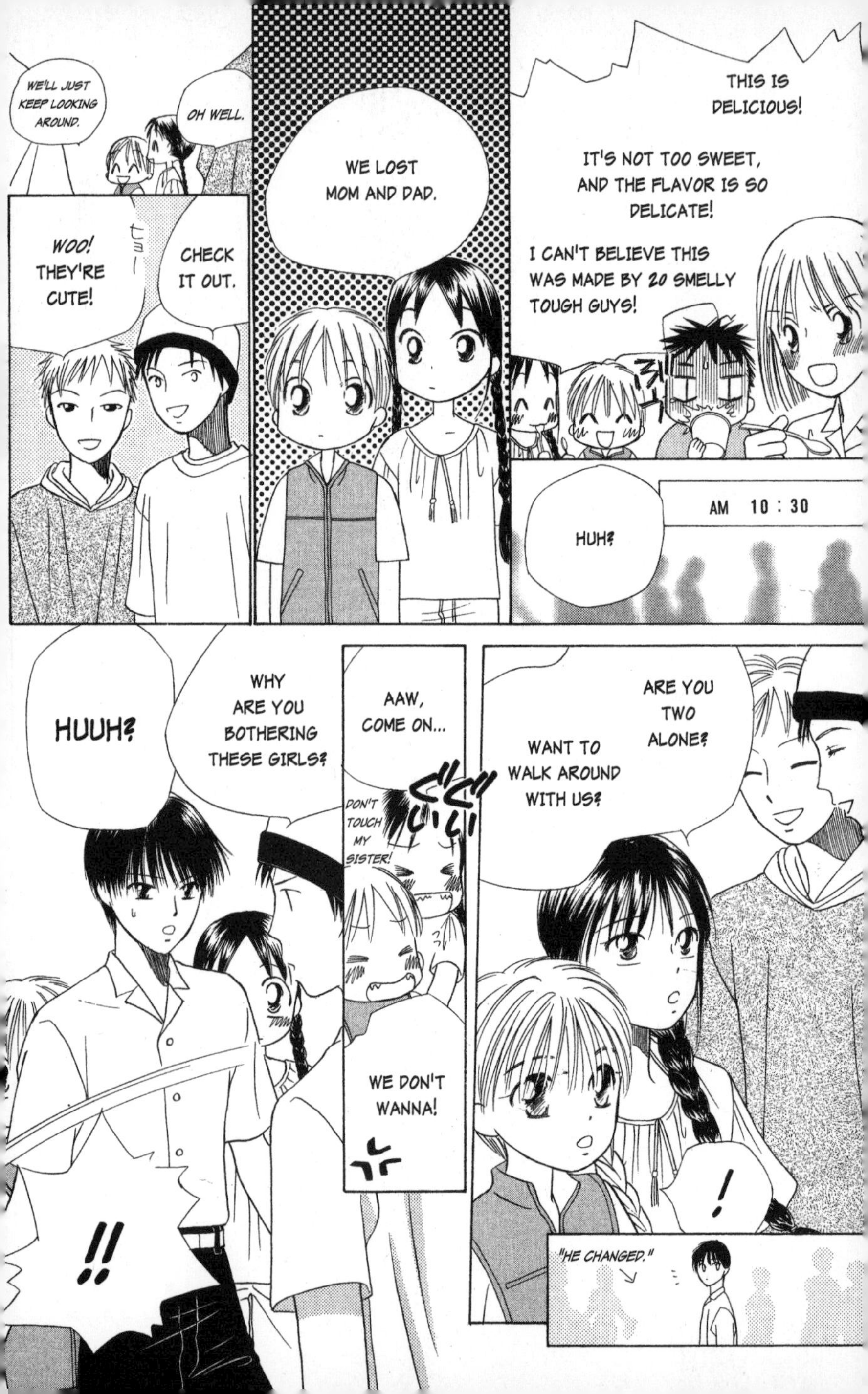
THIS IS DELICIOUS!
IT'S NOT TOO SWEET, AND THE FLAVOR IS SO DELICATE!
I CAN'T BELIEVE THIS WAS MADE BY 20 SMELLY TOUGH GUYS!
AM 10 : 30
HUH?
WE LOST MOM AND DAD.
OH WELL.
WE'LL JUST KEEP LOOKING AROUND.
CHECK IT OUT.
WOO! THEY'RE CUTE!
ヒョー
ARE YOU TWO ALONE?
WANT TO WALK AROUND WITH US?
!
"HE CHANGED."
AAW, COME ON...
DON'T TOUCH MY SISTER!
WE DON'T WANNA!
WHY ARE YOU BOTHERING THESE GIRLS?
HUUH?
!!

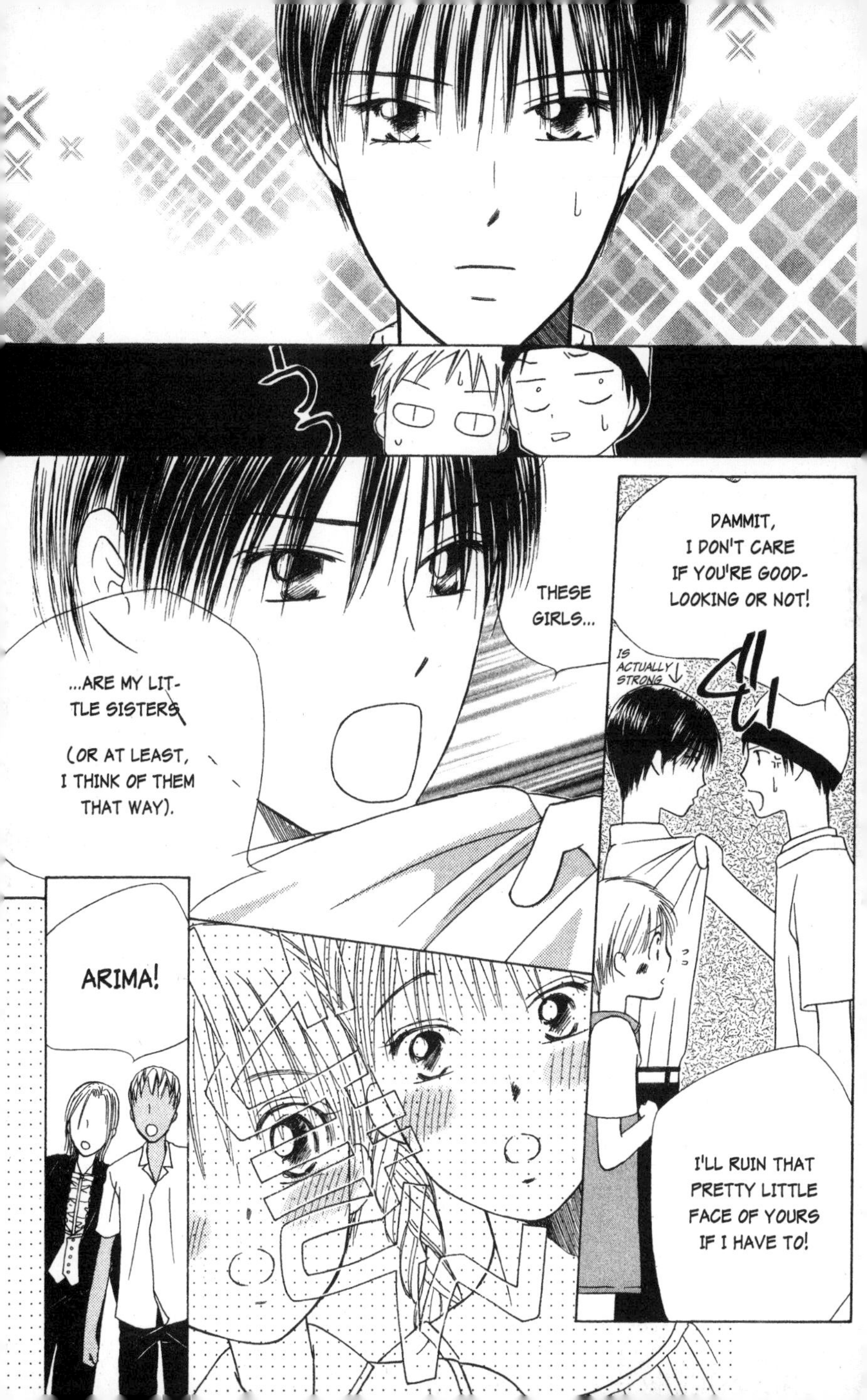
THESE GIRLS...
...ARE MY LIT-TLE SISTERS
(OR AT LEAST, I THINK OF THEM THAT WAY).
DAMMIT, I DON'T CARE IF YOU'RE GOOD-LOOKING OR NOT!
IS ACTUALLY STRONG
I'LL RUIN THAT PRETTY LITTLE FACE OF YOURS IF I HAVE TO!
ARIMA!

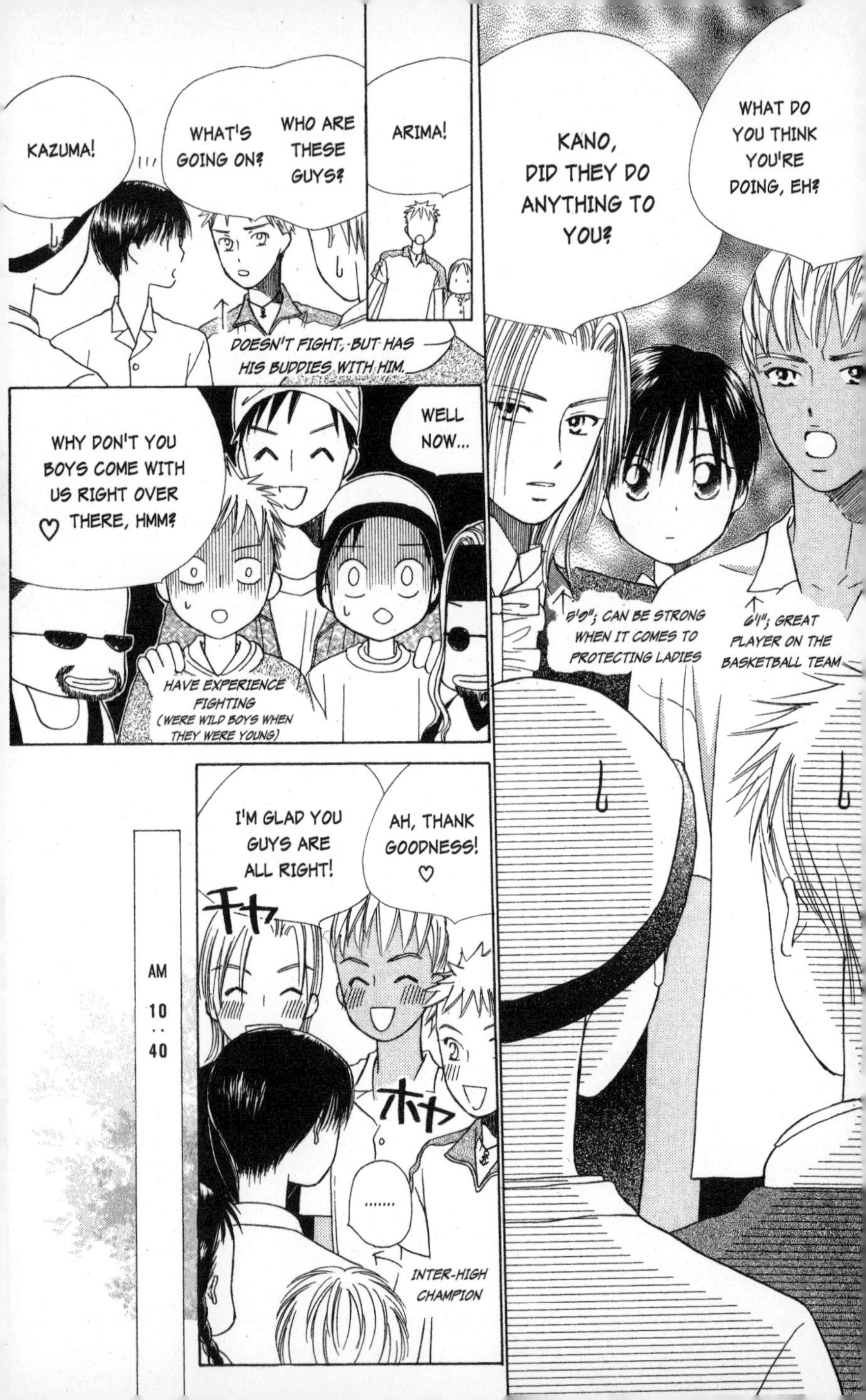

WHAT DO YOU THINK YOU'RE DOING, EH?
KANO, DID THEY DO ANYTHING TO YOU?
5'9"; CAN BE STRONG WHEN IT COMES TO PROTECTING LADIES
6'1"; GREAT PLAYER ON THE BASKETBALL TEAM
ARIMA!
WHO ARE THESE GUYS?
WHAT'S GOING ON?
KAZUMA!
DOESN'T FIGHT, BUT HAS HIS BUDDIES WITH HIM.
WELL NOW...
WHY DON'T YOU BOYS COME WITH US RIGHT OVER ♡ THERE, HMM?
HAVE EXPERIENCE FIGHTING (WERE WILD BOYS WHEN THEY WERE YOUNG)
AH, THANK GOODNESS! ♡
I'M GLAD YOU GUYS ARE ALL RIGHT!
チヤ
ホヤ
....
INTER-HIGH CHAMPION
AM 10:40

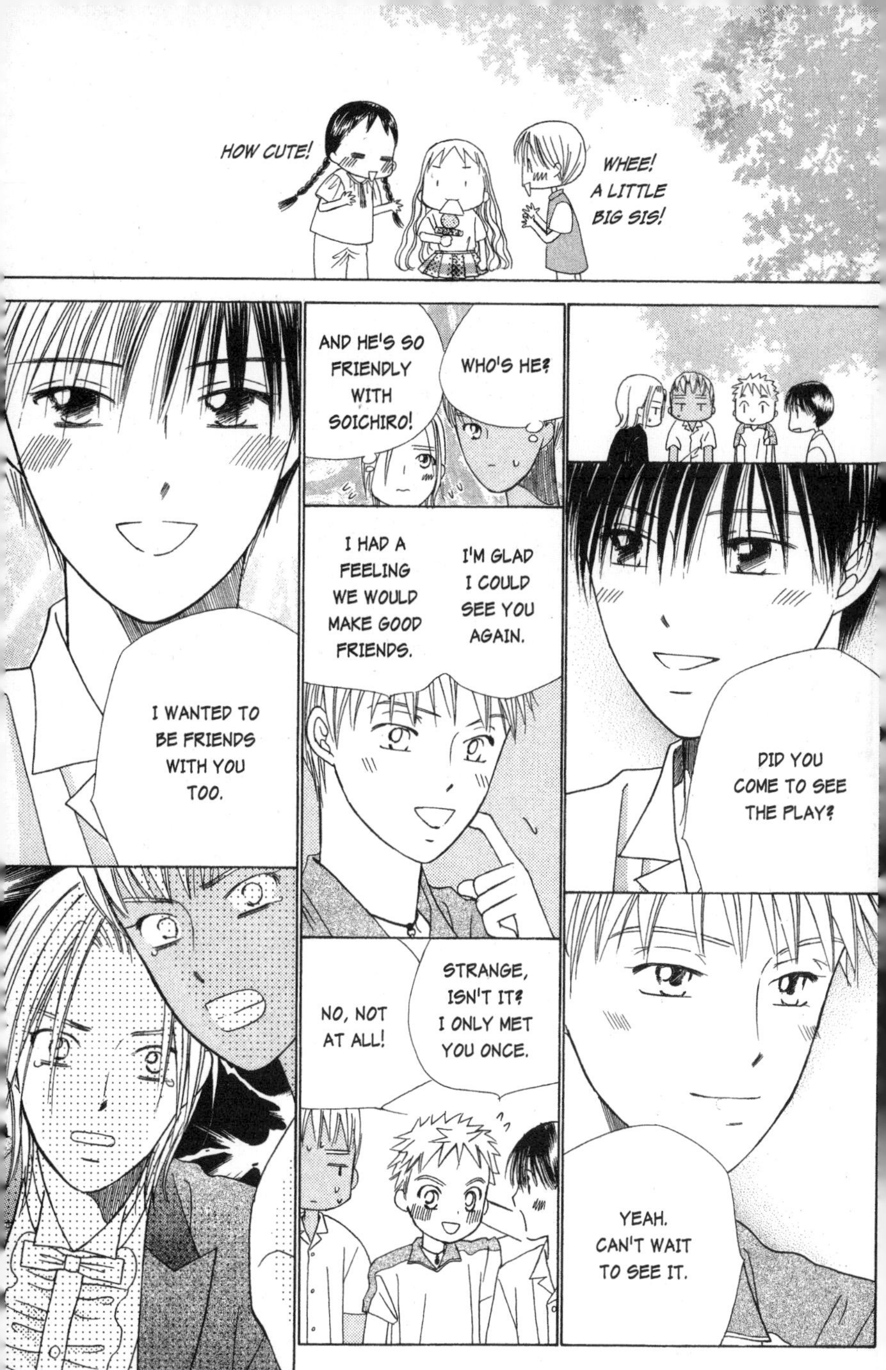

WHEE! A LITTLE BIG SIS!
HOW CUTE!
WHO'S HE?
AND HE'S SO FRIENDLY WITH SOICHIRO!
DID YOU COME TO SEE THE PLAY?
I'M GLAD I COULD SEE YOU AGAIN.
I HAD A FEELING WE WOULD MAKE GOOD FRIENDS.
I WANTED TO BE FRIENDS WITH YOU TOO.
YEAH. CAN'T WAIT TO SEE IT.
STRANGE, ISN'T IT? I ONLY MET YOU ONCE.
NO, NOT AT ALL!

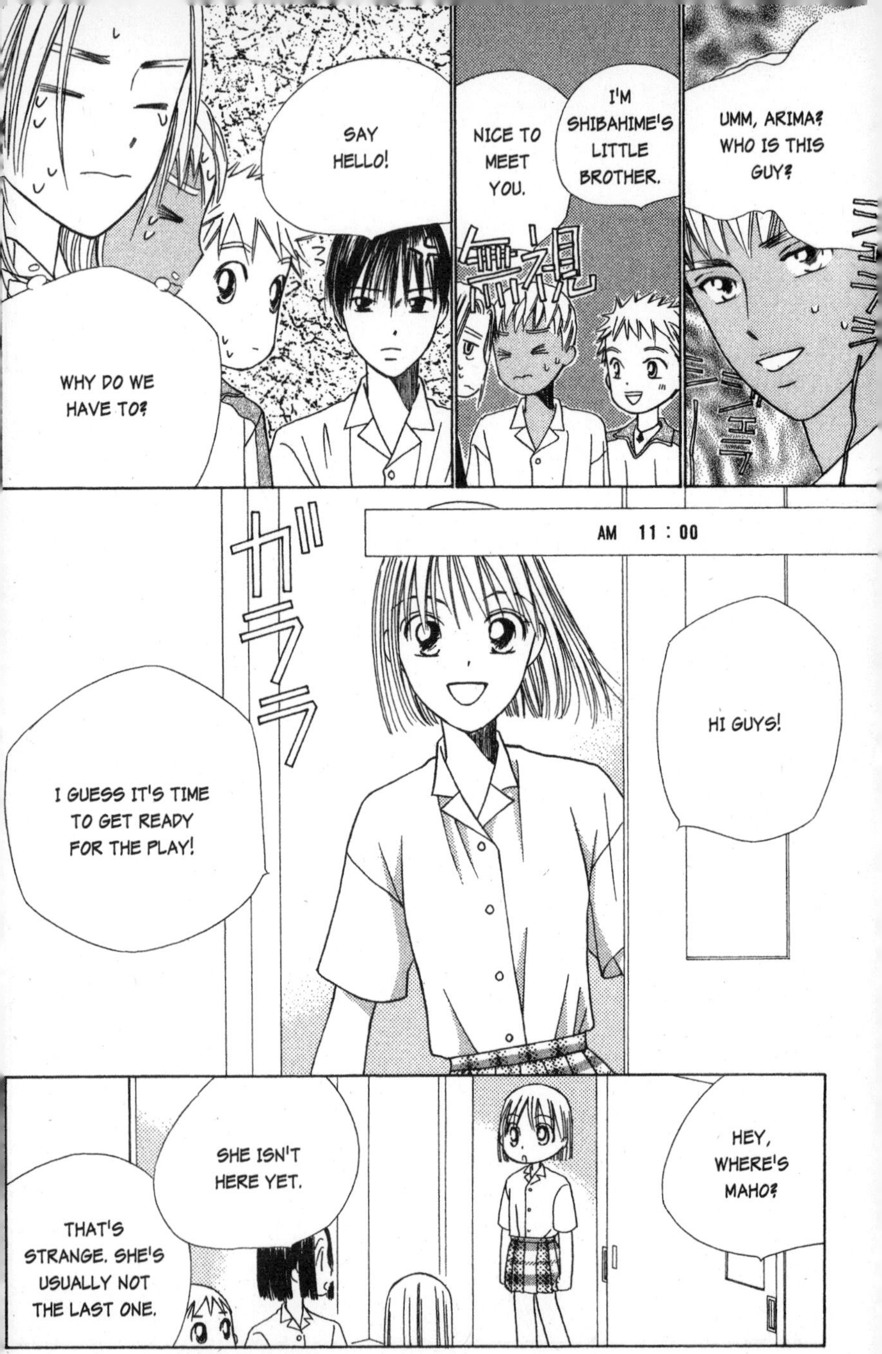
UMM, ARIMA? WHO IS THIS GUY?
I'M SHIBAHIME'S LITTLE BROTHER.
NICE TO MEET YOU.
無視
SAY HELLO!
WHY DO WE HAVE TO?
AM 11 : 00
HI GUYS!
ガラララ
I GUESS IT'S TIME TO GET READY FOR THE PLAY!
HEY, WHERE'S MAHO?
SHE ISN'T HERE YET.
THAT'S STRANGE. SHE'S USUALLY NOT THE LAST ONE.

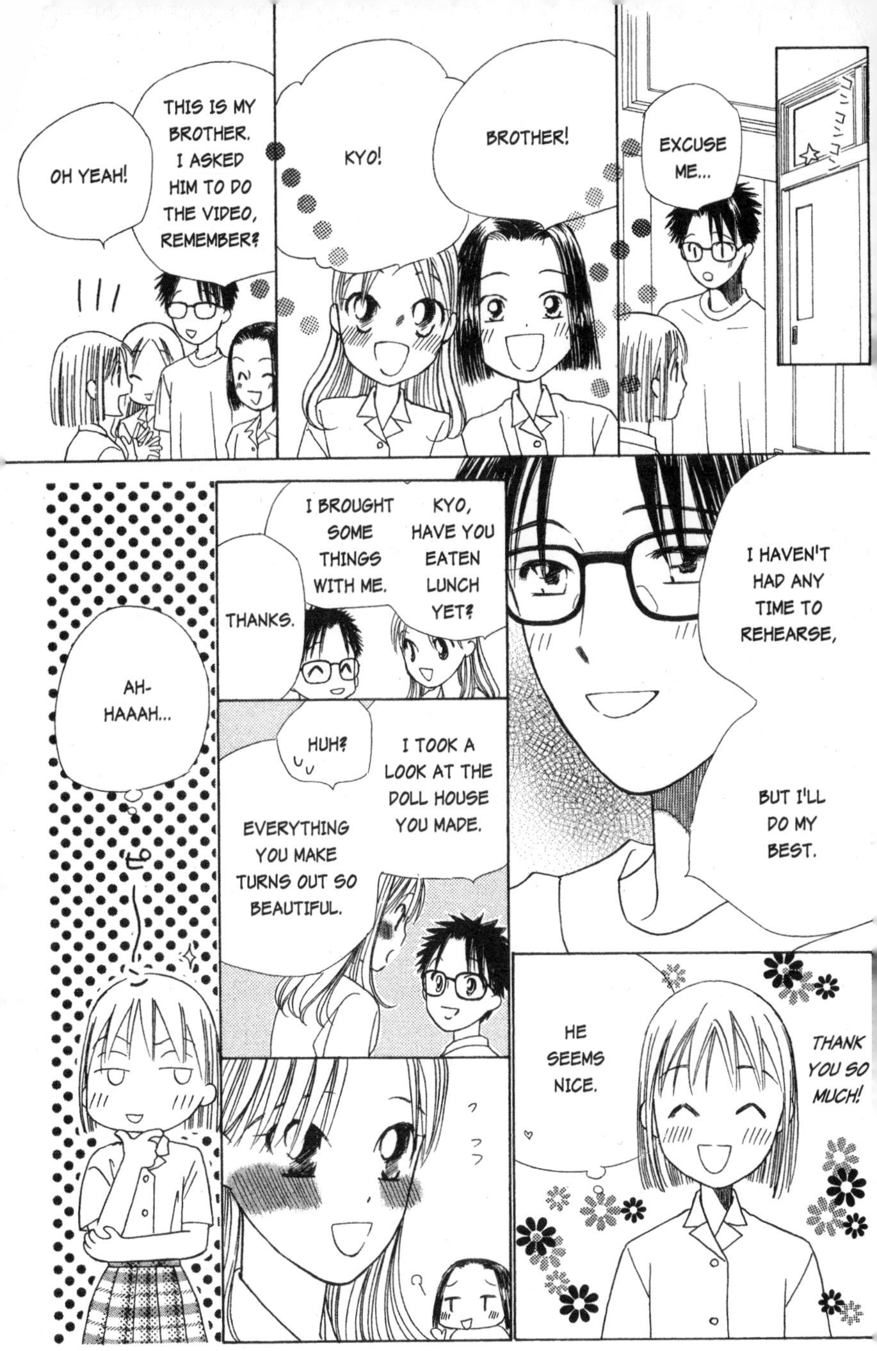
EXCUSE ME...
BROTHER!
KYO!
THIS IS MY BROTHER. I ASKED HIM TO DO THE VIDEO, REMEMBER?
OH YEAH!
I HAVEN'T HAD ANY TIME TO REHEARSE,
BUT I'LL DO MY BEST.
KYO, HAVE YOU EATEN LUNCH YET?
I BROUGHT SOME THINGS WITH ME.
THANKS.
I TOOK A LOOK AT THE DOLL HOUSE YOU MADE.
HUH?
EVERYTHING YOU MAKE TURNS OUT SO BEAUTIFUL.
THANK YOU SO MUCH!
HE SEEMS NICE.
AH-HAAAH...

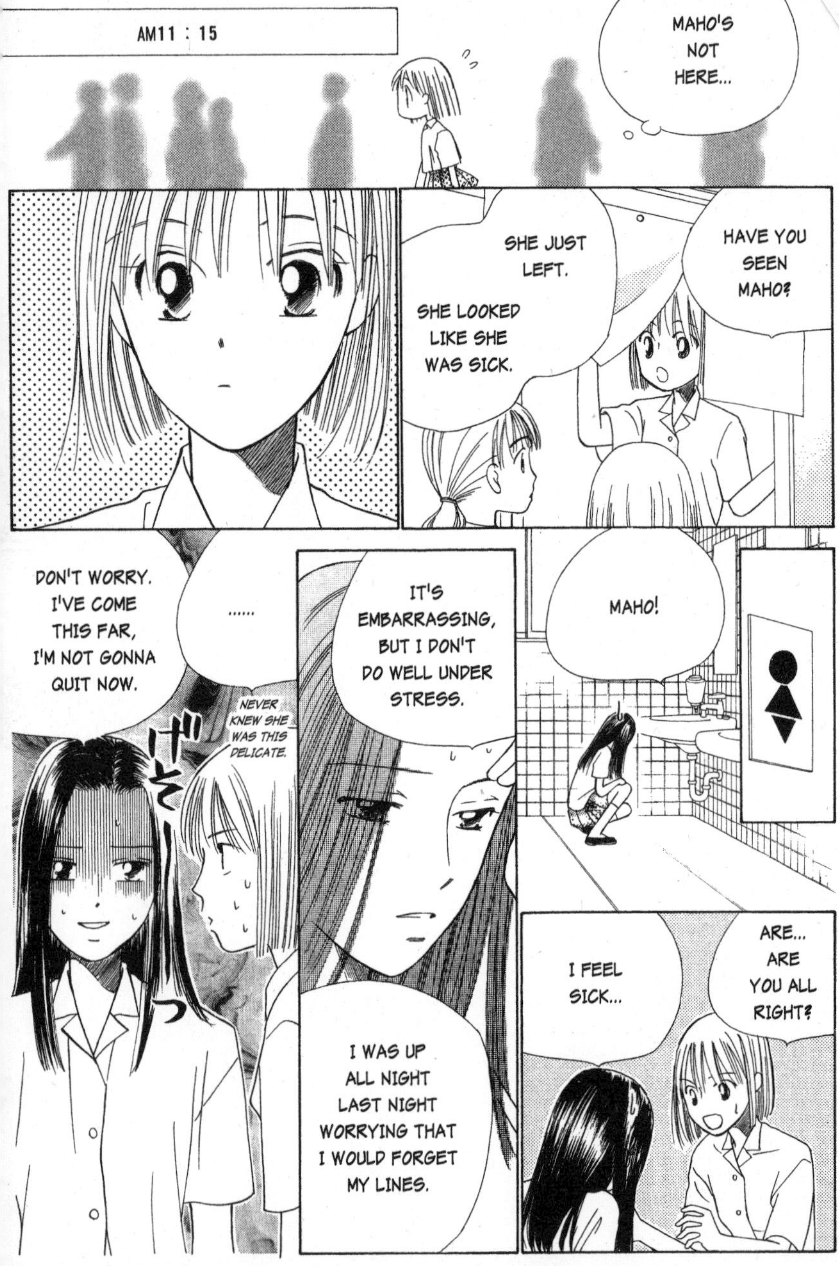
AM11 : 15
MAHO'S NOT HERE...
HAVE YOU SEEN MAHO?
SHE JUST LEFT.
SHE LOOKED LIKE SHE WAS SICK.
MAHO!
ARE... ARE YOU ALL RIGHT?
I FEEL SICK...
IT'S EMBARRASSING, BUT I DON'T DO WELL UNDER STRESS.
I WAS UP ALL NIGHT LAST NIGHT WORRYING THAT I WOULD FORGET MY LINES.
......
DON'T WORRY. I'VE COME THIS FAR, I'M NOT GONNA QUIT NOW.
NEVER KNEW SHE WAS THIS DELICATE.

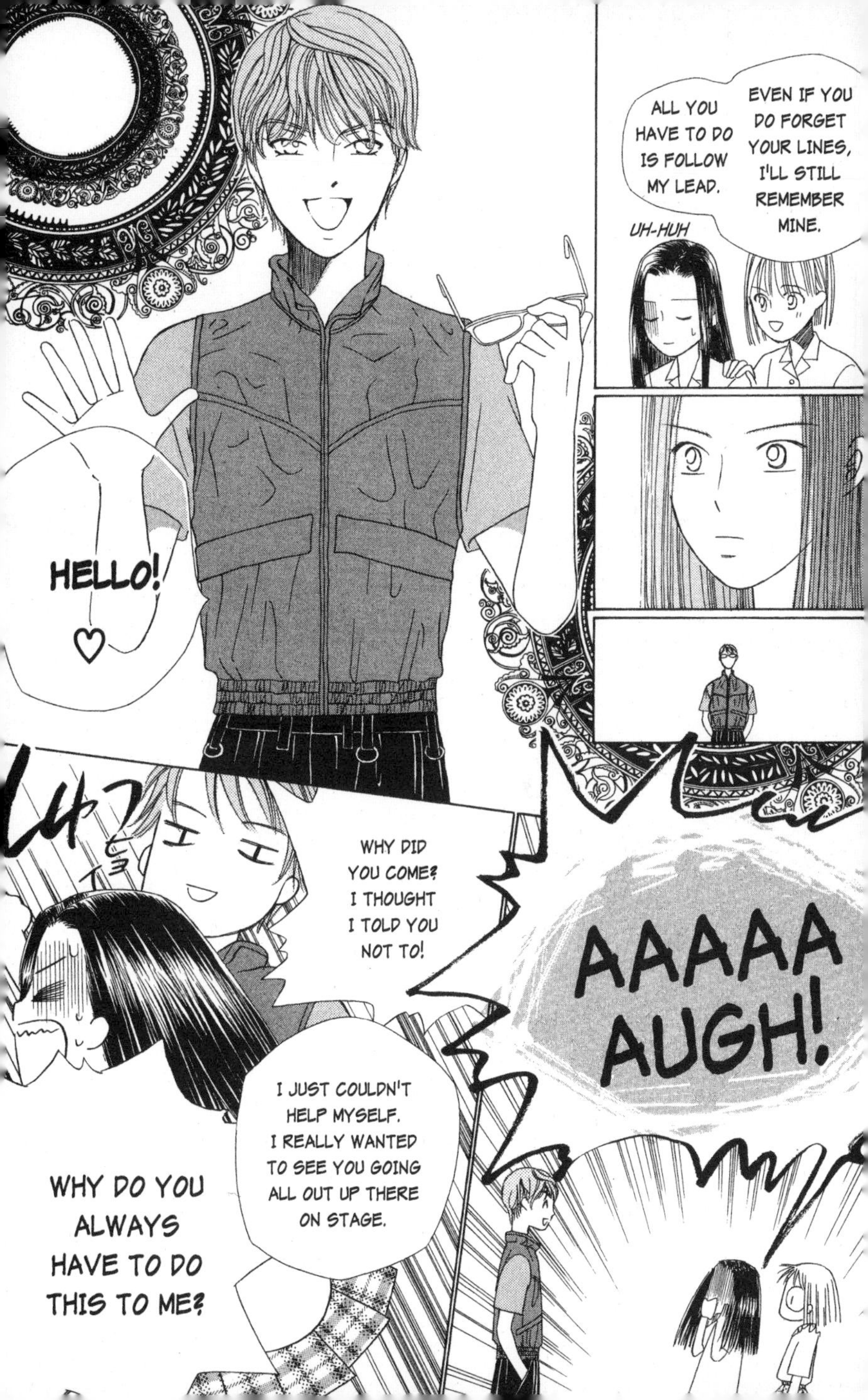
EVEN IF YOU DO FORGET YOUR LINES, I'LL STILL REMEMBER MINE.
ALL YOU HAVE TO DO IS FOLLOW MY LEAD.
UH-HUH
HELLO! ♡
AAAAA AUGH!
WHY DID YOU COME? I THOUGHT I TOLD YOU NOT TO!
I JUST COULDN'T HELP MYSELF. I REALLY WANTED TO SEE YOU GOING ALL OUT UP THERE ON STAGE.
WHY DO YOU ALWAYS HAVE TO DO THIS TO ME?

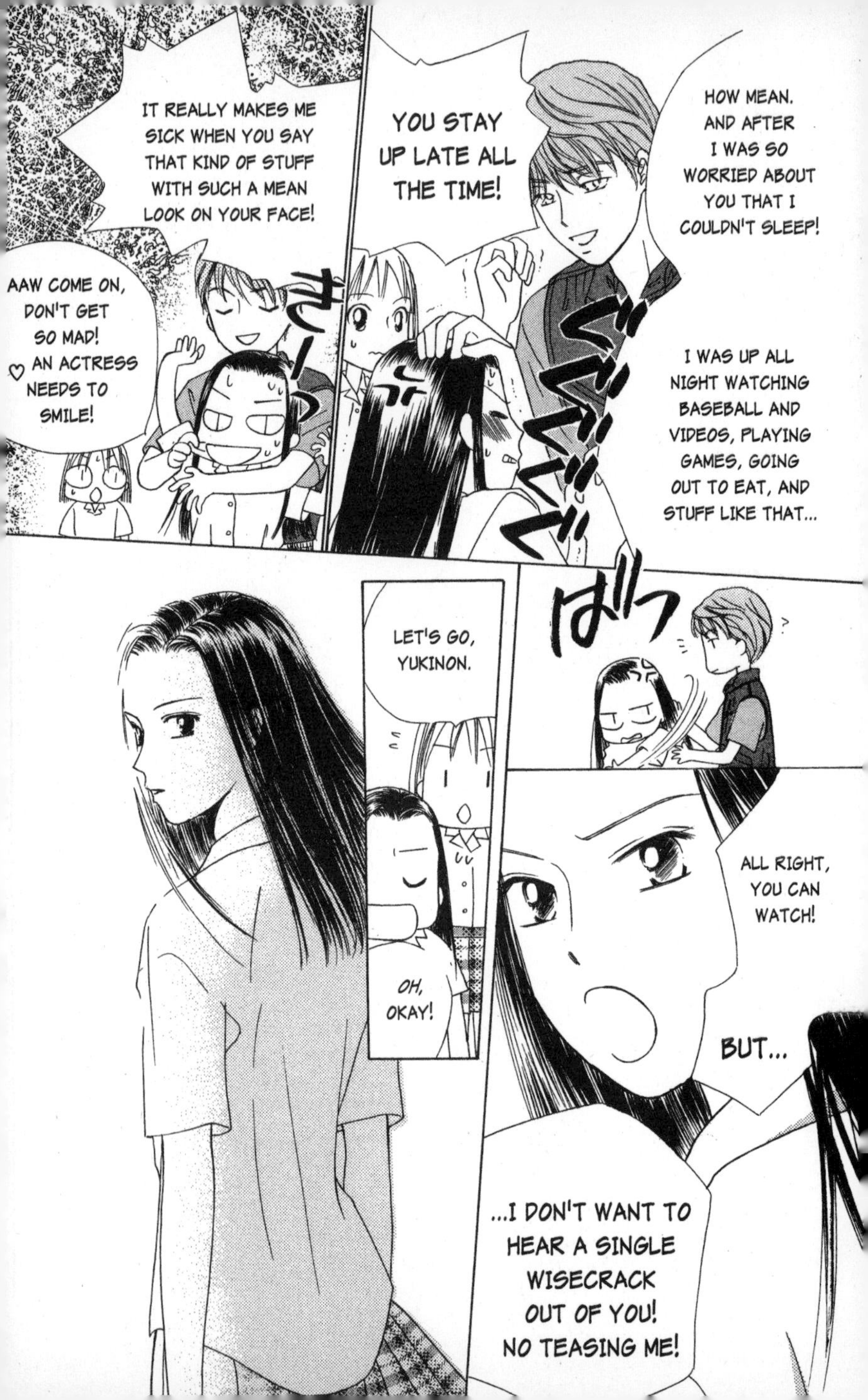
HOW MEAN. AND AFTER I WAS SO WORRIED ABOUT YOU THAT I COULDN'T SLEEP!
YOU STAY UP LATE ALL THE TIME!
I WAS UP ALL NIGHT WATCHING BASEBALL AND VIDEOS, PLAYING GAMES, GOING OUT TO EAT, AND STUFF LIKE THAT...
IT REALLY MAKES ME SICK WHEN YOU SAY THAT KIND OF STUFF WITH SUCH A MEAN LOOK ON YOUR FACE!
AAW COME ON, DON'T GET SO MAD! ♡ AN ACTRESS NEEDS TO SMILE!
ALL RIGHT, YOU CAN WATCH!
BUT...
...I DON'T WANT TO HEAR A SINGLE WISECRACK OUT OF YOU! NO TEASING ME!
LET'S GO, YUKINON.
OH, OKAY!

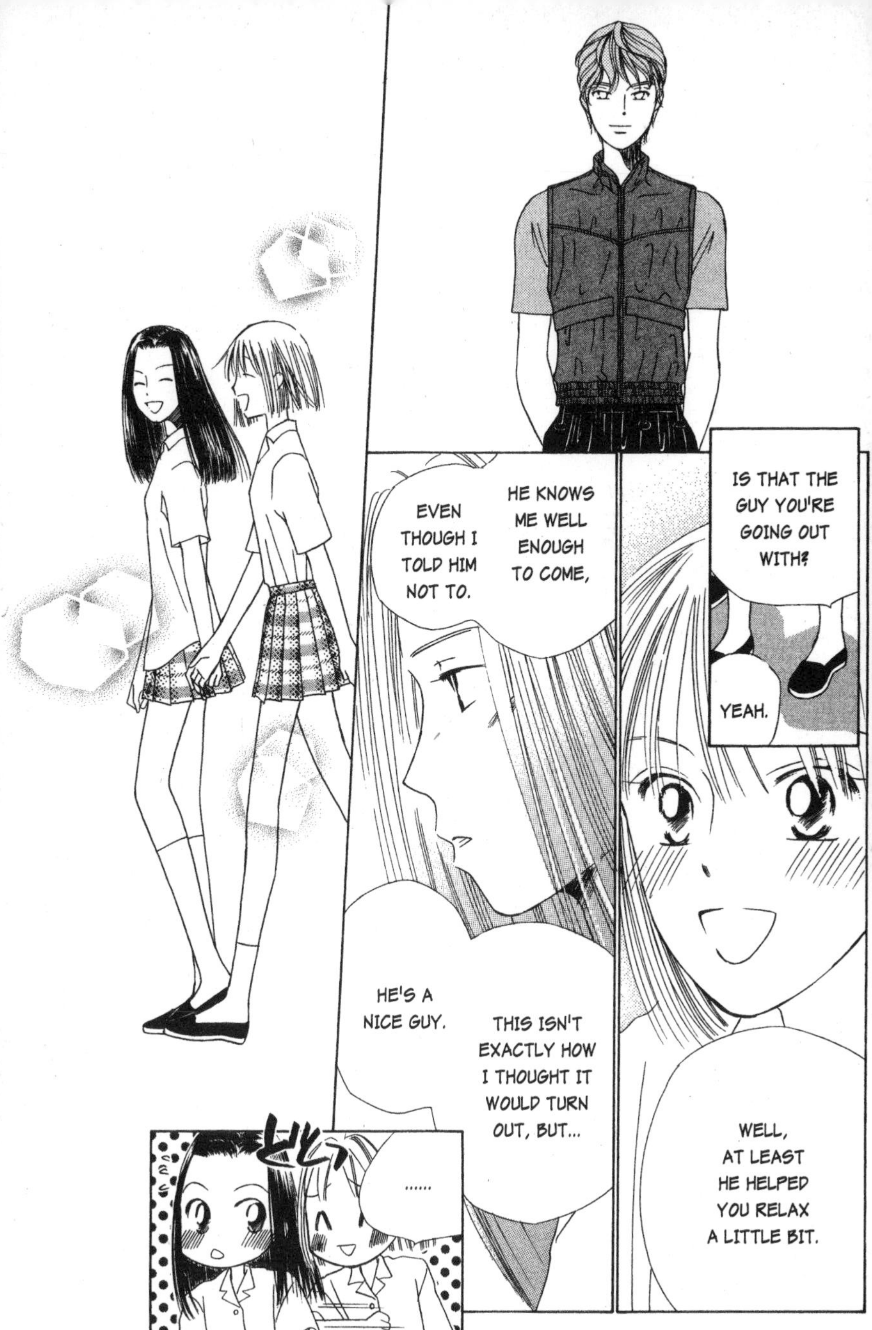
IS THAT THE GUY YOU'RE GOING OUT WITH?
YEAH.
WELL, AT LEAST HE HELPED YOU RELAX A LITTLE BIT.
HE KNOWS ME WELL ENOUGH TO COME,
EVEN THOUGH I TOLD HIM NOT TO.
THIS ISN'T EXACTLY HOW I THOUGHT IT WOULD TURN OUT, BUT...
HE'S A NICE GUY.
......

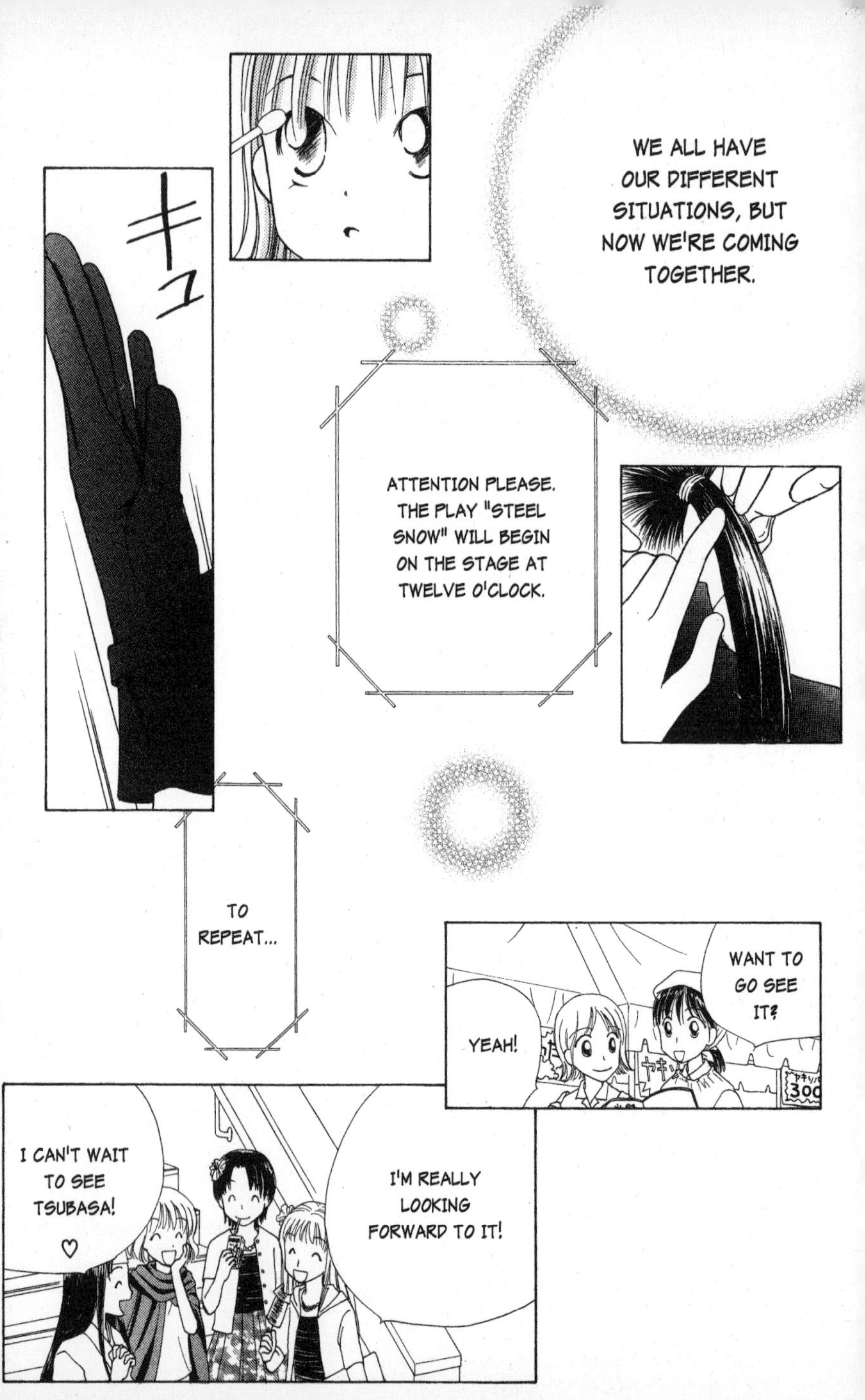
WE ALL HAVE OUR DIFFERENT SITUATIONS, BUT NOW WE'RE COMING TOGETHER.
キュ
ATTENTION PLEASE. THE PLAY "STEEL SNOW" WILL BEGIN ON THE STAGE AT TWELVE O'CLOCK.
TO REPEAT...
WANT TO GO SEE IT?
YEAH!
I'M REALLY LOOKING FORWARD TO IT!
I CAN'T WAIT TO SEE TSUBASA! ♡

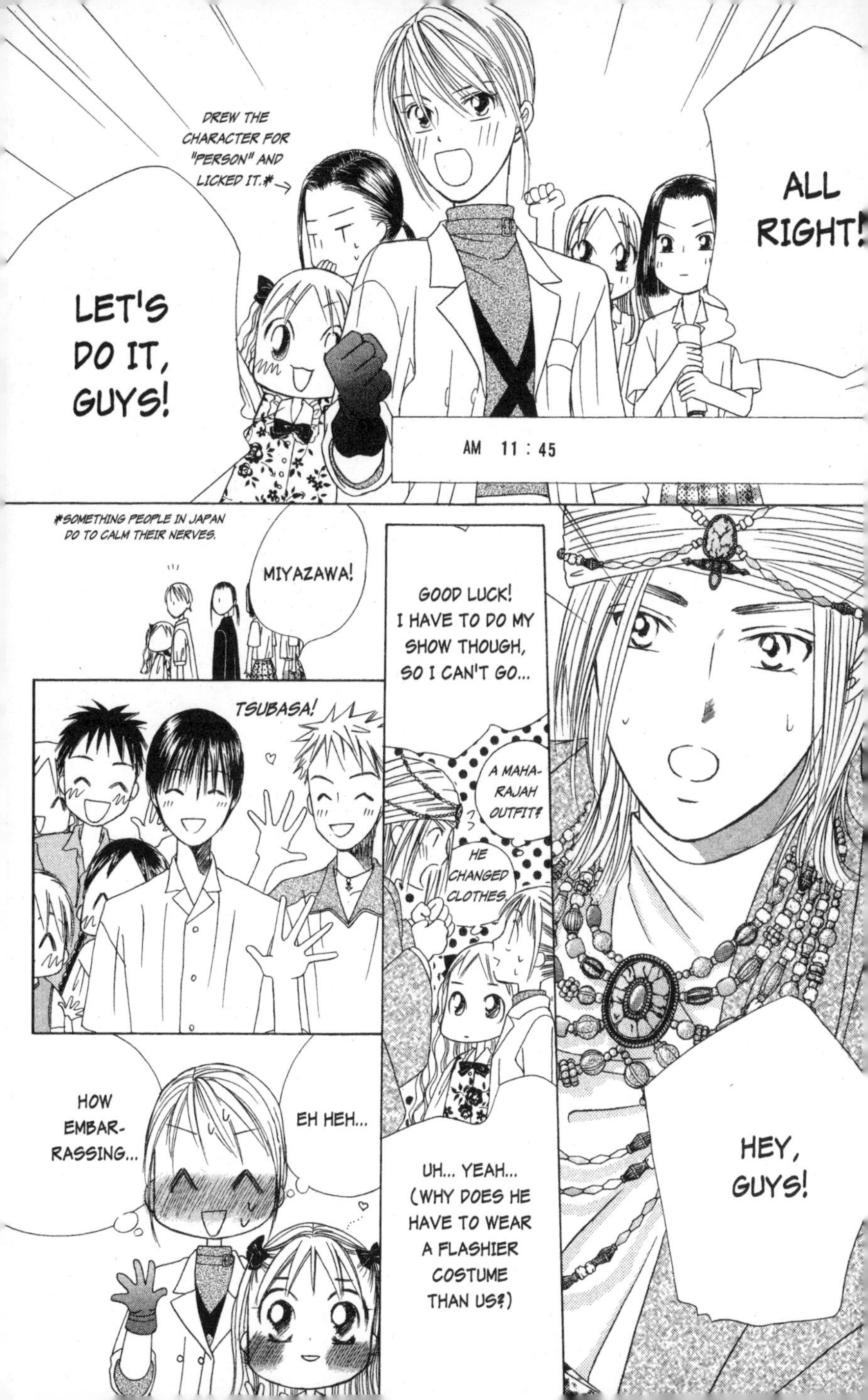
ALL RIGHT!
LET'S DO IT, GUYS!
DREW THE CHARACTER FOR "PERSON" AND LICKED IT.*
AM 11 : 45
HEY, GUYS!
GOOD LUCK! I HAVE TO DO MY SHOW THOUGH, SO I CAN'T GO...
A MAHA-RAJAH OUTFIT?
HE CHANGED CLOTHES.
UH... YEAH... (WHY DOES HE HAVE TO WEAR A FLASHIER COSTUME THAN US?)
MIYAZAWA!
TSUBASA!
EH HEH...
HOW EMBAR-RASSING...
*SOMETHING PEOPLE IN JAPAN DO TO CALM THEIR NERVES.

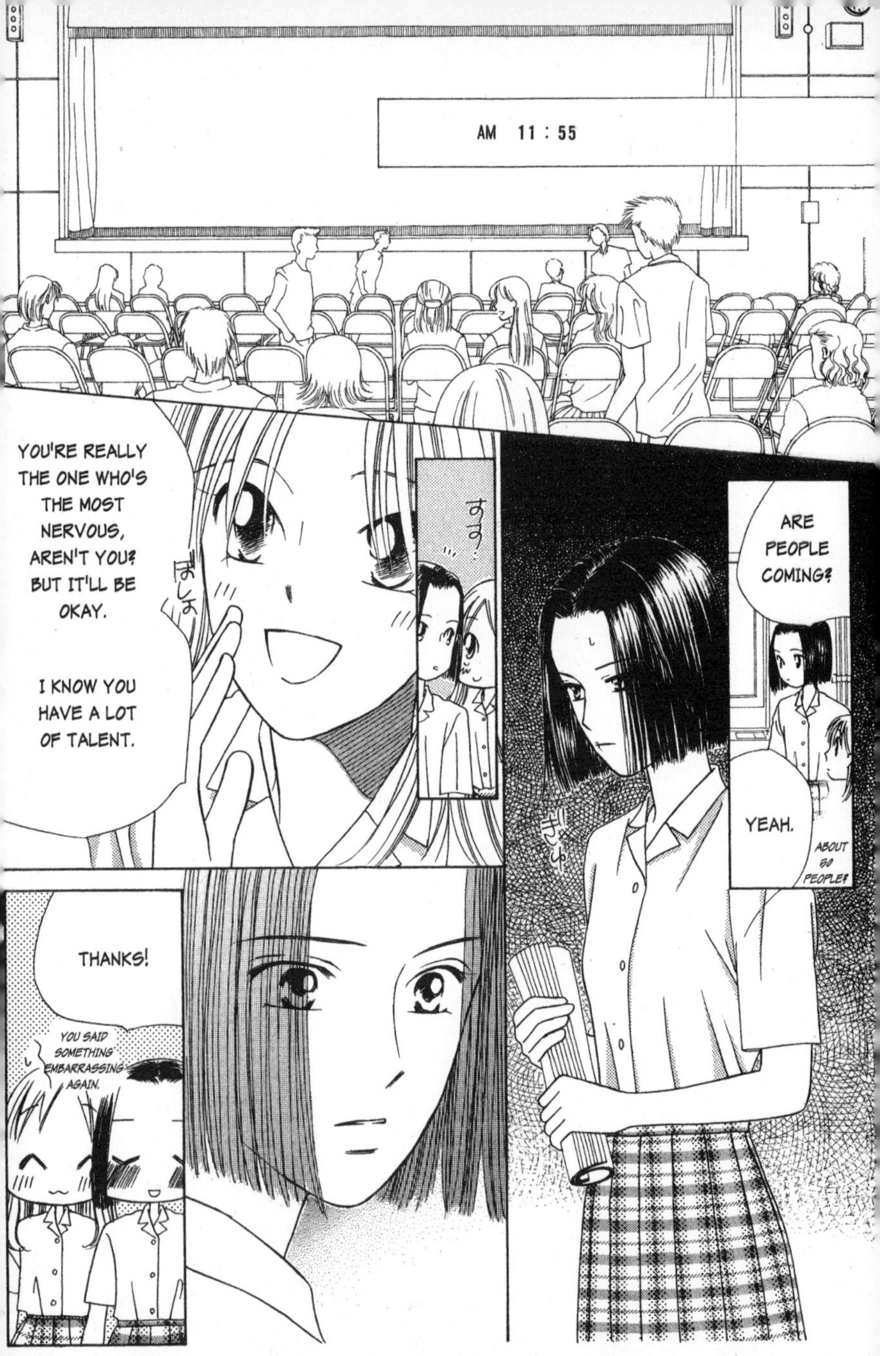

AM 11 : 55
ARE PEOPLE COMING?
YEAH.
ABOUT 50 PEOPLE?
YOU'RE REALLY THE ONE WHO'S THE MOST NERVOUS, AREN'T YOU? BUT IT'LL BE OKAY.
I KNOW YOU HAVE A LOT OF TALENT.
THANKS!
YOU SAID SOMETHING EMBARRASSING AGAIN.

2

That's right, Kazuma's band is called Yin and Yang.

The words Yin and Yang have deep meanings, so I've always wanted to use them. I'm glad I finally got the chance!

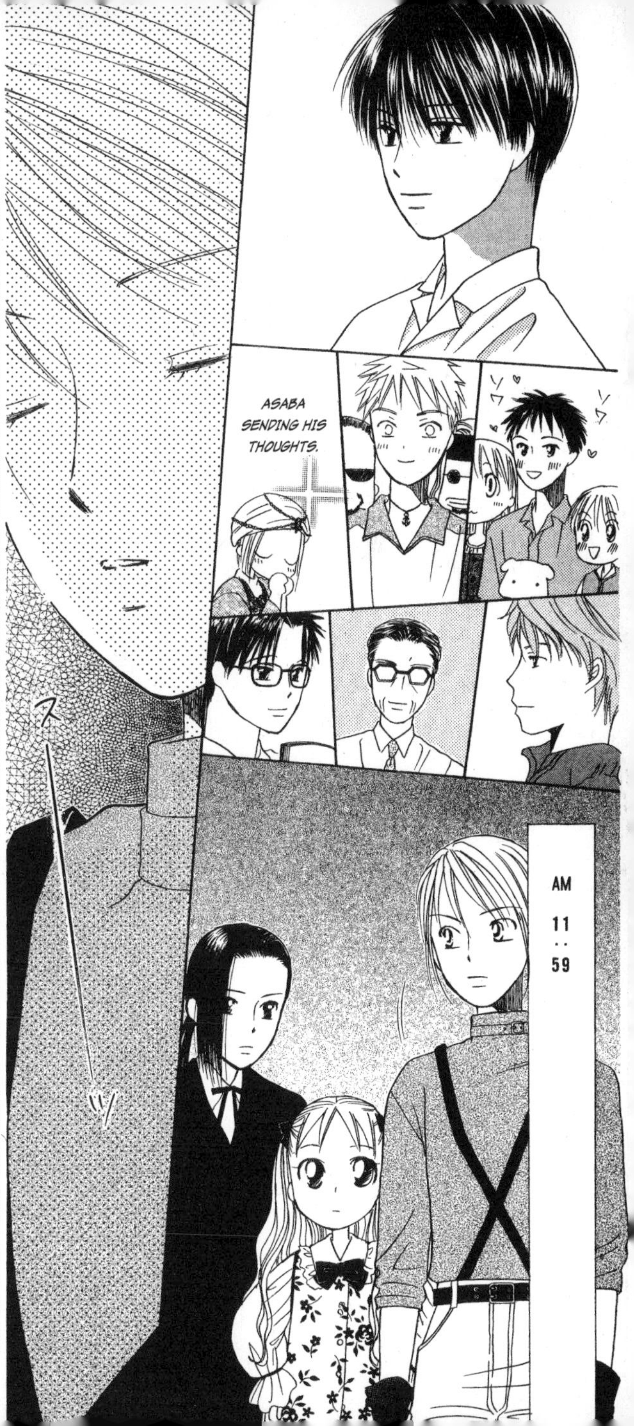
ASABA SENDING HIS THOUGHTS.
AM 11:59

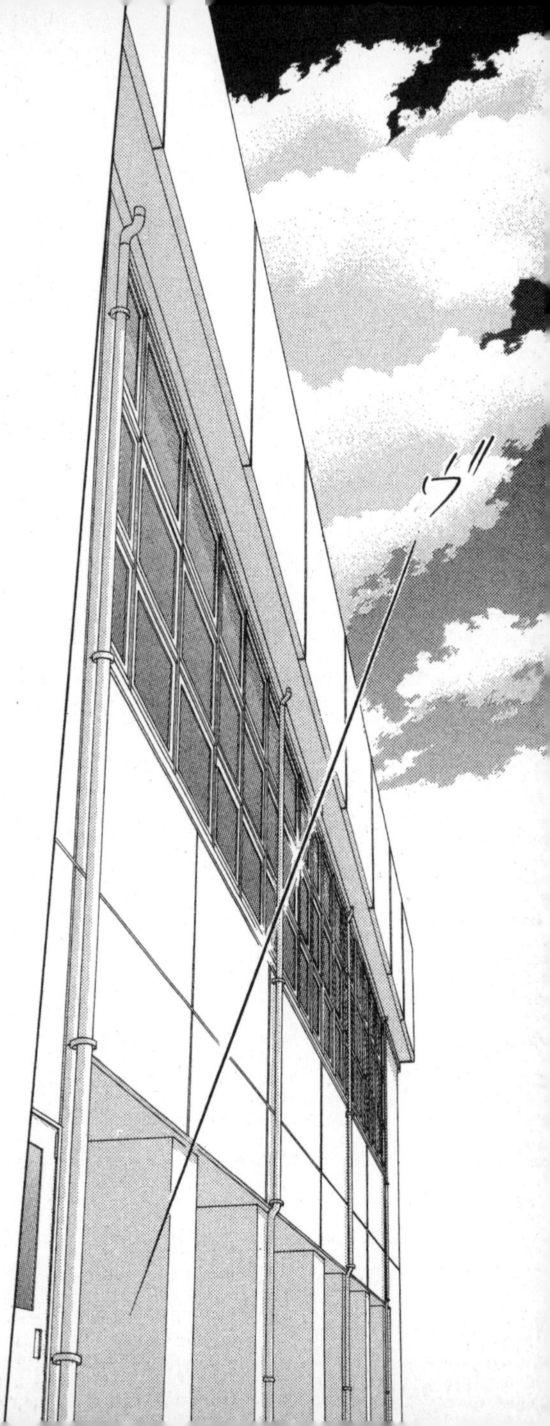
ヴ

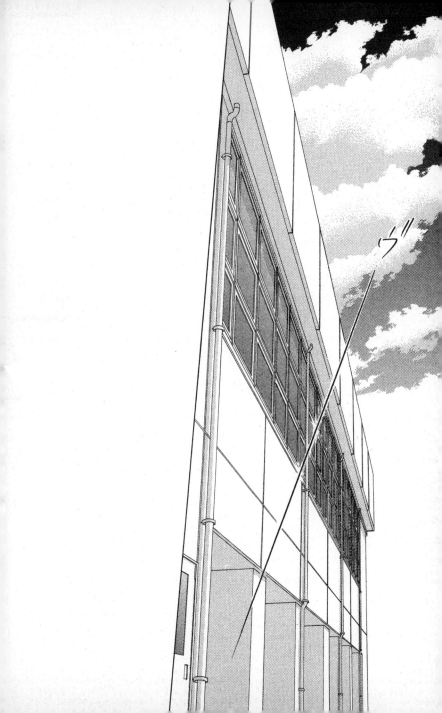

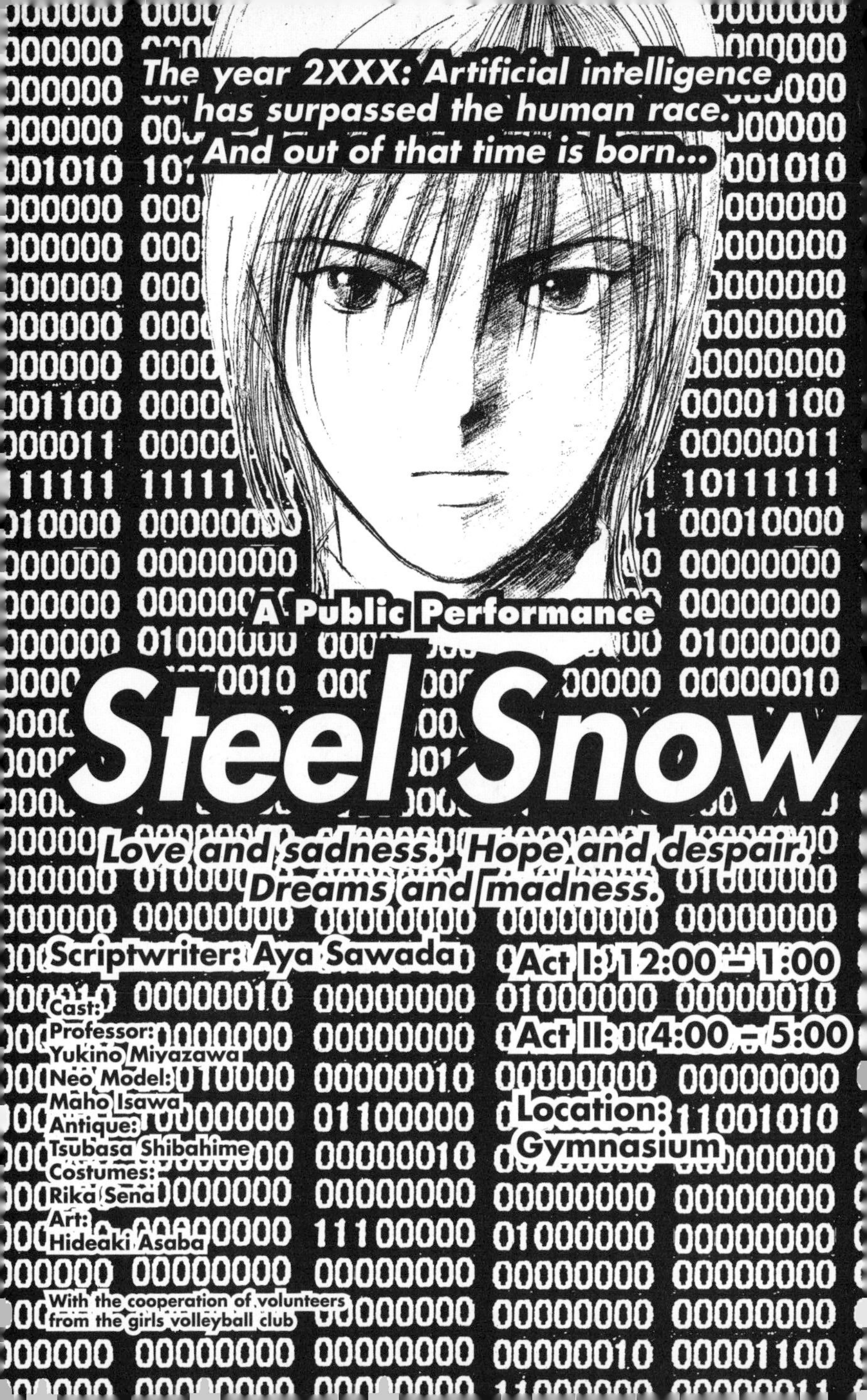
The year 2XXX: Artificial intelligence has surpassed the human race. And out of that time is born...
A Public Performance
Steel Snow
Love and sadness. Hope and despair. Dreams and madness.
Scriptwriter: Aya Sawada
Cast:
Professor: Yukino Miyazawa
Neo Model: Maho Isawa
Antique: Tsubasa Shibahime
Costumes: Rika Sena
Art: Hideaki Asaba
With the cooperation of volunteers from the girls volleyball club
Act I: 12:00 – 1:00
Act II: 4:00 – 5:00
Location: Gymnasium

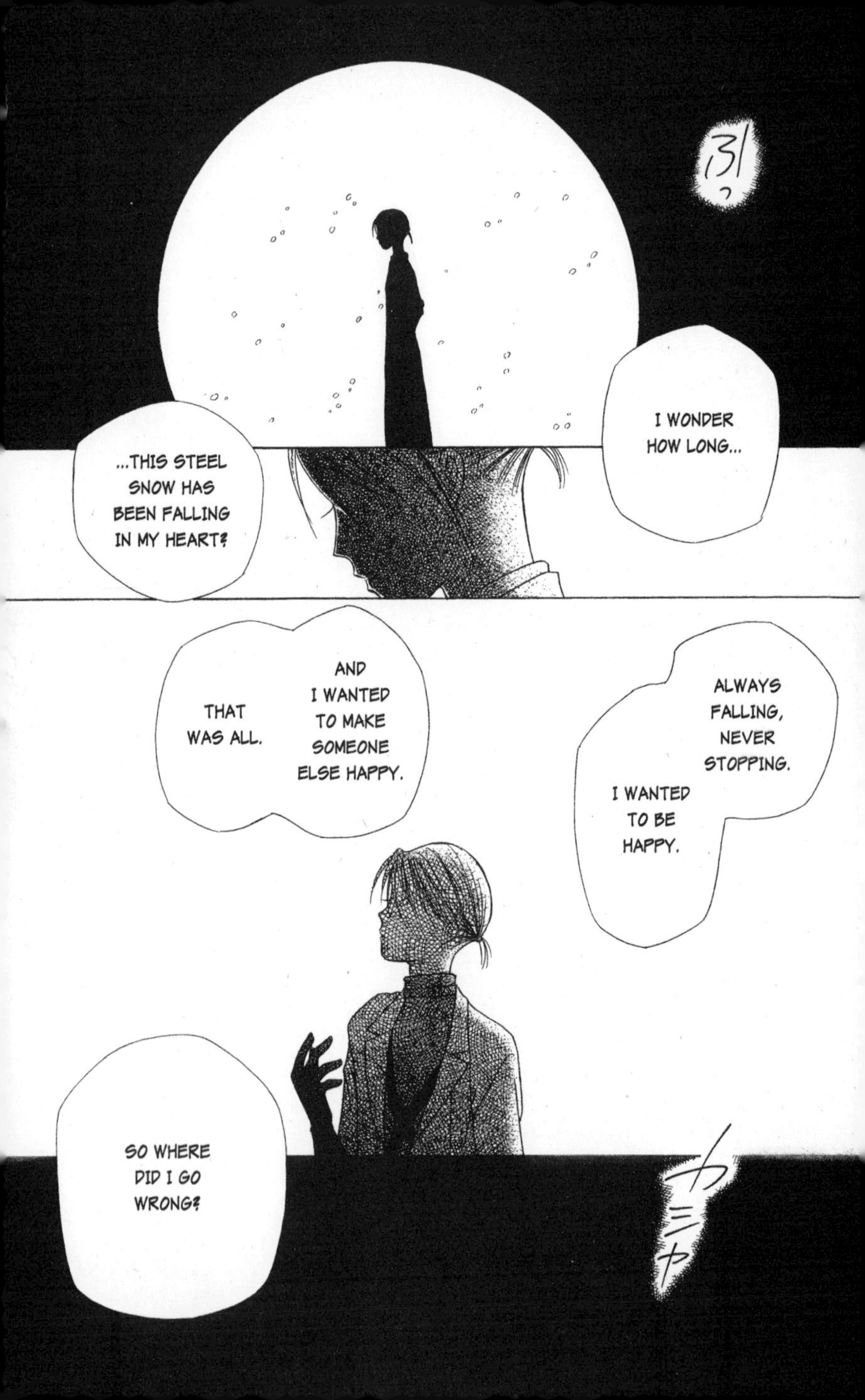
I WONDER HOW LONG...
...THIS STEEL SNOW HAS BEEN FALLING IN MY HEART?
ALWAYS FALLING, NEVER STOPPING.
I WANTED TO BE HAPPY.
AND I WANTED TO MAKE SOMEONE ELSE HAPPY.
THAT WAS ALL.
SO WHERE DID I GO WRONG?

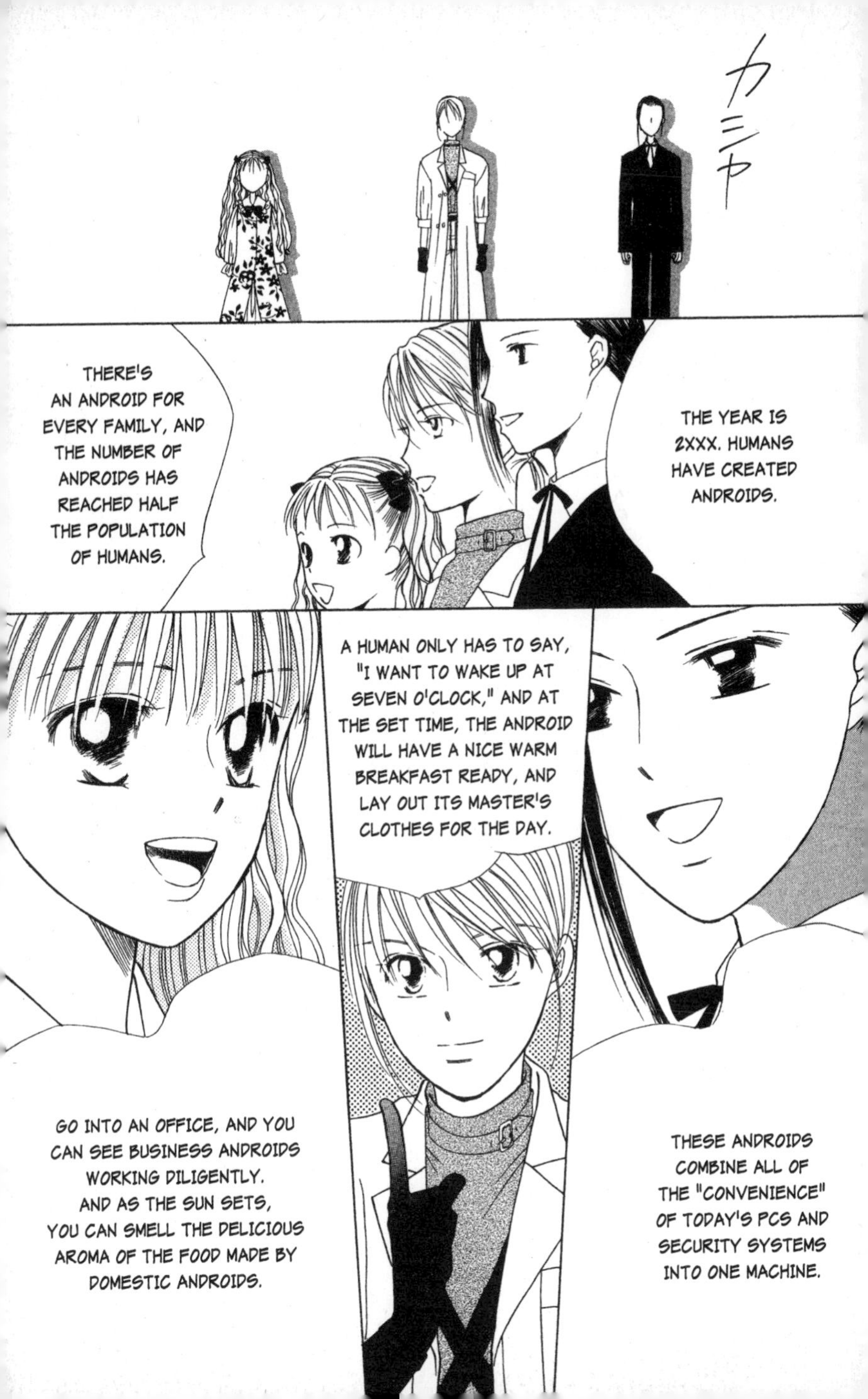
カシャ
THE YEAR IS 2XXX. HUMANS HAVE CREATED ANDROIDS.
THERE'S AN ANDROID FOR EVERY FAMILY, AND THE NUMBER OF ANDROIDS HAS REACHED HALF THE POPULATION OF HUMANS.
A HUMAN ONLY HAS TO SAY, "I WANT TO WAKE UP AT SEVEN O'CLOCK," AND AT THE SET TIME, THE ANDROID WILL HAVE A NICE WARM BREAKFAST READY, AND LAY OUT ITS MASTER'S CLOTHES FOR THE DAY.
THESE ANDROIDS COMBINE ALL OF THE "CONVENIENCE" OF TODAY'S PCS AND SECURITY SYSTEMS INTO ONE MACHINE.
GO INTO AN OFFICE, AND YOU CAN SEE BUSINESS ANDROIDS WORKING DILIGENTLY. AND AS THE SUN SETS, YOU CAN SMELL THE DELICIOUS AROMA OF THE FOOD MADE BY DOMESTIC ANDROIDS.

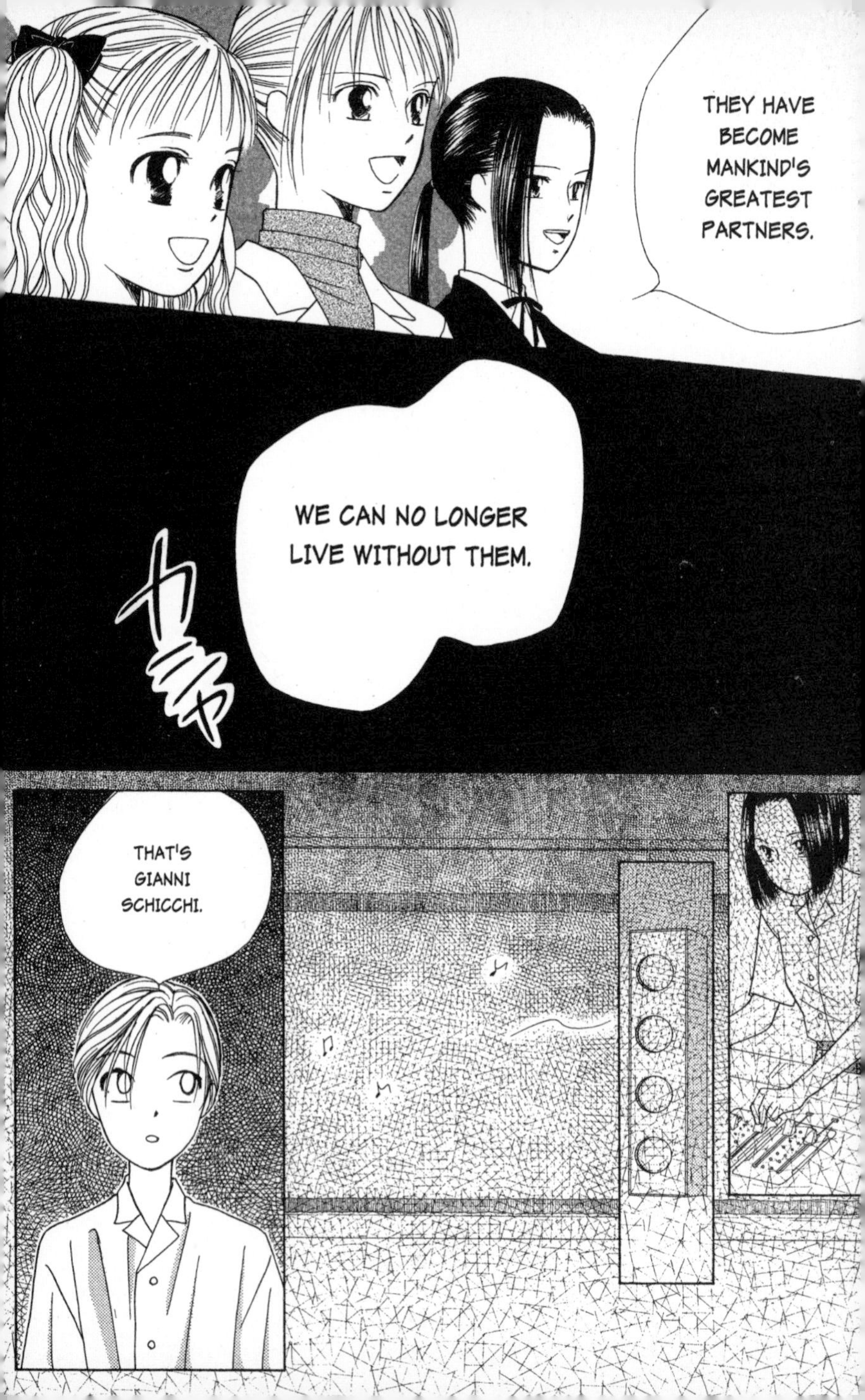
THEY HAVE BECOME MANKIND'S GREATEST PARTNERS.
WE CAN NO LONGER LIVE WITHOUT THEM.
THAT'S GIANNI SCHICCHI.

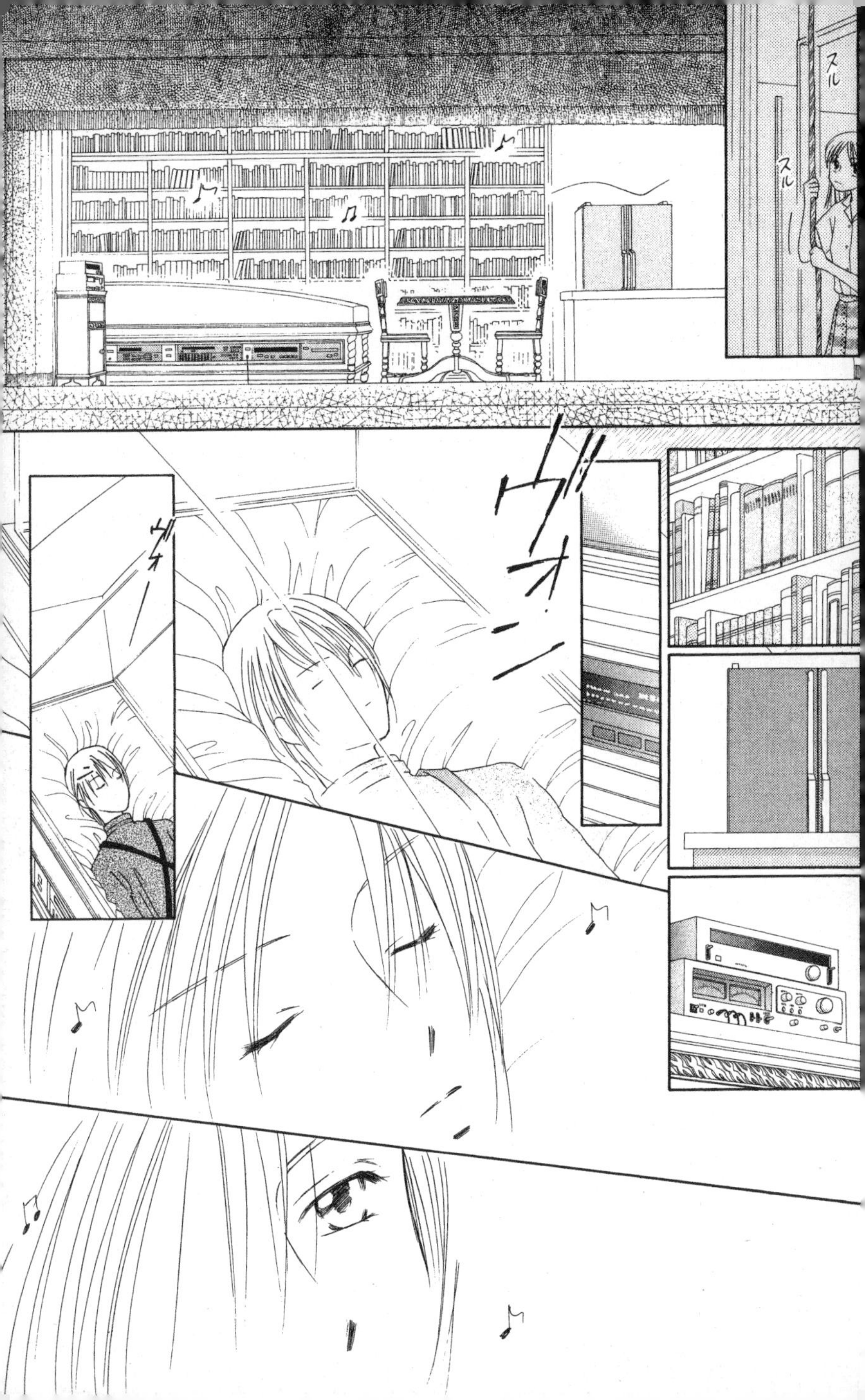
スル
スル
ヴォ!ーン
ヴォー

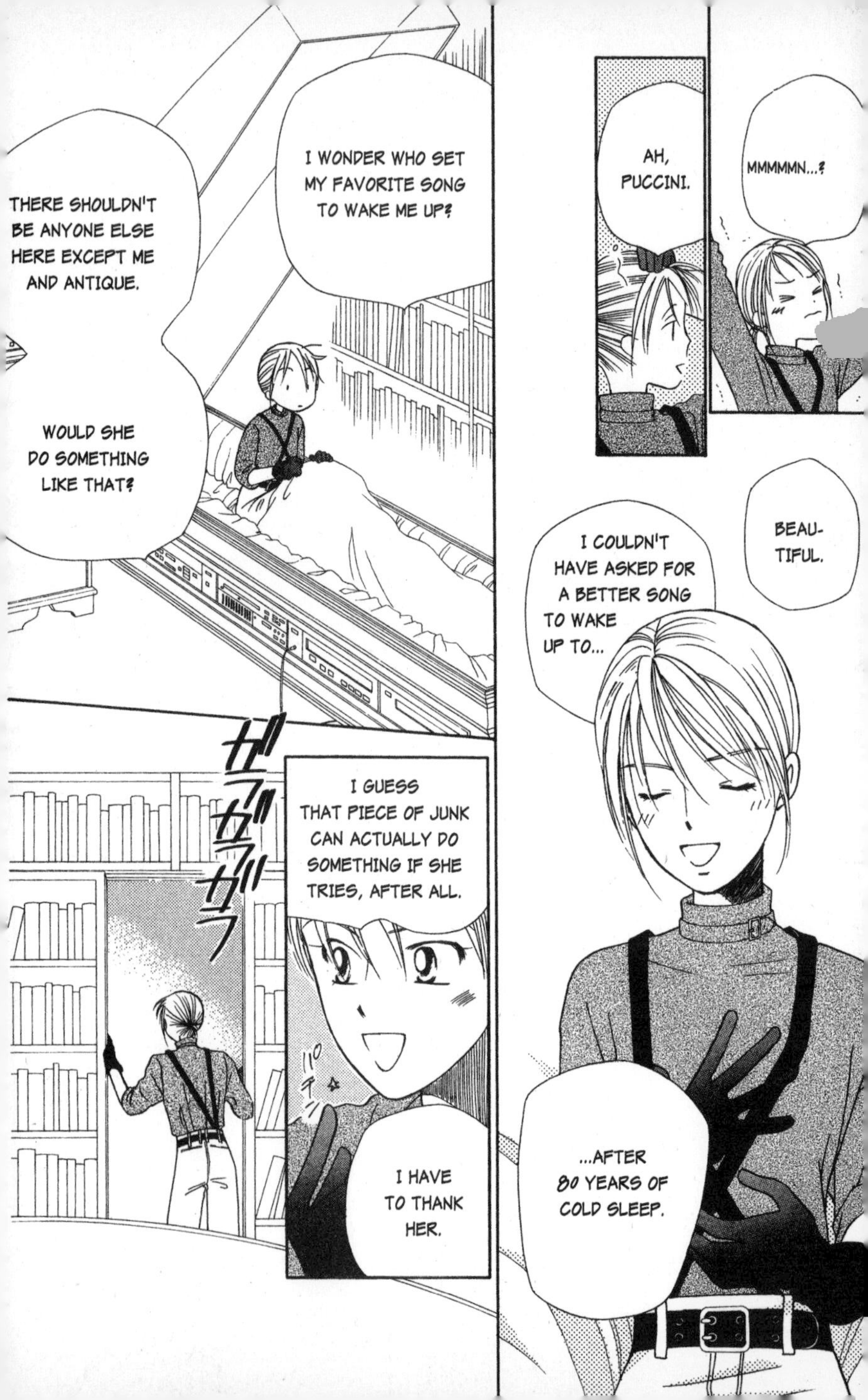
MMMMMN...?
AH, PUCCINI.
BEAUTIFUL.
I COULDN'T HAVE ASKED FOR A BETTER SONG TO WAKE UP TO...
...AFTER 80 YEARS OF COLD SLEEP.
I WONDER WHO SET MY FAVORITE SONG TO WAKE ME UP?
THERE SHOULDN'T BE ANYONE ELSE HERE EXCEPT ME AND ANTIQUE.
WOULD SHE DO SOMETHING LIKE THAT?
I GUESS THAT PIECE OF JUNK CAN ACTUALLY DO SOMETHING IF SHE TRIES, AFTER ALL.
I HAVE TO THANK HER.

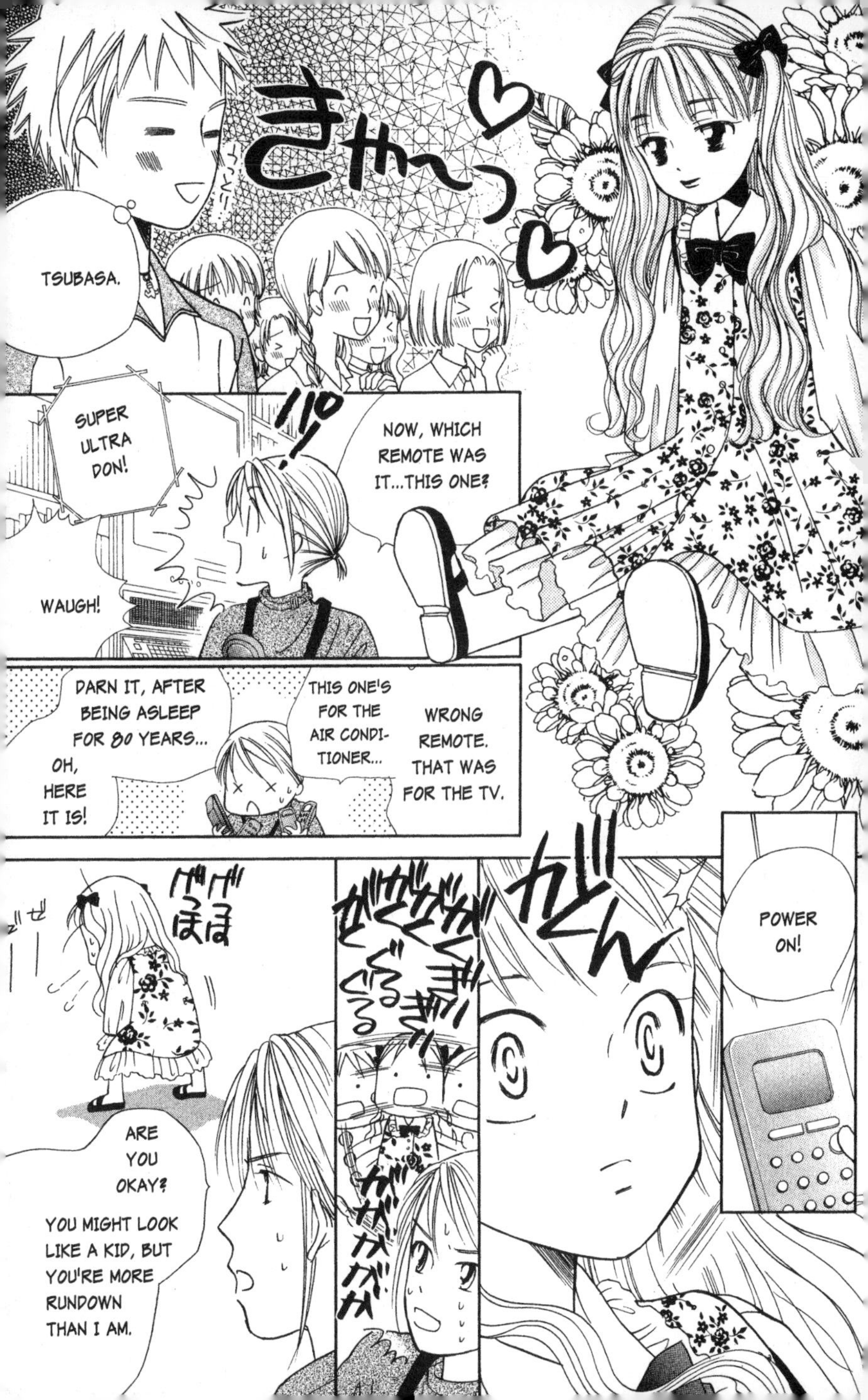
きゃ〜っ
TSUBASA.
NOW, WHICH REMOTE WAS IT...THIS ONE?
SUPER ULTRA DON!
WAUGH!
WRONG REMOTE. THAT WAS FOR THE TV.
THIS ONE'S FOR THE AIR CONDITIONER...
DARN IT, AFTER BEING ASLEEP FOR 80 YEARS...
OH, HERE IT IS!
POWER ON!
ARE YOU OKAY?
YOU MIGHT LOOK LIKE A KID, BUT YOU'RE MORE RUNDOWN THAN I AM.

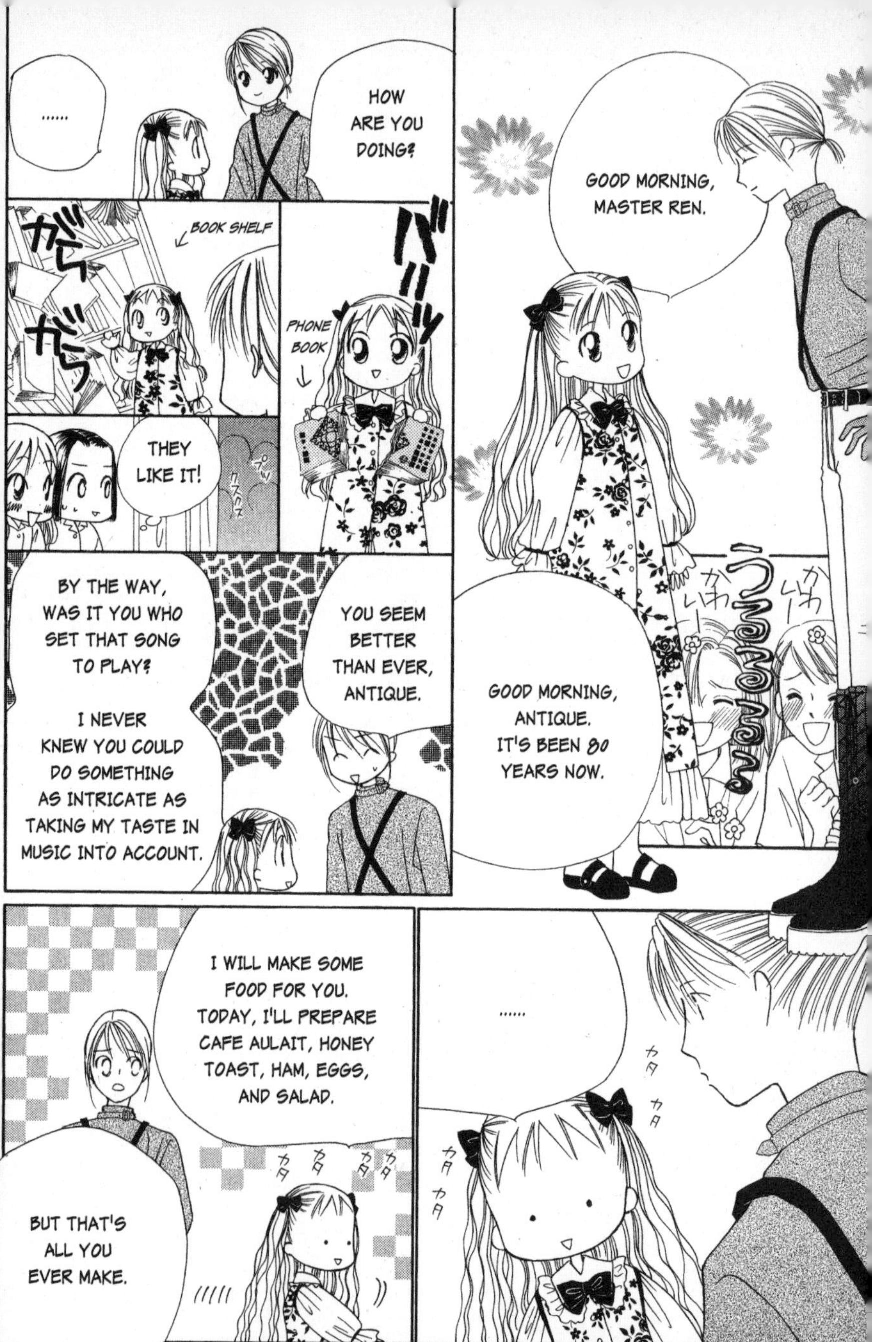
GOOD MORNING, MASTER REN.
GOOD MORNING, ANTIQUE. IT'S BEEN 80 YEARS NOW.
HOW ARE YOU DOING?
......
PHONE BOOK
BOOK SHELF
THEY LIKE IT!
YOU SEEM BETTER THAN EVER, ANTIQUE.
BY THE WAY, WAS IT YOU WHO SET THAT SONG TO PLAY?
I NEVER KNEW YOU COULD DO SOMETHING AS INTRICATE AS TAKING MY TASTE IN MUSIC INTO ACCOUNT.
......
I WILL MAKE SOME FOOD FOR YOU. TODAY, I'LL PREPARE CAFE AULAIT, HONEY TOAST, HAM, EGGS, AND SALAD.
BUT THAT'S ALL YOU EVER MAKE.

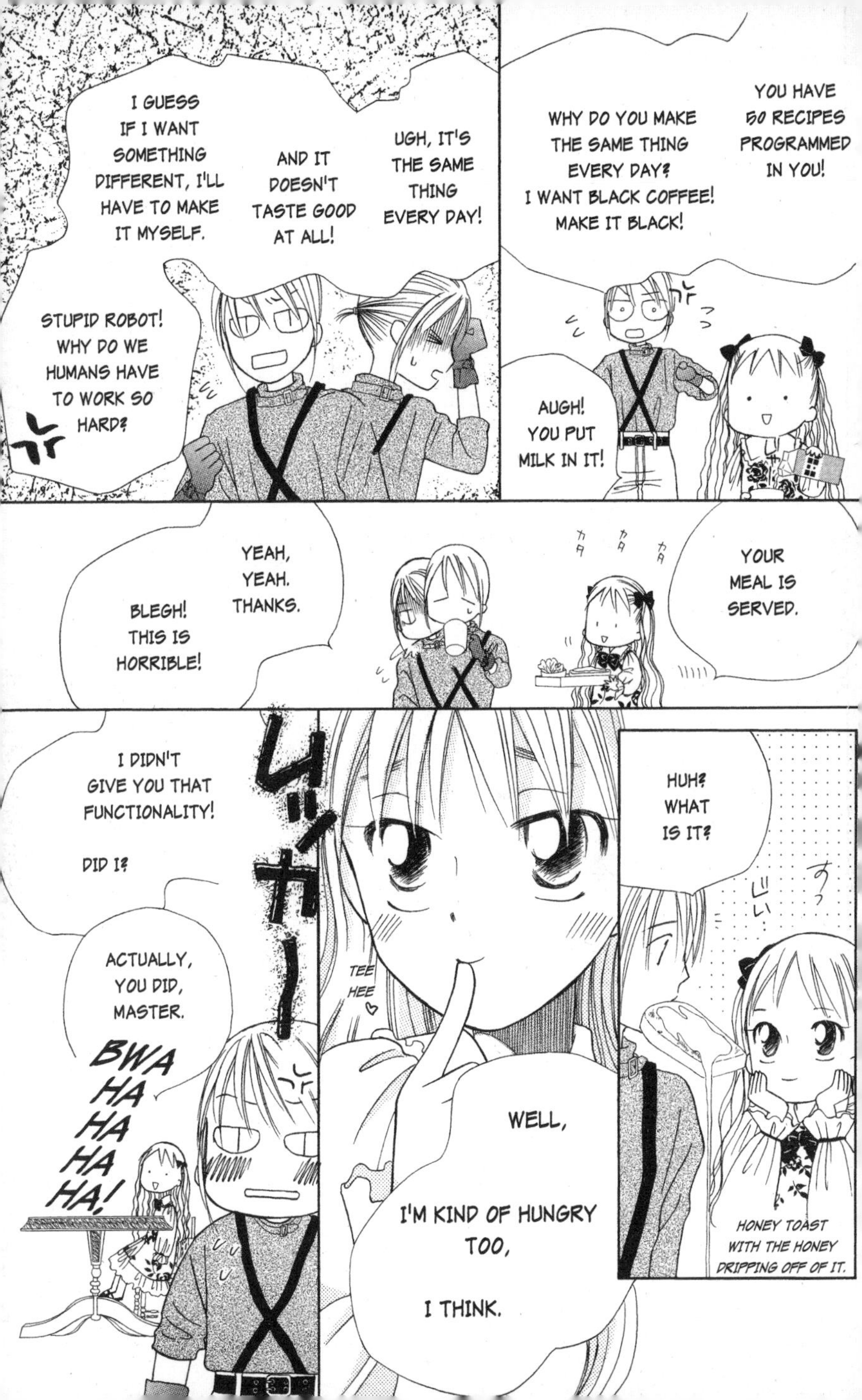
YOU HAVE 50 RECIPES PROGRAMMED IN YOU!
WHY DO YOU MAKE THE SAME THING EVERY DAY? I WANT BLACK COFFEE! MAKE IT BLACK!
AUGH! YOU PUT MILK IN IT!
UGH, IT'S THE SAME THING EVERY DAY!
AND IT DOESN'T TASTE GOOD AT ALL!
I GUESS IF I WANT SOMETHING DIFFERENT, I'LL HAVE TO MAKE IT MYSELF.
STUPID ROBOT! WHY DO WE HUMANS HAVE TO WORK SO HARD?
YOUR MEAL IS SERVED.
YEAH, YEAH. THANKS.
BLEGH! THIS IS HORRIBLE!
HUH? WHAT IS IT?
HONEY TOAST WITH THE HONEY DRIPPING OFF OF IT.
WELL,
I'M KIND OF HUNGRY TOO,
I THINK.
TEE HEE
I DIDN'T GIVE YOU THAT FUNCTIONALITY!
DID I?
ACTUALLY, YOU DID, MASTER.
BWA HA HA HA HA!

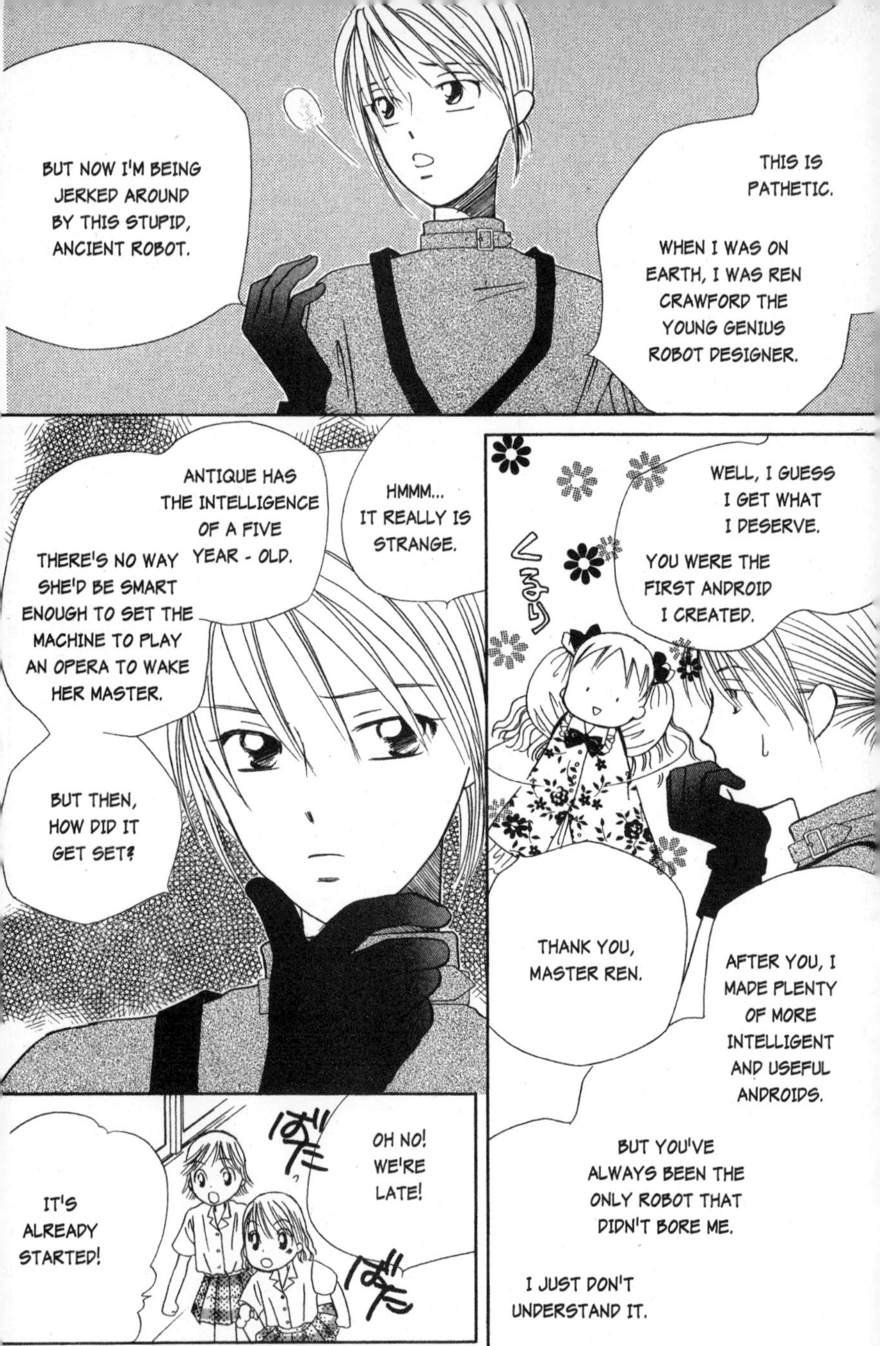
THIS IS PATHETIC.
WHEN I WAS ON EARTH, I WAS REN CRAWFORD THE YOUNG GENIUS ROBOT DESIGNER.
BUT NOW I'M BEING JERKED AROUND BY THIS STUPID, ANCIENT ROBOT.
WELL, I GUESS I GET WHAT I DESERVE.
YOU WERE THE FIRST ANDROID I CREATED.
くるり
THANK YOU, MASTER REN.
AFTER YOU, I MADE PLENTY OF MORE INTELLIGENT AND USEFUL ANDROIDS.
BUT YOU'VE ALWAYS BEEN THE ONLY ROBOT THAT DIDN'T BORE ME.
I JUST DON'T UNDERSTAND IT.
HMMM... IT REALLY IS STRANGE.
ANTIQUE HAS THE INTELLIGENCE OF A FIVE YEAR - OLD.
THERE'S NO WAY SHE'D BE SMART ENOUGH TO SET THE MACHINE TO PLAY AN OPERA TO WAKE HER MASTER.
BUT THEN, HOW DID IT GET SET?
OH NO! WE'RE LATE!
ばた
ばた
IT'S ALREADY STARTED!

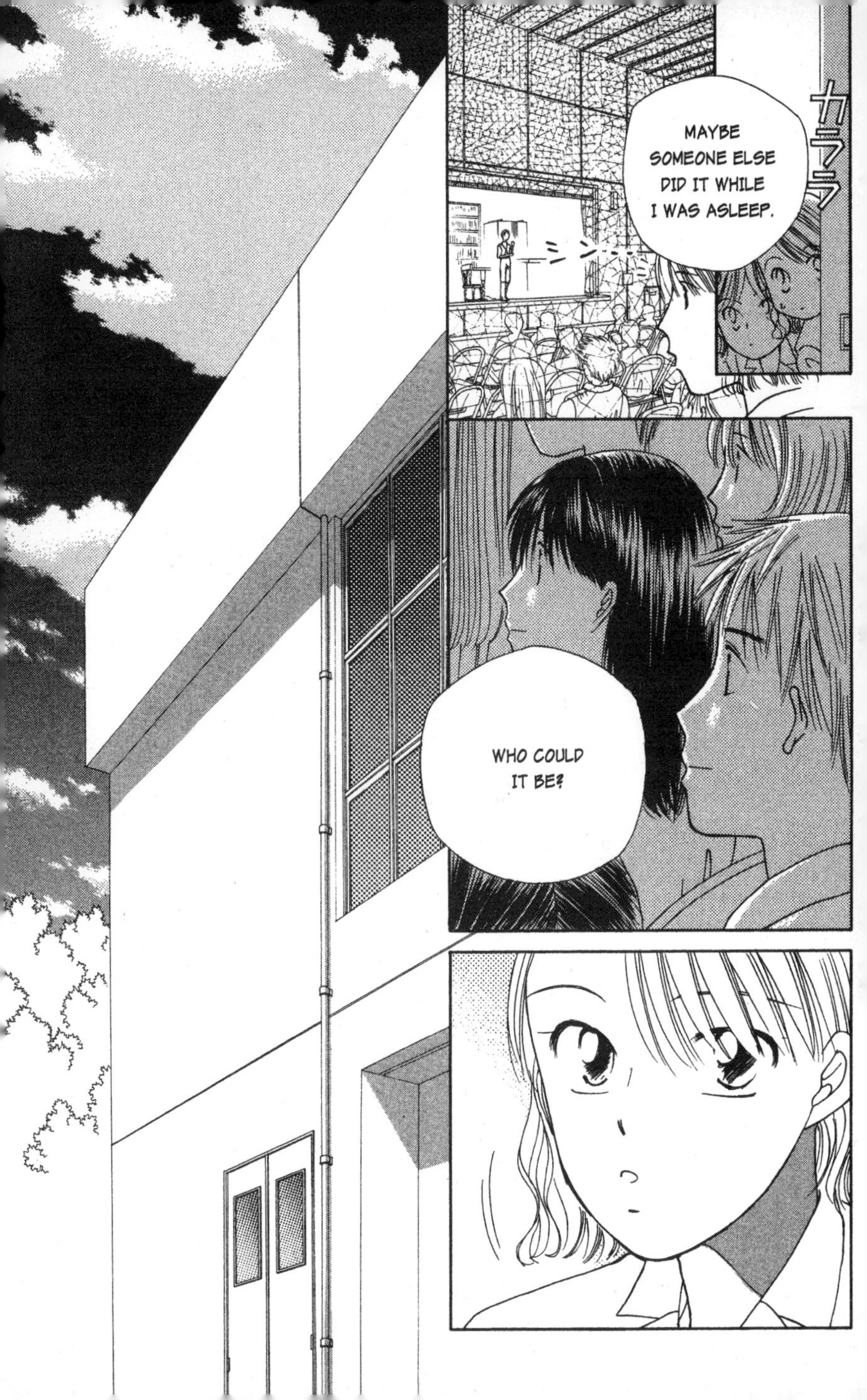
カラ
MAYBE SOMEONE ELSE DID IT WHILE I WAS ASLEEP.
シン…
WHO COULD IT BE?

ACT 39 * CULTURE FESTIVAL 2

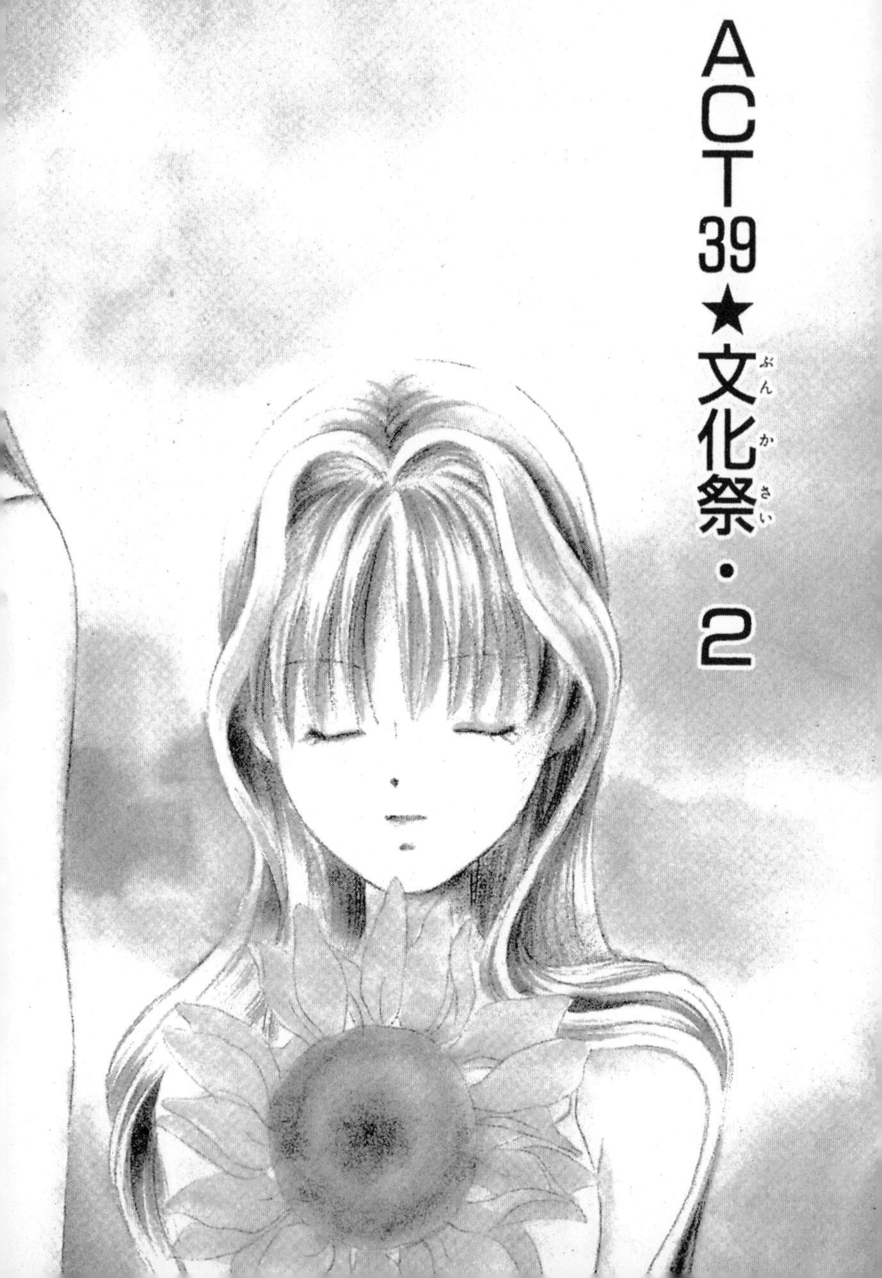
ACT39★文化祭・2

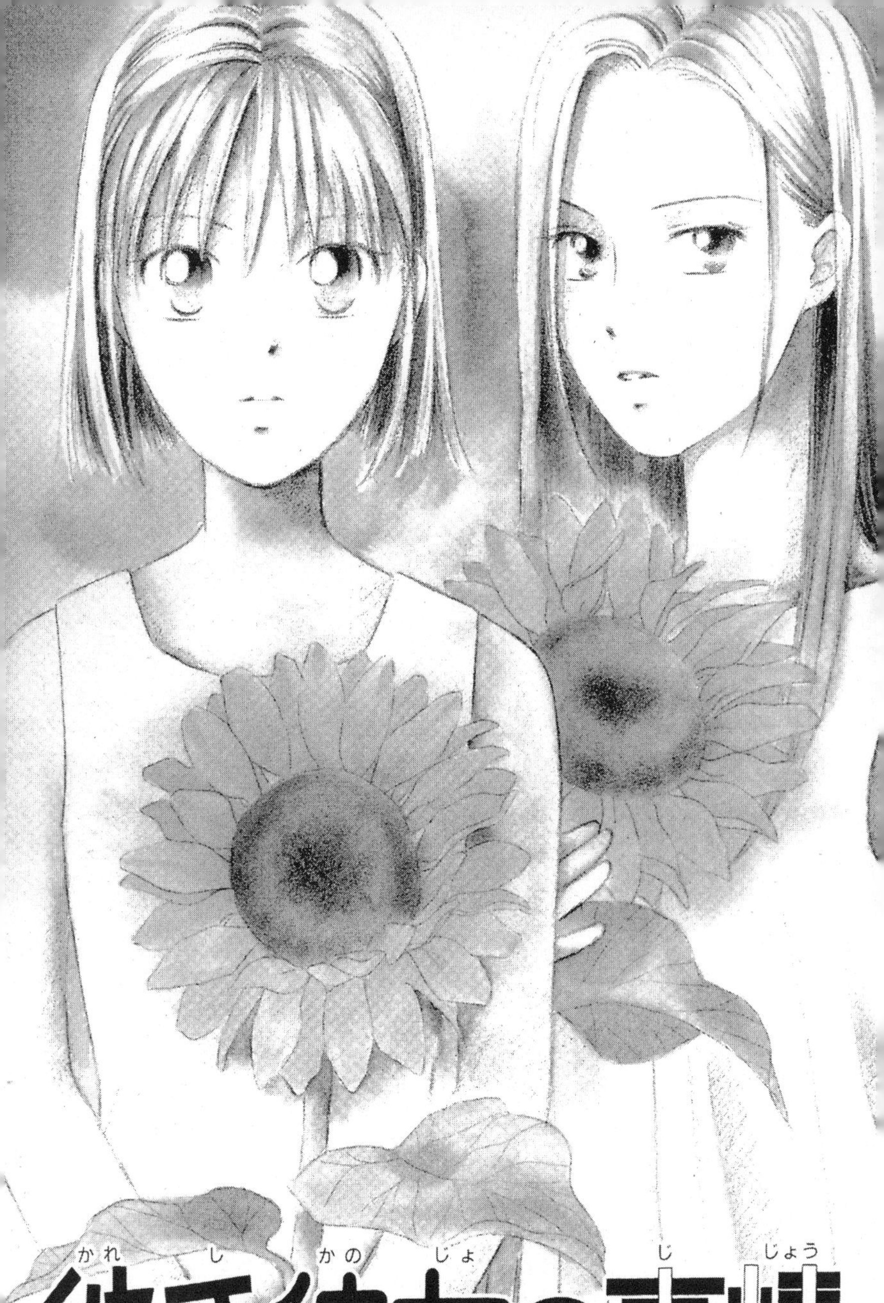

彼氏彼女の事情

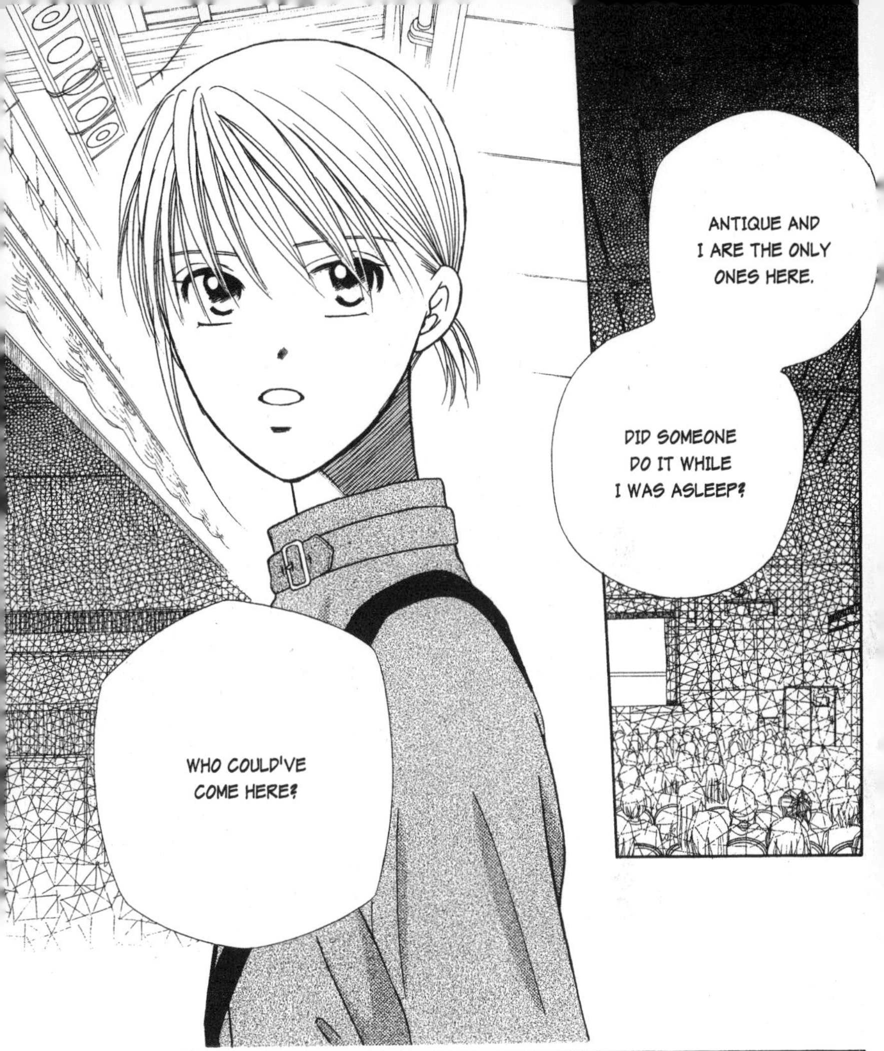
ANTIQUE AND I ARE THE ONLY ONES HERE.
DID SOMEONE DO IT WHILE I WAS ASLEEP?
WHO COULD'VE COME HERE?

Computers:

I bought a computer: an NEC Simplem.

Lowbrow? More flash than substance? You bet!

Well anyway, I can get on the Internet now. Now looking for materials and information will be even easier (well, eventually).

But it's not actually going so well.

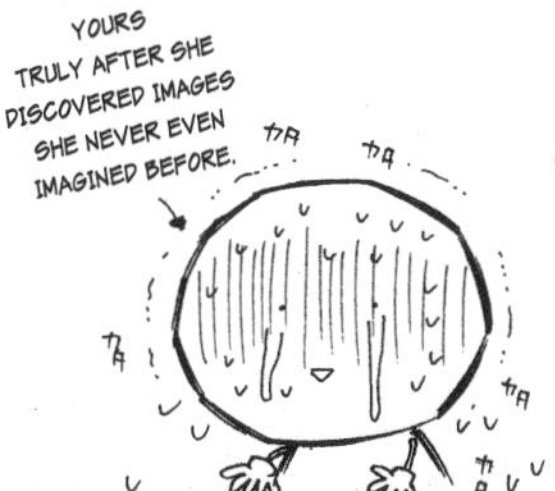
YOURS TRULY AFTER SHE DISCOVERED IMAGES SHE NEVER EVEN IMAGINED BEFORE.

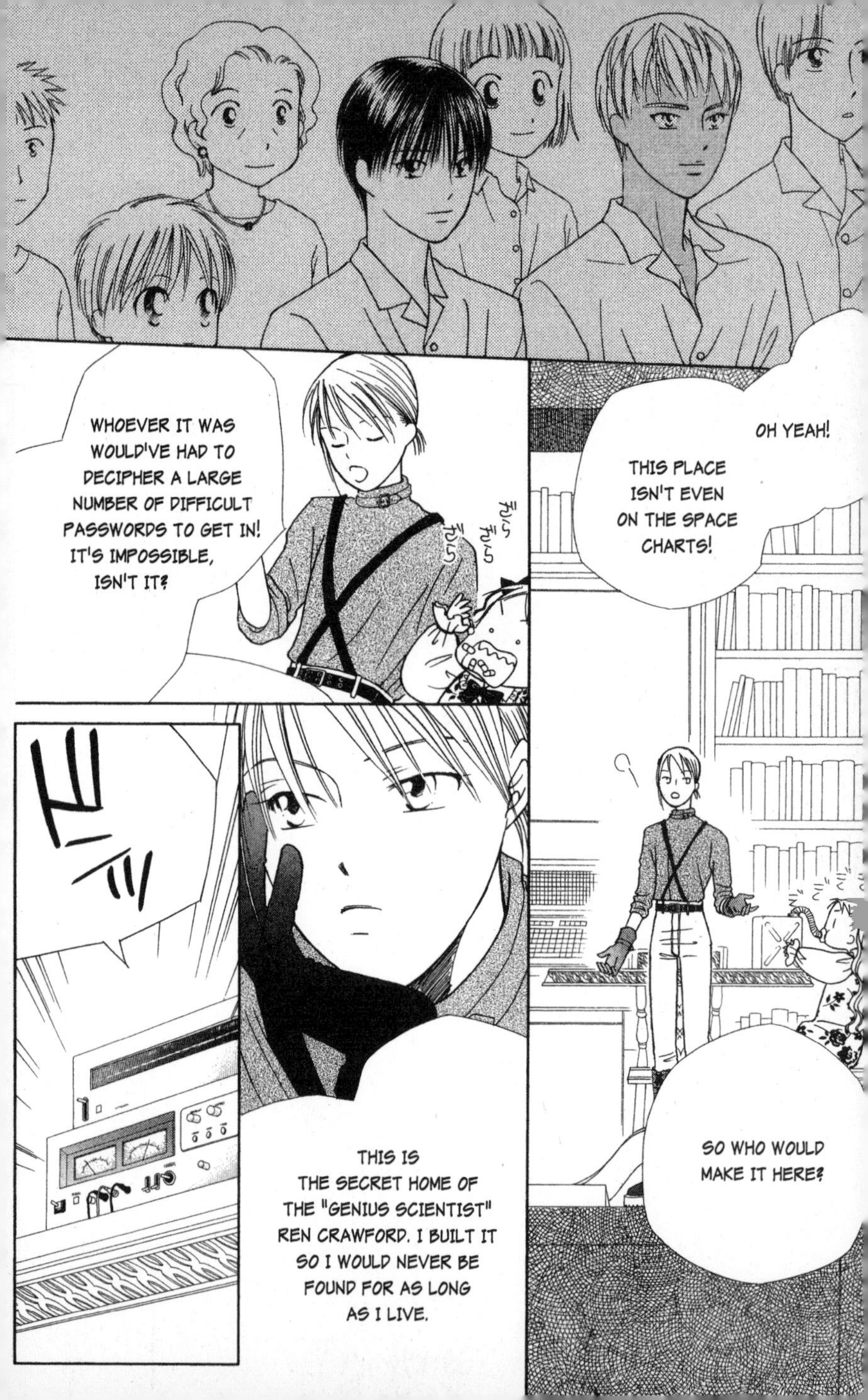
WHOEVER IT WAS WOULD'VE HAD TO DECIPHER A LARGE NUMBER OF DIFFICULT PASSWORDS TO GET IN! IT'S IMPOSSIBLE, ISN'T IT?
OH YEAH!
THIS PLACE ISN'T EVEN ON THE SPACE CHARTS!
SO WHO WOULD MAKE IT HERE?
THIS IS THE SECRET HOME OF THE "GENIUS SCIENTIST" REN CRAWFORD. I BUILT IT SO I WOULD NEVER BE FOUND FOR AS LONG AS I LIVE.

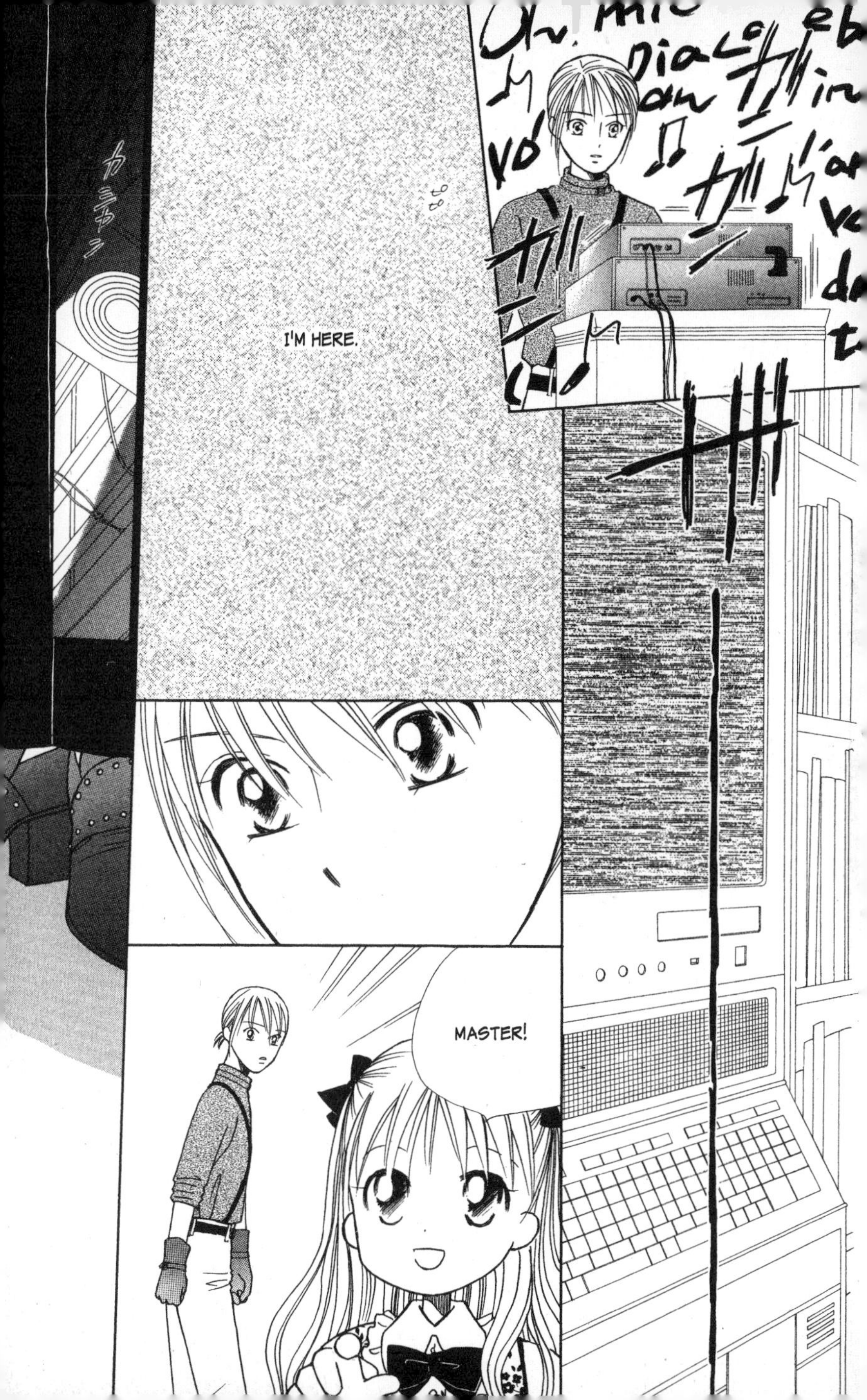
I'M HERE.
MASTER!

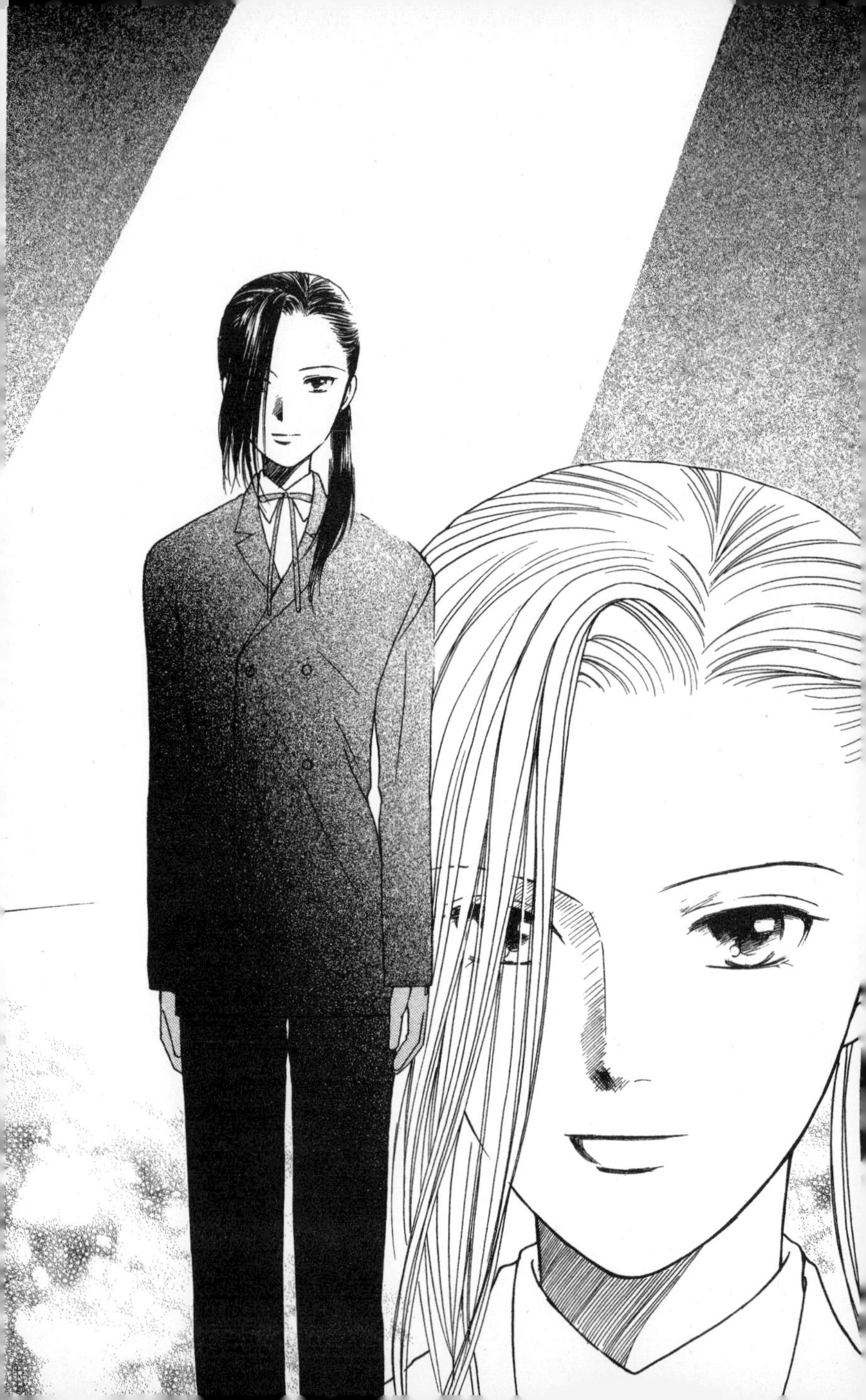

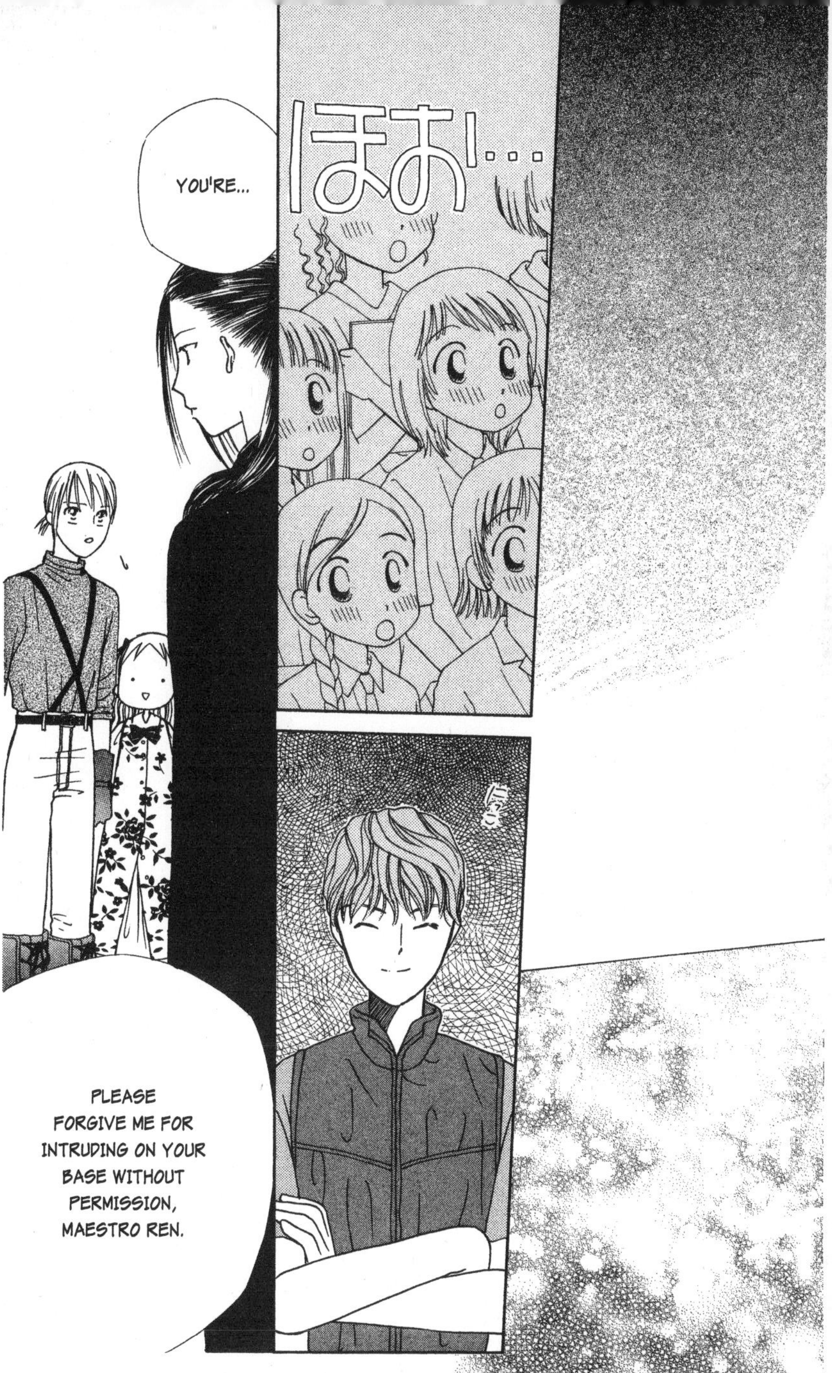
ほお...
YOU'RE...
PLEASE FORGIVE ME FOR INTRUDING ON YOUR BASE WITHOUT PERMISSION, MAESTRO REN.

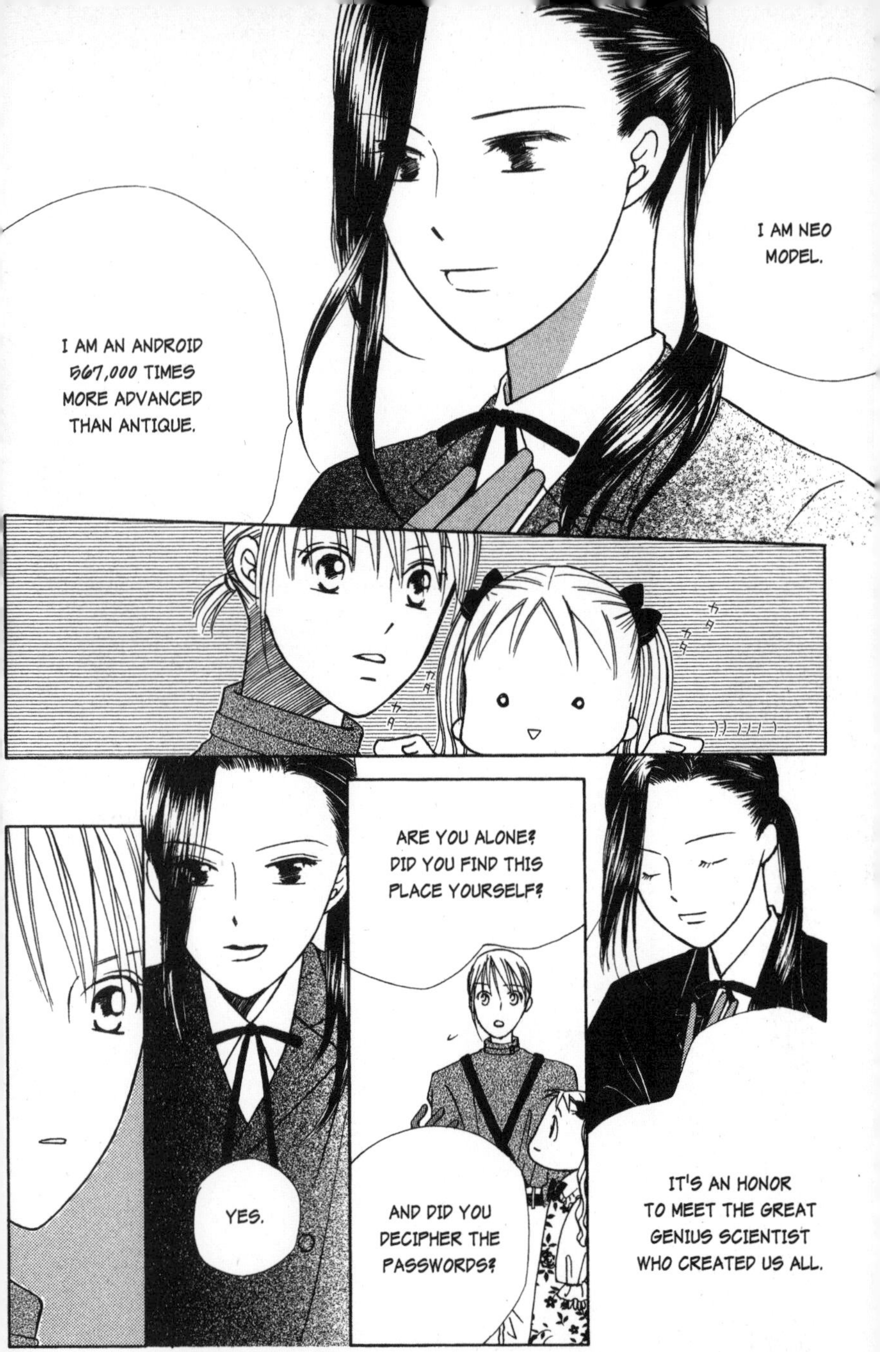
I AM NEO MODEL.
I AM AN ANDROID 567,000 TIMES MORE ADVANCED THAN ANTIQUE.
IT'S AN HONOR TO MEET THE GREAT GENIUS SCIENTIST WHO CREATED US ALL.
ARE YOU ALONE? DID YOU FIND THIS PLACE YOURSELF?
AND DID YOU DECIPHER THE PASSWORDS?
YES.

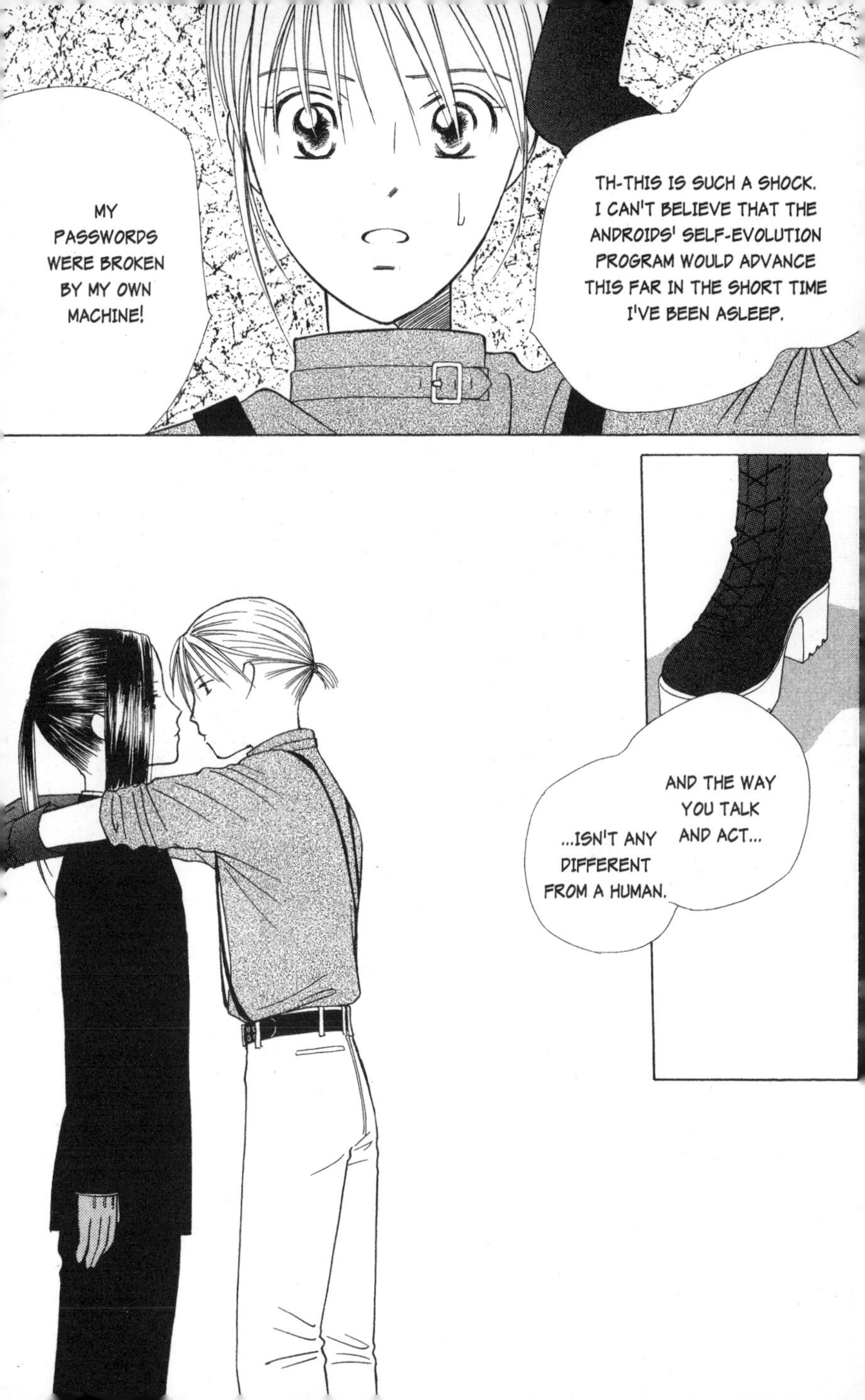
TH-THIS IS SUCH A SHOCK. I CAN'T BELIEVE THAT THE ANDROIDS' SELF-EVOLUTION PROGRAM WOULD ADVANCE THIS FAR IN THE SHORT TIME I'VE BEEN ASLEEP.
MY PASSWORDS WERE BROKEN BY MY OWN MACHINE!
AND THE WAY YOU TALK AND ACT...
...ISN'T ANY DIFFERENT FROM A HUMAN.

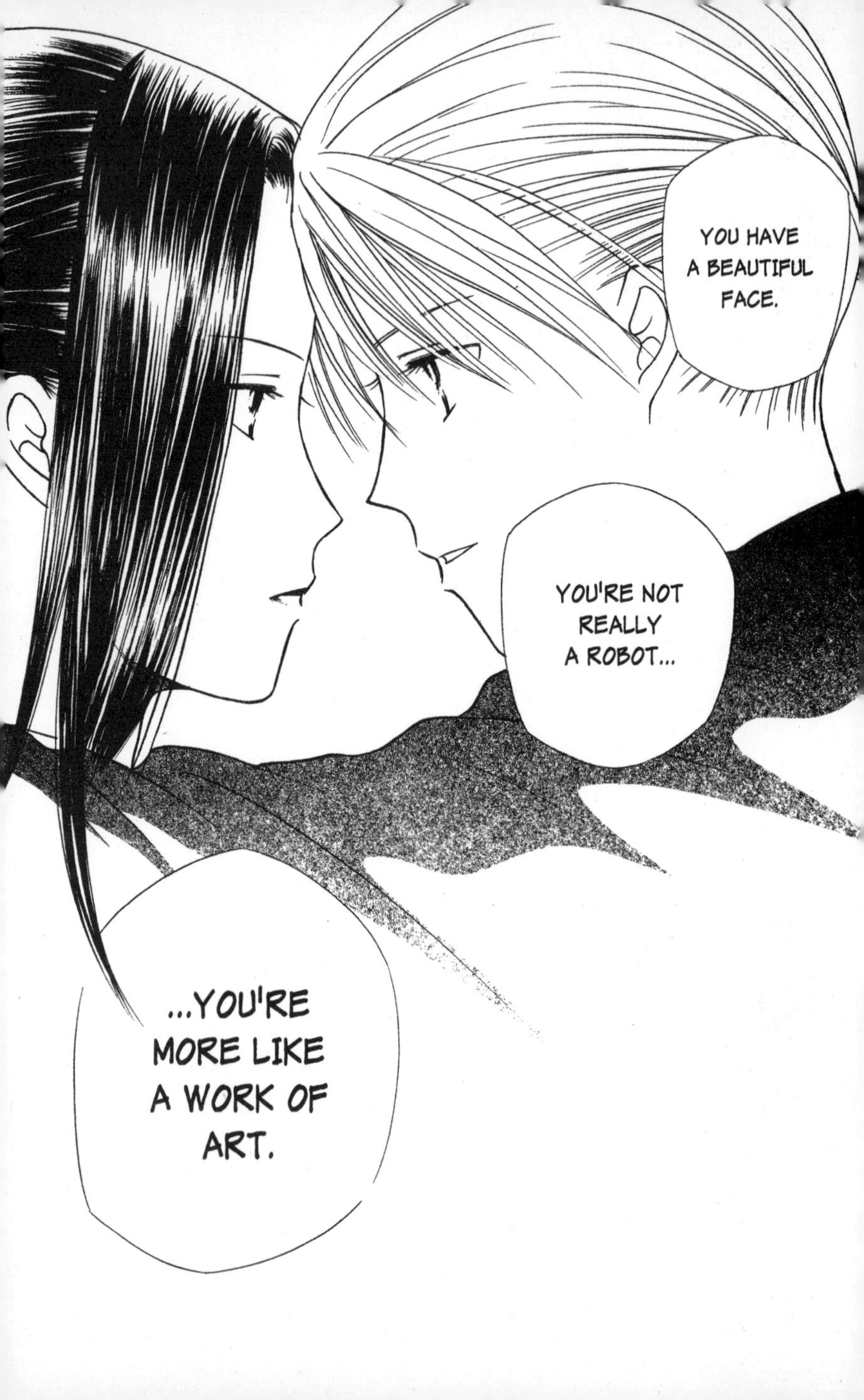
YOU HAVE A BEAUTIFUL FACE.
YOU'RE NOT REALLY A ROBOT...
...YOU'RE MORE LIKE A WORK OF ART.

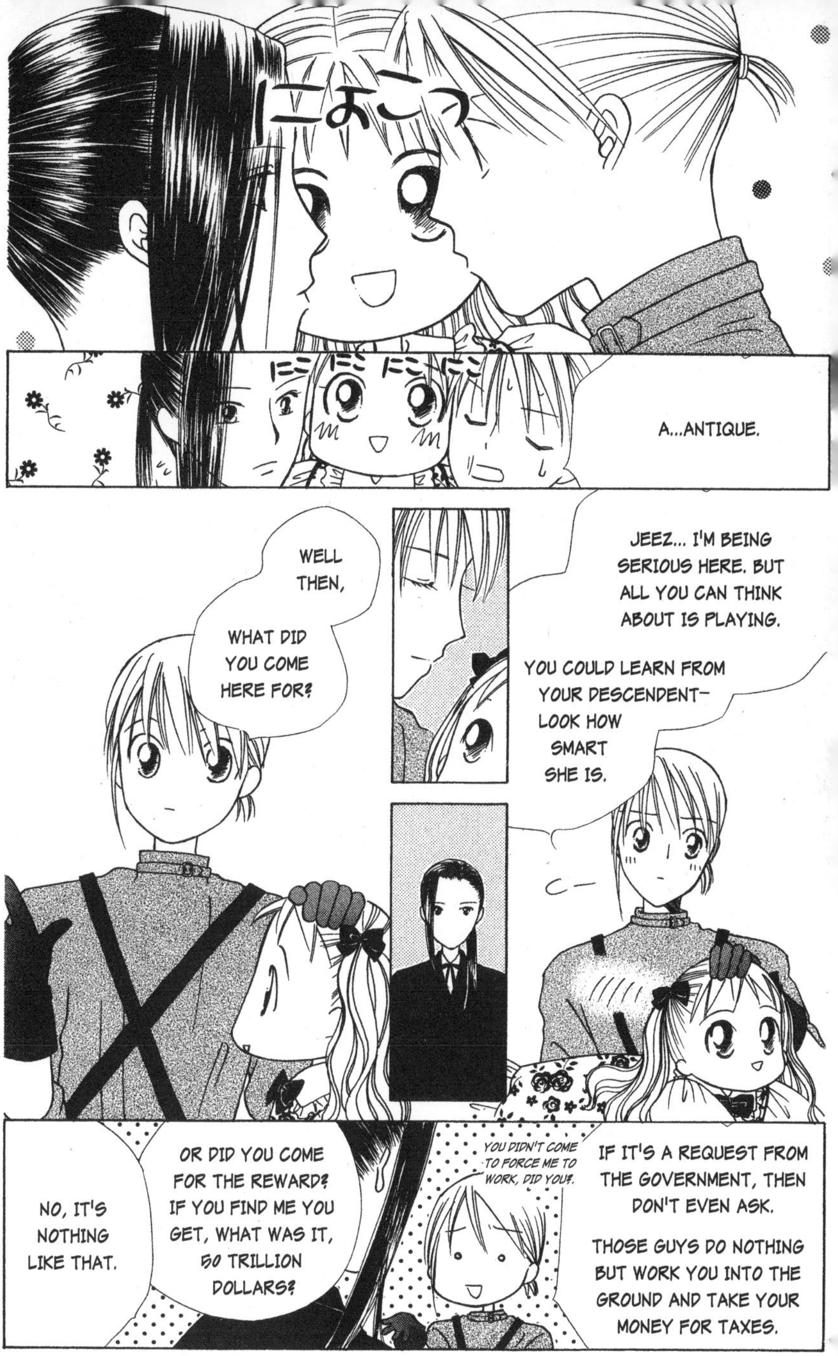
にょこっ
にこにこ にこにこ
A...ANTIQUE.
JEEZ... I'M BEING SERIOUS HERE. BUT ALL YOU CAN THINK ABOUT IS PLAYING.
YOU COULD LEARN FROM YOUR DESCENDENT—LOOK HOW SMART SHE IS.
WELL THEN,
WHAT DID YOU COME HERE FOR?
IF IT'S A REQUEST FROM THE GOVERNMENT, THEN DON'T EVEN ASK.
THOSE GUYS DO NOTHING BUT WORK YOU INTO THE GROUND AND TAKE YOUR MONEY FOR TAXES.
YOU DIDN'T COME TO FORCE ME TO WORK, DID YOU?
OR DID YOU COME FOR THE REWARD? IF YOU FIND ME YOU GET, WHAT WAS IT, 50 TRILLION DOLLARS?
NO, IT'S NOTHING LIKE THAT.

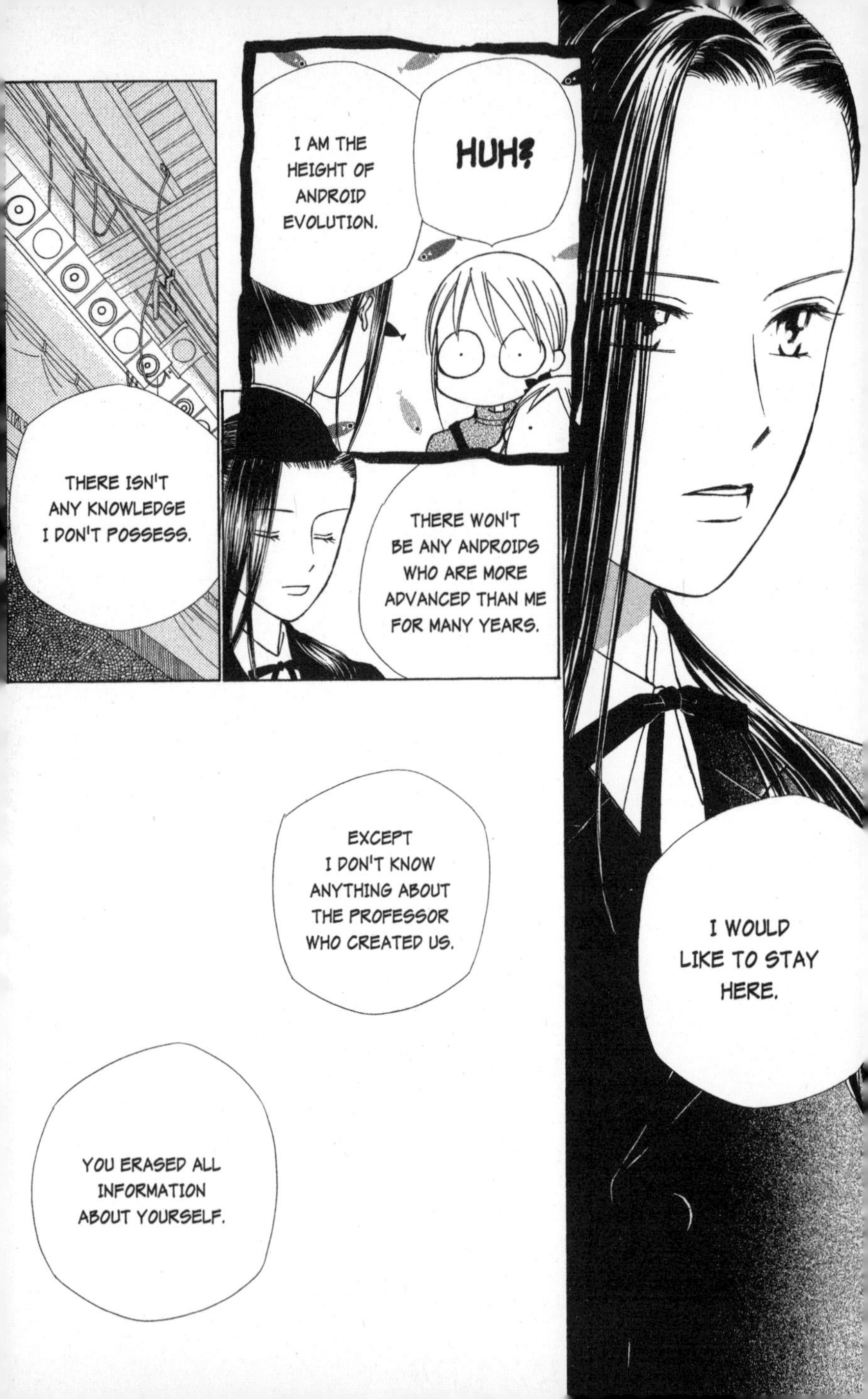
I AM THE HEIGHT OF ANDROID EVOLUTION.
HUH?
THERE WON'T BE ANY ANDROIDS WHO ARE MORE ADVANCED THAN ME FOR MANY YEARS.
THERE ISN'T ANY KNOWLEDGE I DON'T POSSESS.
EXCEPT I DON'T KNOW ANYTHING ABOUT THE PROFESSOR WHO CREATED US.
YOU ERASED ALL INFORMATION ABOUT YOURSELF.
I WOULD LIKE TO STAY HERE.

3

I love the Japanese language (and Chinese poetry, too), so right now I'm reading the Kojiki.

Just looking at the shape of letters like "Yomotsu Hirasaka" and saying them out loud makes me kinda happy.

White Rabbit in Inaba (Japanese mythology)

"Crab" = "Shark"

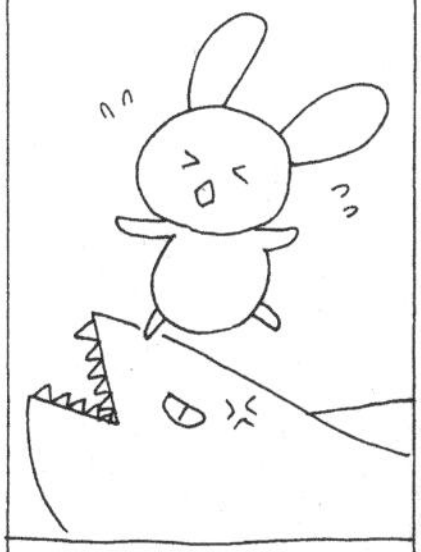

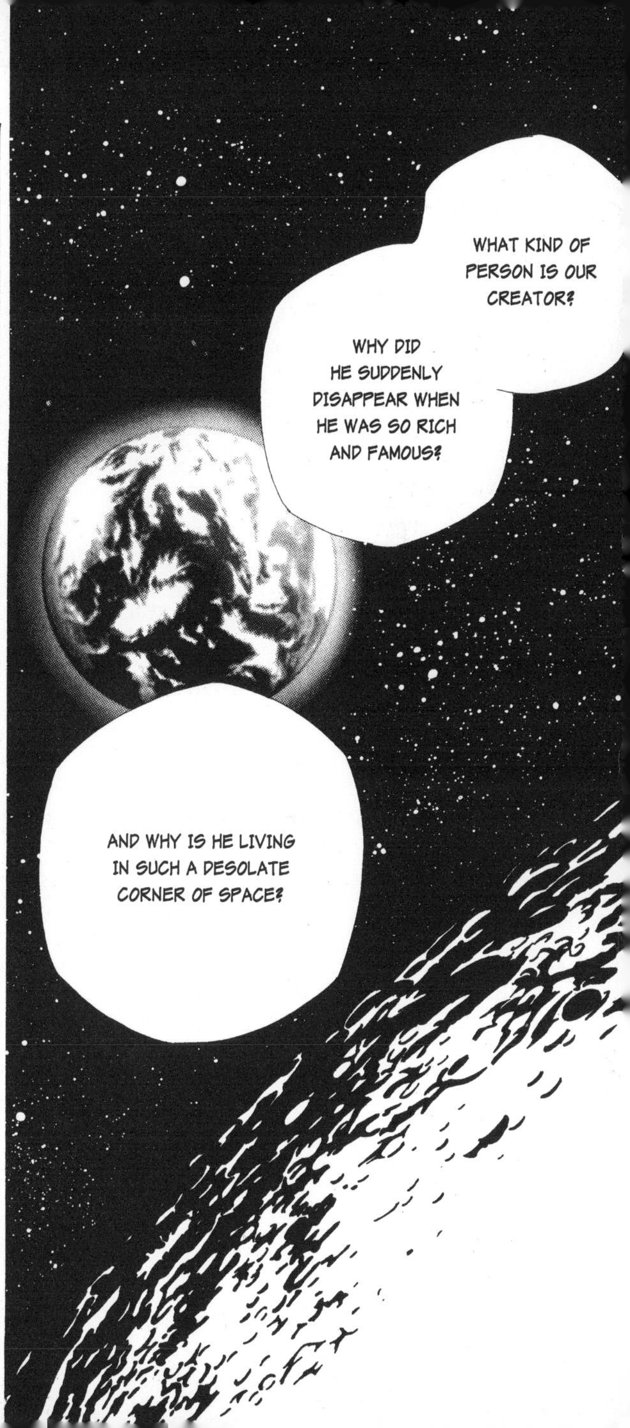
WHAT KIND OF PERSON IS OUR CREATOR?
WHY DID HE SUDDENLY DISAPPEAR WHEN HE WAS SO RICH AND FAMOUS?
AND WHY IS HE LIVING IN SUCH A DESOLATE CORNER OF SPACE?

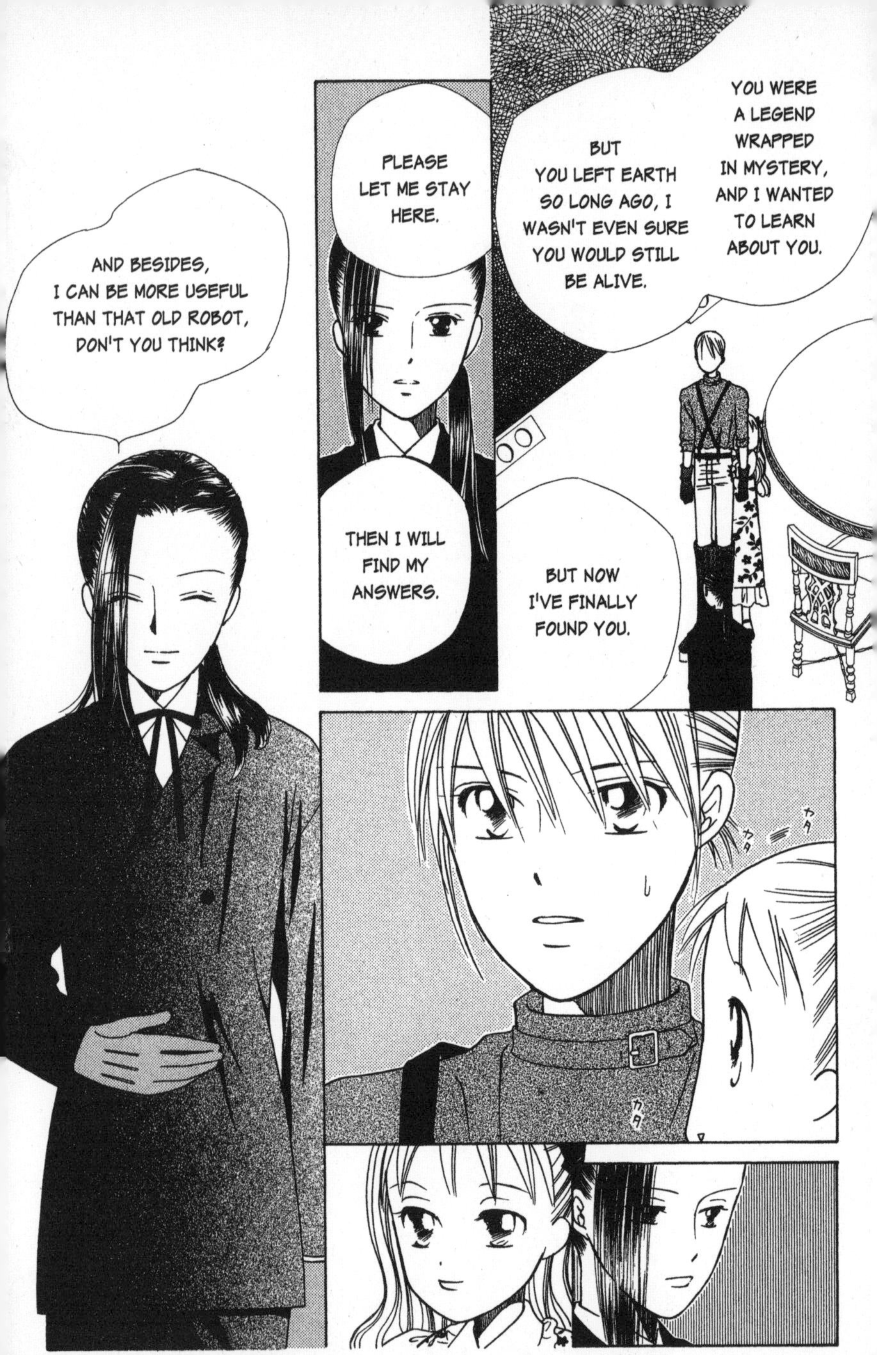
YOU WERE A LEGEND WRAPPED IN MYSTERY, AND I WANTED TO LEARN ABOUT YOU.
BUT YOU LEFT EARTH SO LONG AGO, I WASN'T EVEN SURE YOU WOULD STILL BE ALIVE.
BUT NOW I'VE FINALLY FOUND YOU.
PLEASE LET ME STAY HERE.
THEN I WILL FIND MY ANSWERS.
AND BESIDES, I CAN BE MORE USEFUL THAN THAT OLD ROBOT, DON'T YOU THINK?

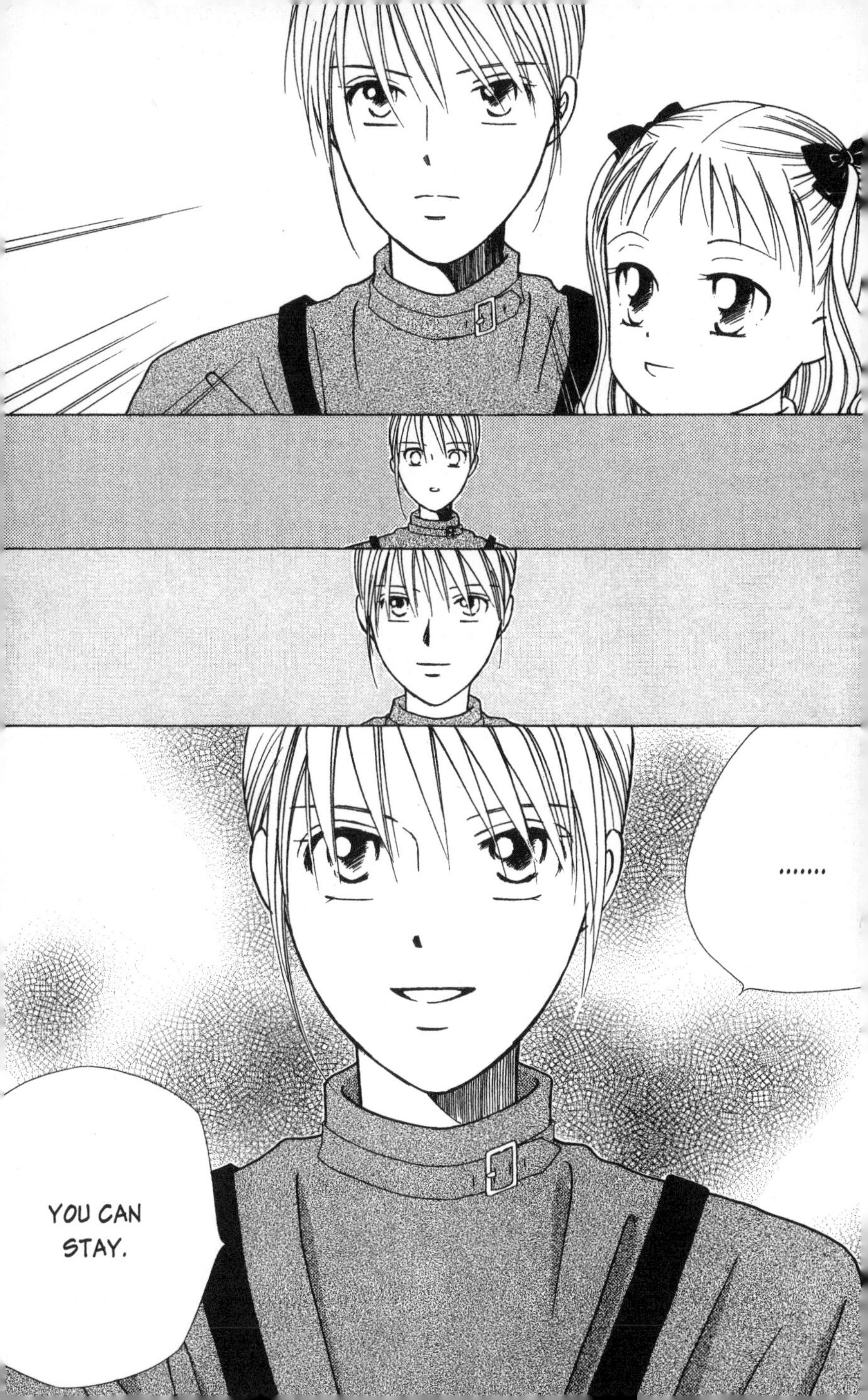
....
YOU CAN STAY.

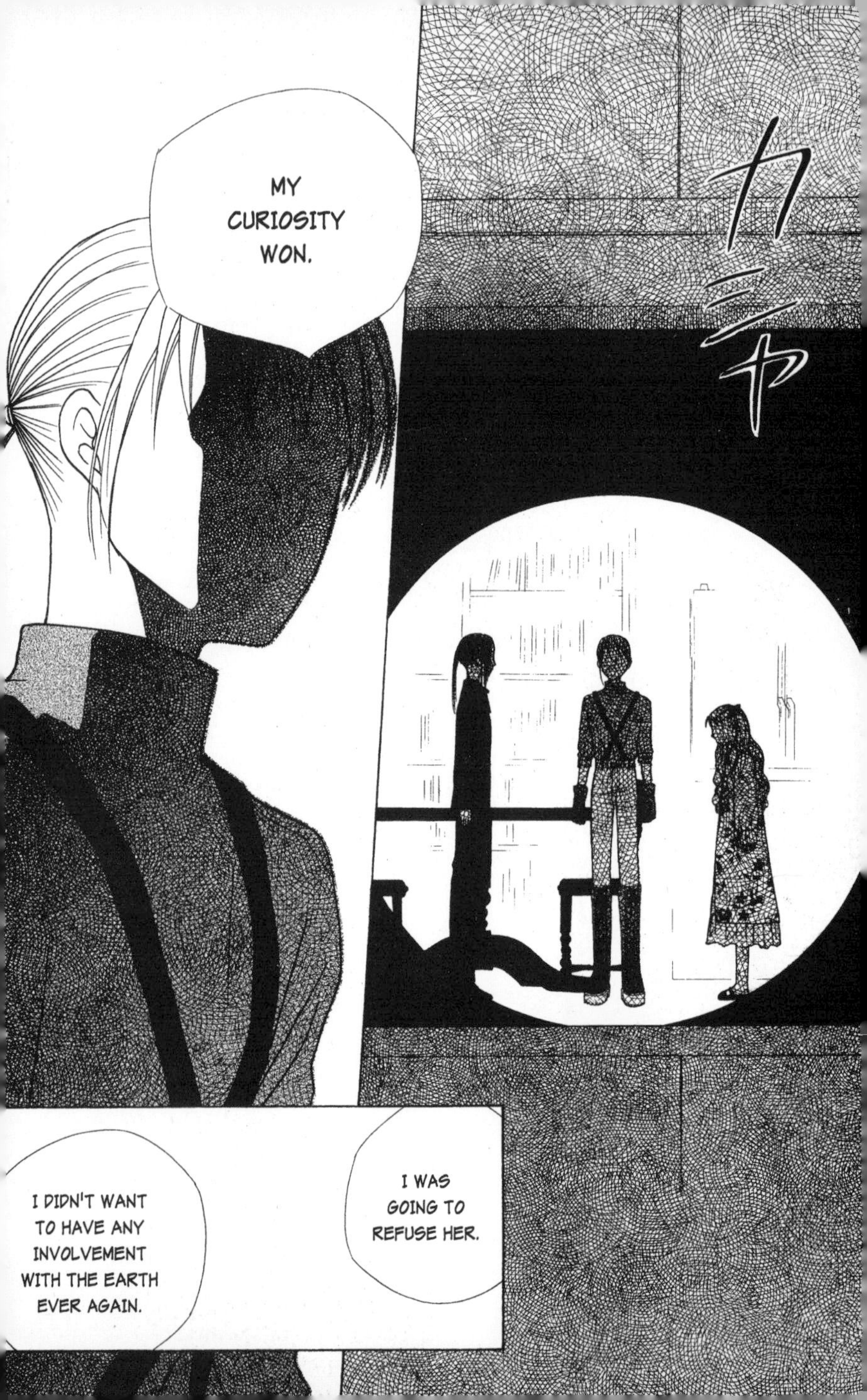
MY CURIOSITY WON.
カミャ
I WAS GOING TO REFUSE HER.
I DIDN'T WANT TO HAVE ANY INVOLVEMENT WITH THE EARTH EVER AGAIN.

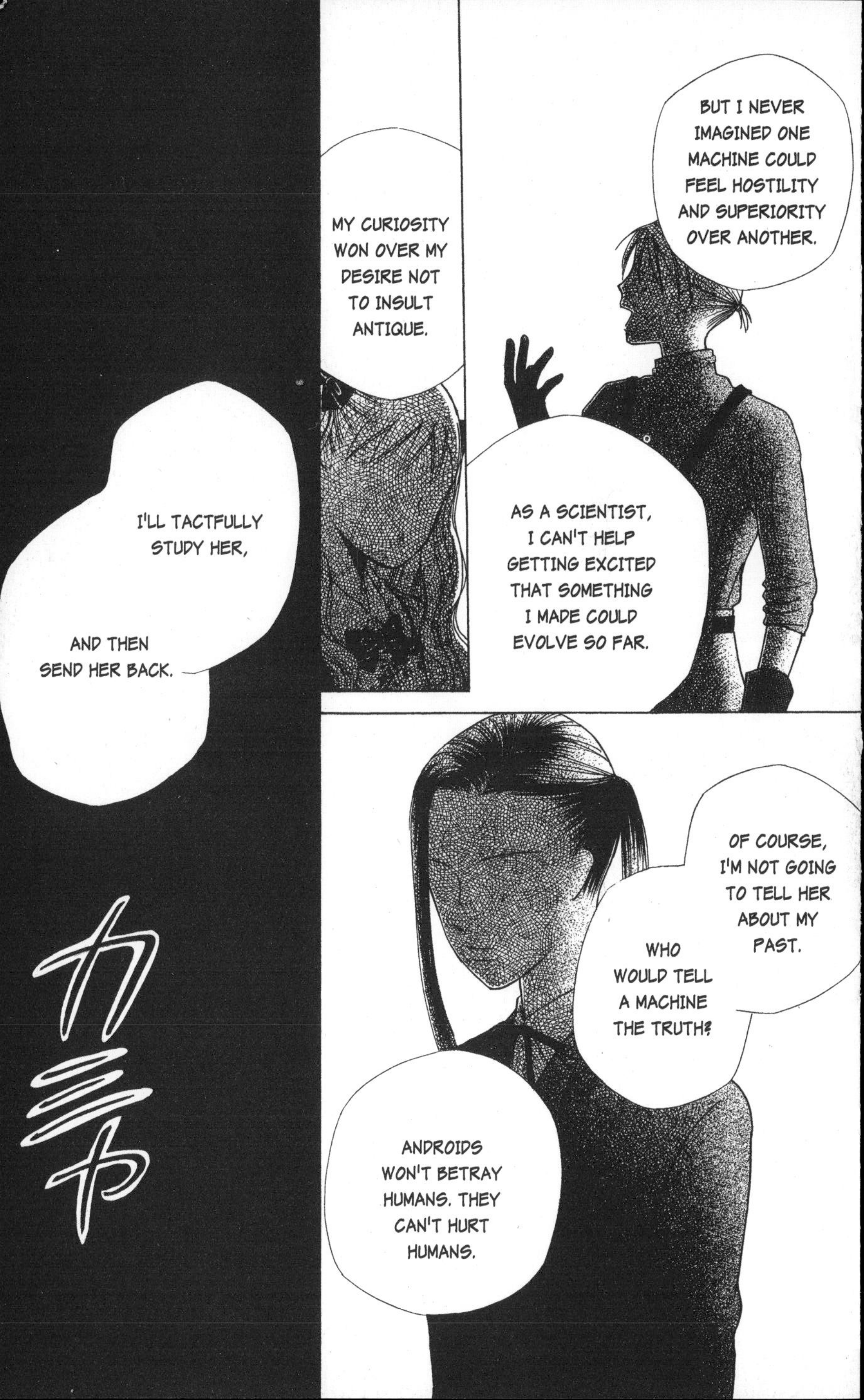

BUT I NEVER IMAGINED ONE MACHINE COULD FEEL HOSTILITY AND SUPERIORITY OVER ANOTHER.
AS A SCIENTIST, I CAN'T HELP GETTING EXCITED THAT SOMETHING I MADE COULD EVOLVE SO FAR.
MY CURIOSITY WON OVER MY DESIRE NOT TO INSULT ANTIQUE.
OF COURSE, I'M NOT GOING TO TELL HER ABOUT MY PAST.
WHO WOULD TELL A MACHINE THE TRUTH?
ANDROIDS WON'T BETRAY HUMANS. THEY CAN'T HURT HUMANS.
I'LL TACTFULLY STUDY HER,
AND THEN SEND HER BACK.
カミヤ

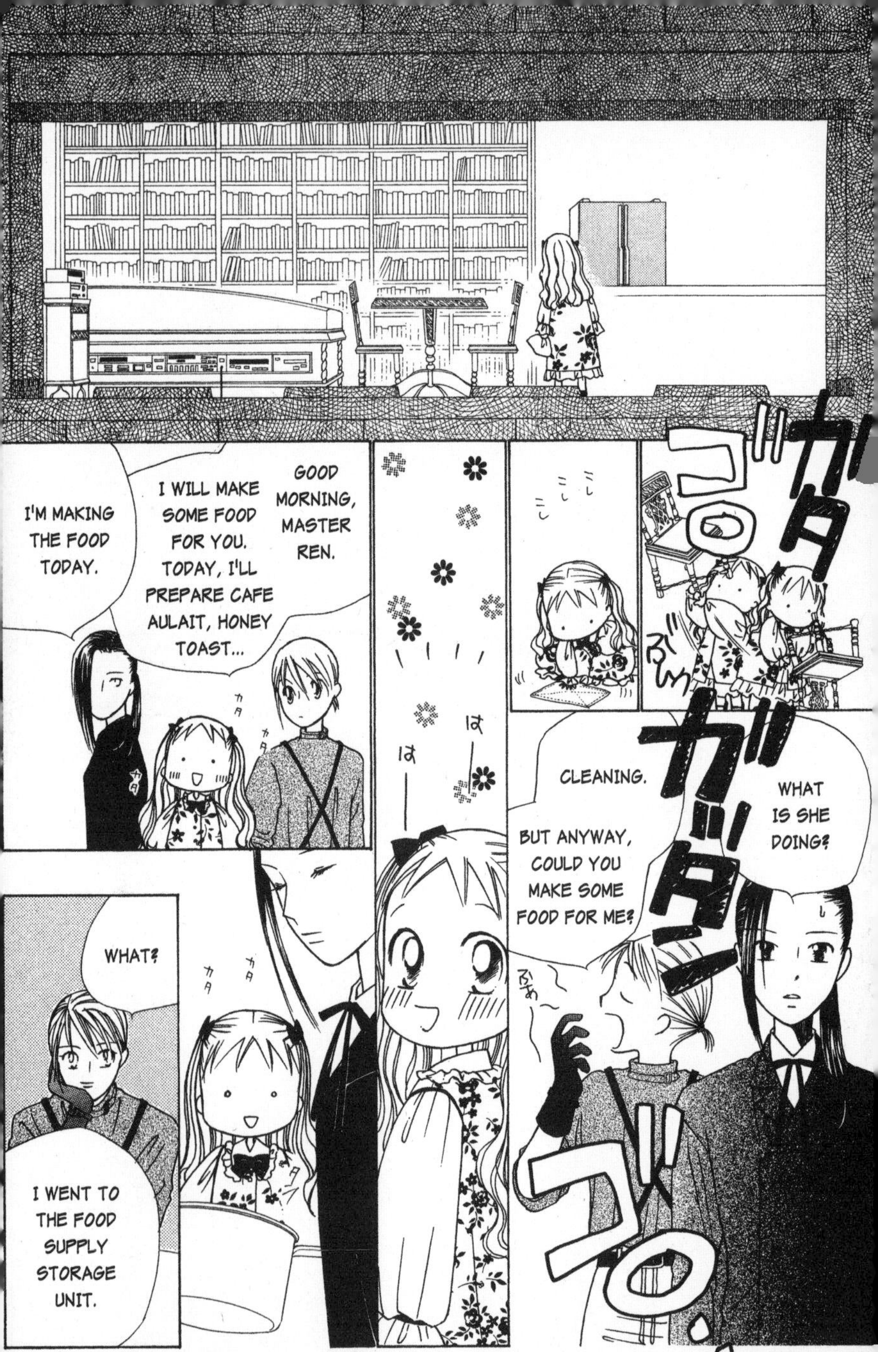
GOOD MORNING, MASTER REN.
I WILL MAKE SOME FOOD FOR YOU. TODAY, I'LL PREPARE CAFE AULAIT, HONEY TOAST...
I'M MAKING THE FOOD TODAY.
WHAT IS SHE DOING?
CLEANING.
BUT ANYWAY, COULD YOU MAKE SOME FOOD FOR ME?
WHAT?
I WENT TO THE FOOD SUPPLY STORAGE UNIT.

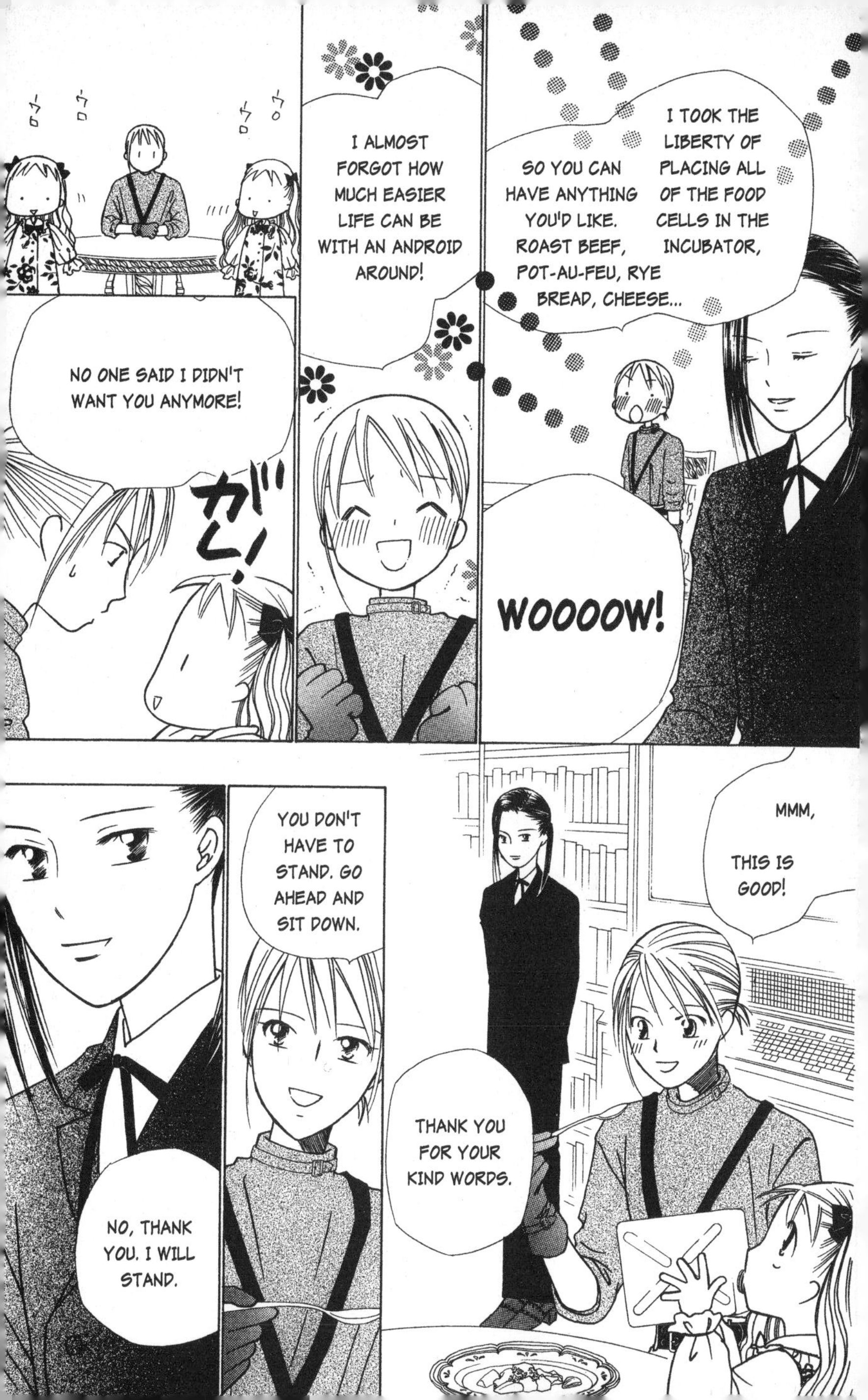
I TOOK THE LIBERTY OF PLACING ALL OF THE FOOD CELLS IN THE INCUBATOR,
SO YOU CAN HAVE ANYTHING YOU'D LIKE. ROAST BEEF, POT-AU-FEU, RYE BREAD, CHEESE...
WOOOOW!
I ALMOST FORGOT HOW MUCH EASIER LIFE CAN BE WITH AN ANDROID AROUND!
NO ONE SAID I DIDN'T WANT YOU ANYMORE!
MMM,
THIS IS GOOD!
THANK YOU FOR YOUR KIND WORDS.
YOU DON'T HAVE TO STAND. GO AHEAD AND SIT DOWN.
NO, THANK YOU. I WILL STAND.

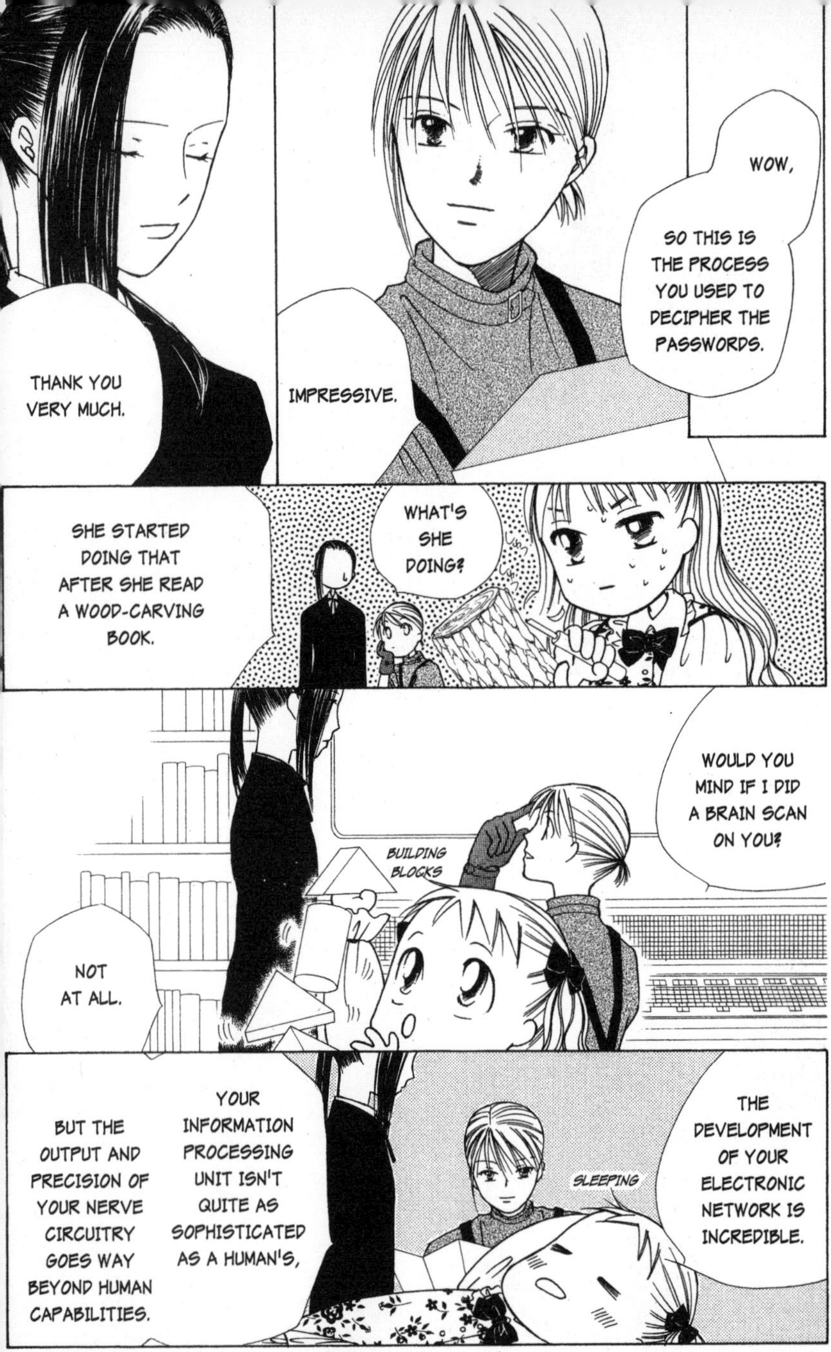
WOW,
SO THIS IS THE PROCESS YOU USED TO DECIPHER THE PASSWORDS.
IMPRESSIVE.
THANK YOU VERY MUCH.
WHAT'S SHE DOING?
SHE STARTED DOING THAT AFTER SHE READ A WOOD-CARVING BOOK.
WOULD YOU MIND IF I DID A BRAIN SCAN ON YOU?
BUILDING BLOCKS
NOT AT ALL.
THE DEVELOPMENT OF YOUR ELECTRONIC NETWORK IS INCREDIBLE.
SLEEPING
YOUR INFORMATION PROCESSING UNIT ISN'T QUITE AS SOPHISTICATED AS A HUMAN'S,
BUT THE OUTPUT AND PRECISION OF YOUR NERVE CIRCUITRY GOES WAY BEYOND HUMAN CAPABILITIES.

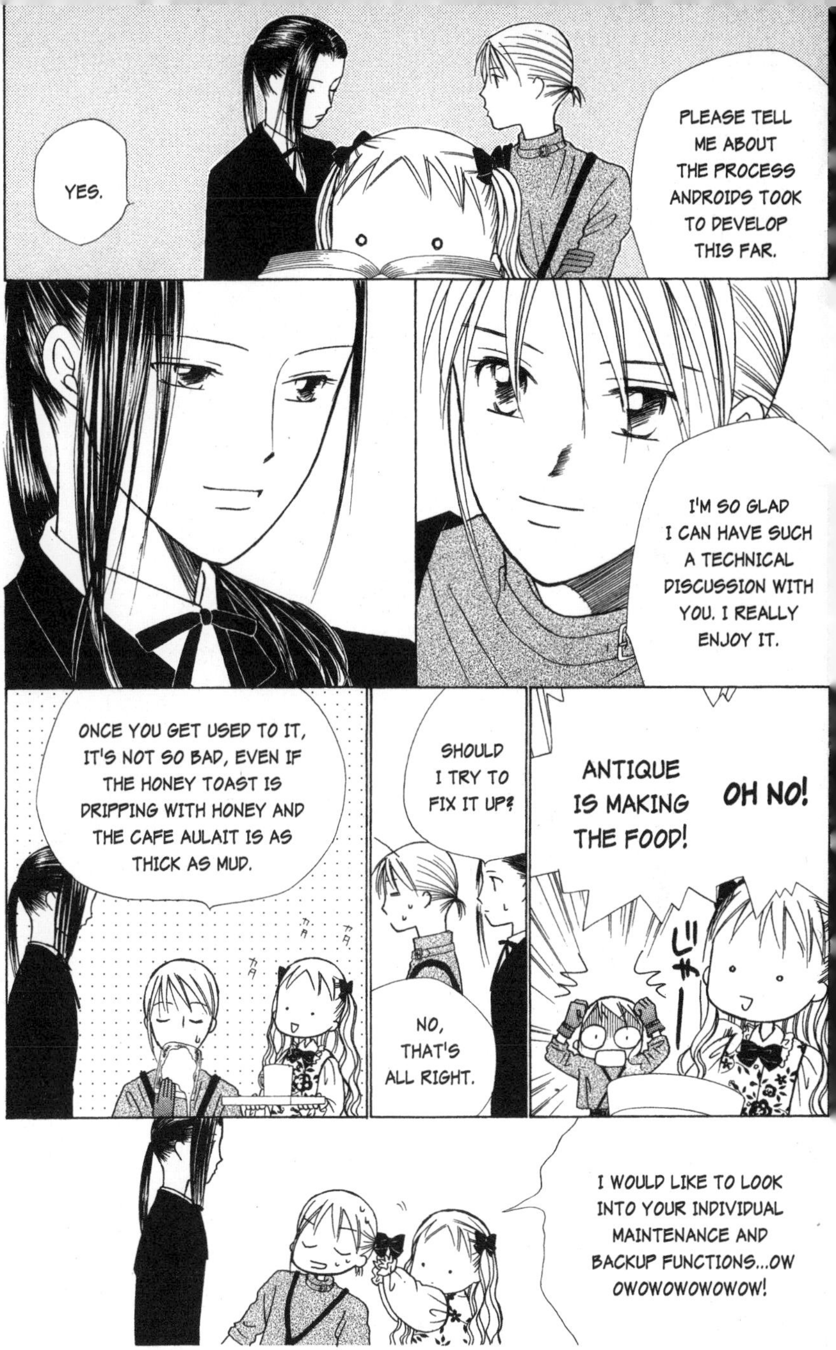
PLEASE TELL ME ABOUT THE PROCESS ANDROIDS TOOK TO DEVELOP THIS FAR.
YES.
I'M SO GLAD I CAN HAVE SUCH A TECHNICAL DISCUSSION WITH YOU. I REALLY ENJOY IT.
OH NO!
ANTIQUE IS MAKING THE FOOD!
じゃー
SHOULD I TRY TO FIX IT UP?
NO, THAT'S ALL RIGHT.
ONCE YOU GET USED TO IT, IT'S NOT SO BAD, EVEN IF THE HONEY TOAST IS DRIPPING WITH HONEY AND THE CAFE AULAIT IS AS THICK AS MUD.
I WOULD LIKE TO LOOK INTO YOUR INDIVIDUAL MAINTENANCE AND BACKUP FUNCTIONS...OW OWOWOWOWOWOW!

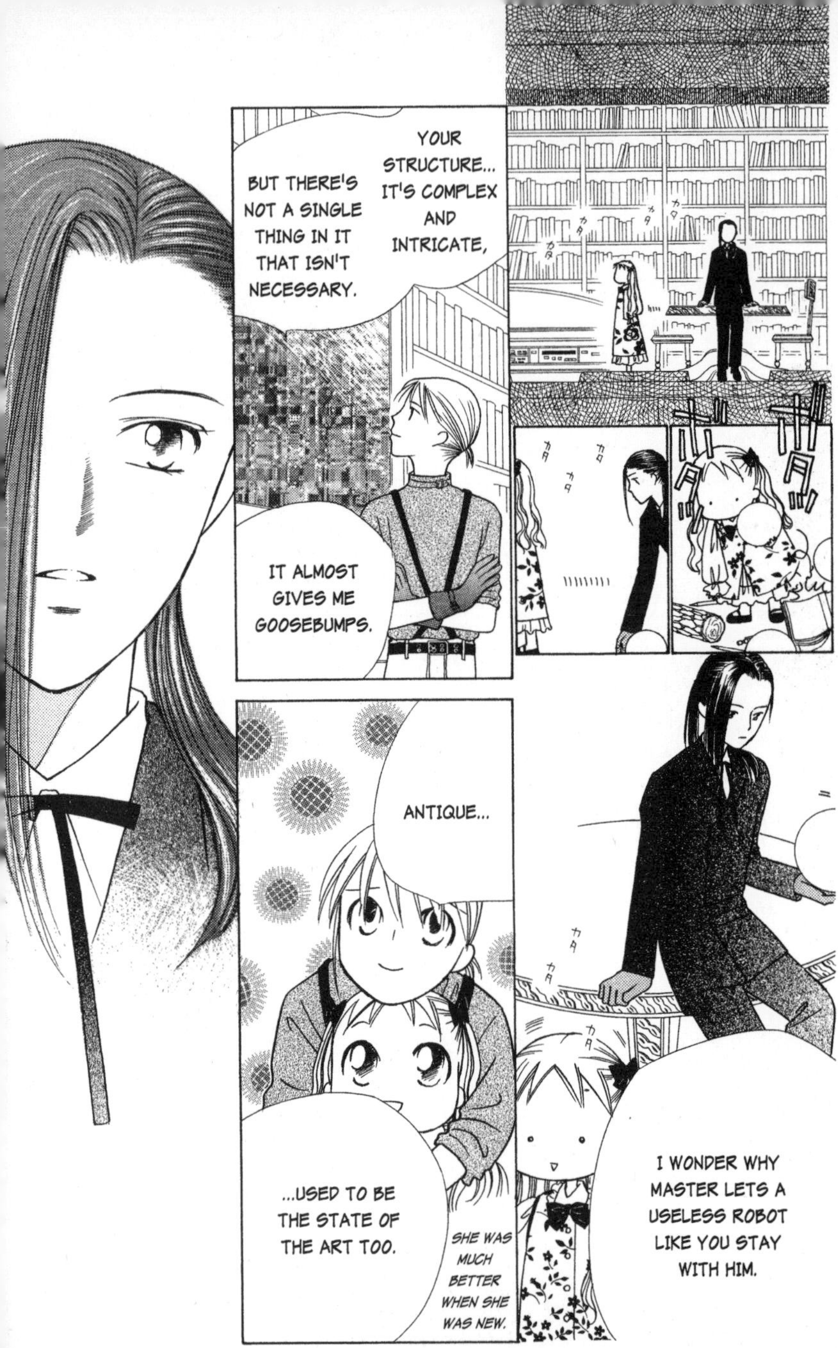
YOUR STRUCTURE... IT'S COMPLEX AND INTRICATE,
BUT THERE'S NOT A SINGLE THING IN IT THAT ISN'T NECESSARY.
IT ALMOST GIVES ME GOOSEBUMPS.
I WONDER WHY MASTER LETS A USELESS ROBOT LIKE YOU STAY WITH HIM.
ANTIQUE...
...USED TO BE THE STATE OF THE ART TOO.
SHE WAS MUCH BETTER WHEN SHE WAS NEW.

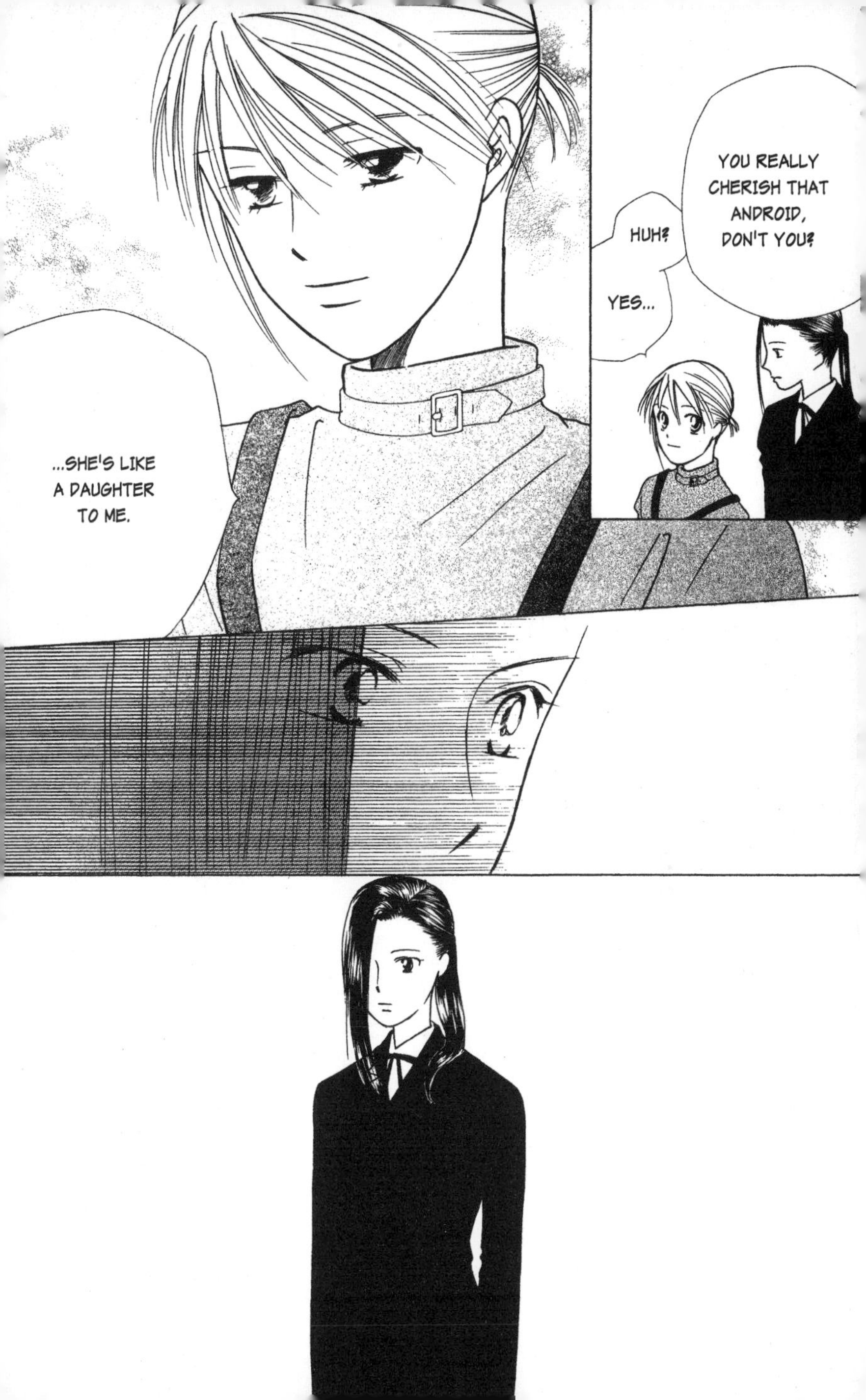
YOU REALLY CHERISH THAT ANDROID, DON'T YOU?
HUH?
YES...
...SHE'S LIKE A DAUGHTER TO ME.

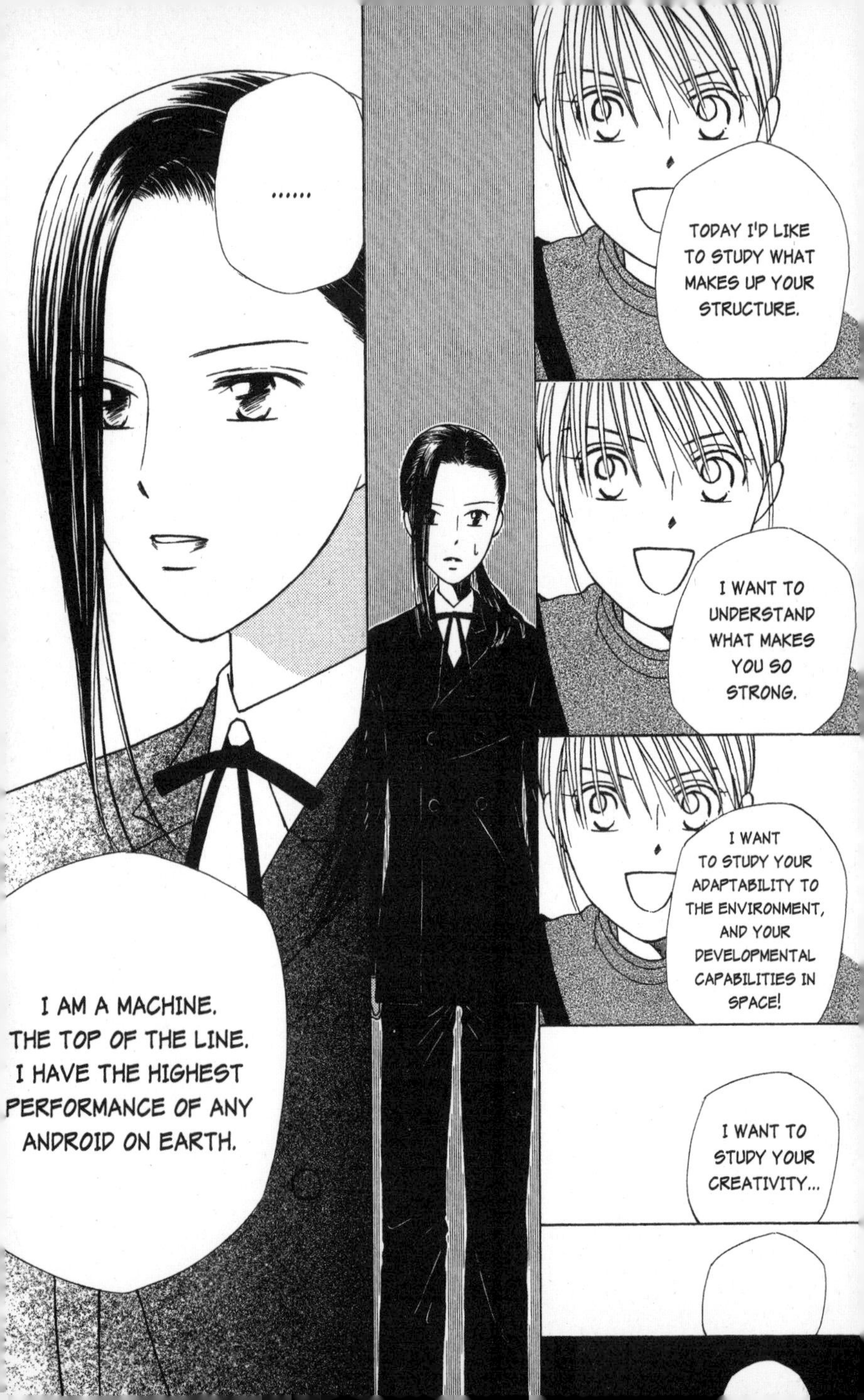
TODAY I'D LIKE TO STUDY WHAT MAKES UP YOUR STRUCTURE.
I WANT TO UNDERSTAND WHAT MAKES YOU SO STRONG.
I WANT TO STUDY YOUR ADAPTABILITY TO THE ENVIRONMENT, AND YOUR DEVELOPMENTAL CAPABILITIES IN SPACE!
I WANT TO STUDY YOUR CREATIVITY...
......
I AM A MACHINE. THE TOP OF THE LINE. I HAVE THE HIGHEST PERFORMANCE OF ANY ANDROID ON EARTH.

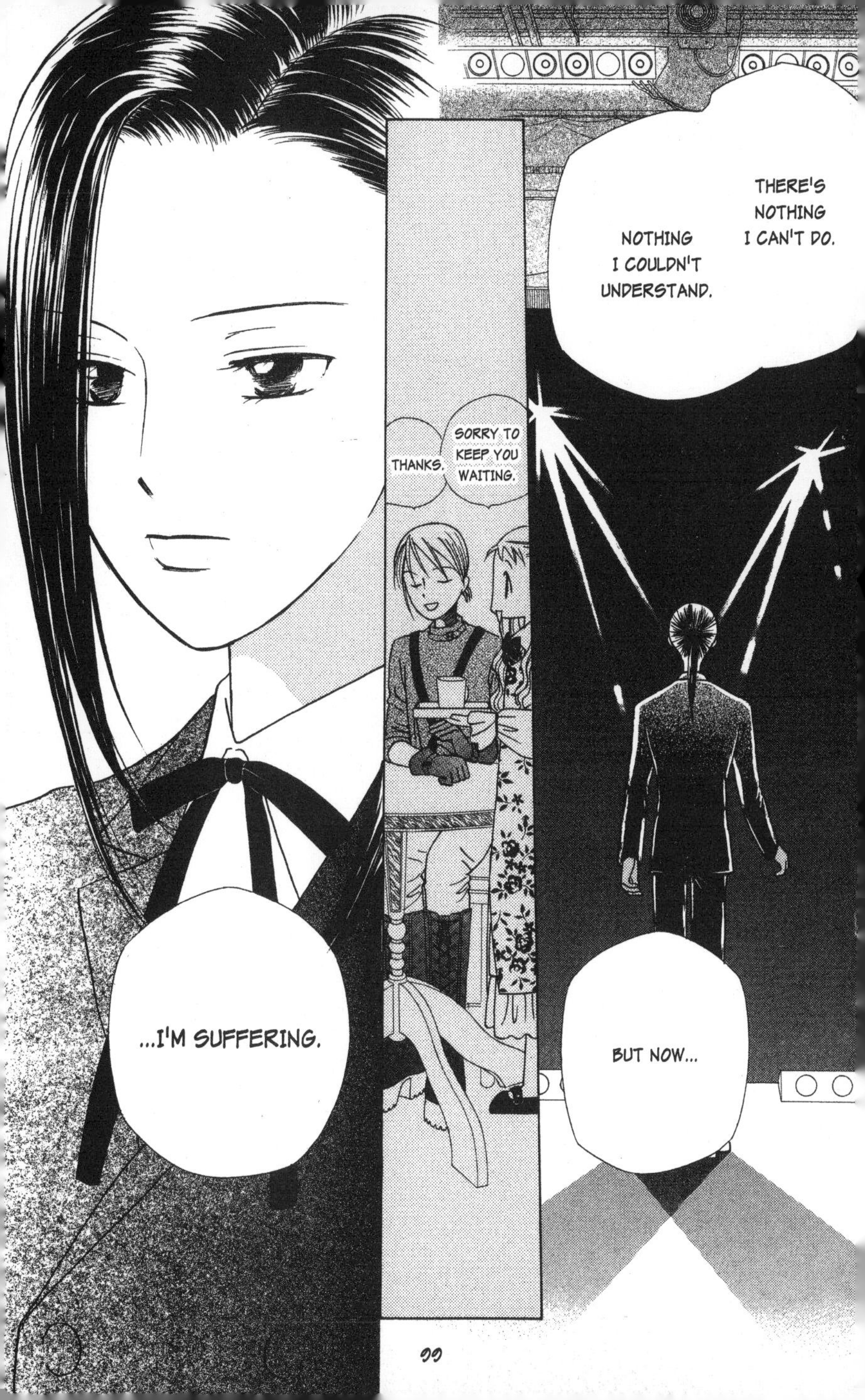
THERE'S NOTHING I CAN'T DO.
NOTHING I COULDN'T UNDERSTAND.
SORRY TO KEEP YOU WAITING.
THANKS.
BUT NOW...
...I'M SUFFERING.

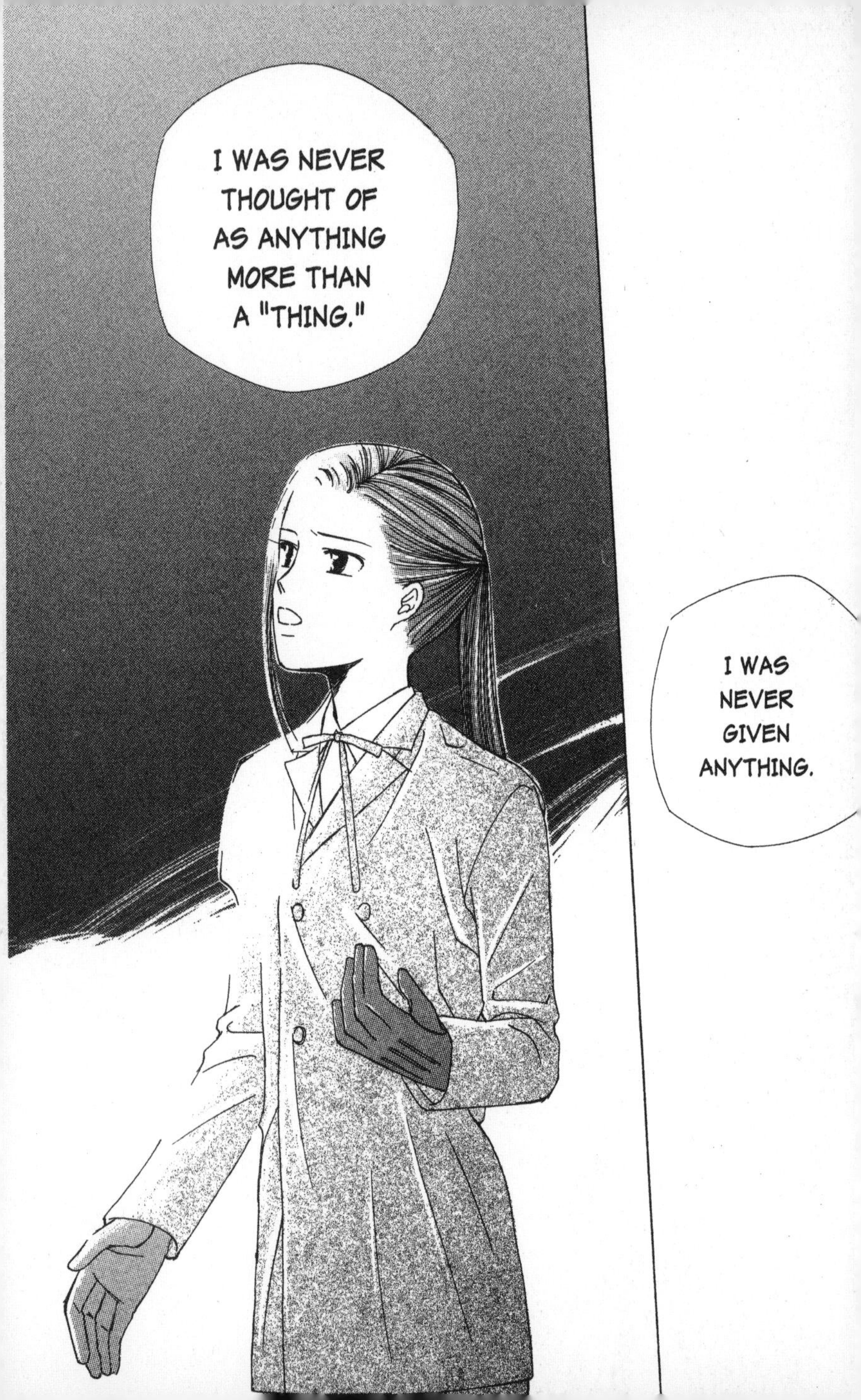
I WAS NEVER GIVEN ANYTHING.
I WAS NEVER THOUGHT OF AS ANYTHING MORE THAN A "THING."

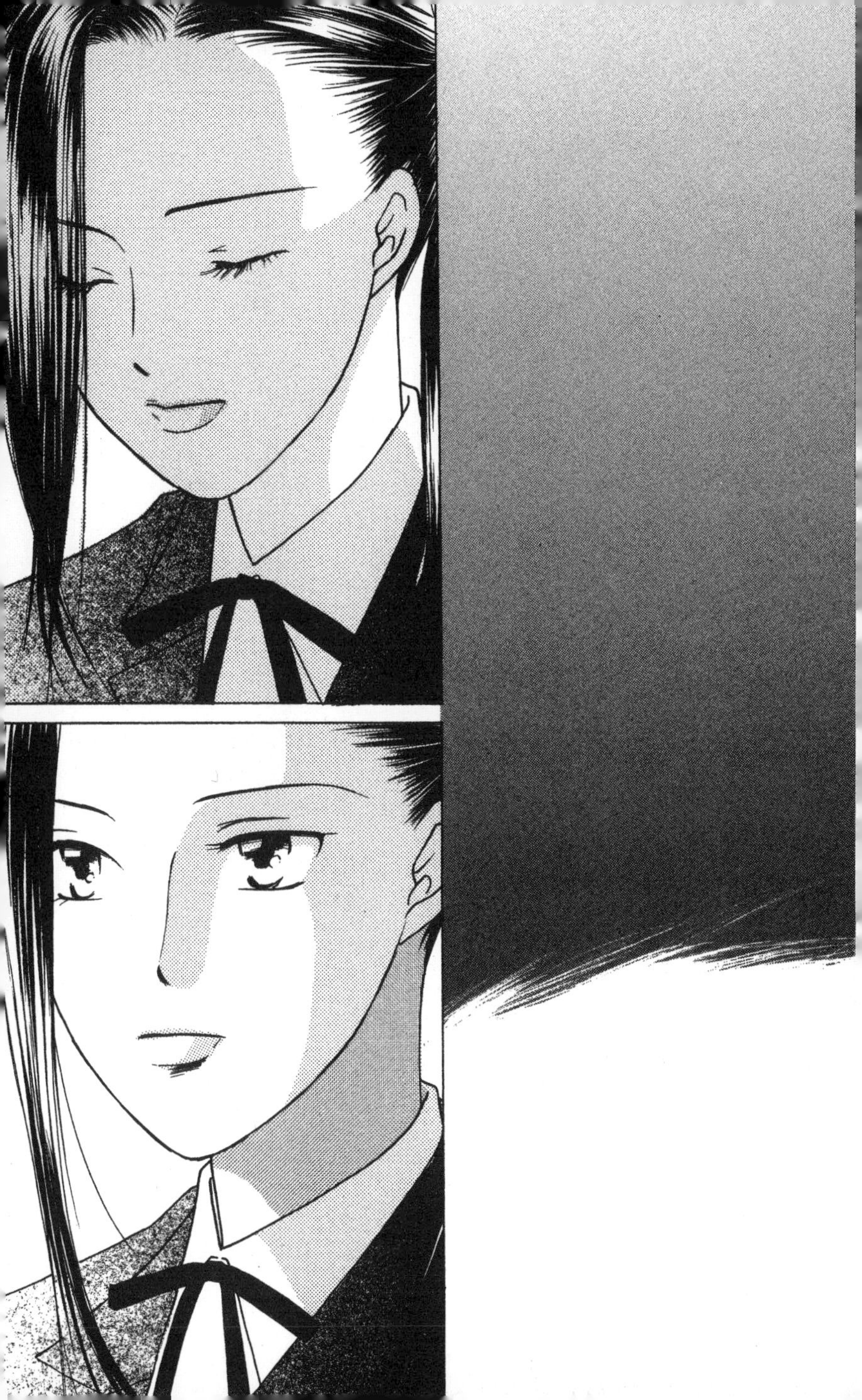

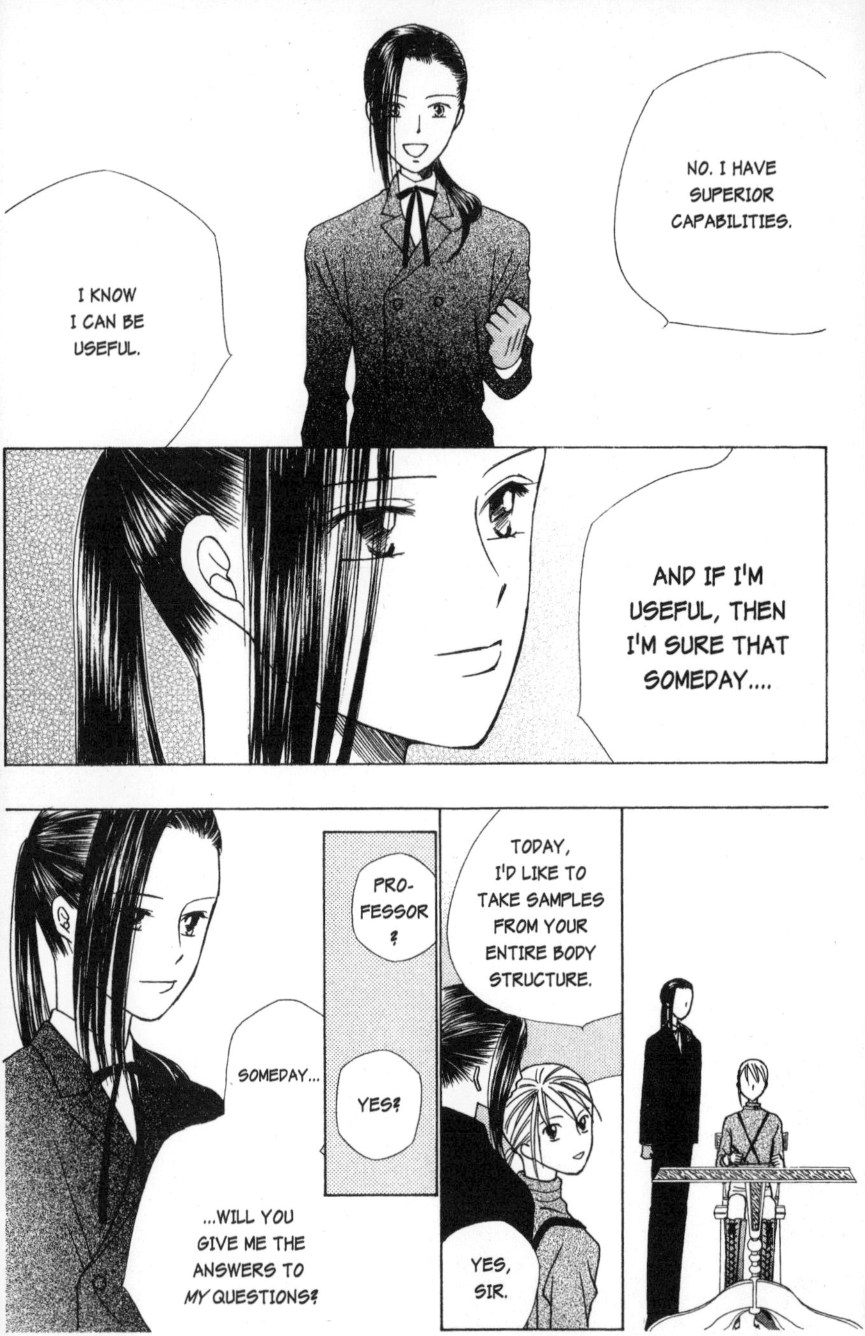
NO. I HAVE SUPERIOR CAPABILITIES.
I KNOW I CAN BE USEFUL.
AND IF I'M USEFUL, THEN I'M SURE THAT SOMEDAY....
TODAY, I'D LIKE TO TAKE SAMPLES FROM YOUR ENTIRE BODY STRUCTURE.
YES, SIR.
PRO-FESSOR?
YES?
SOMEDAY...
...WILL YOU GIVE ME THE ANSWERS TO *MY* QUESTIONS?

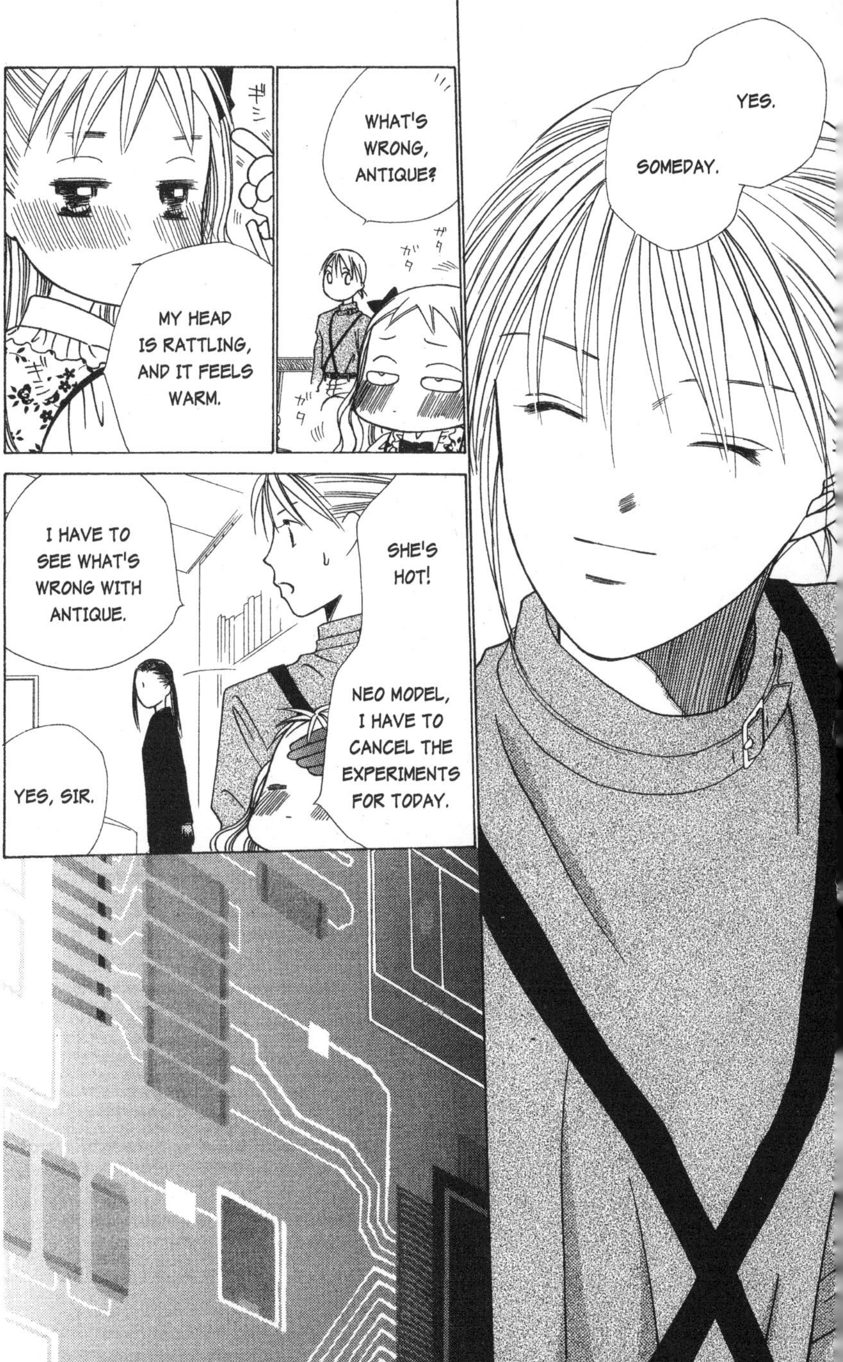
YES.
SOMEDAY.
WHAT'S WRONG, ANTIQUE?
MY HEAD IS RATTLING, AND IT FEELS WARM.
SHE'S HOT!
NEO MODEL, I HAVE TO CANCEL THE EXPERIMENTS FOR TODAY.
I HAVE TO SEE WHAT'S WRONG WITH ANTIQUE.
YES, SIR.

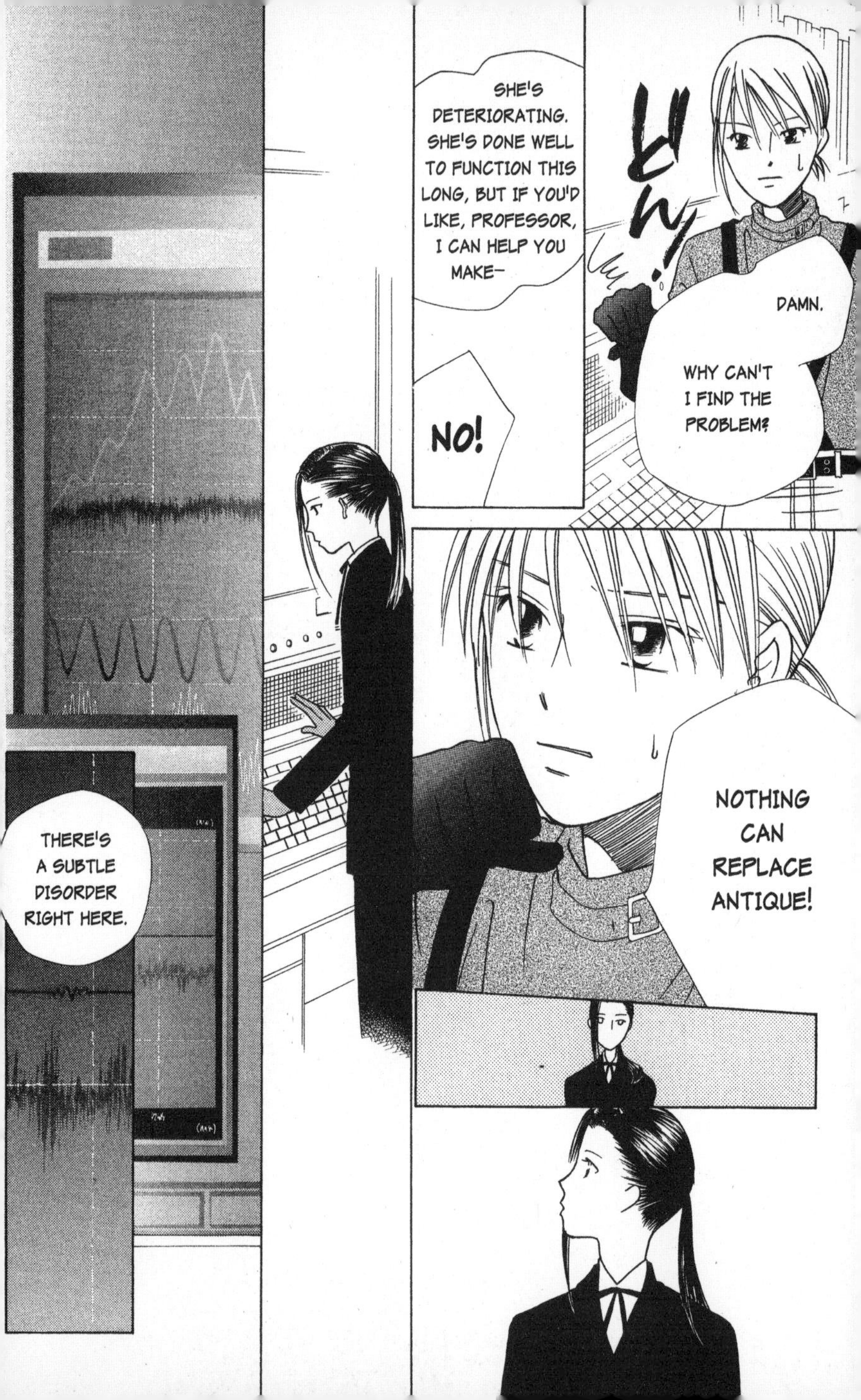
どん！
SHE'S DETERIORATING. SHE'S DONE WELL TO FUNCTION THIS LONG, BUT IF YOU'D LIKE, PROFESSOR, I CAN HELP YOU MAKE–
NO!
DAMN.
WHY CAN'T I FIND THE PROBLEM?
NOTHING CAN REPLACE ANTIQUE!
THERE'S A SUBTLE DISORDER RIGHT HERE.

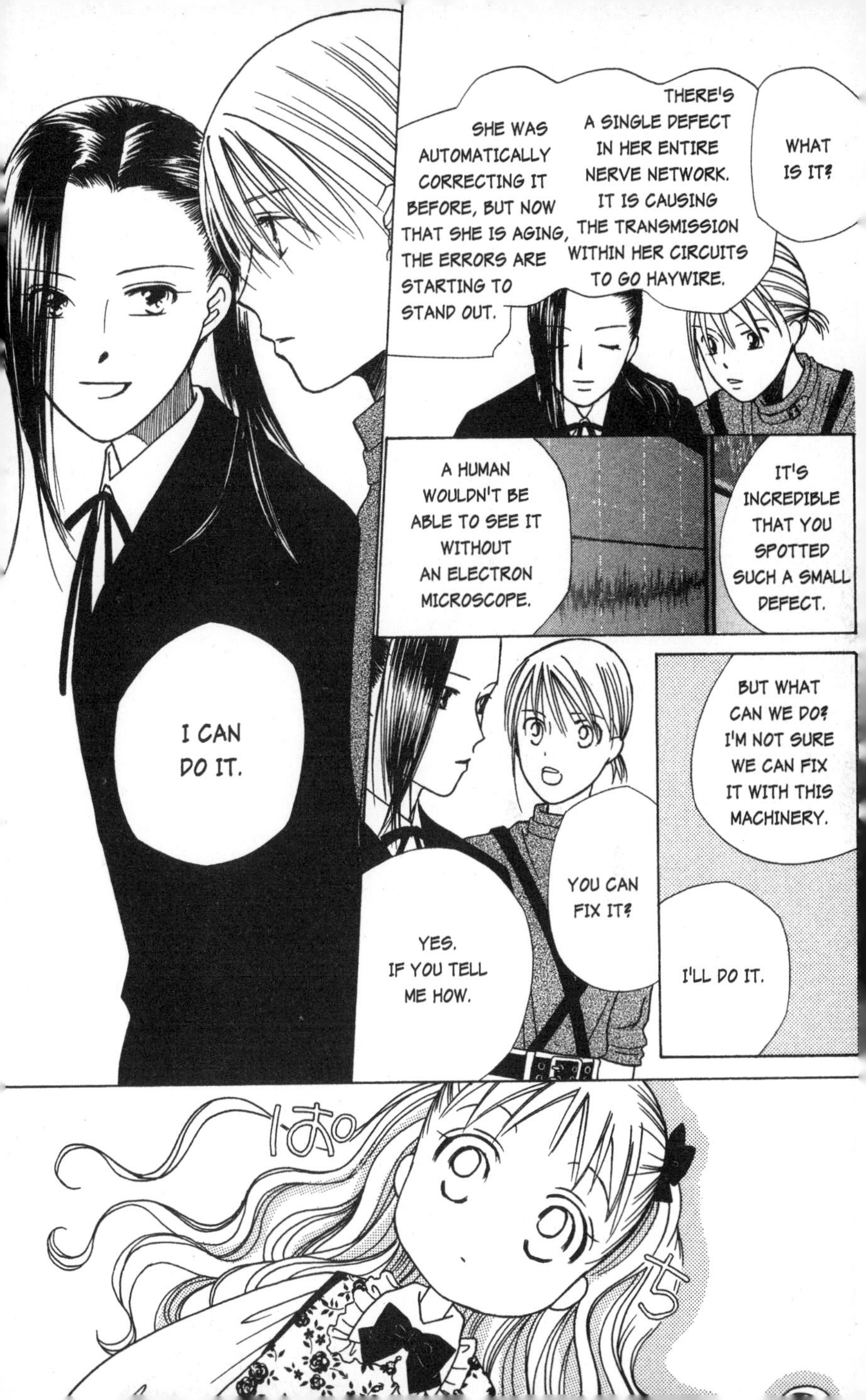
WHAT IS IT?
THERE'S A SINGLE DEFECT IN HER ENTIRE NERVE NETWORK. IT IS CAUSING THE TRANSMISSION WITHIN HER CIRCUITS TO GO HAYWIRE.
SHE WAS AUTOMATICALLY CORRECTING IT BEFORE, BUT NOW THAT SHE IS AGING, THE ERRORS ARE STARTING TO STAND OUT.
IT'S INCREDIBLE THAT YOU SPOTTED SUCH A SMALL DEFECT.
A HUMAN WOULDN'T BE ABLE TO SEE IT WITHOUT AN ELECTRON MICROSCOPE.
BUT WHAT CAN WE DO? I'M NOT SURE WE CAN FIX IT WITH THIS MACHINERY.
I'LL DO IT.
YOU CAN FIX IT?
YES. IF YOU TELL ME HOW.
I CAN DO IT.

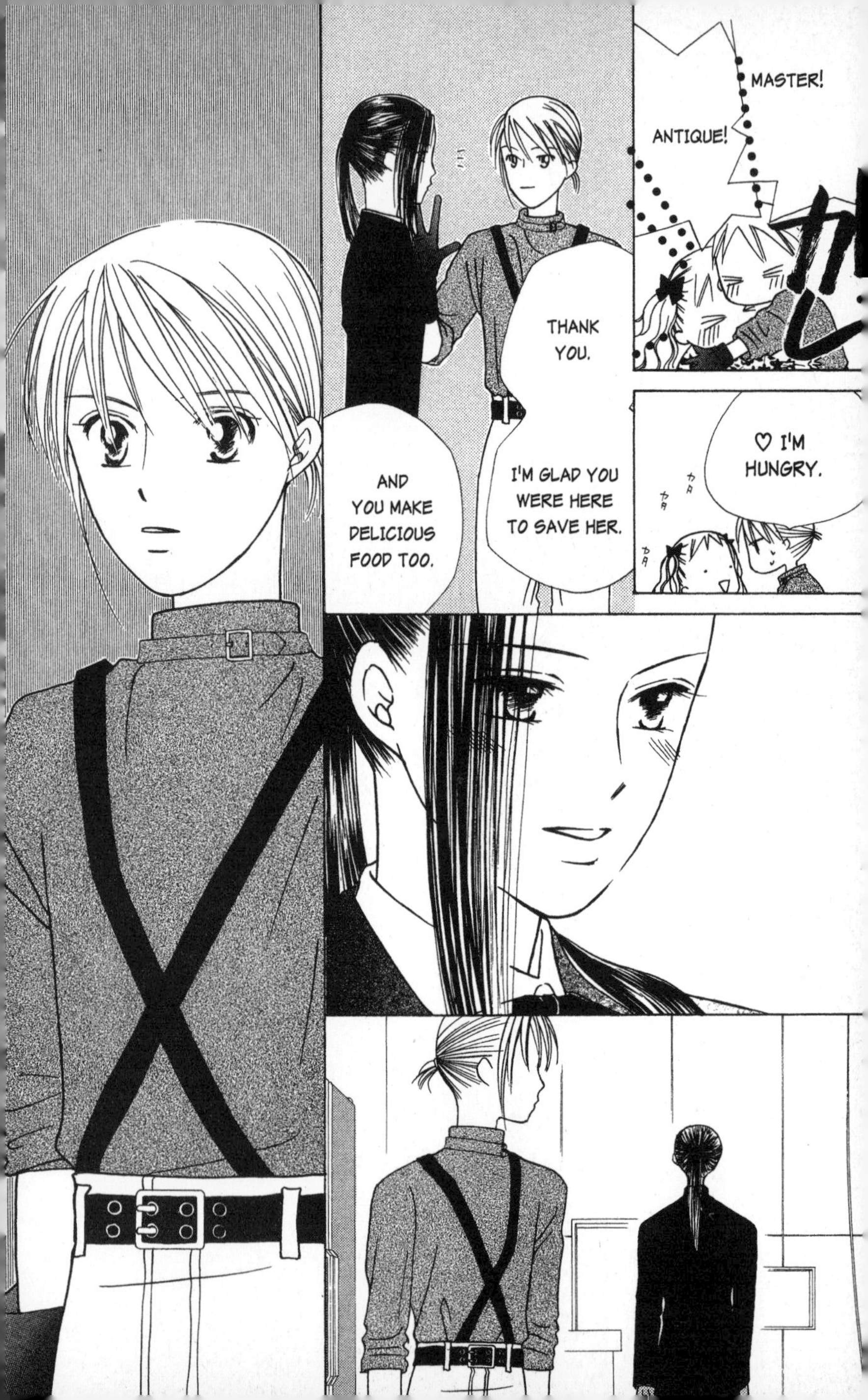
MASTER!
ANTIQUE!
♡ I'M HUNGRY.
THANK YOU.
I'M GLAD YOU WERE HERE TO SAVE HER.
AND YOU MAKE DELICIOUS FOOD TOO.

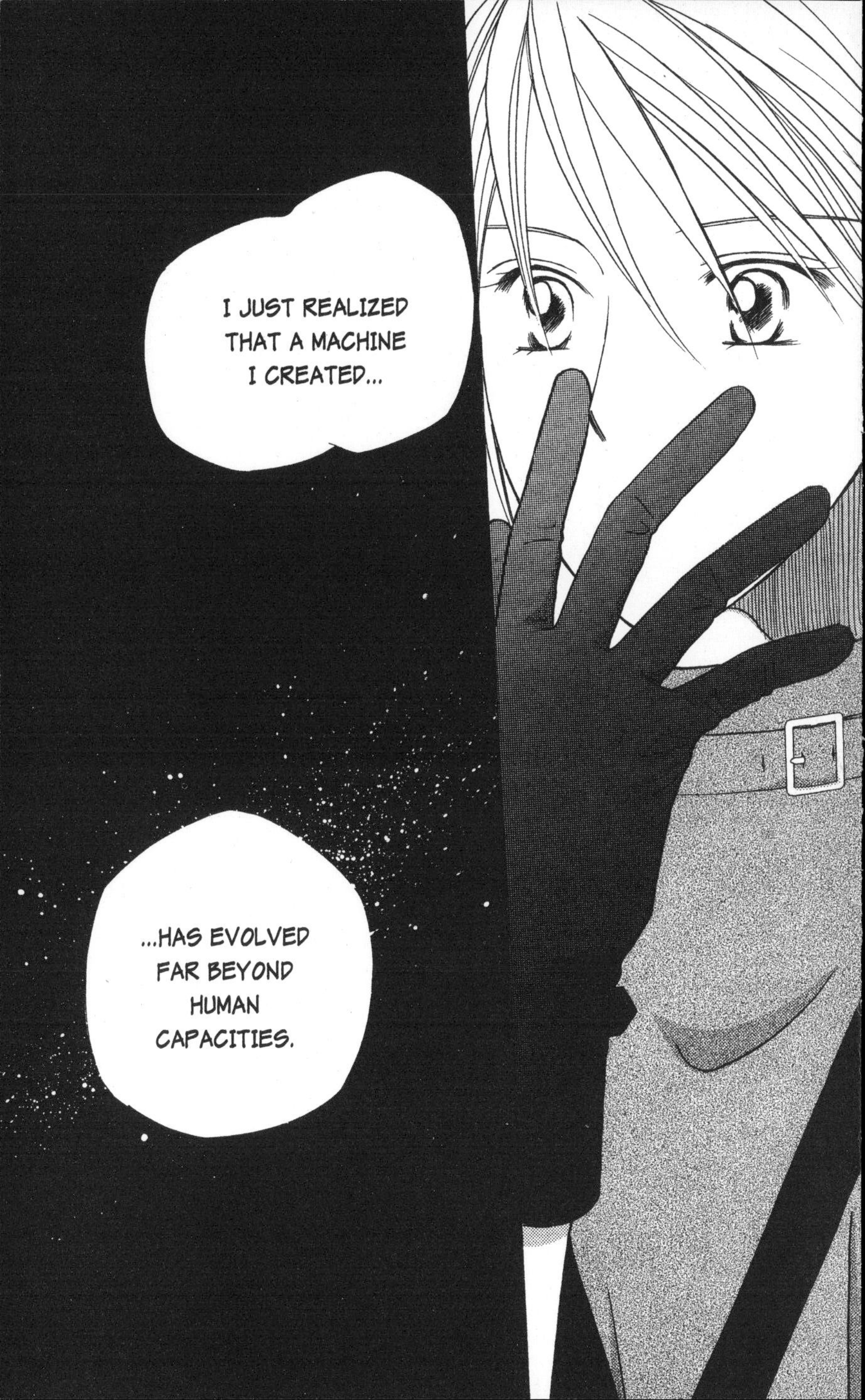
I JUST REALIZED THAT A MACHINE I CREATED...
...HAS EVOLVED FAR BEYOND HUMAN CAPACITIES.

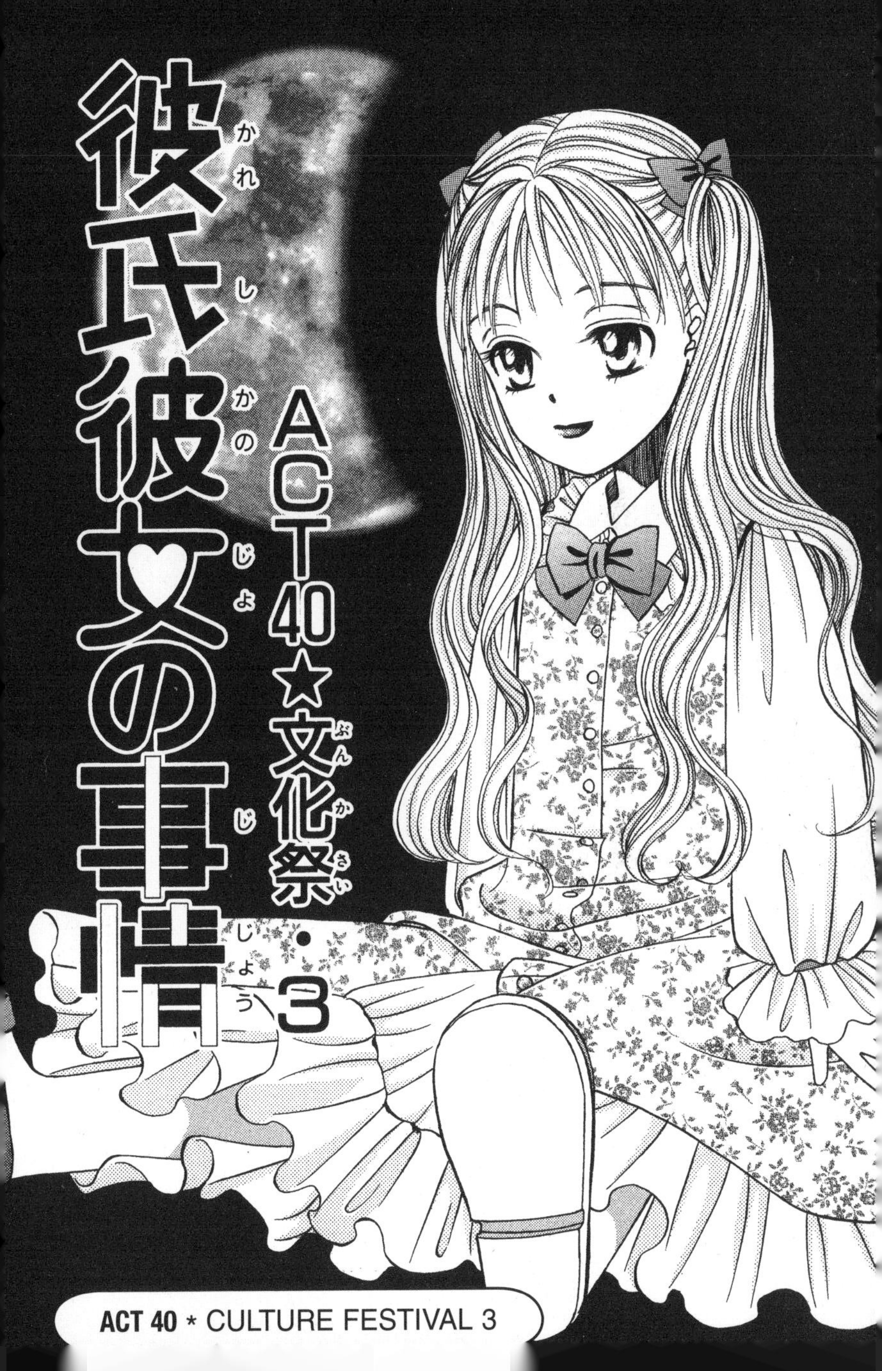
彼氏彼女の事情
ACT40★文化祭・3
ACT 40 * CULTURE FESTIVAL 3

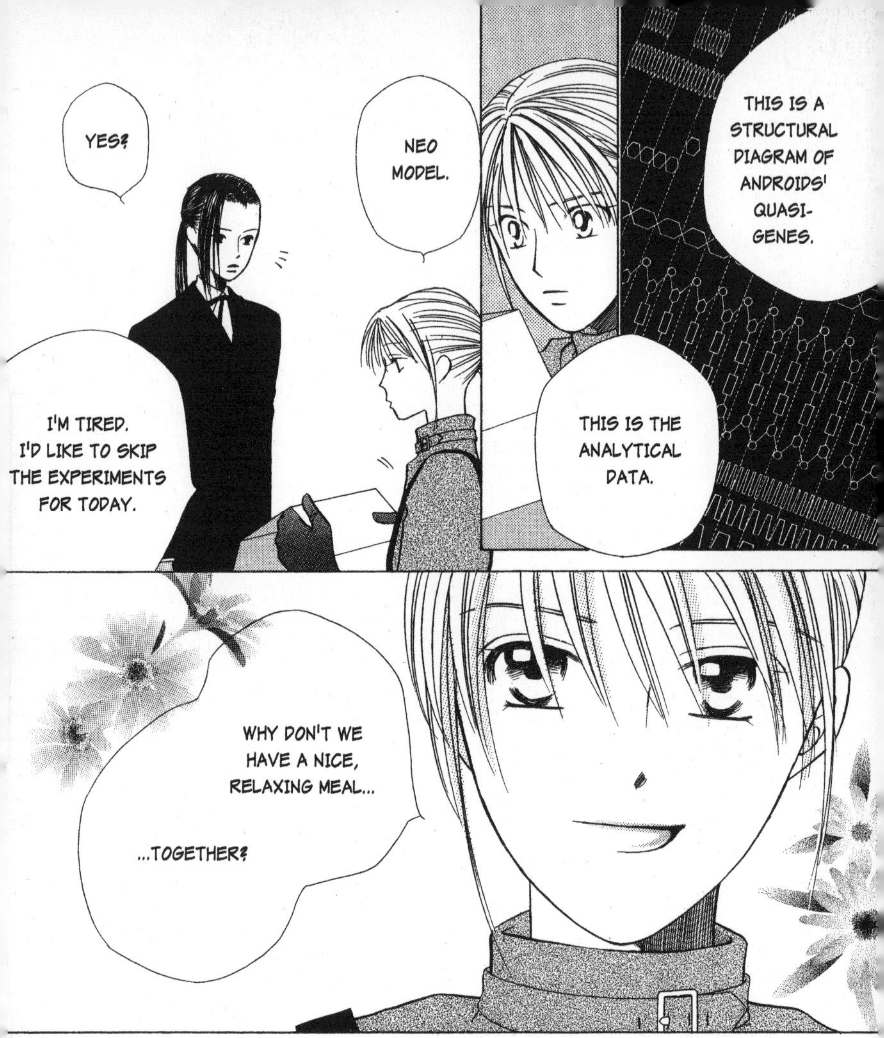
THIS IS A STRUCTURAL DIAGRAM OF ANDROIDS' QUASI-GENES.
THIS IS THE ANALYTICAL DATA.
NEO MODEL.
YES?
I'M TIRED. I'D LIKE TO SKIP THE EXPERIMENTS FOR TODAY.
WHY DON'T WE HAVE A NICE, RELAXING MEAL...
...TOGETHER?

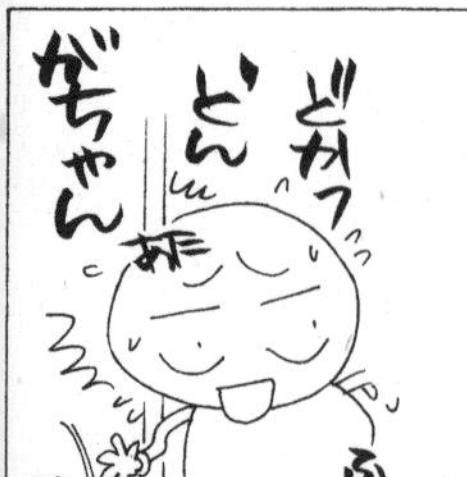
どかっ
どん
がちゃん
ふた
ぱき

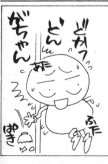

Ever since I started reading the Kojiki, I've fallen even more in love with Japanese history. (But that doesn't mean I know much about it! I'd like to learn though.)

I want to learn the tea ceremony or calligraphy, or wear a kimono. But yours truly is a very fidgety person, so I don't think I'll ever be able to handle the tea ceremony.

And a kimono? Where would yours truly wear a kimono? So the only thing left is calligraphy.

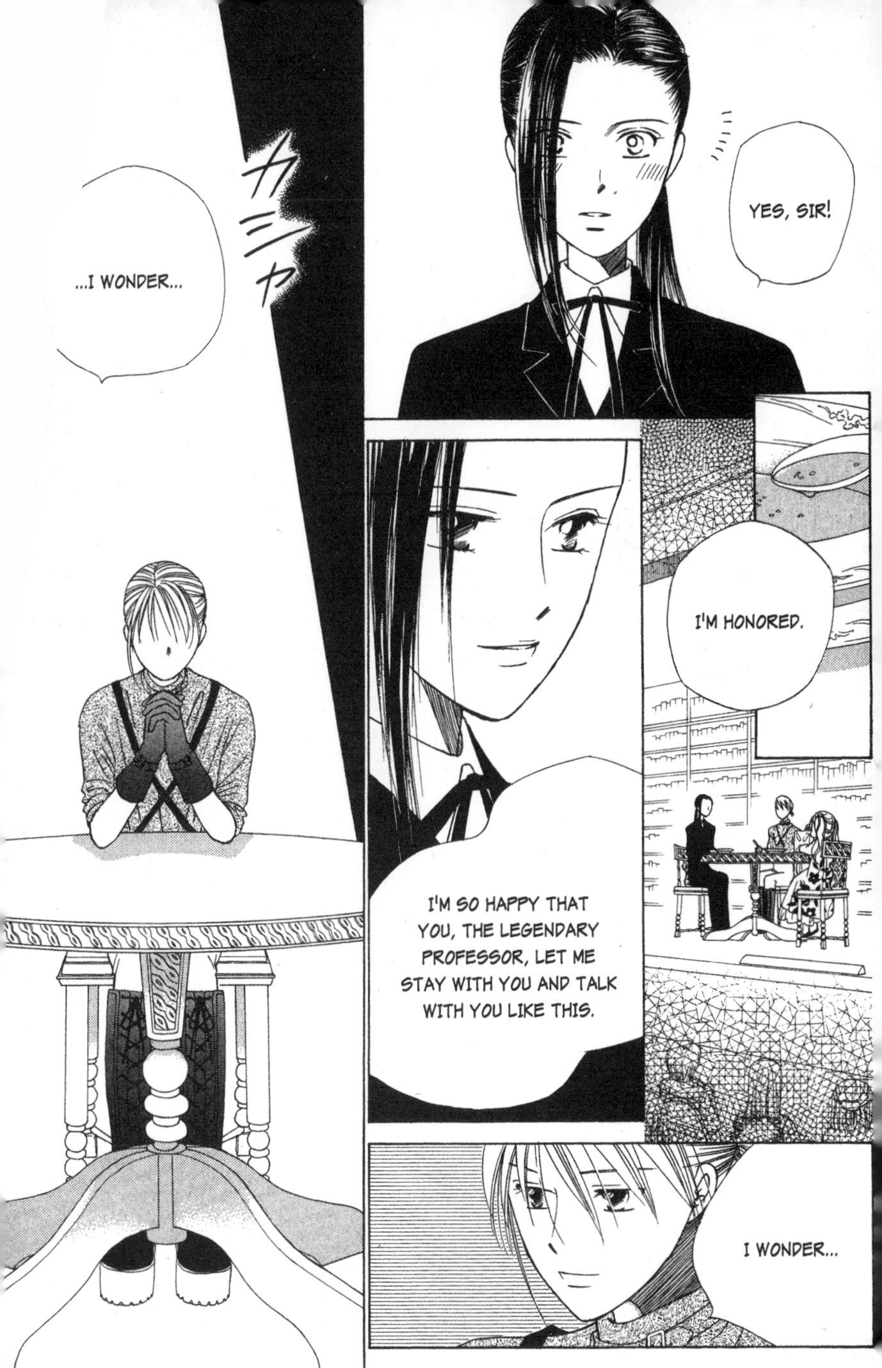
YES, SIR!
I'M HONORED.
I'M SO HAPPY THAT YOU, THE LEGENDARY PROFESSOR, LET ME STAY WITH YOU AND TALK WITH YOU LIKE THIS.
I WONDER...
カシャ
...I WONDER...

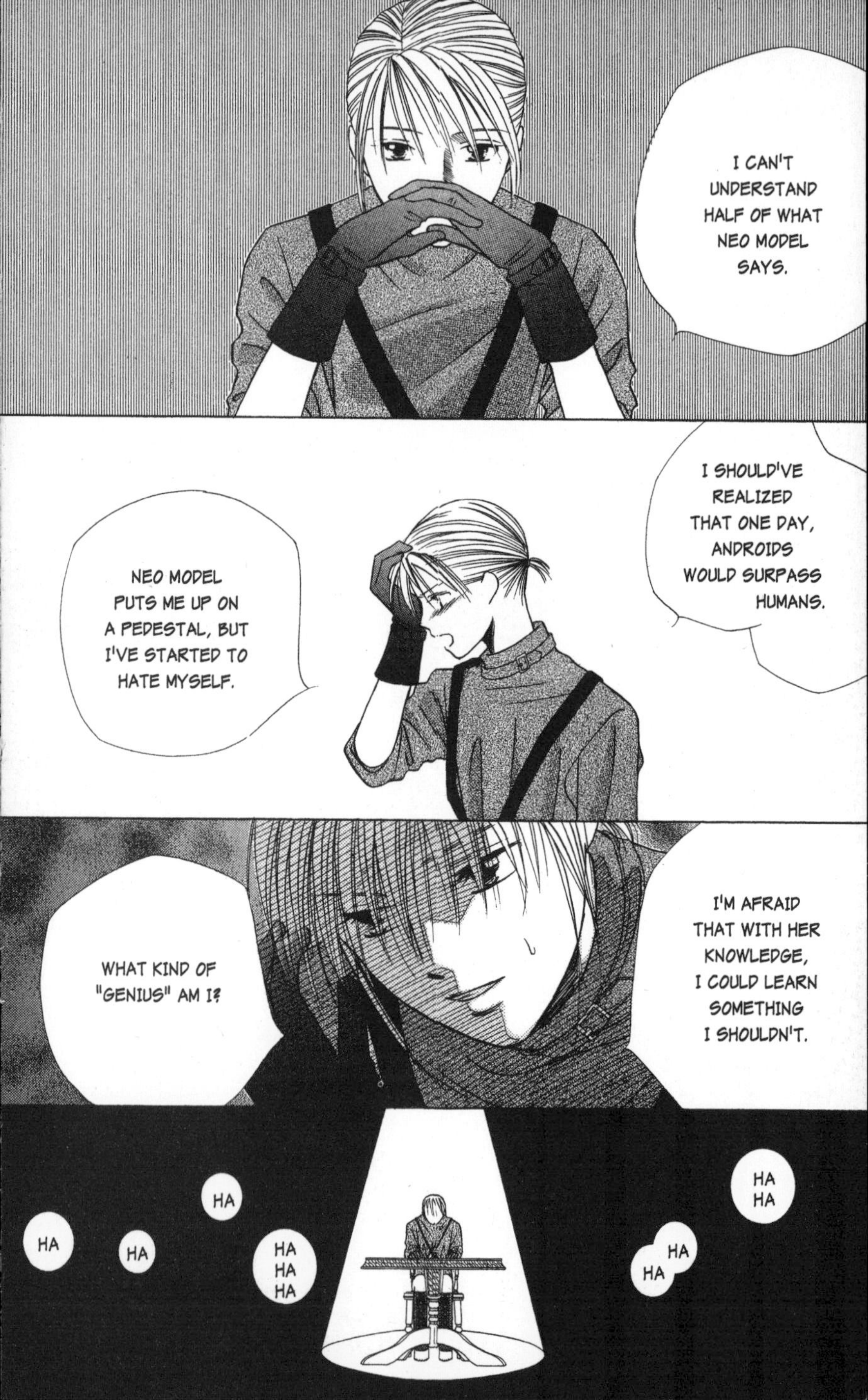
I CAN'T UNDERSTAND HALF OF WHAT NEO MODEL SAYS.
I SHOULD'VE REALIZED THAT ONE DAY, ANDROIDS WOULD SURPASS HUMANS.
NEO MODEL PUTS ME UP ON A PEDESTAL, BUT I'VE STARTED TO HATE MYSELF.
I'M AFRAID THAT WITH HER KNOWLEDGE, I COULD LEARN SOMETHING I SHOULDN'T.
WHAT KIND OF "GENIUS" AM I?
HA HA
HA HA
HA
HA HA HA
HA
HA
HA

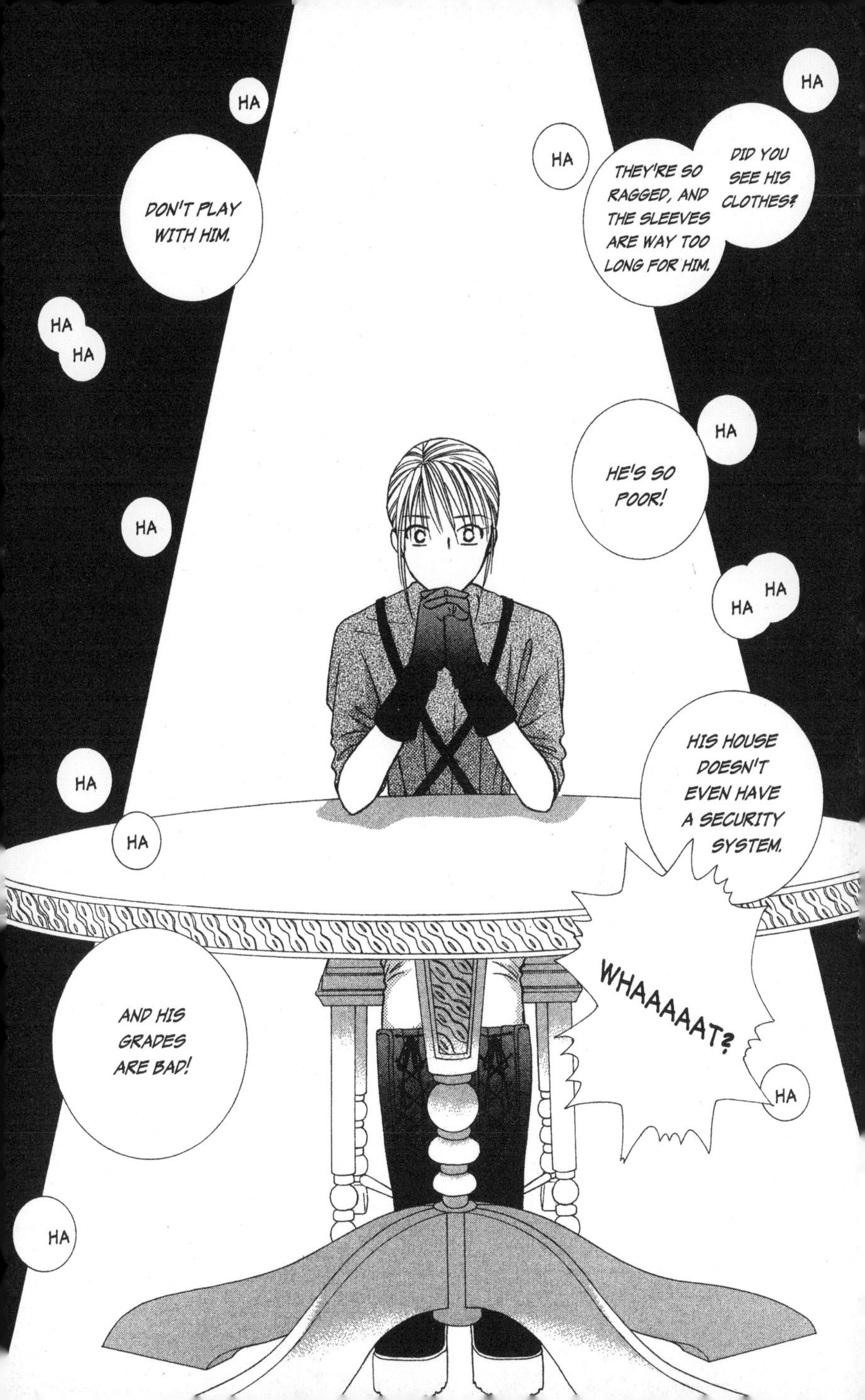
HA
DID YOU SEE HIS CLOTHES?
THEY'RE SO RAGGED, AND THE SLEEVES ARE WAY TOO LONG FOR HIM.
HA
HA
DON'T PLAY WITH HIM.
HA
HA
HA
HE'S SO POOR!
HA
HA
HA
HA
HIS HOUSE DOESN'T EVEN HAVE A SECURITY SYSTEM.
HA
WHAAAAAT?
HA
AND HIS GRADES ARE BAD!
HA

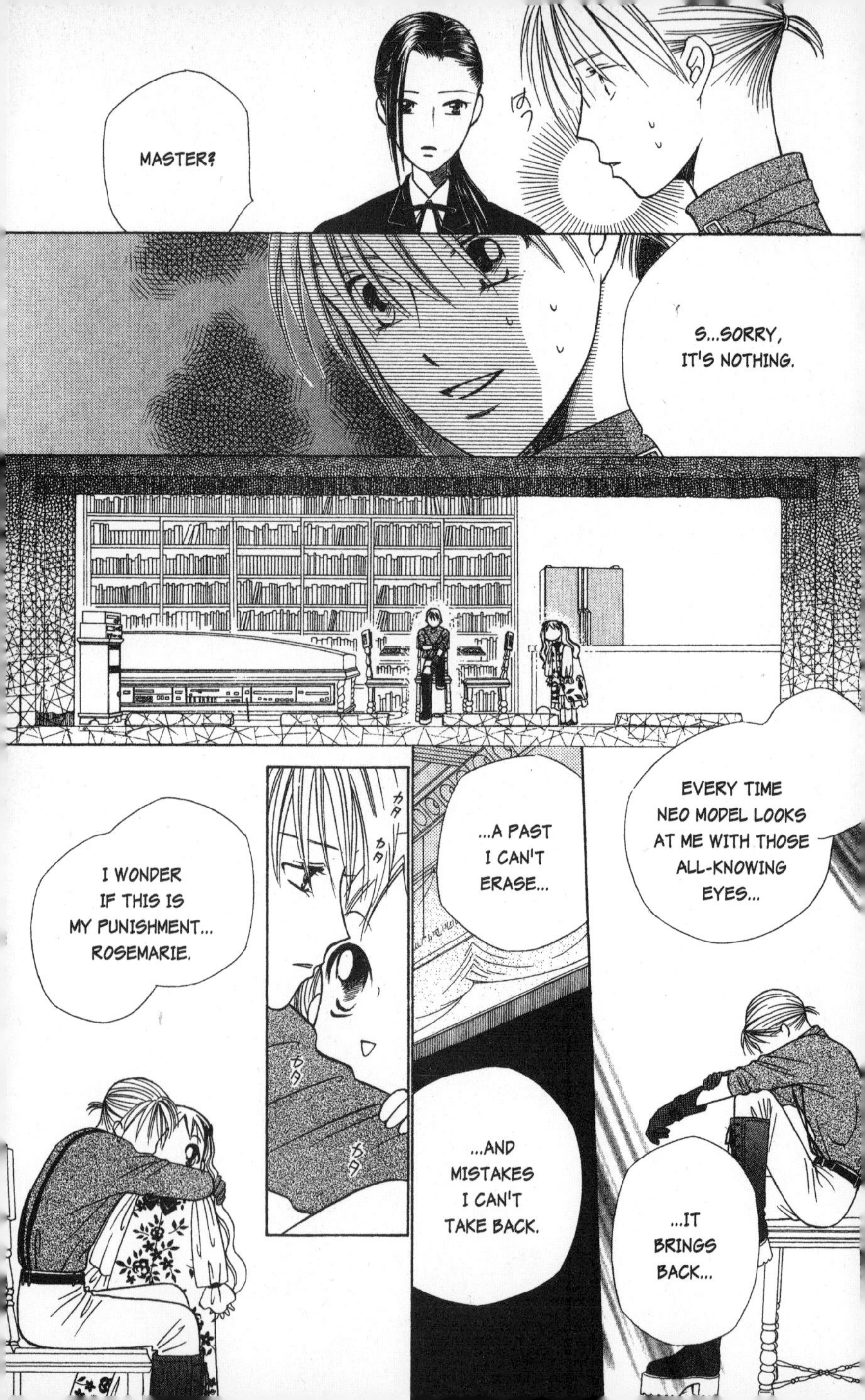
MASTER?
はっ
S...SORRY, IT'S NOTHING.
EVERY TIME NEO MODEL LOOKS AT ME WITH THOSE ALL-KNOWING EYES...
...IT BRINGS BACK...
...A PAST I CAN'T ERASE...
...AND MISTAKES I CAN'T TAKE BACK.
I WONDER IF THIS IS MY PUNISHMENT... ROSEMARIE.

4

Children of Heaven

I saw a movie from Iran called Children of Heaven.

It was suuuuch a GREAT movie! And the ending was just the kind I like: happy.

It was only shown on one screen...

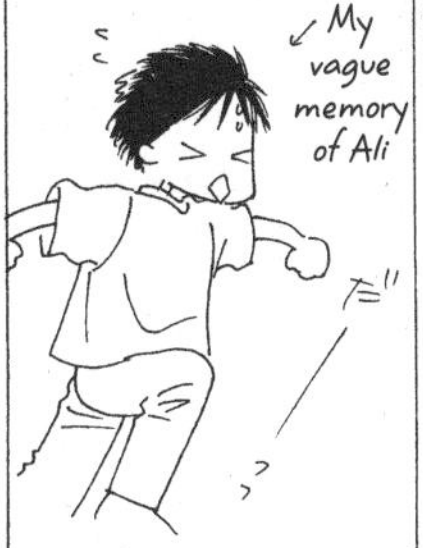
My vague memory of Ali

...but I HIGHLY recommend you watch it when it comes out on video.

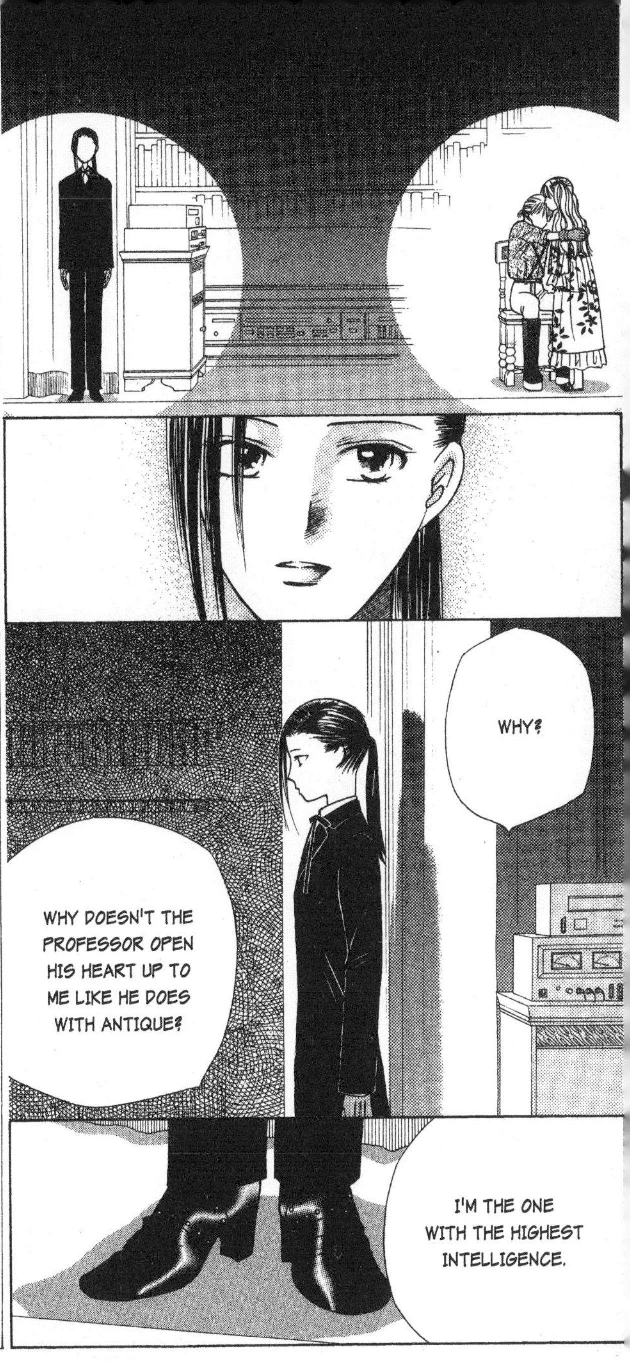
WHY?
WHY DOESN'T THE PROFESSOR OPEN HIS HEART UP TO ME LIKE HE DOES WITH ANTIQUE?
I'M THE ONE WITH THE HIGHEST INTELLIGENCE.

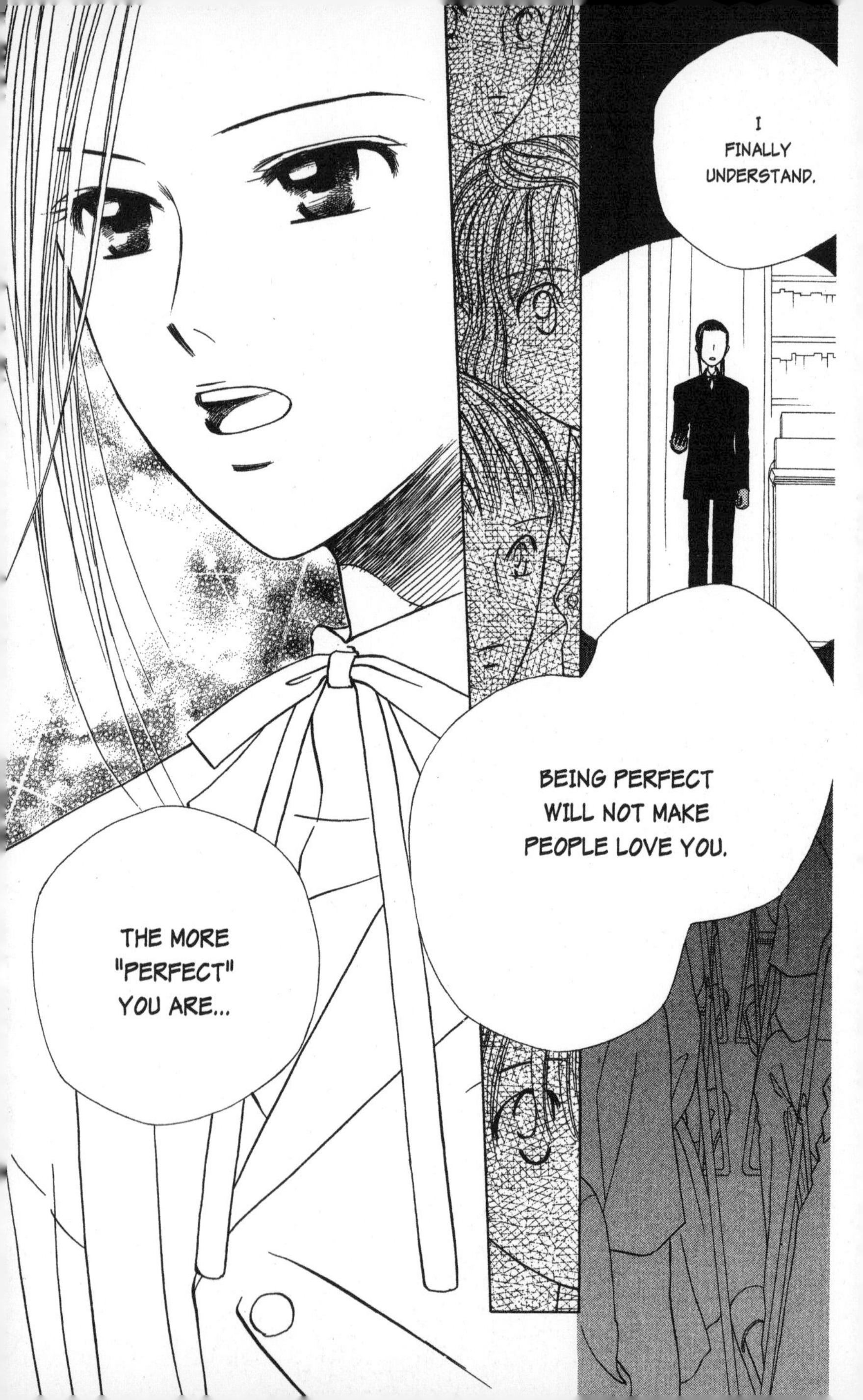
I FINALLY UNDERSTAND.
BEING PERFECT WILL NOT MAKE PEOPLE LOVE YOU.
THE MORE "PERFECT" YOU ARE...

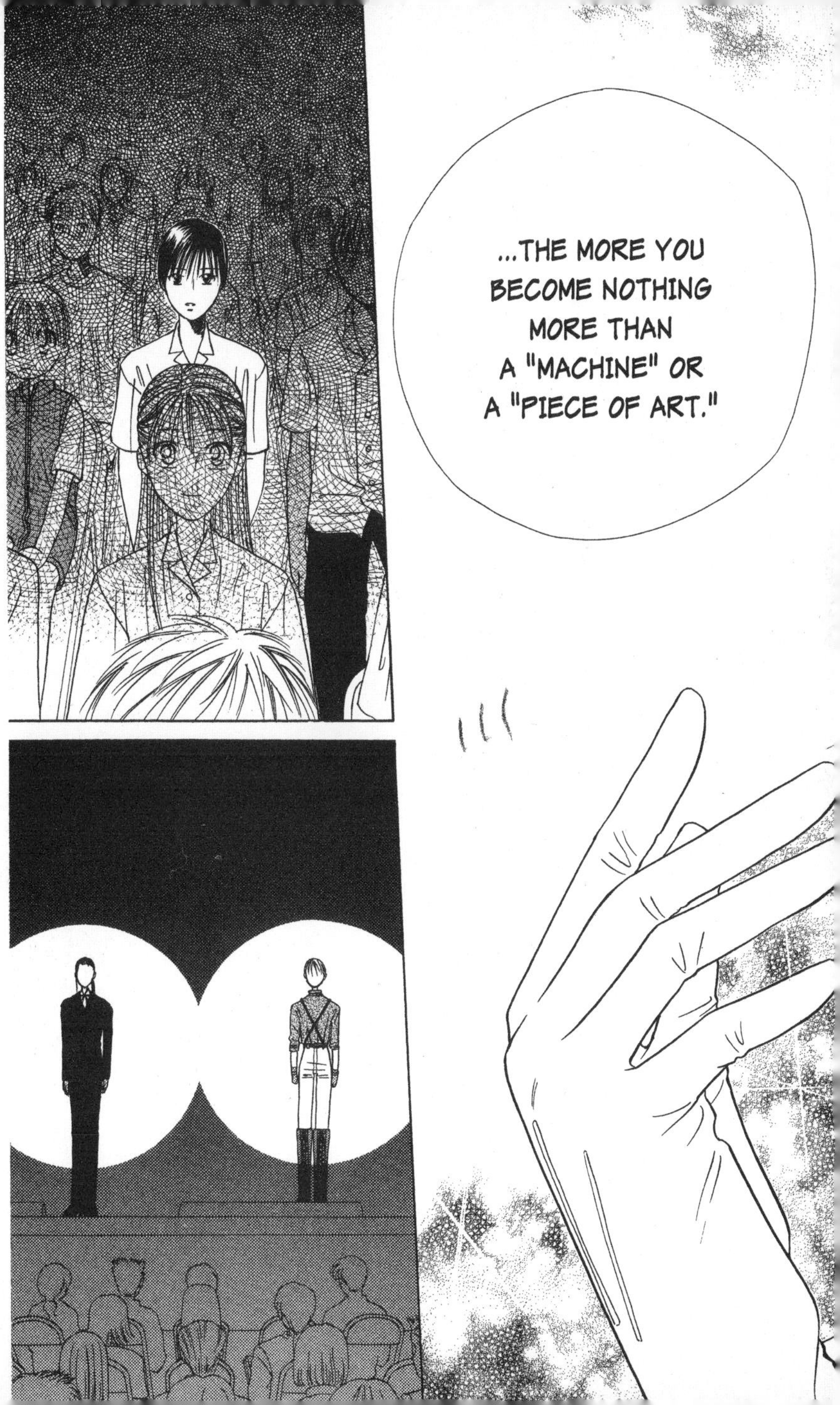
...THE MORE YOU BECOME NOTHING MORE THAN A "MACHINE" OR A "PIECE OF ART."

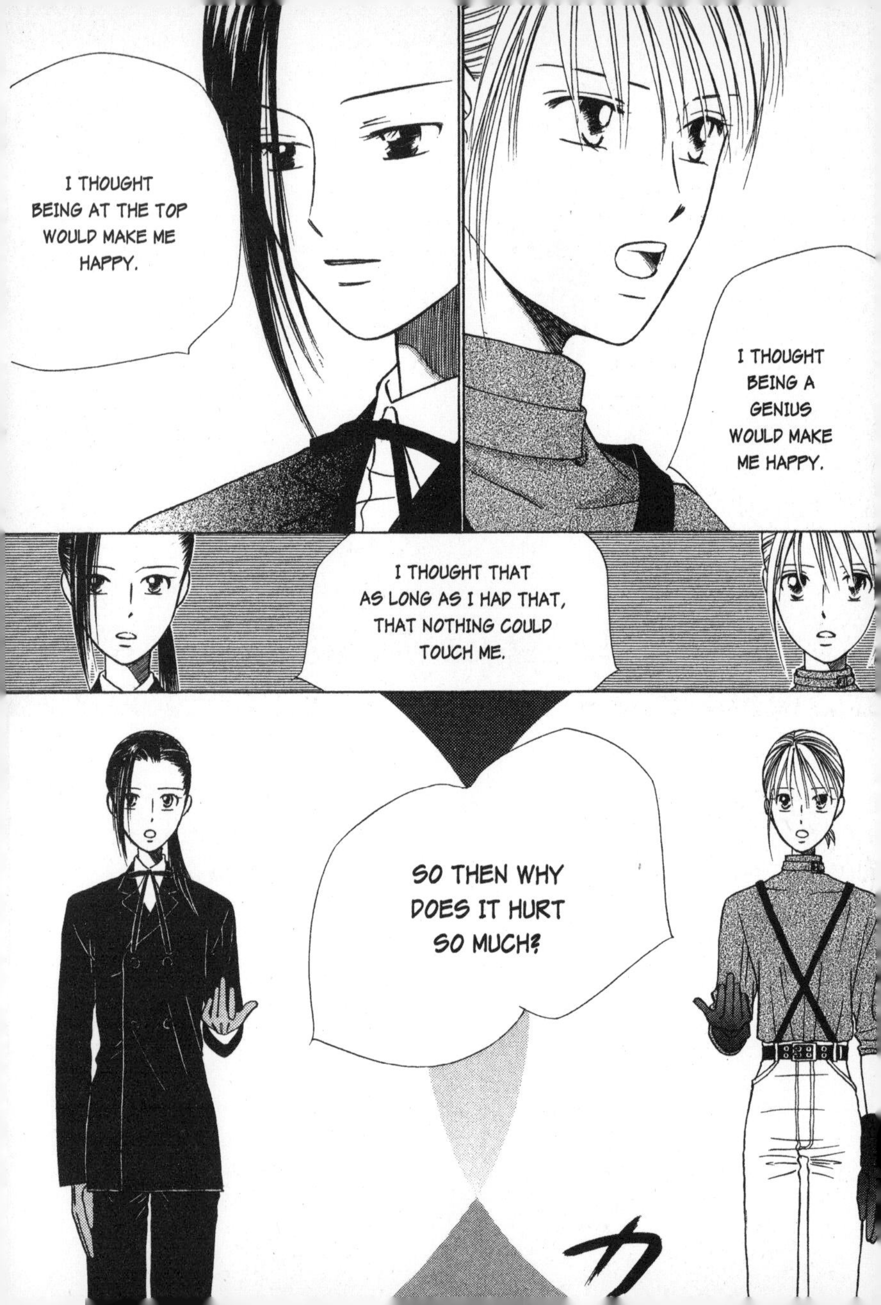
I THOUGHT BEING A GENIUS WOULD MAKE ME HAPPY.
I THOUGHT BEING AT THE TOP WOULD MAKE ME HAPPY.
I THOUGHT THAT AS LONG AS I HAD THAT, THAT NOTHING COULD TOUCH ME.
SO THEN WHY DOES IT HURT SO MUCH?
カ

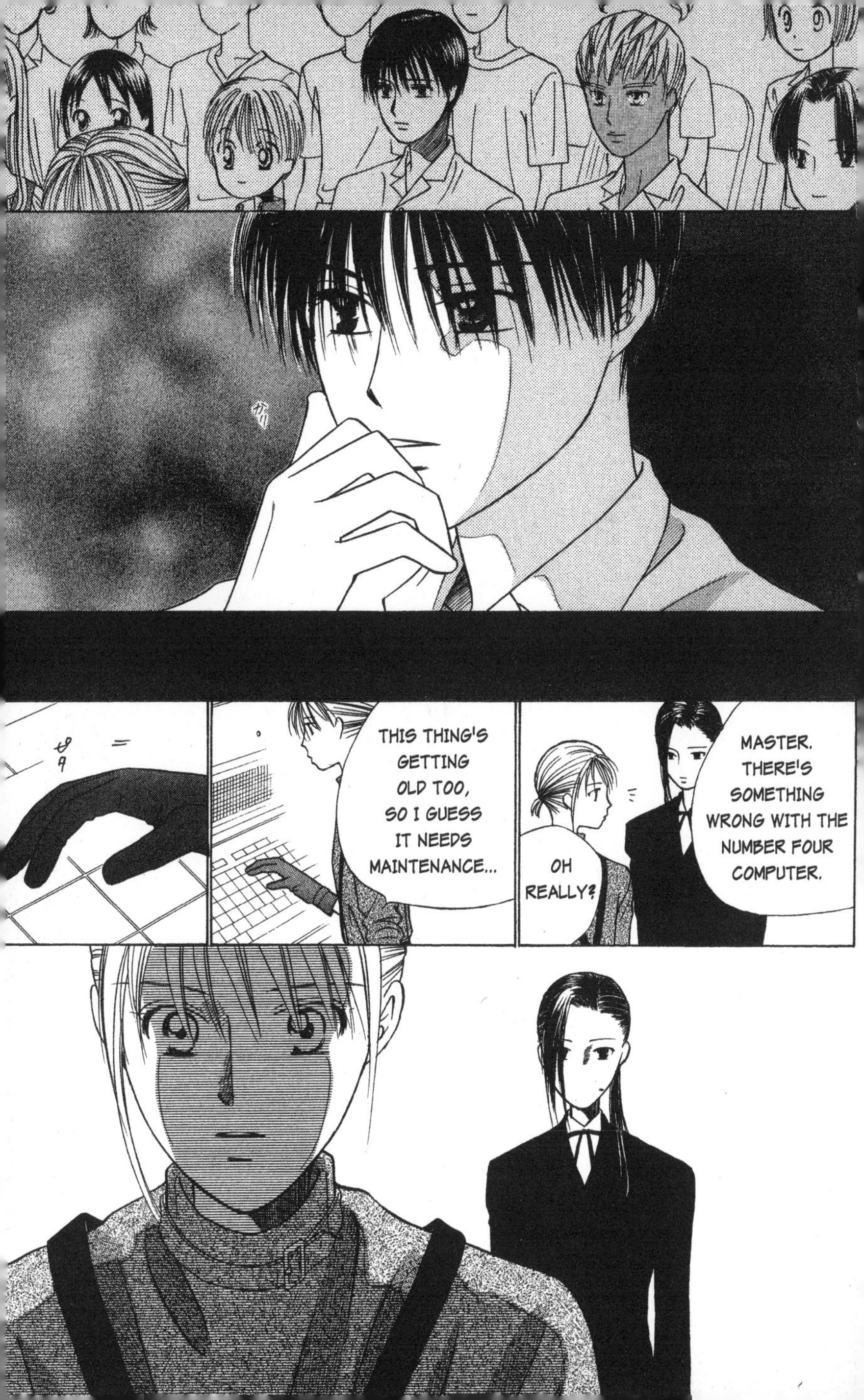
MASTER. THERE'S SOMETHING WRONG WITH THE NUMBER FOUR COMPUTER.
OH REALLY?
THIS THING'S GETTING OLD TOO, SO I GUESS IT NEEDS MAINTENANCE...

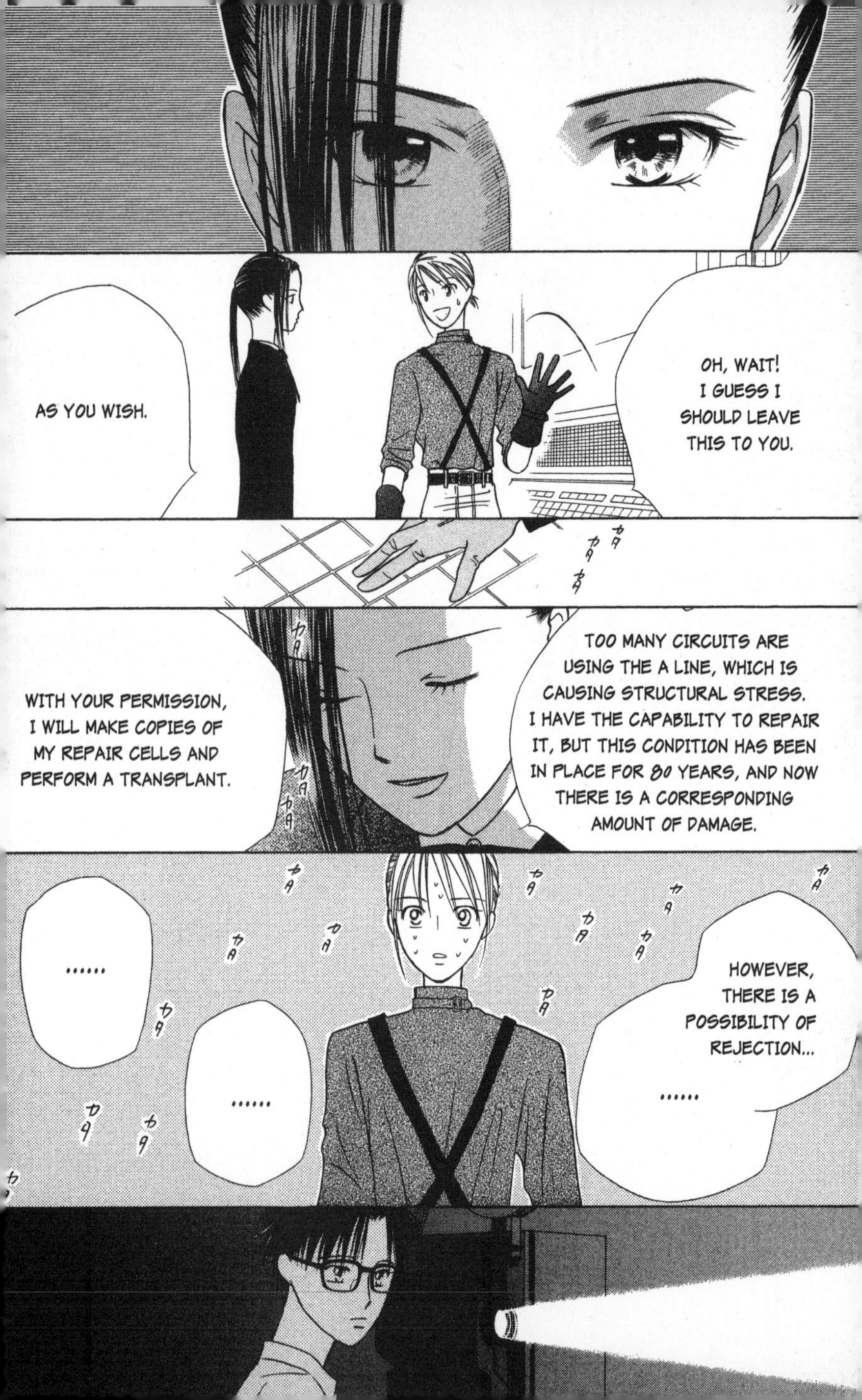
OH, WAIT! I GUESS I SHOULD LEAVE THIS TO YOU.
AS YOU WISH.
TOO MANY CIRCUITS ARE USING THE A LINE, WHICH IS CAUSING STRUCTURAL STRESS. I HAVE THE CAPABILITY TO REPAIR IT, BUT THIS CONDITION HAS BEEN IN PLACE FOR 80 YEARS, AND NOW THERE IS A CORRESPONDING AMOUNT OF DAMAGE.
WITH YOUR PERMISSION, I WILL MAKE COPIES OF MY REPAIR CELLS AND PERFORM A TRANSPLANT.
HOWEVER, THERE IS A POSSIBILITY OF REJECTION...
......
......
......

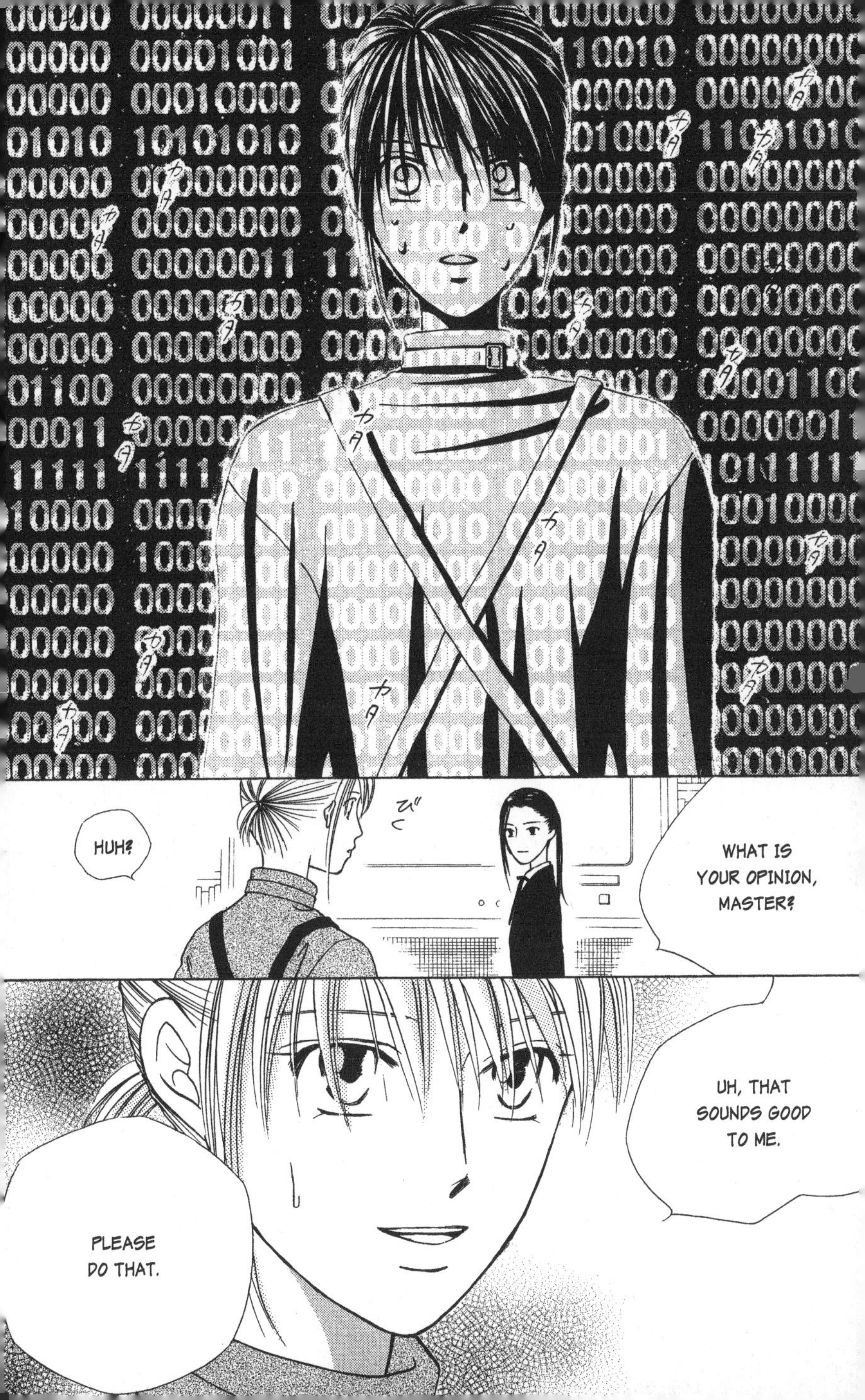
WHAT IS YOUR OPINION, MASTER?
HUH?
UH, THAT SOUNDS GOOD TO ME.
PLEASE DO THAT.

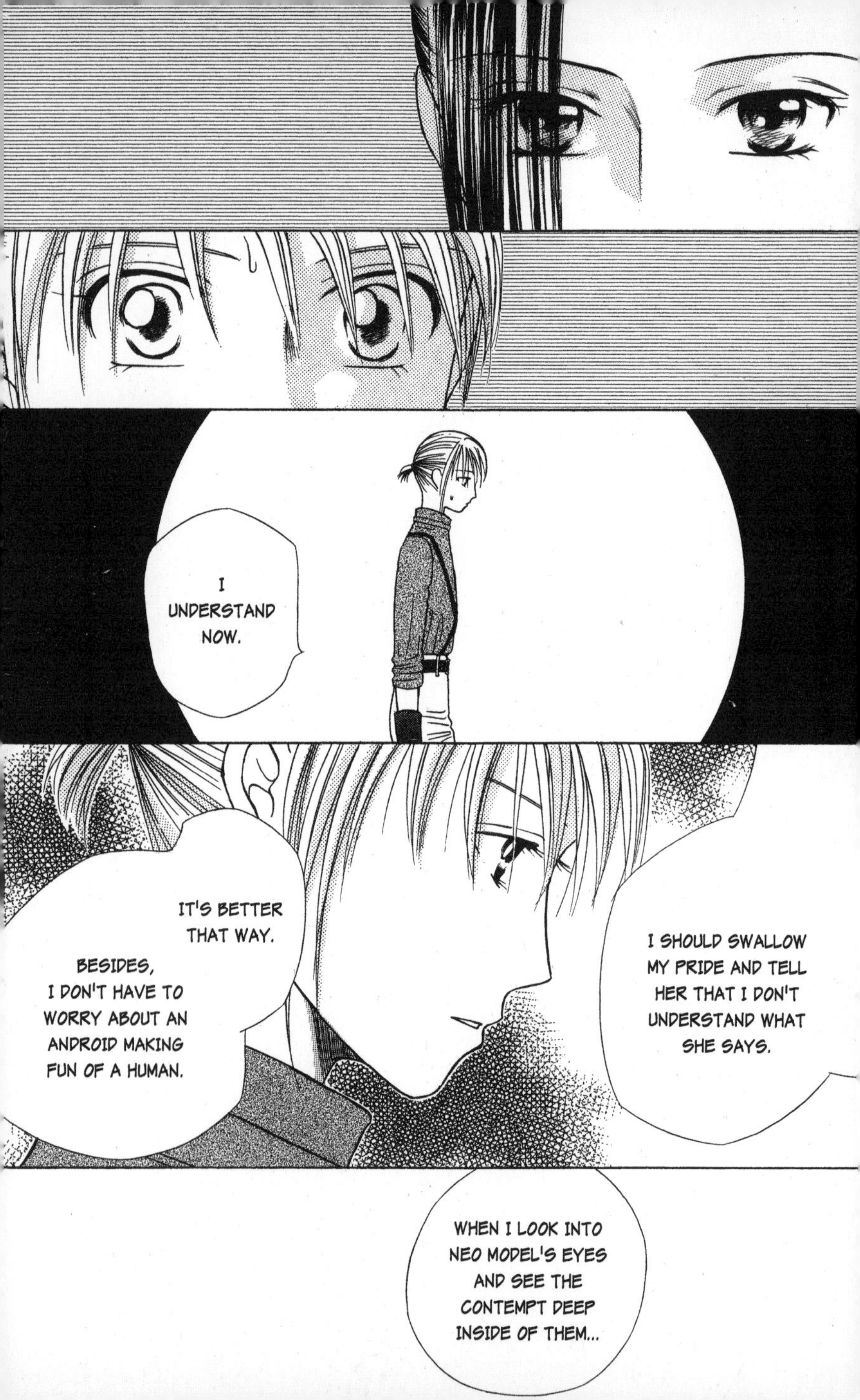
I UNDERSTAND NOW.
I SHOULD SWALLOW MY PRIDE AND TELL HER THAT I DON'T UNDERSTAND WHAT SHE SAYS.
IT'S BETTER THAT WAY.
BESIDES, I DON'T HAVE TO WORRY ABOUT AN ANDROID MAKING FUN OF A HUMAN.
WHEN I LOOK INTO NEO MODEL'S EYES AND SEE THE CONTEMPT DEEP INSIDE OF THEM...

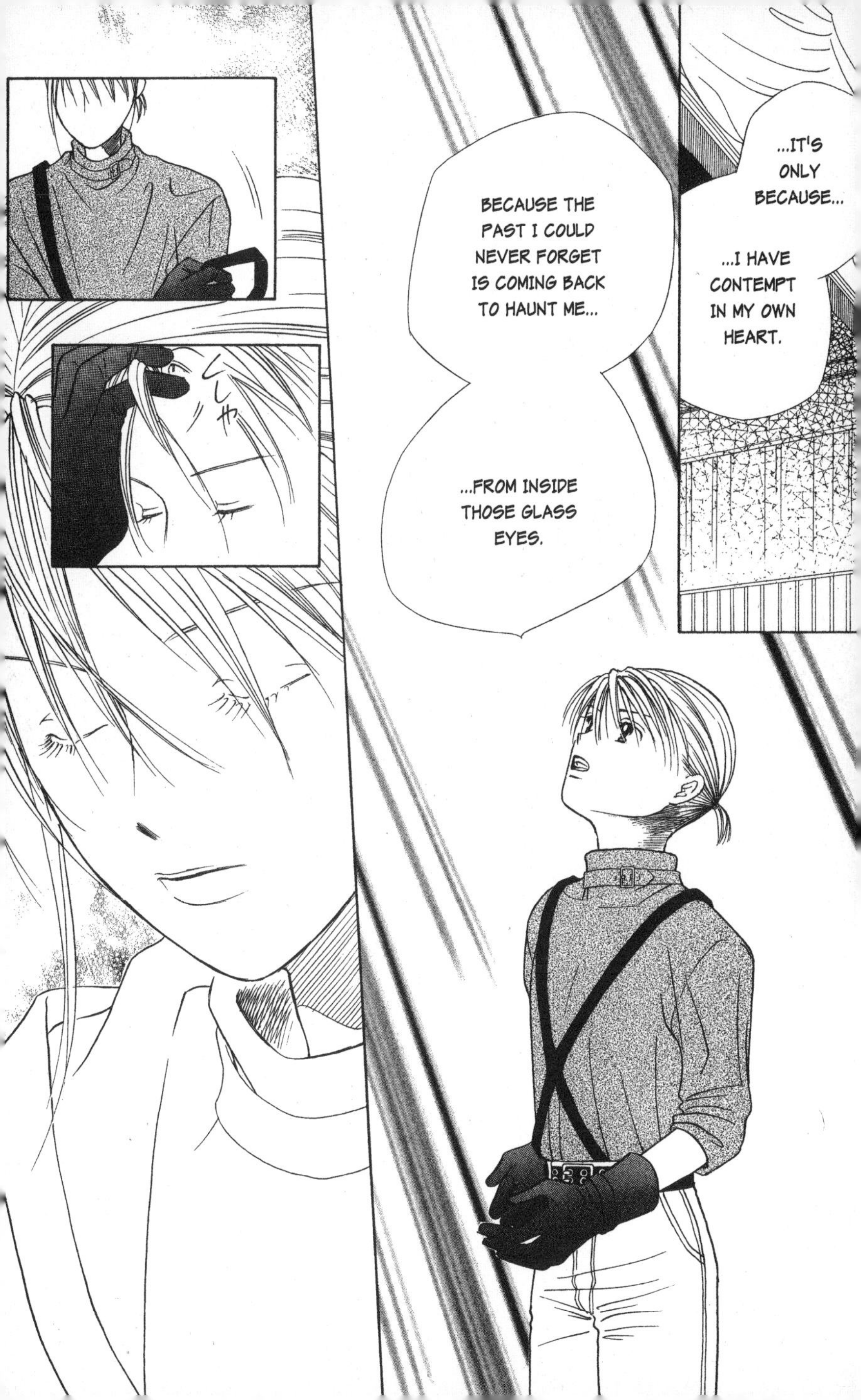
...IT'S ONLY BECAUSE...
...I HAVE CONTEMPT IN MY OWN HEART.
BECAUSE THE PAST I COULD NEVER FORGET IS COMING BACK TO HAUNT ME...
...FROM INSIDE THOSE GLASS EYES.

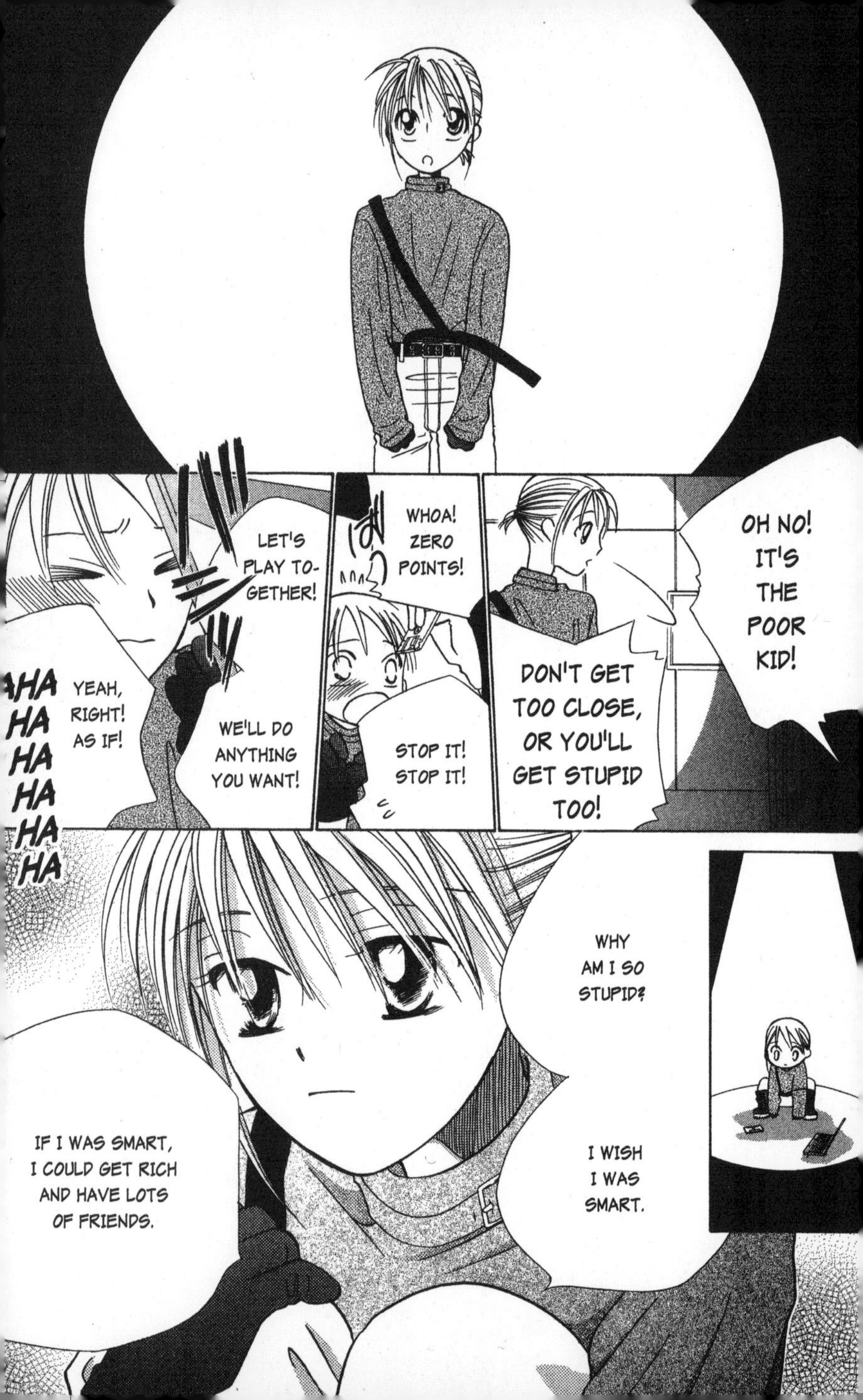
OH NO! IT'S THE POOR KID!
DON'T GET TOO CLOSE, OR YOU'LL GET STUPID TOO!
WHOA! ZERO POINTS!
STOP IT! STOP IT!
LET'S PLAY TO-GETHER!
WE'LL DO ANYTHING YOU WANT!
YEAH, RIGHT! AS IF!
HA HA HA HA HA HA
WHY AM I SO STUPID?
I WISH I WAS SMART.
IF I WAS SMART, I COULD GET RICH AND HAVE LOTS OF FRIENDS.

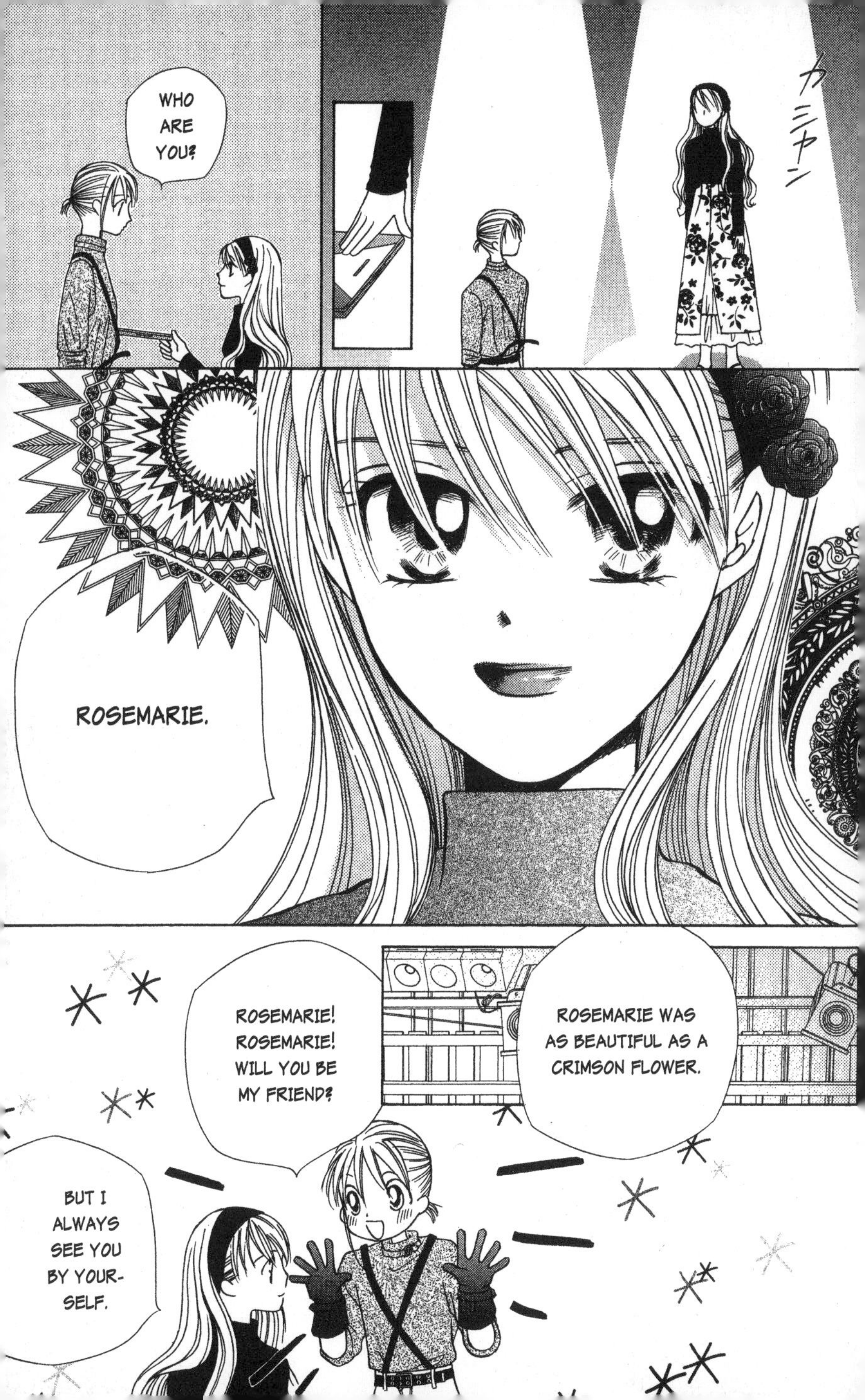

カシャン
WHO ARE YOU?
ROSEMARIE.
ROSEMARIE WAS AS BEAUTIFUL AS A CRIMSON FLOWER.
ROSEMARIE! ROSEMARIE! WILL YOU BE MY FRIEND?
BUT I ALWAYS SEE YOU BY YOUR-SELF.

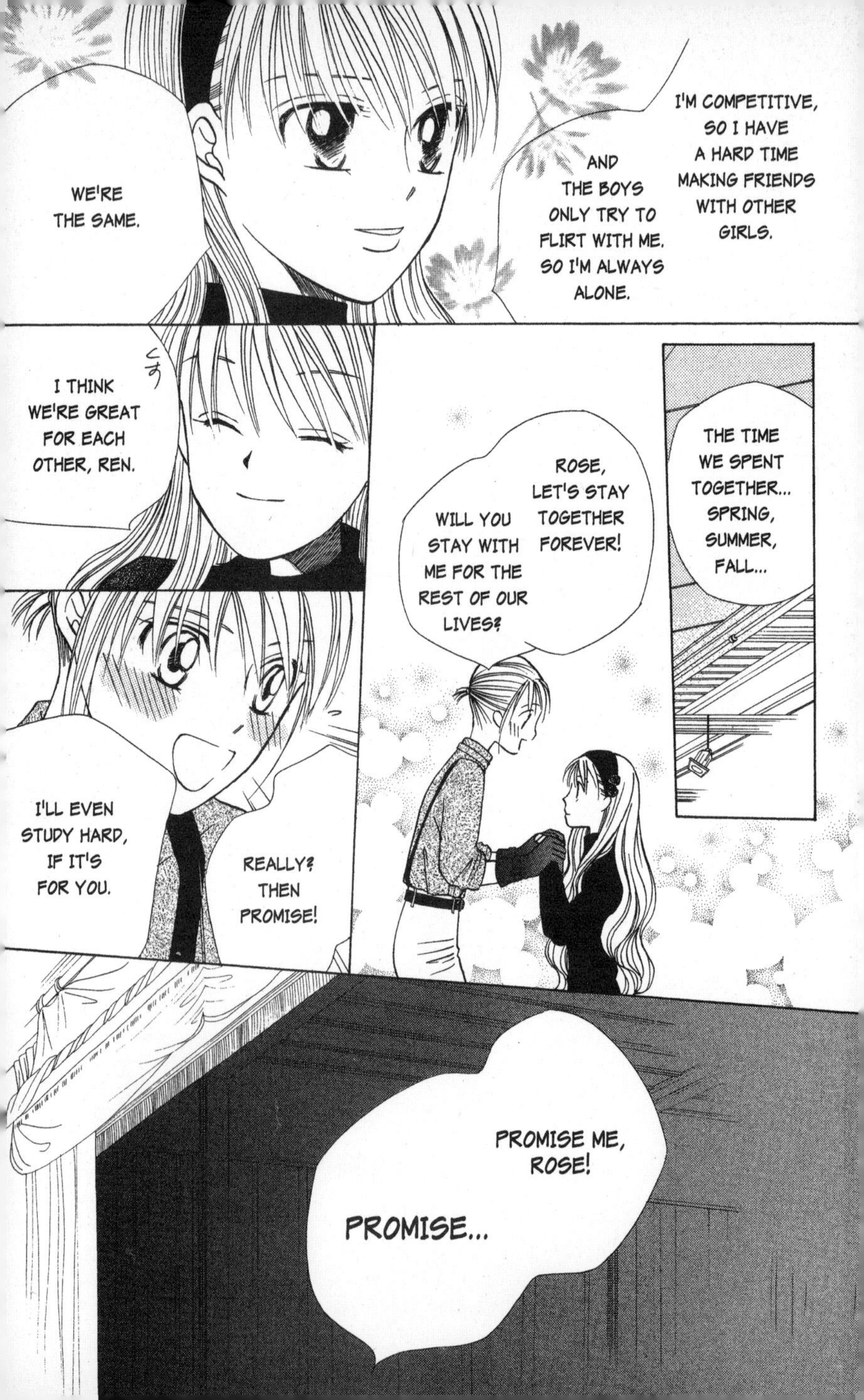
I'M COMPETITIVE, SO I HAVE A HARD TIME MAKING FRIENDS WITH OTHER GIRLS.
AND THE BOYS ONLY TRY TO FLIRT WITH ME. SO I'M ALWAYS ALONE.
WE'RE THE SAME.
THE TIME WE SPENT TOGETHER... SPRING, SUMMER, FALL...
ROSE, LET'S STAY TOGETHER FOREVER!
WILL YOU STAY WITH ME FOR THE REST OF OUR LIVES?
I THINK WE'RE GREAT FOR EACH OTHER, REN.
REALLY? THEN PROMISE!
I'LL EVEN STUDY HARD, IF IT'S FOR YOU.
PROMISE ME, ROSE!
PROMISE...

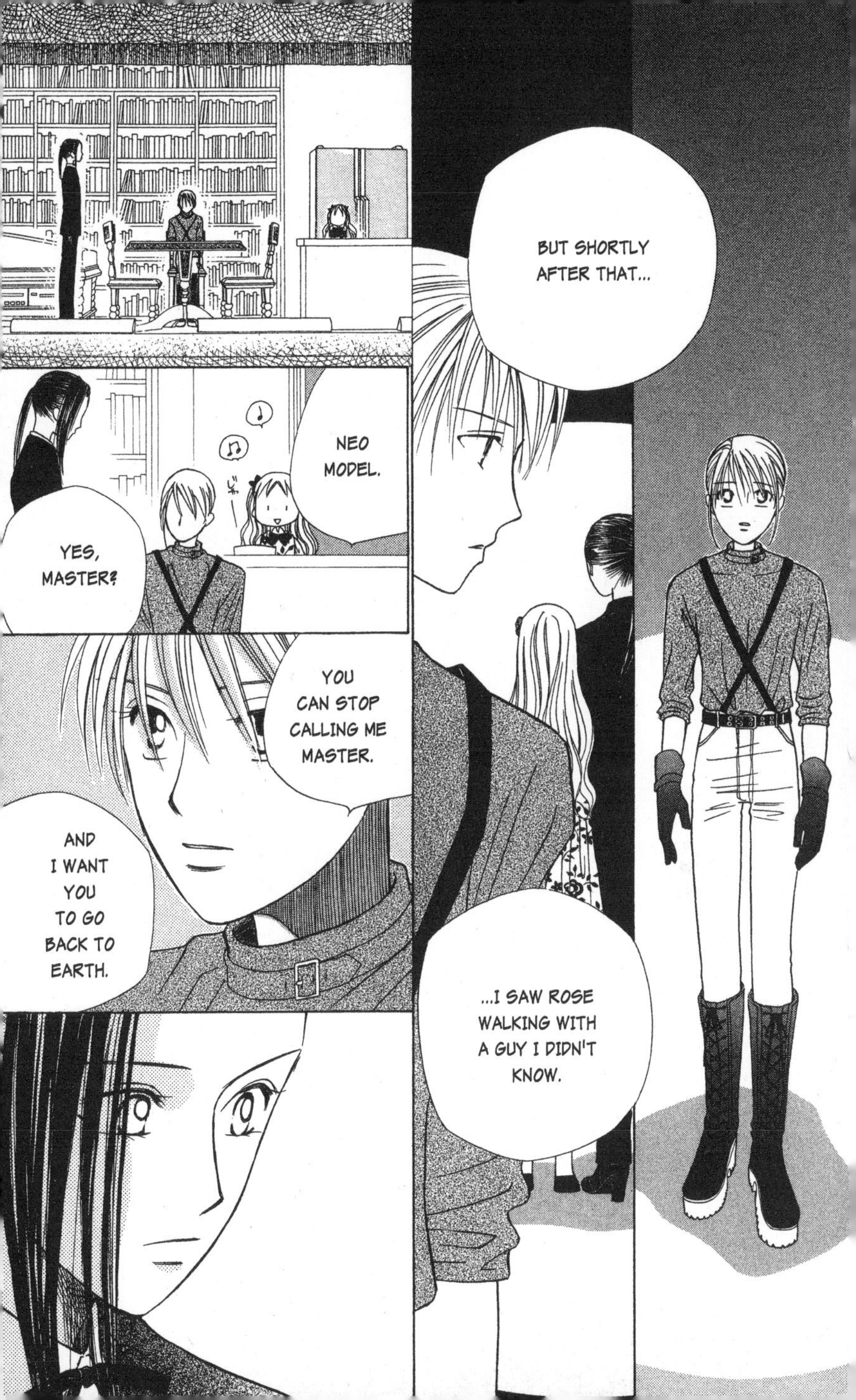
NEO MODEL.
YES, MASTER?
YOU CAN STOP CALLING ME MASTER.
AND I WANT YOU TO GO BACK TO EARTH.
BUT SHORTLY AFTER THAT...
...I SAW ROSE WALKING WITH A GUY I DIDN'T KNOW.

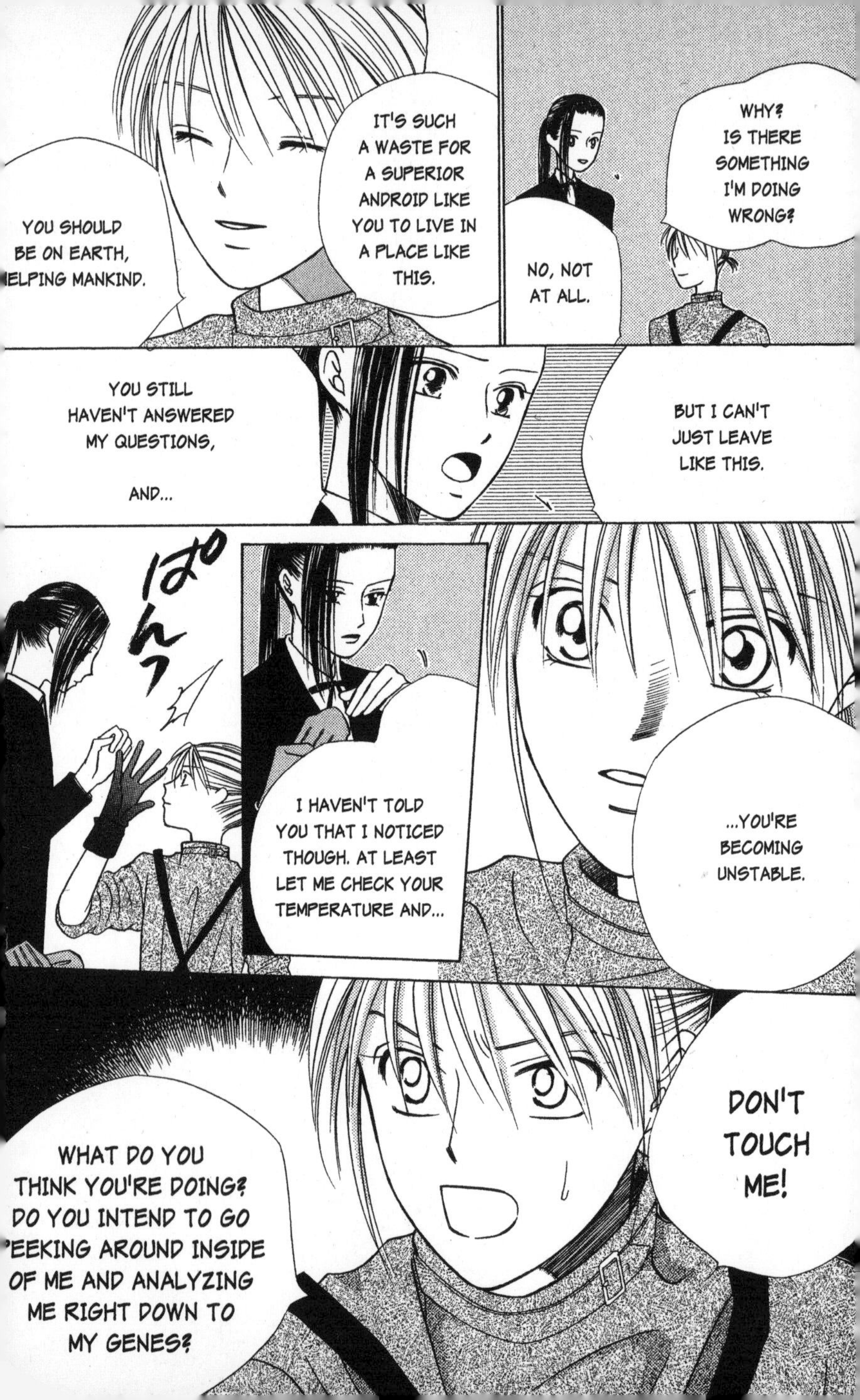
WHY? IS THERE SOMETHING I'M DOING WRONG?
NO, NOT AT ALL.
IT'S SUCH A WASTE FOR A SUPERIOR ANDROID LIKE YOU TO LIVE IN A PLACE LIKE THIS.
YOU SHOULD BE ON EARTH, ELPING MANKIND.
BUT I CAN'T JUST LEAVE LIKE THIS.
YOU STILL HAVEN'T ANSWERED MY QUESTIONS,
AND...
...YOU'RE BECOMING UNSTABLE.
I HAVEN'T TOLD YOU THAT I NOTICED THOUGH. AT LEAST LET ME CHECK YOUR TEMPERATURE AND...
ぱんっ
DON'T TOUCH ME!
WHAT DO YOU THINK YOU'RE DOING? DO YOU INTEND TO GO EEKING AROUND INSIDE OF ME AND ANALYZING ME RIGHT DOWN TO MY GENES?

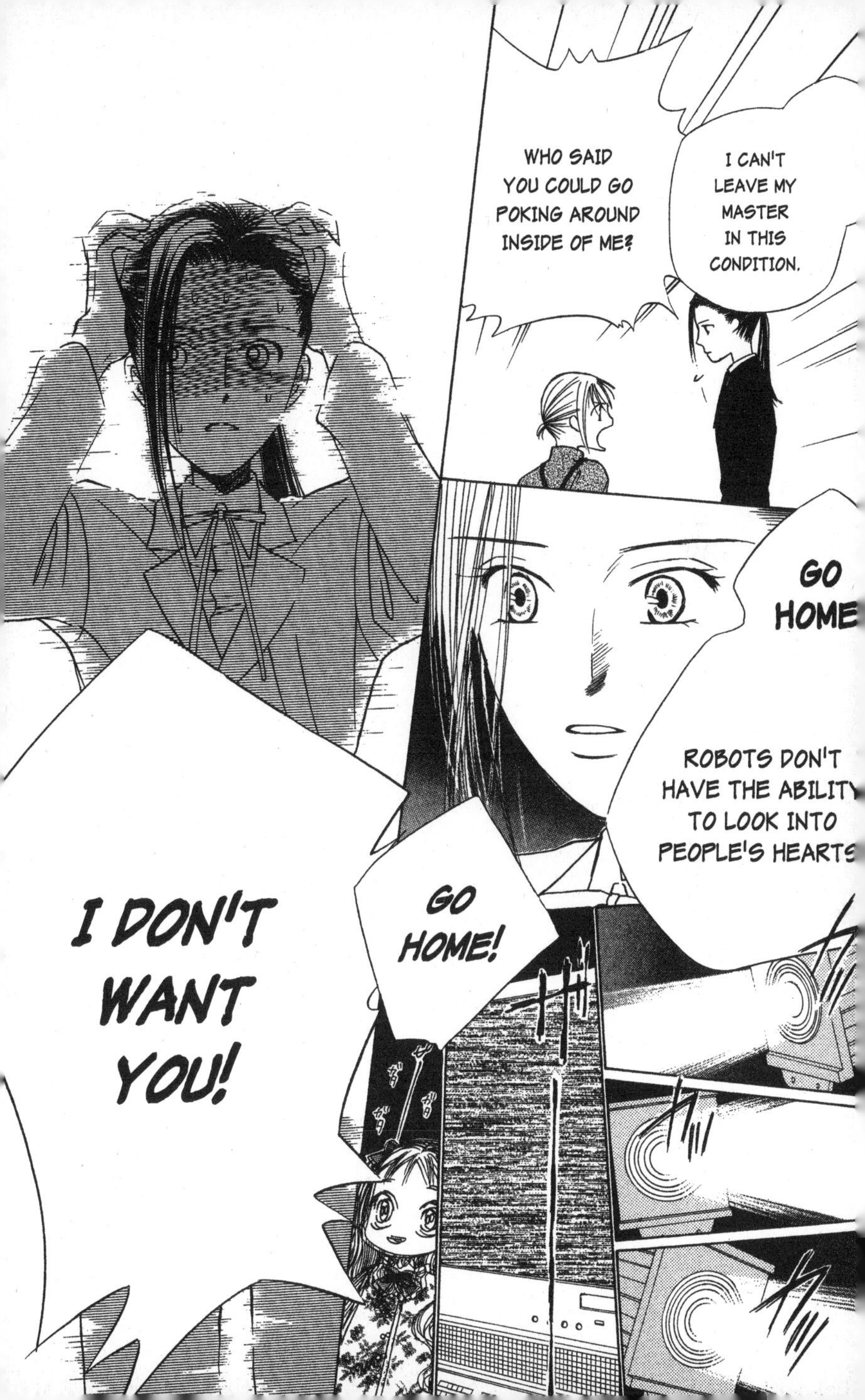
I CAN'T LEAVE MY MASTER IN THIS CONDITION.
WHO SAID YOU COULD GO POKING AROUND INSIDE OF ME?
GO HOME
ROBOTS DON'T HAVE THE ABILITY TO LOOK INTO PEOPLE'S HEARTS
GO HOME!
I DON'T WANT YOU!

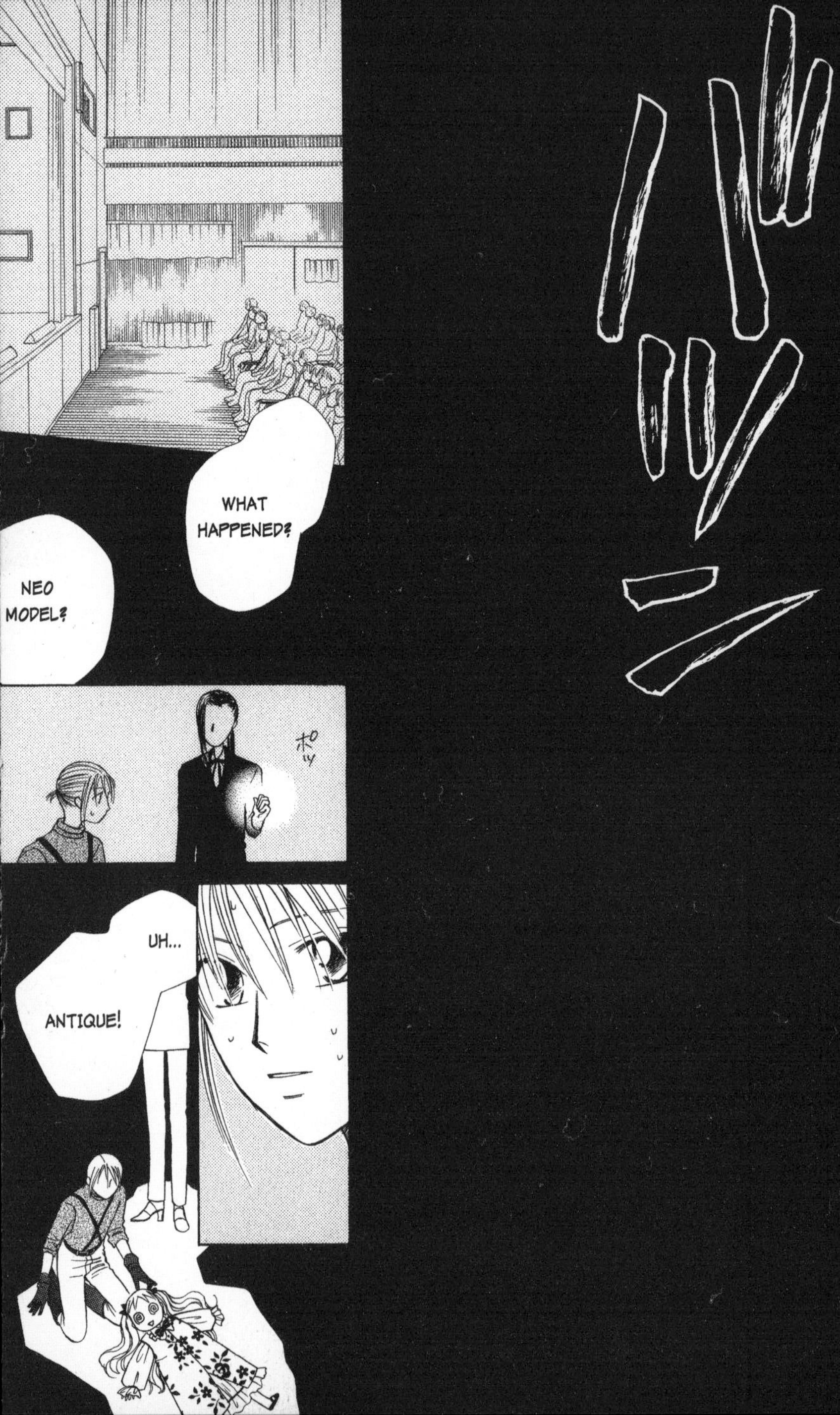
バツン
WHAT HAPPENED?
NEO MODEL?
ポッ
UH...
ANTIQUE!

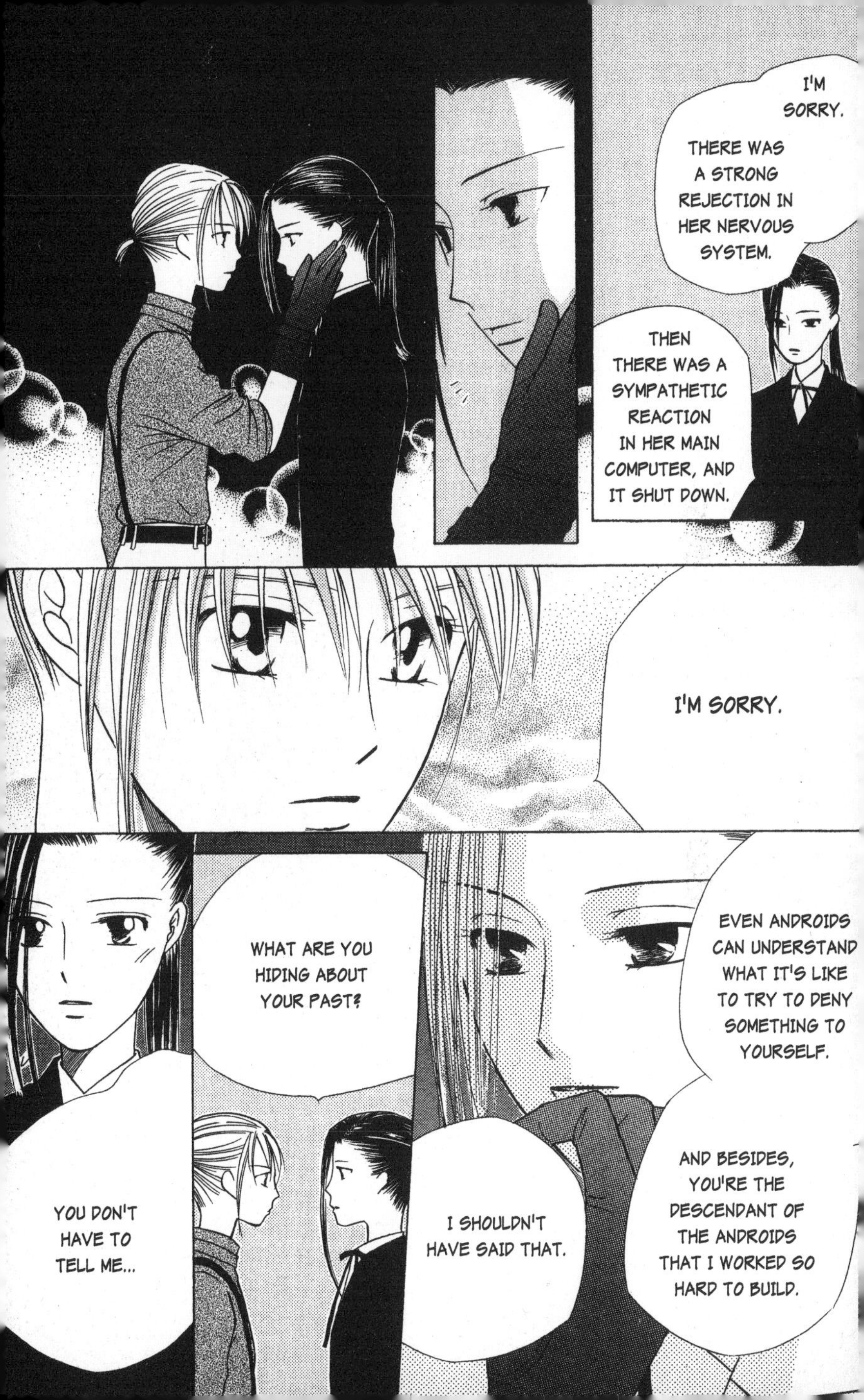
I'M SORRY.
THERE WAS A STRONG REJECTION IN HER NERVOUS SYSTEM.
THEN THERE WAS A SYMPATHETIC REACTION IN HER MAIN COMPUTER, AND IT SHUT DOWN.
I'M SORRY.
EVEN ANDROIDS CAN UNDERSTAND WHAT IT'S LIKE TO TRY TO DENY SOMETHING TO YOURSELF.
AND BESIDES, YOU'RE THE DESCENDANT OF THE ANDROIDS THAT I WORKED SO HARD TO BUILD.
I SHOULDN'T HAVE SAID THAT.
WHAT ARE YOU HIDING ABOUT YOUR PAST?
YOU DON'T HAVE TO TELL ME...

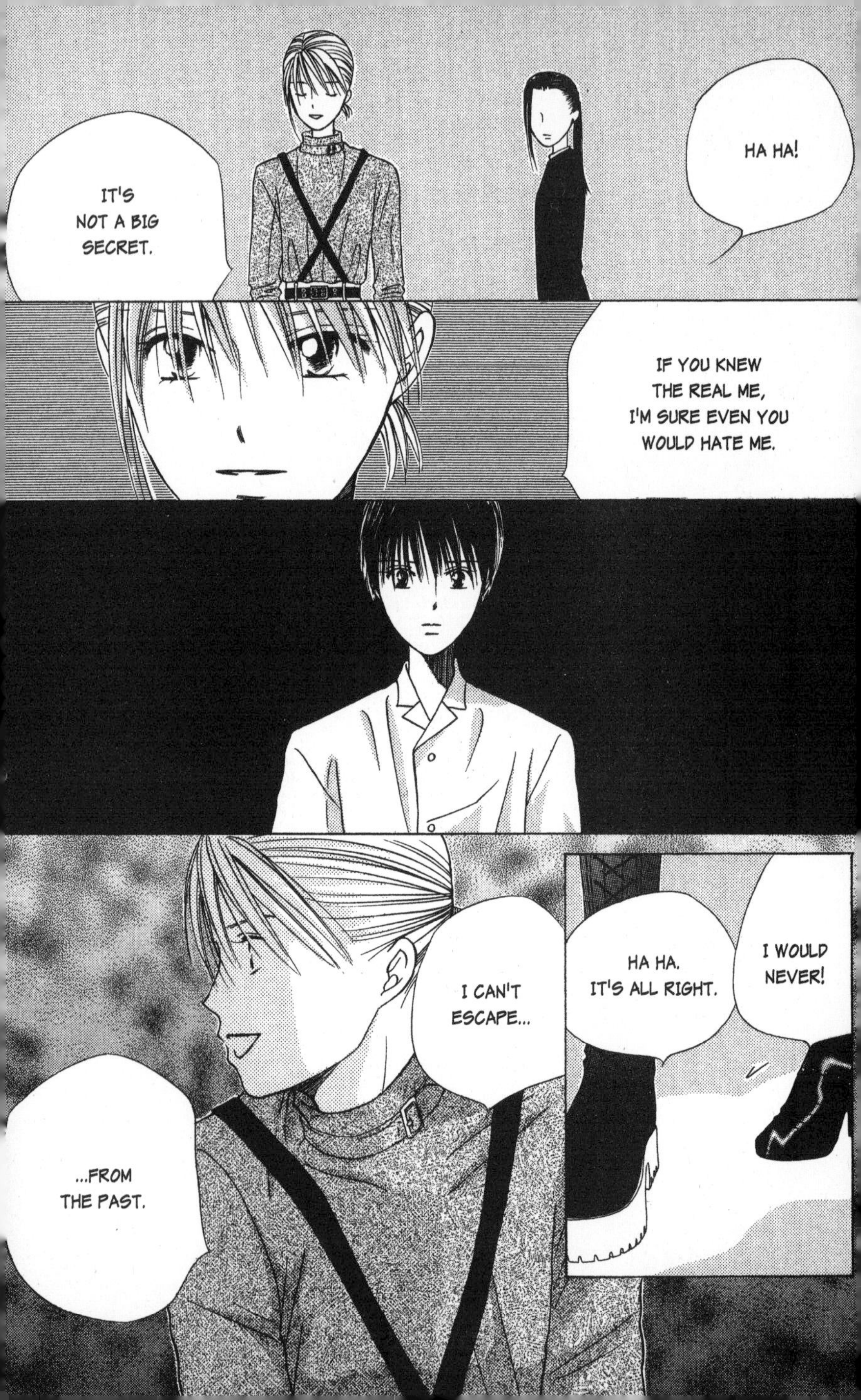
HA HA!
IT'S NOT A BIG SECRET.
IF YOU KNEW THE REAL ME, I'M SURE EVEN YOU WOULD HATE ME.
I WOULD NEVER!
HA HA. IT'S ALL RIGHT.
I CAN'T ESCAPE...
...FROM THE PAST.

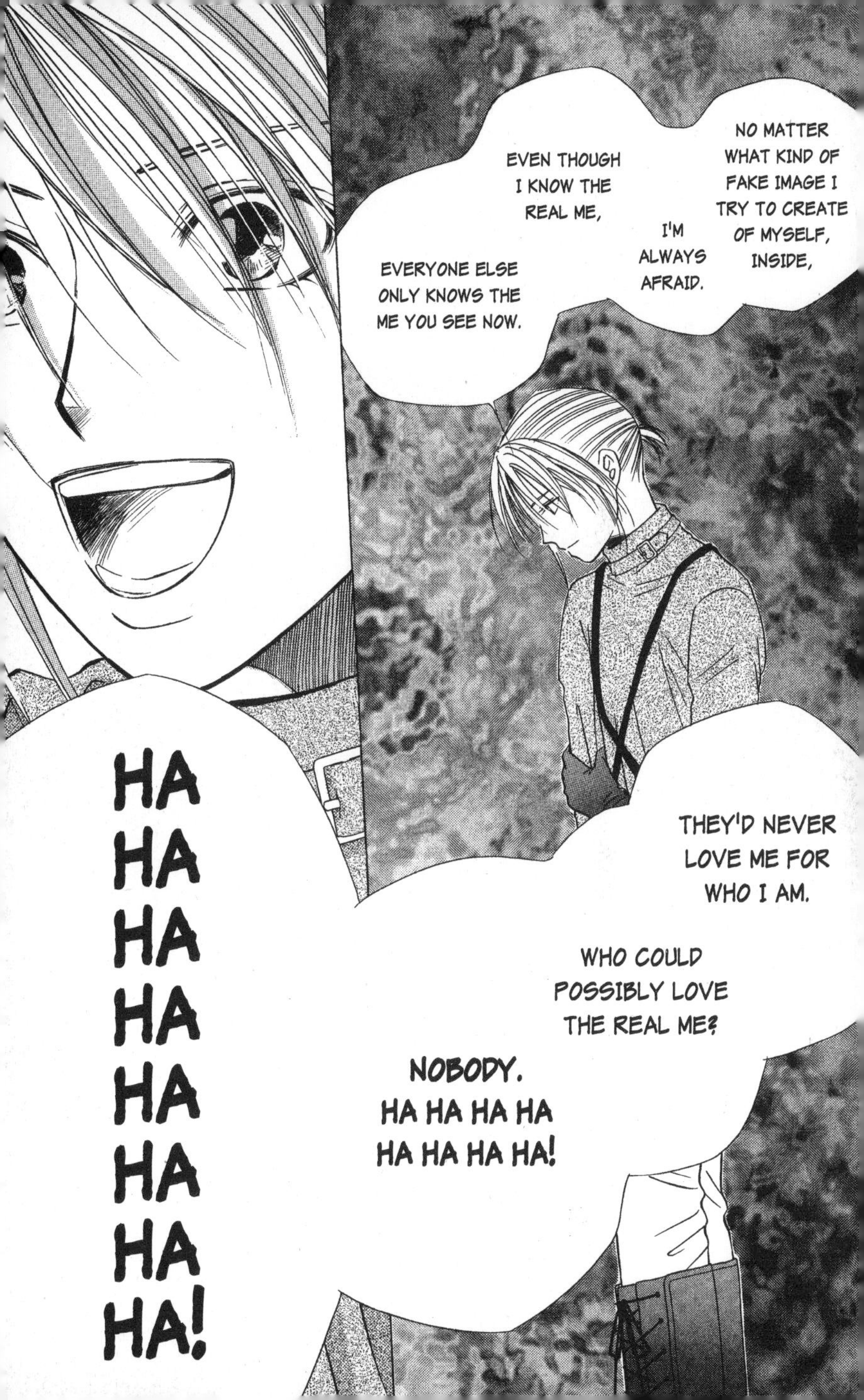
NO MATTER WHAT KIND OF FAKE IMAGE I TRY TO CREATE OF MYSELF, INSIDE,
I'M ALWAYS AFRAID.
EVEN THOUGH I KNOW THE REAL ME,
EVERYONE ELSE ONLY KNOWS THE ME YOU SEE NOW.
THEY'D NEVER LOVE ME FOR WHO I AM.
WHO COULD POSSIBLY LOVE THE REAL ME?
NOBODY. HA HA HA HA HA HA HA HA!
HA HA HA HA HA HA HA HA!

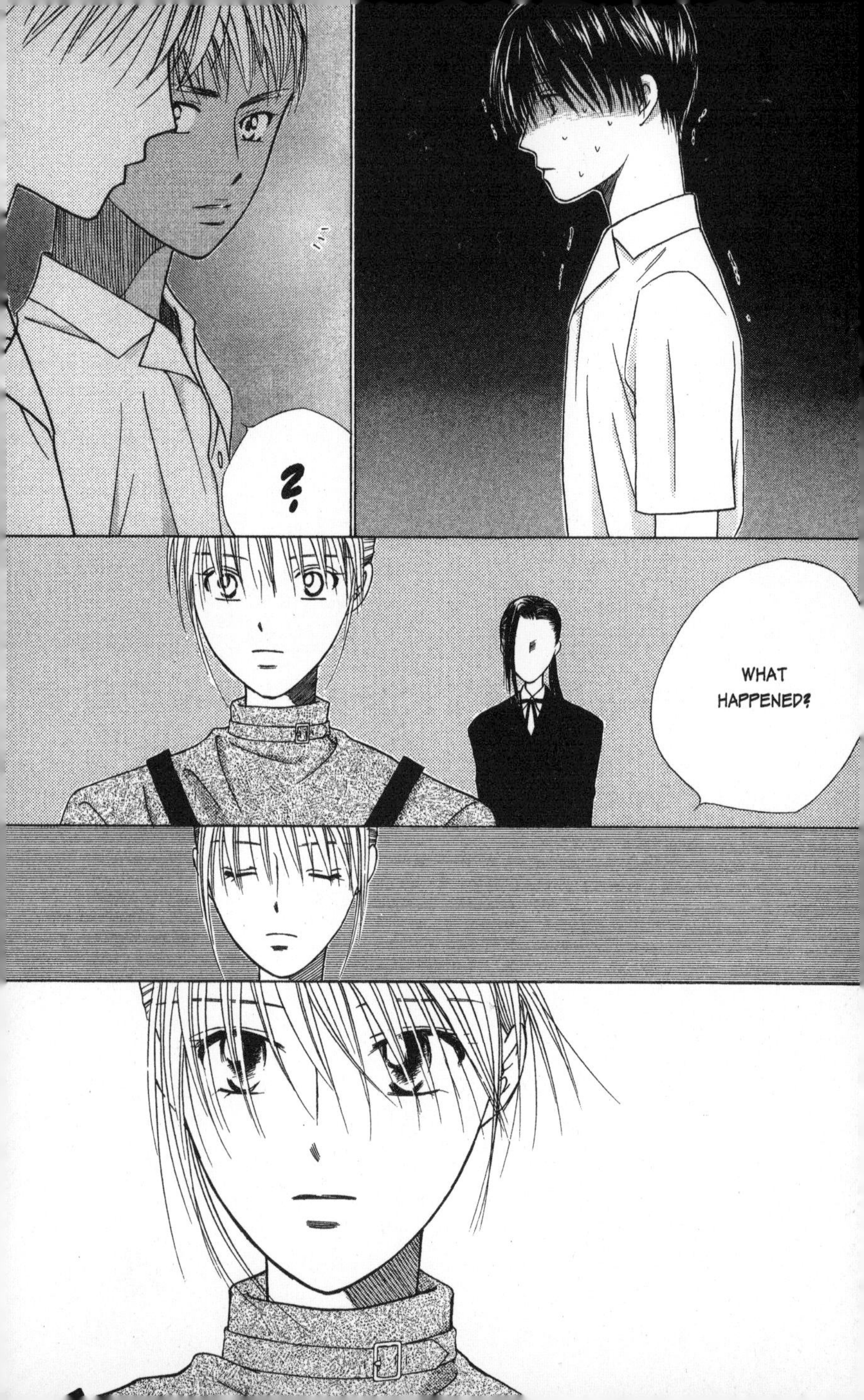

?
WHAT HAPPENED?

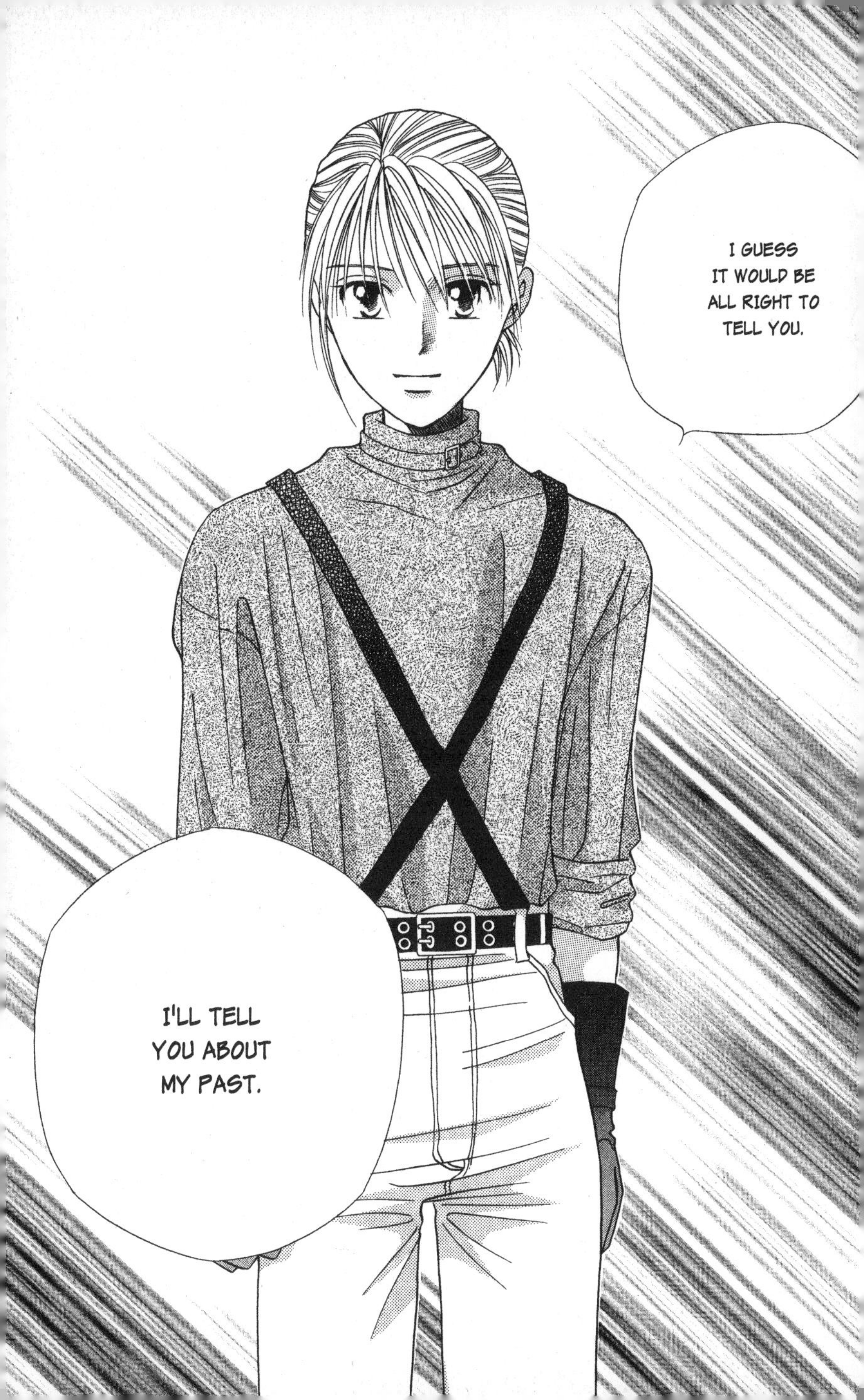
I GUESS IT WOULD BE ALL RIGHT TO TELL YOU.
I'LL TELL YOU ABOUT MY PAST.

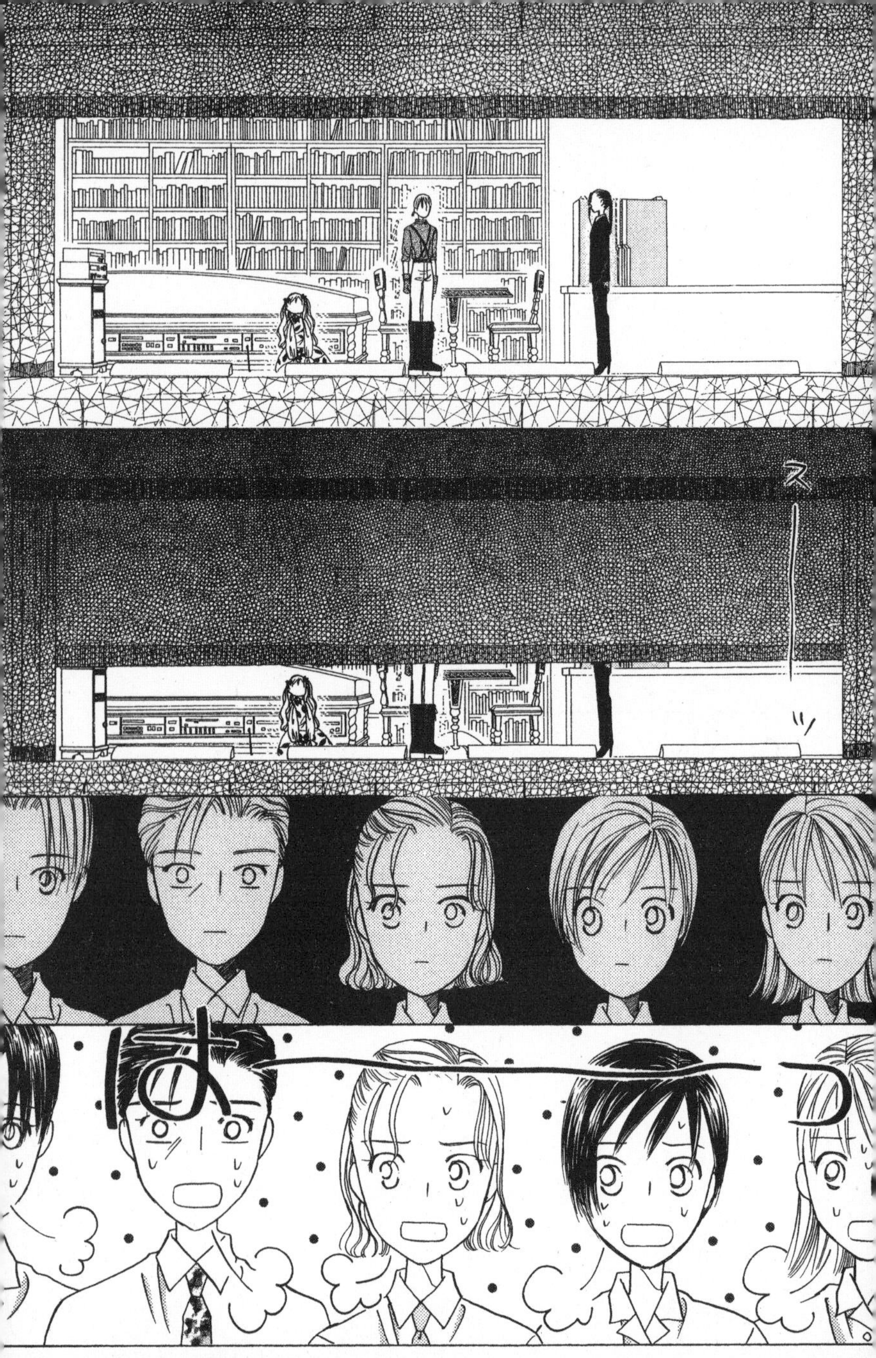

スーッ
はーっ

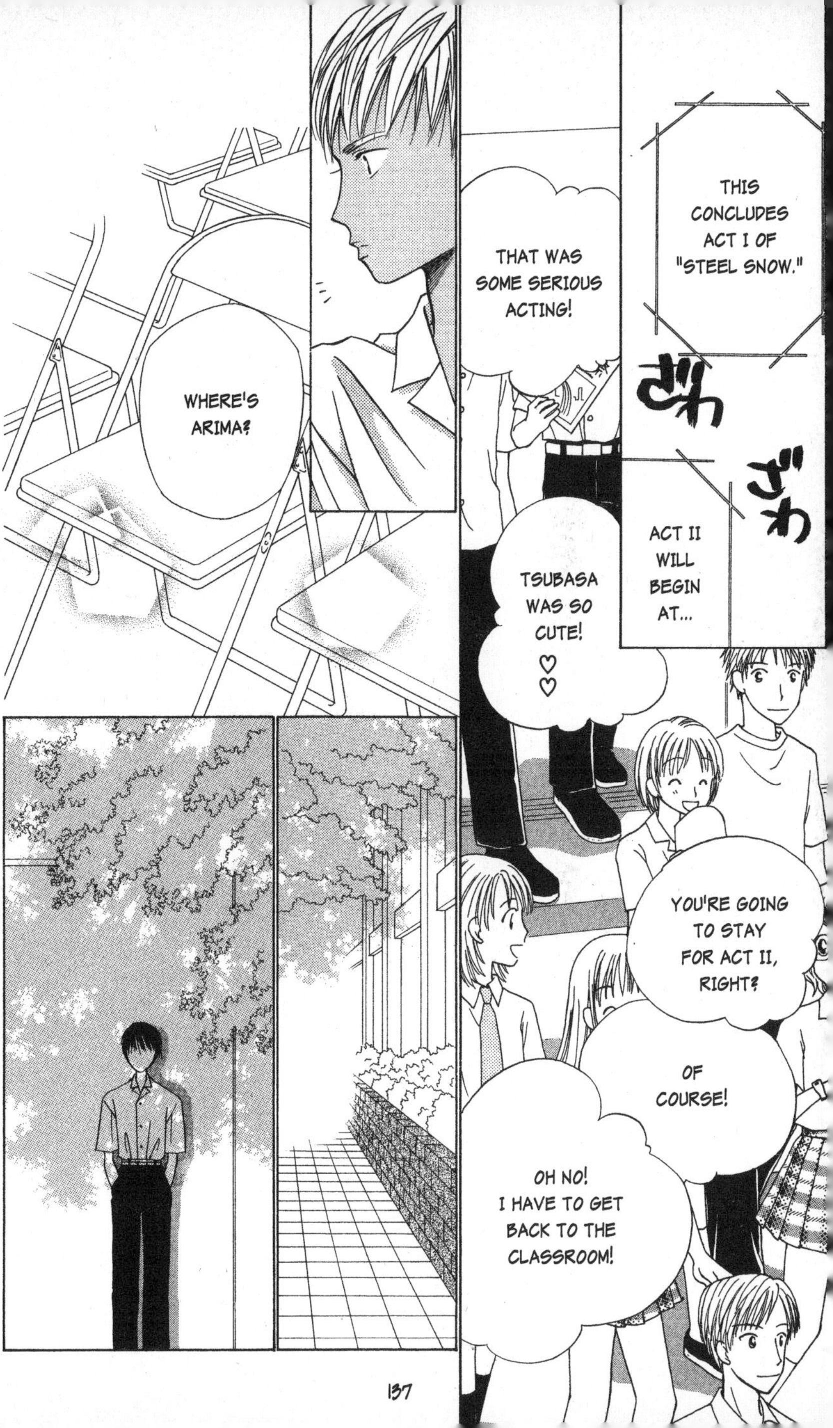
THIS CONCLUDES ACT I OF "STEEL SNOW."
ざわ
ざわ
ACT II WILL BEGIN AT...
THAT WAS SOME SERIOUS ACTING!
TSUBASA WAS SO CUTE! ♡ ♡
YOU'RE GOING TO STAY FOR ACT II, RIGHT?
OF COURSE!
OH NO! I HAVE TO GET BACK TO THE CLASSROOM!
WHERE'S ARIMA?

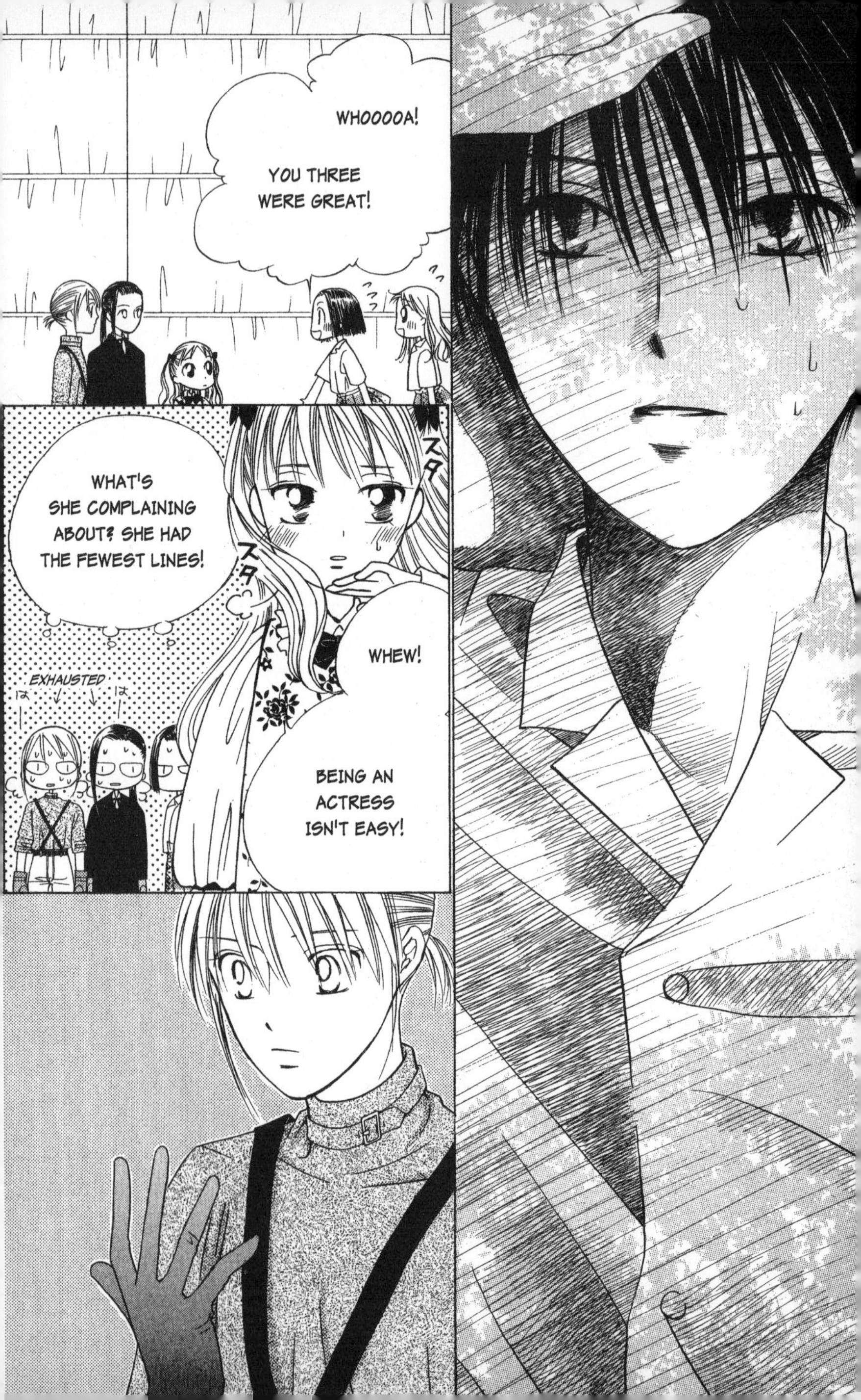
WHOOOOA!
YOU THREE WERE GREAT!
スタ
スタ
WHEW!
BEING AN ACTRESS ISN'T EASY!
WHAT'S SHE COMPLAINING ABOUT? SHE HAD THE FEWEST LINES!
EXHAUSTED
は
は

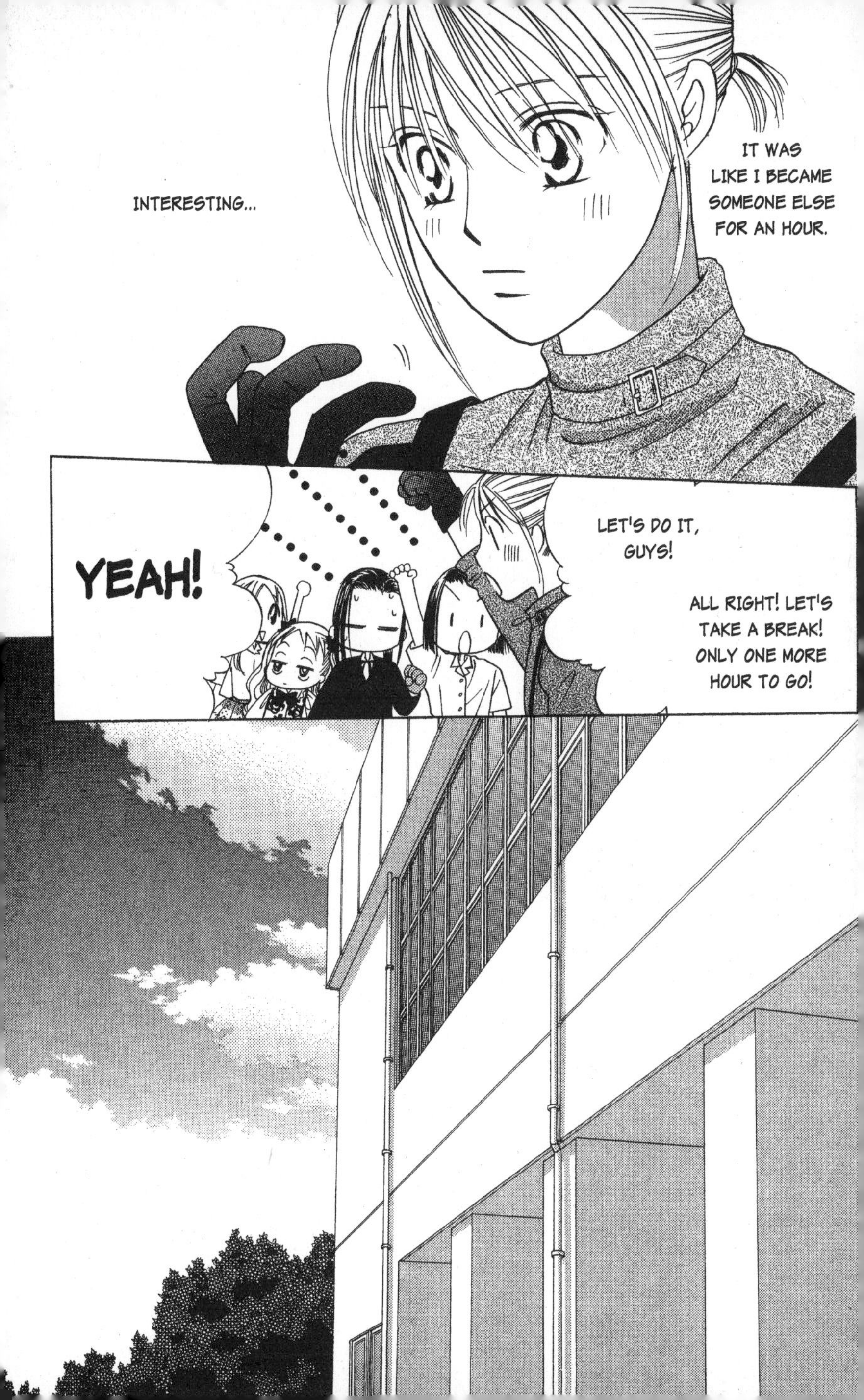
IT WAS LIKE I BECAME SOMEONE ELSE FOR AN HOUR.
INTERESTING...
ALL RIGHT! LET'S TAKE A BREAK! ONLY ONE MORE HOUR TO GO!
LET'S DO IT, GUYS!
YEAH!

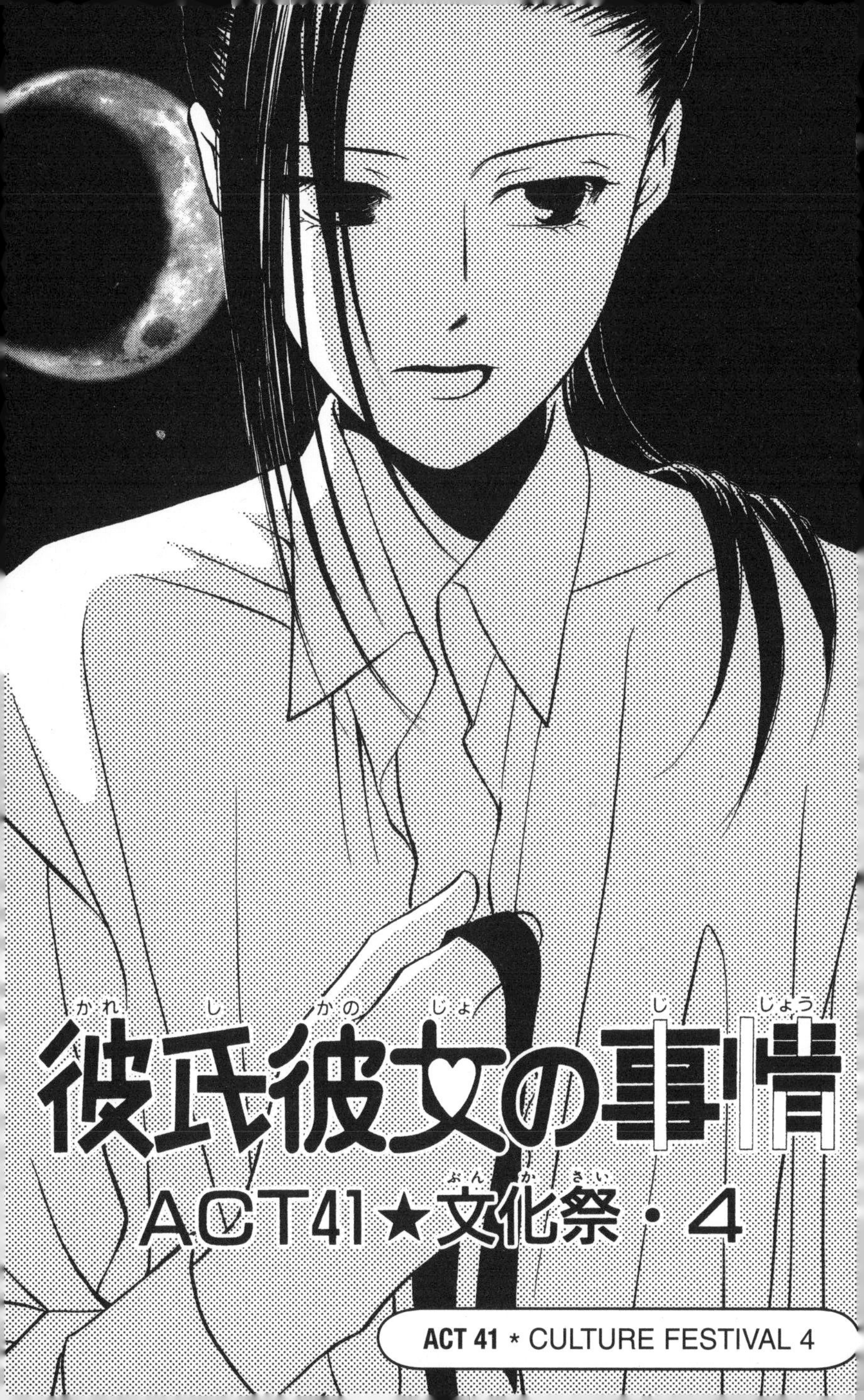
彼氏彼女の事情
ACT41★文化祭・4
ACT 41 ★ CULTURE FESTIVAL 4

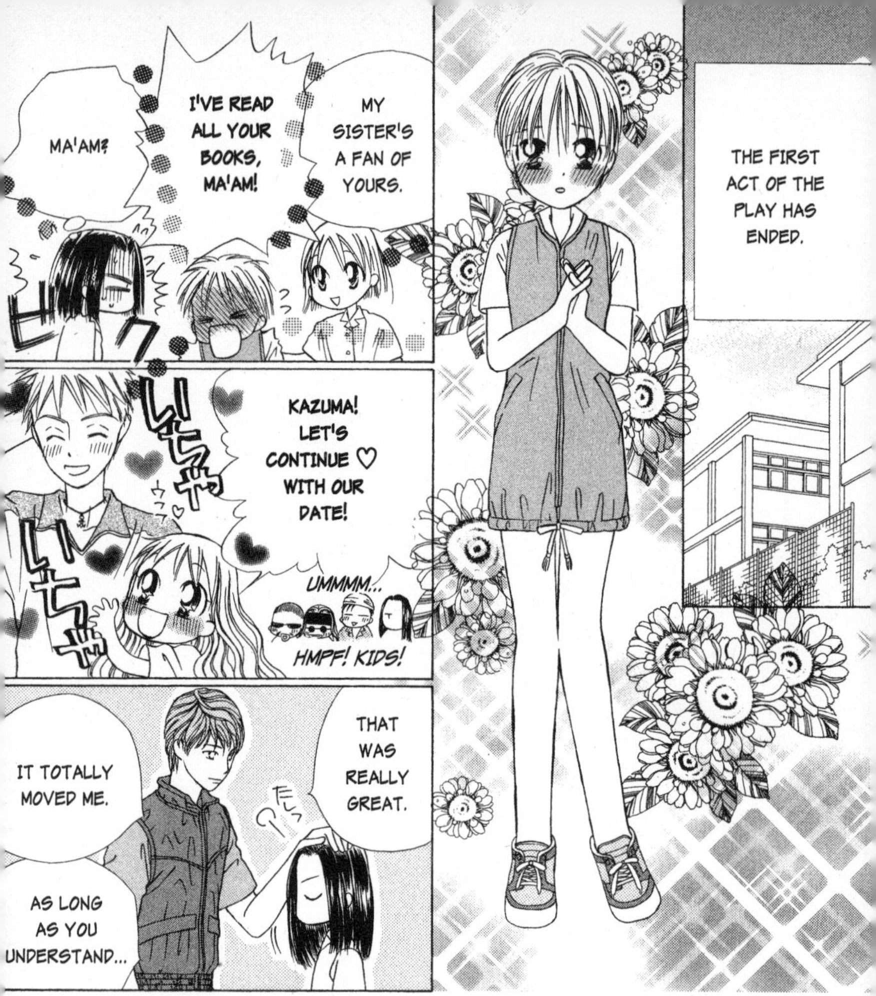
THE FIRST ACT OF THE PLAY HAS ENDED.
MY SISTER'S A FAN OF YOURS.
I'VE READ ALL YOUR BOOKS, MA'AM!
MA'AM?
KAZUMA! LET'S CONTINUE ♡ WITH OUR DATE!
UMMMM...
HMPF! KIDS!
THAT WAS REALLY GREAT.
IT TOTALLY MOVED ME.
AS LONG AS YOU UNDERSTAND...

I did calligraphy from the time I was in kinder-garten up until my junior high graduation, so it looks like going back to it now will work out fine. (Really?) I got a lot of "special honors" and "grand prizes" in exhibitions. But which was higher, those prizes or the "gold prize" Which was lower? I didn't understand, and so I lost interest until I didn't even go to exhibitions any more. I disappointed my poor teacher a lot... Even now, I still can't tell if my calligraphy was good or what.

But when I was a child, I hated the letters I drew. Because you see, in calligraphy, your personality comes through in the letters you draw, and mine looked positively EVIL and looked like they were drawn by a very stubborn person. I really wanted to be the kind of person who could draw breezy, lively letters.

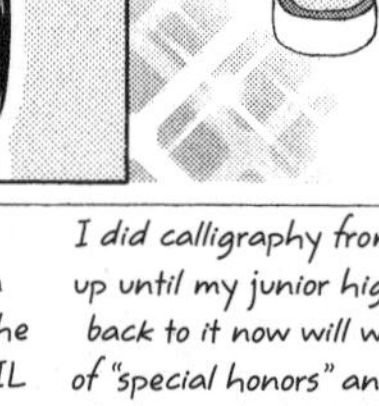

Uuugh, I HATE it! Maybe I just shouldn't do ANYthing?

5

"Seven Brides for Seven Brothers"

and

"All About Eve"...

I love those kinds of movies. I guess I really like old American movies.

For a whole day after I watch one, I'm in a really happy mood, and I sleep well. I think it's amazing.

"Beauty and the Beast" (the old Jean Cocteau version) is SO beautiful!

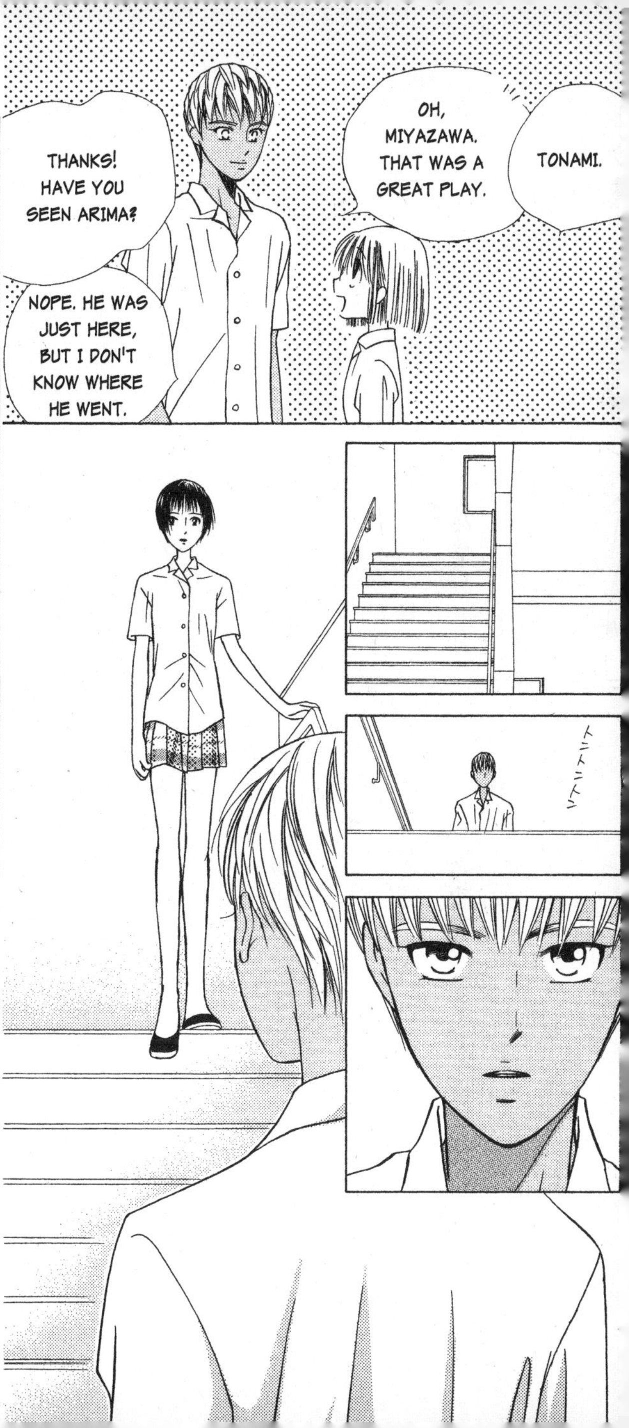
TONAMI.
OH, MIYAZAWA. THAT WAS A GREAT PLAY.
THANKS! HAVE YOU SEEN ARIMA?
NOPE. HE WAS JUST HERE, BUT I DON'T KNOW WHERE HE WENT.
トントントン

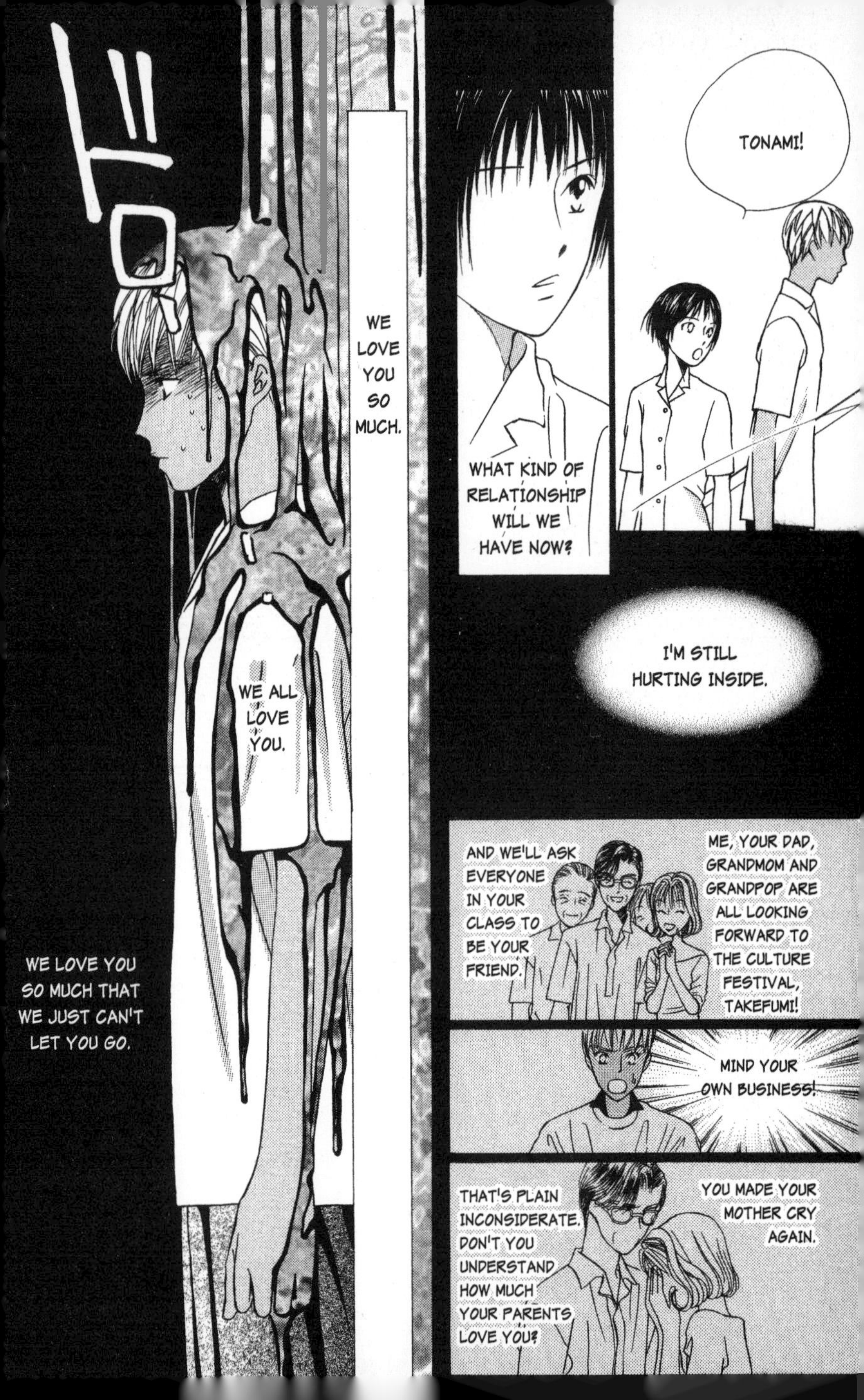
TONAMI!
WHAT KIND OF RELATIONSHIP WILL WE HAVE NOW?
I'M STILL HURTING INSIDE.
ME, YOUR DAD, GRANDMOM AND GRANDPOP ARE ALL LOOKING FORWARD TO THE CULTURE FESTIVAL, TAKEFUMI!
AND WE'LL ASK EVERYONE IN YOUR CLASS TO BE YOUR FRIEND.
MIND YOUR OWN BUSINESS!
YOU MADE YOUR MOTHER CRY AGAIN.
THAT'S PLAIN INCONSIDERATE. DON'T YOU UNDERSTAND HOW MUCH YOUR PARENTS LOVE YOU?
WE LOVE YOU SO MUCH.
WE ALL LOVE YOU.
WE LOVE YOU SO MUCH THAT WE JUST CAN'T LET YOU GO.

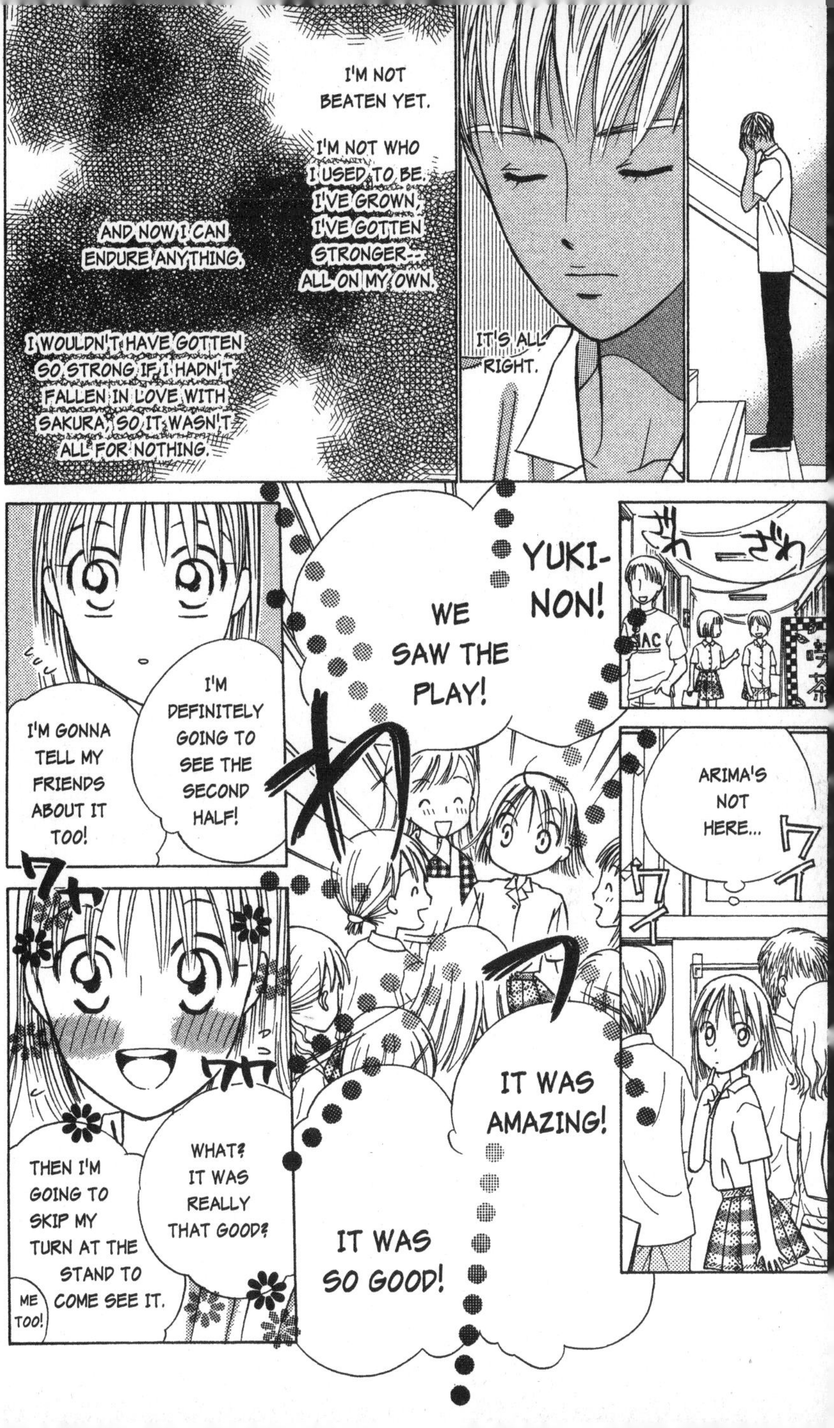
IT'S ALL RIGHT.
I'M NOT BEATEN YET.
I'M NOT WHO I USED TO BE. I'VE GROWN, I'VE GOTTEN STRONGER-- ALL ON MY OWN.
AND NOW I CAN ENDURE ANYTHING.
I WOULDN'T HAVE GOTTEN SO STRONG IF I HADN'T FALLEN IN LOVE WITH SAKURA, SO IT WASN'T ALL FOR NOTHING.
ざわ ざわ
YUKI-NON!
WE SAW THE PLAY!
ARIMA'S NOT HERE...
ワイワイ
I'M DEFINITELY GOING TO SEE THE SECOND HALF!
I'M GONNA TELL MY FRIENDS ABOUT IT TOO!
IT WAS AMAZING!
IT WAS SO GOOD!
WHAT? IT WAS REALLY THAT GOOD?
THEN I'M GOING TO SKIP MY TURN AT THE STAND TO COME SEE IT.
ME TOO!

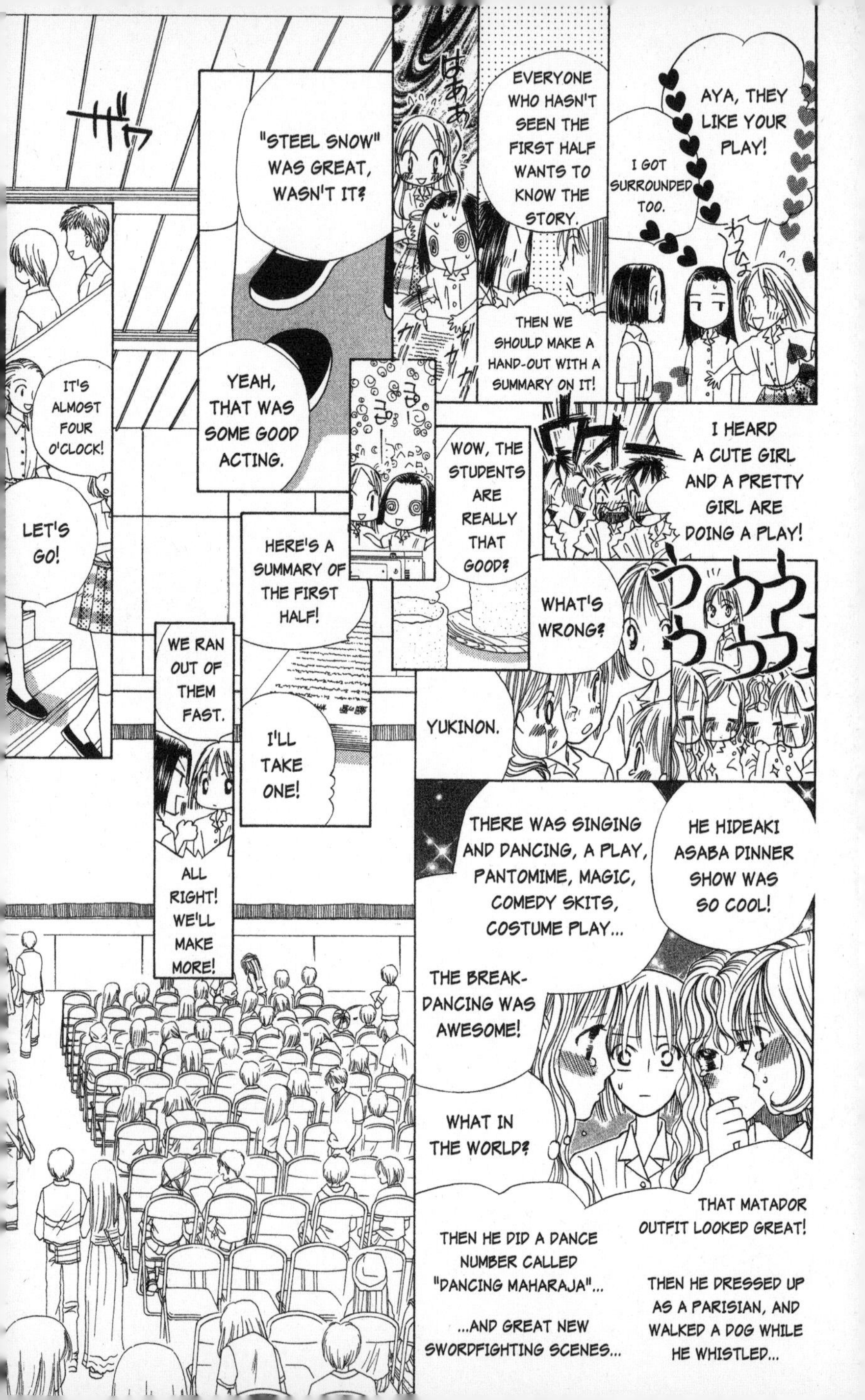
AYA, THEY LIKE YOUR PLAY!
I GOT SURROUNDED TOO.
EVERYONE WHO HASN'T SEEN THE FIRST HALF WANTS TO KNOW THE STORY.
THEN WE SHOULD MAKE A HAND-OUT WITH A SUMMARY ON IT!
I HEARD A CUTE GIRL AND A PRETTY GIRL ARE DOING A PLAY!
WOW, THE STUDENTS ARE REALLY THAT GOOD?
WHAT'S WRONG?
YUKINON.
HE HIDEAKI ASABA DINNER SHOW WAS SO COOL!
THERE WAS SINGING AND DANCING, A PLAY, PANTOMIME, MAGIC, COMEDY SKITS, COSTUME PLAY...
THE BREAK-DANCING WAS AWESOME!
WHAT IN THE WORLD?
THAT MATADOR OUTFIT LOOKED GREAT!
THEN HE DRESSED UP AS A PARISIAN, AND WALKED A DOG WHILE HE WHISTLED...
THEN HE DID A DANCE NUMBER CALLED "DANCING MAHARAJA"...
...AND GREAT NEW SWORDFIGHTING SCENES...
"STEEL SNOW" WAS GREAT, WASN'T IT?
YEAH, THAT WAS SOME GOOD ACTING.
HERE'S A SUMMARY OF THE FIRST HALF!
I'LL TAKE ONE!
WE RAN OUT OF THEM FAST.
ALL RIGHT! WE'LL MAKE MORE!
IT'S ALMOST FOUR O'CLOCK!
LET'S GO!

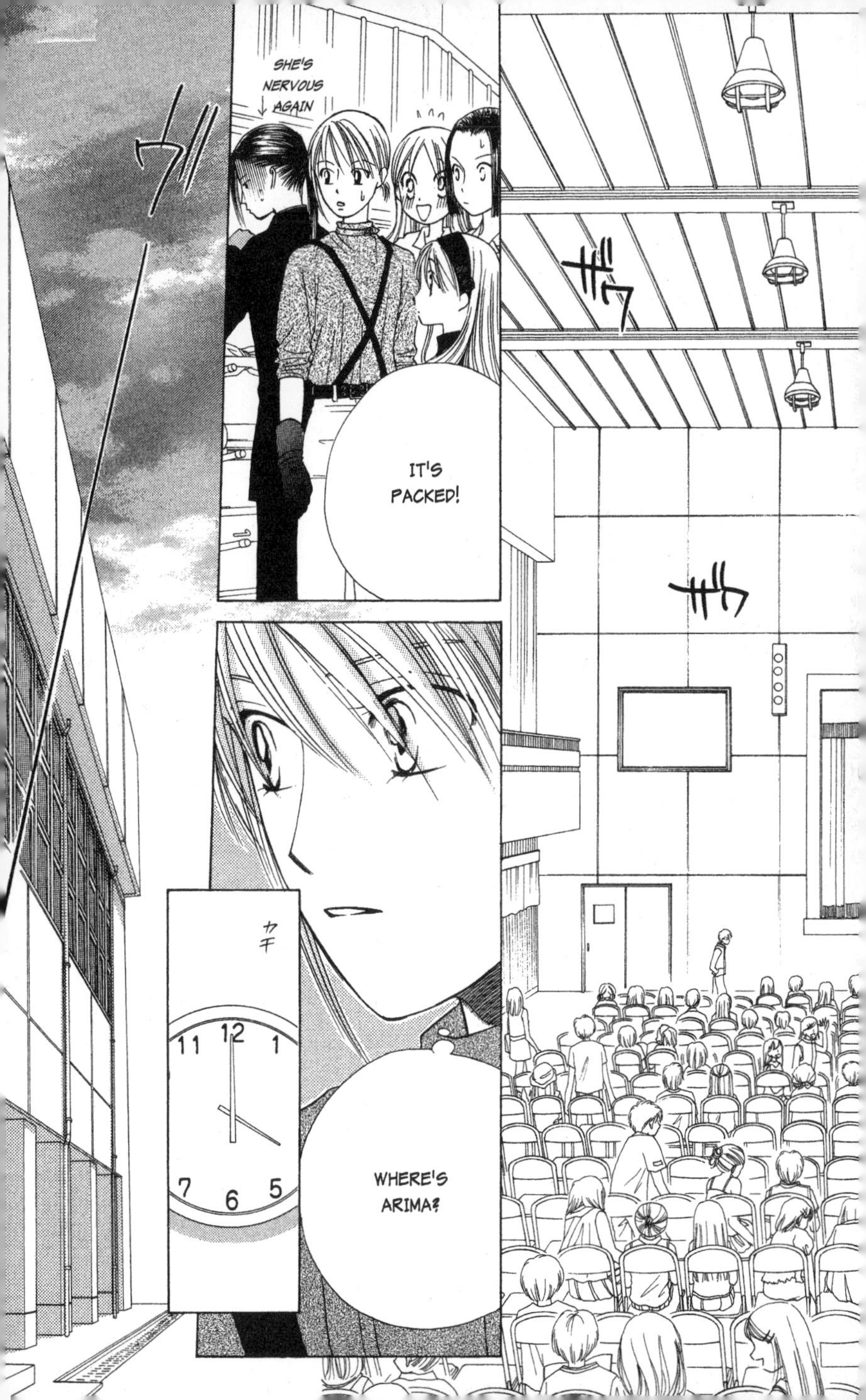
ザワ
ザワ
SHE'S NERVOUS AGAIN
IT'S PACKED!
カチ
WHERE'S ARIMA?

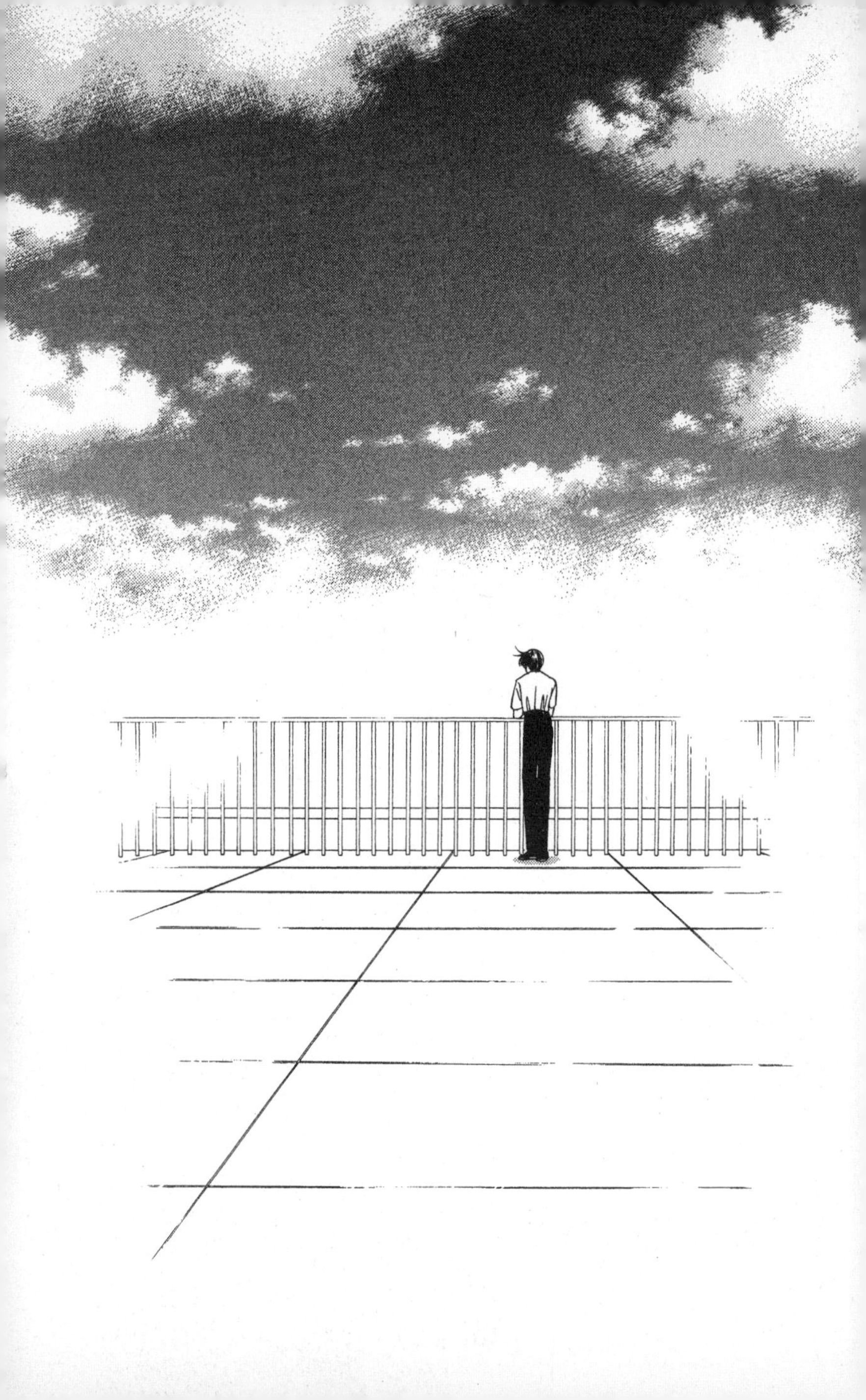

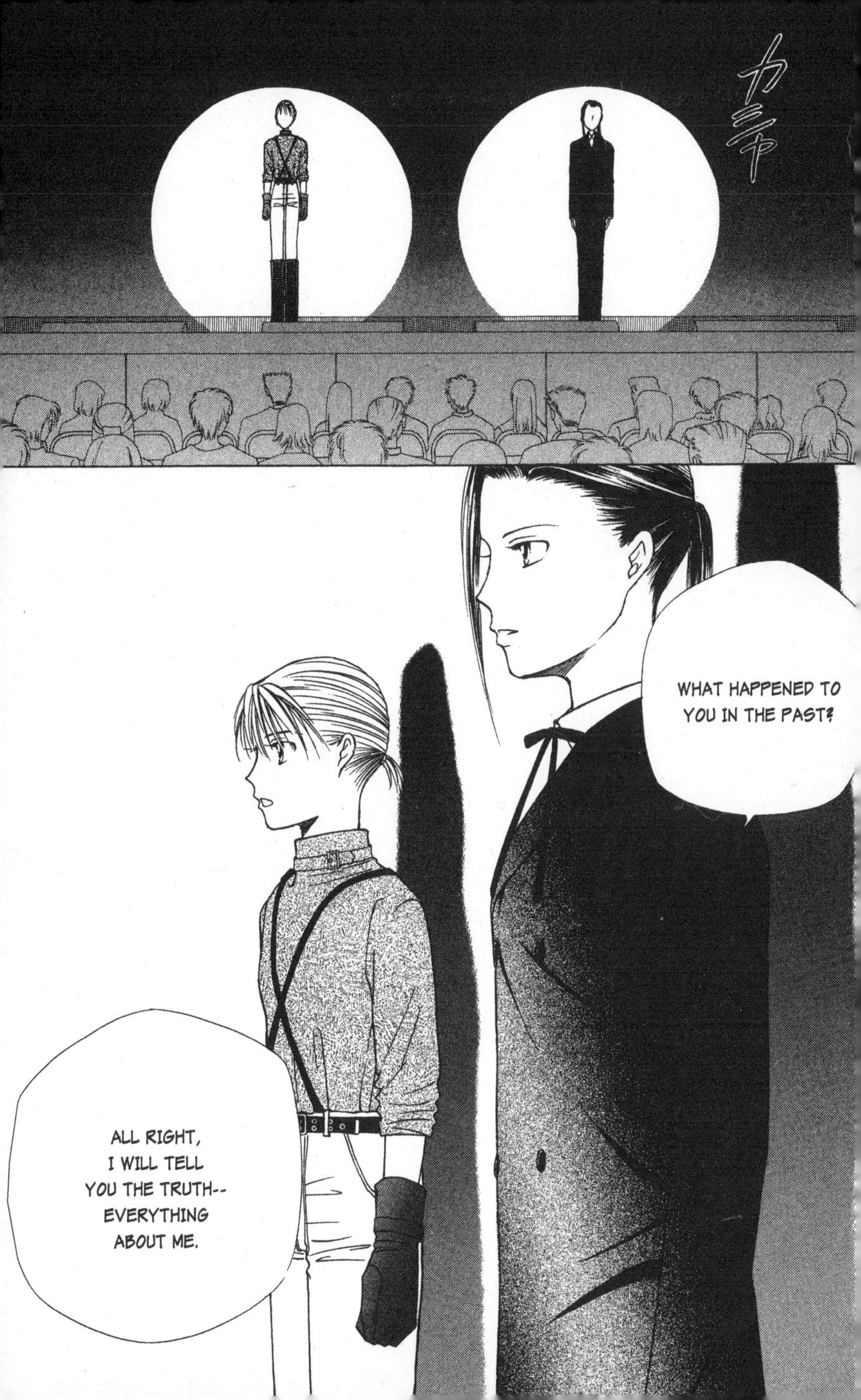
WHAT HAPPENED TO YOU IN THE PAST?
ALL RIGHT, I WILL TELL YOU THE TRUTH-- EVERYTHING ABOUT ME.

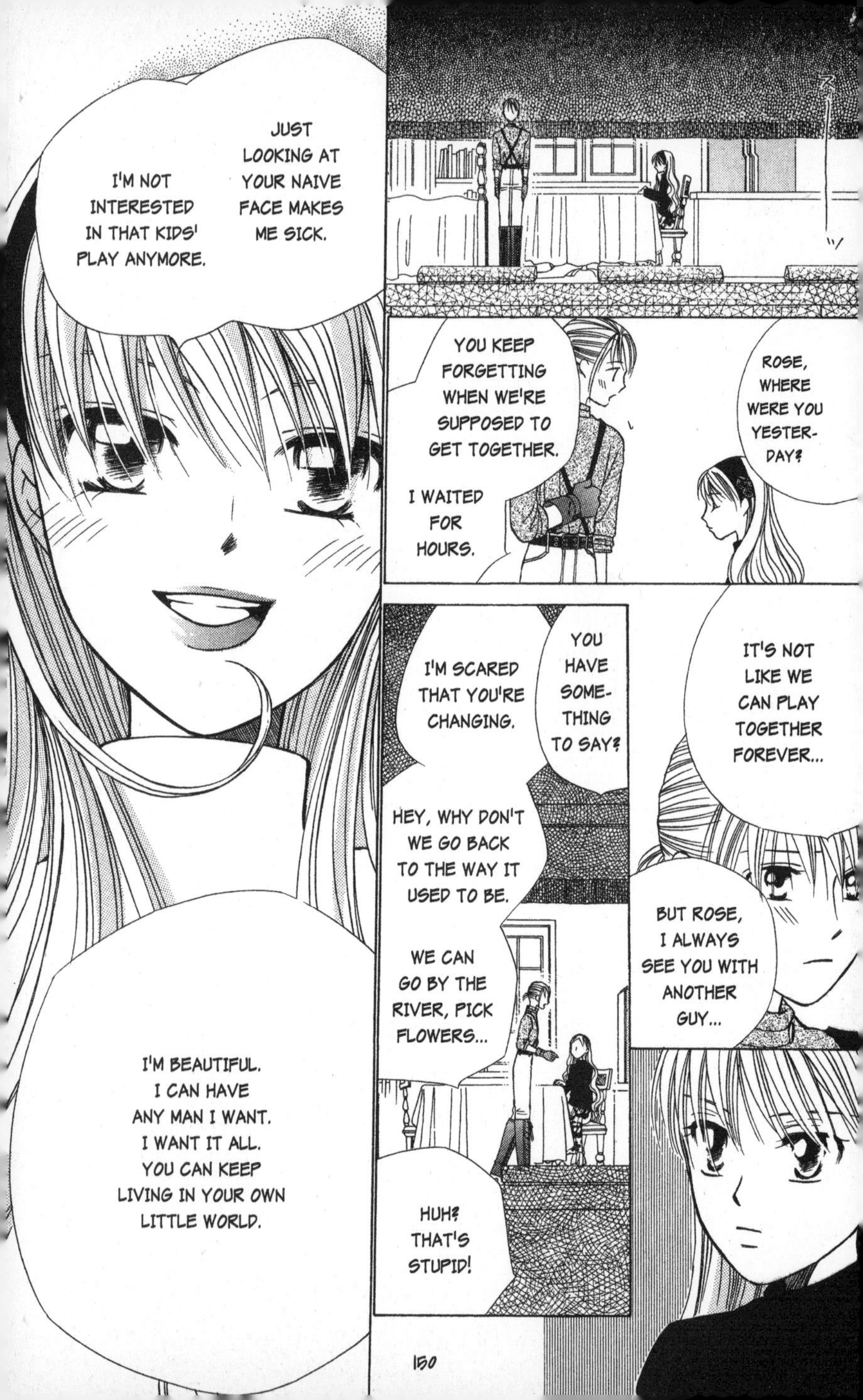
ROSE, WHERE WERE YOU YESTERDAY?
YOU KEEP FORGETTING WHEN WE'RE SUPPOSED TO GET TOGETHER.
I WAITED FOR HOURS.
IT'S NOT LIKE WE CAN PLAY TOGETHER FOREVER...
YOU HAVE SOMETHING TO SAY?
I'M SCARED THAT YOU'RE CHANGING.
HEY, WHY DON'T WE GO BACK TO THE WAY IT USED TO BE.
WE CAN GO BY THE RIVER, PICK FLOWERS...
HUH? THAT'S STUPID!
BUT ROSE, I ALWAYS SEE YOU WITH ANOTHER GUY...
JUST LOOKING AT YOUR NAIVE FACE MAKES ME SICK.
I'M NOT INTERESTED IN THAT KIDS' PLAY ANYMORE.
I'M BEAUTIFUL. I CAN HAVE ANY MAN I WANT. I WANT IT ALL. YOU CAN KEEP LIVING IN YOUR OWN LITTLE WORLD.

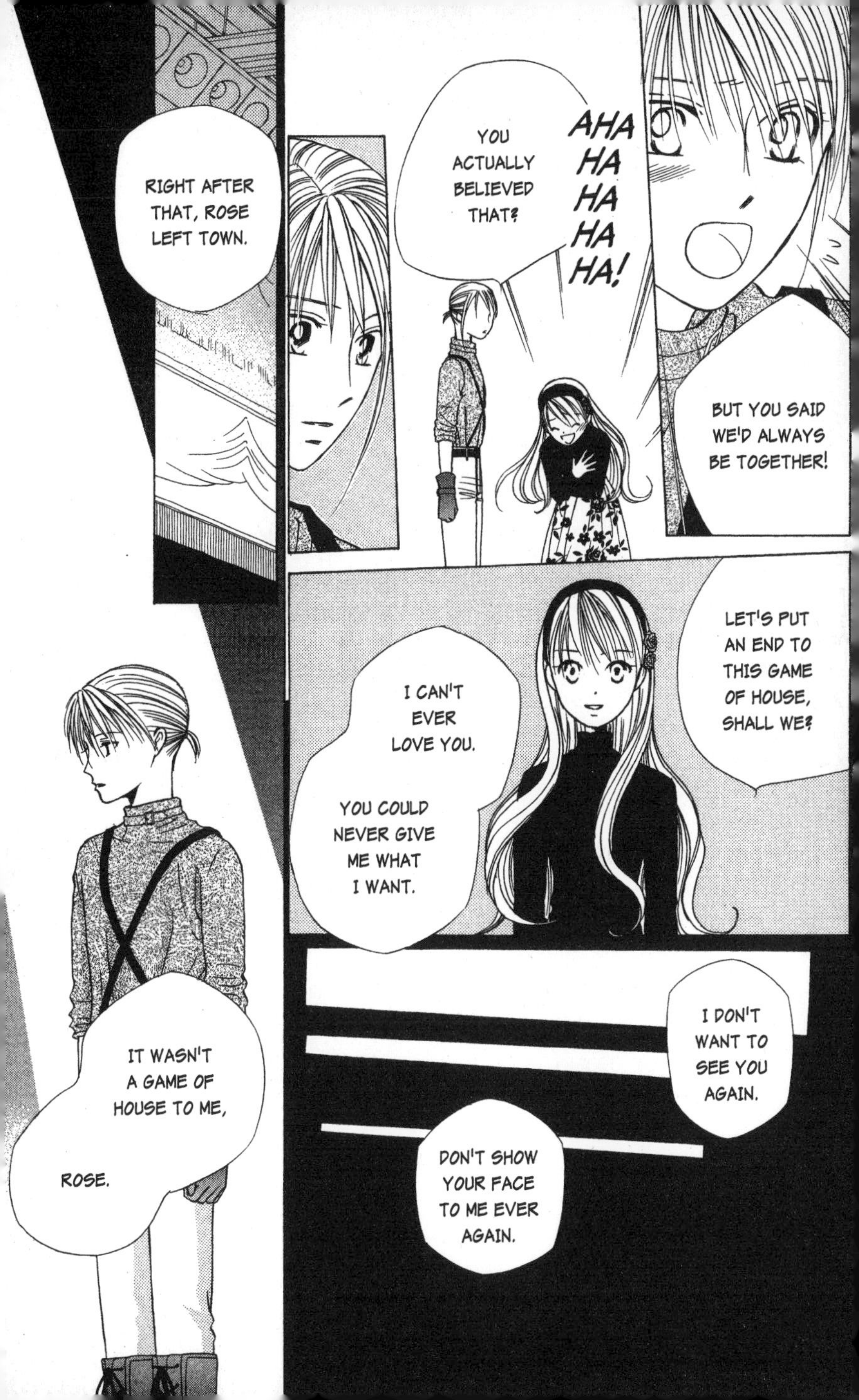
BUT YOU SAID WE'D ALWAYS BE TOGETHER!
AHA HA HA HA HA!
YOU ACTUALLY BELIEVED THAT?
LET'S PUT AN END TO THIS GAME OF HOUSE, SHALL WE?
I CAN'T EVER LOVE YOU.
YOU COULD NEVER GIVE ME WHAT I WANT.
I DON'T WANT TO SEE YOU AGAIN.
DON'T SHOW YOUR FACE TO ME EVER AGAIN.
RIGHT AFTER THAT, ROSE LEFT TOWN.
IT WASN'T A GAME OF HOUSE TO ME,
ROSE.

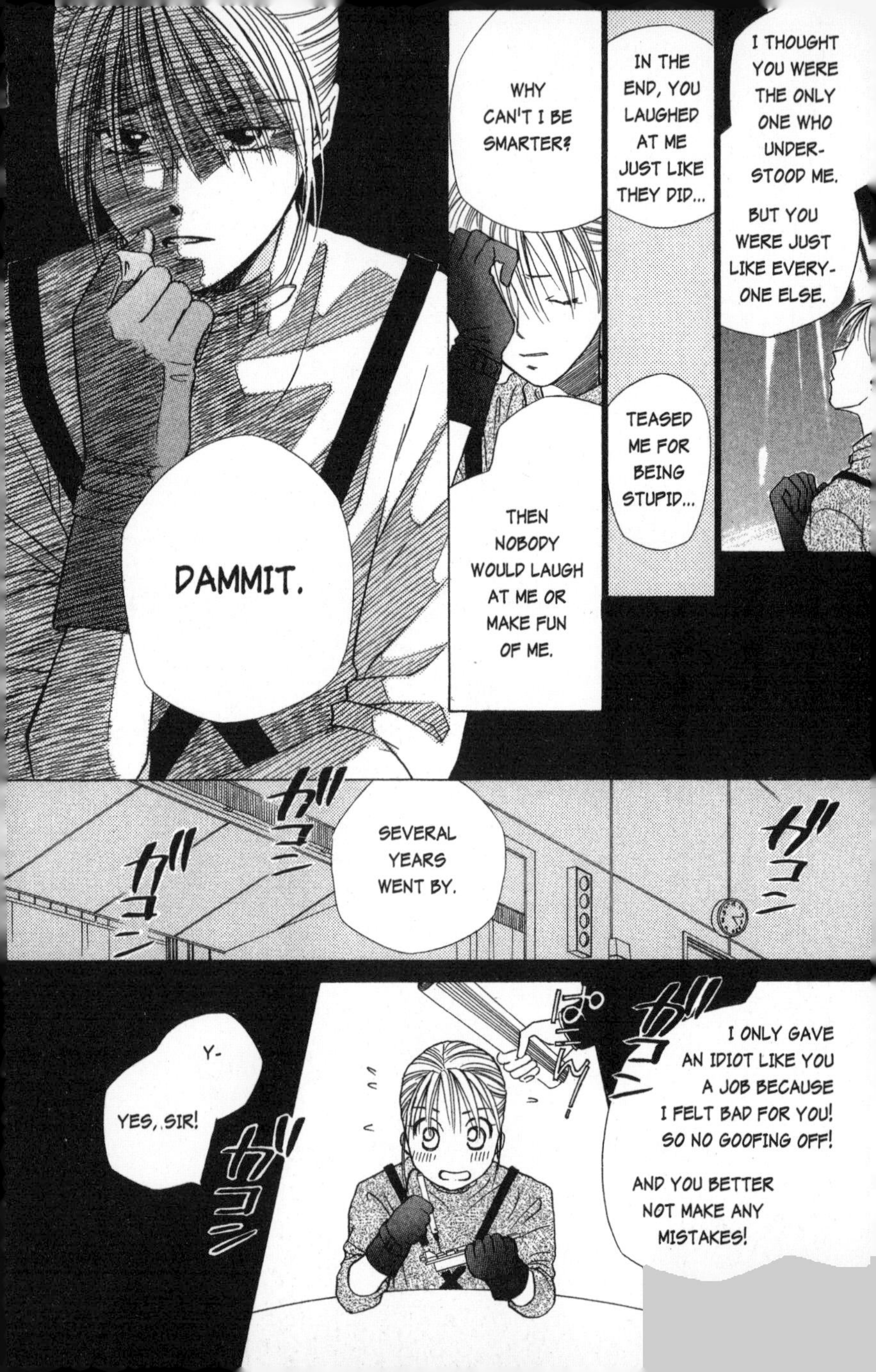
I THOUGHT YOU WERE THE ONLY ONE WHO UNDER-STOOD ME.
BUT YOU WERE JUST LIKE EVERY-ONE ELSE.
IN THE END, YOU LAUGHED AT ME JUST LIKE THEY DID...
TEASED ME FOR BEING STUPID...
WHY CAN'T I BE SMARTER?
THEN NOBODY WOULD LAUGH AT ME OR MAKE FUN OF ME.
DAMMIT.
SEVERAL YEARS WENT BY.
I ONLY GAVE AN IDIOT LIKE YOU A JOB BECAUSE I FELT BAD FOR YOU! SO NO GOOFING OFF!
AND YOU BETTER NOT MAKE ANY MISTAKES!
Y-
YES, SIR!

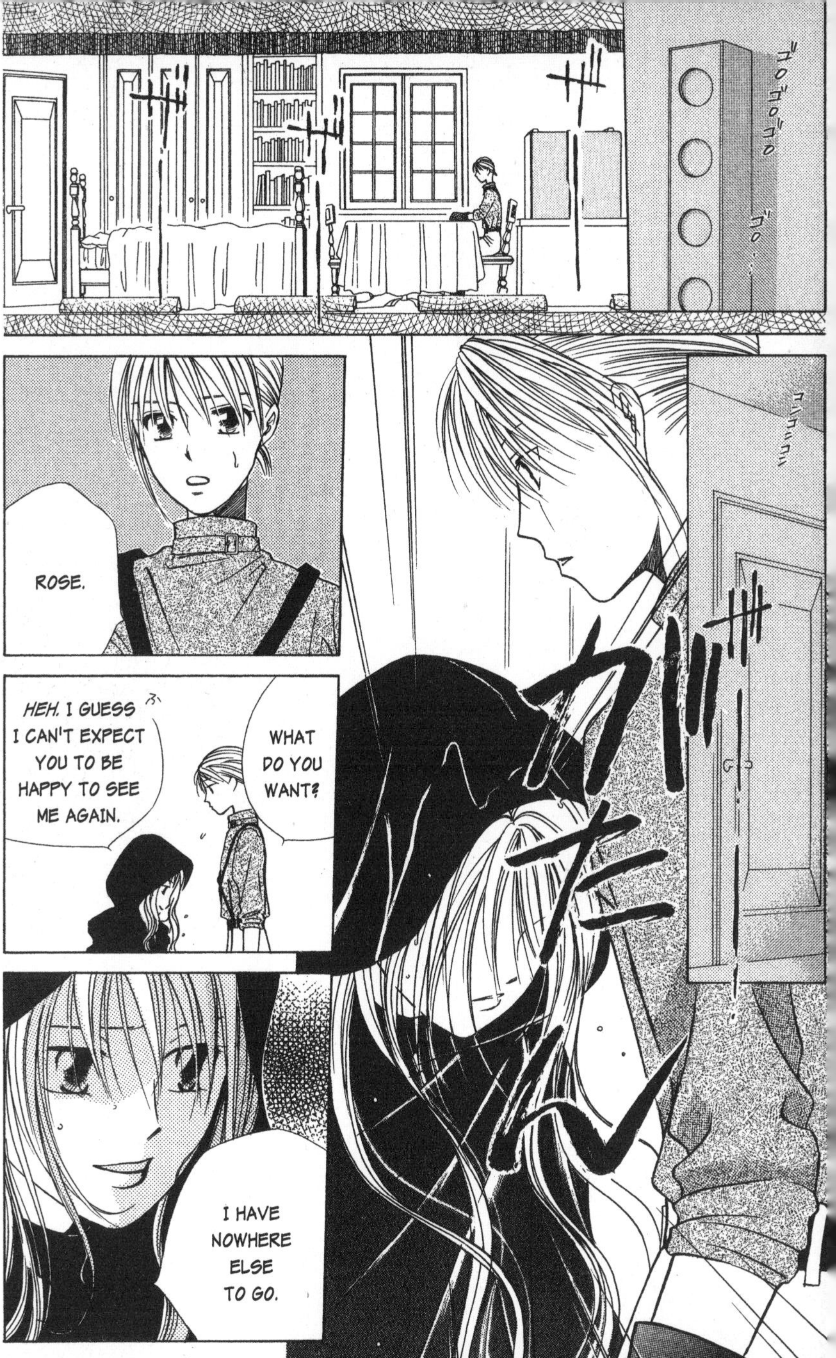
ゴロゴロゴロ
ゴロ…
コッコッ
ROSE.
WHAT DO YOU WANT?
HEH. I GUESS I CAN'T EXPECT YOU TO BE HAPPY TO SEE ME AGAIN.
ふ
I HAVE NOWHERE ELSE TO GO.

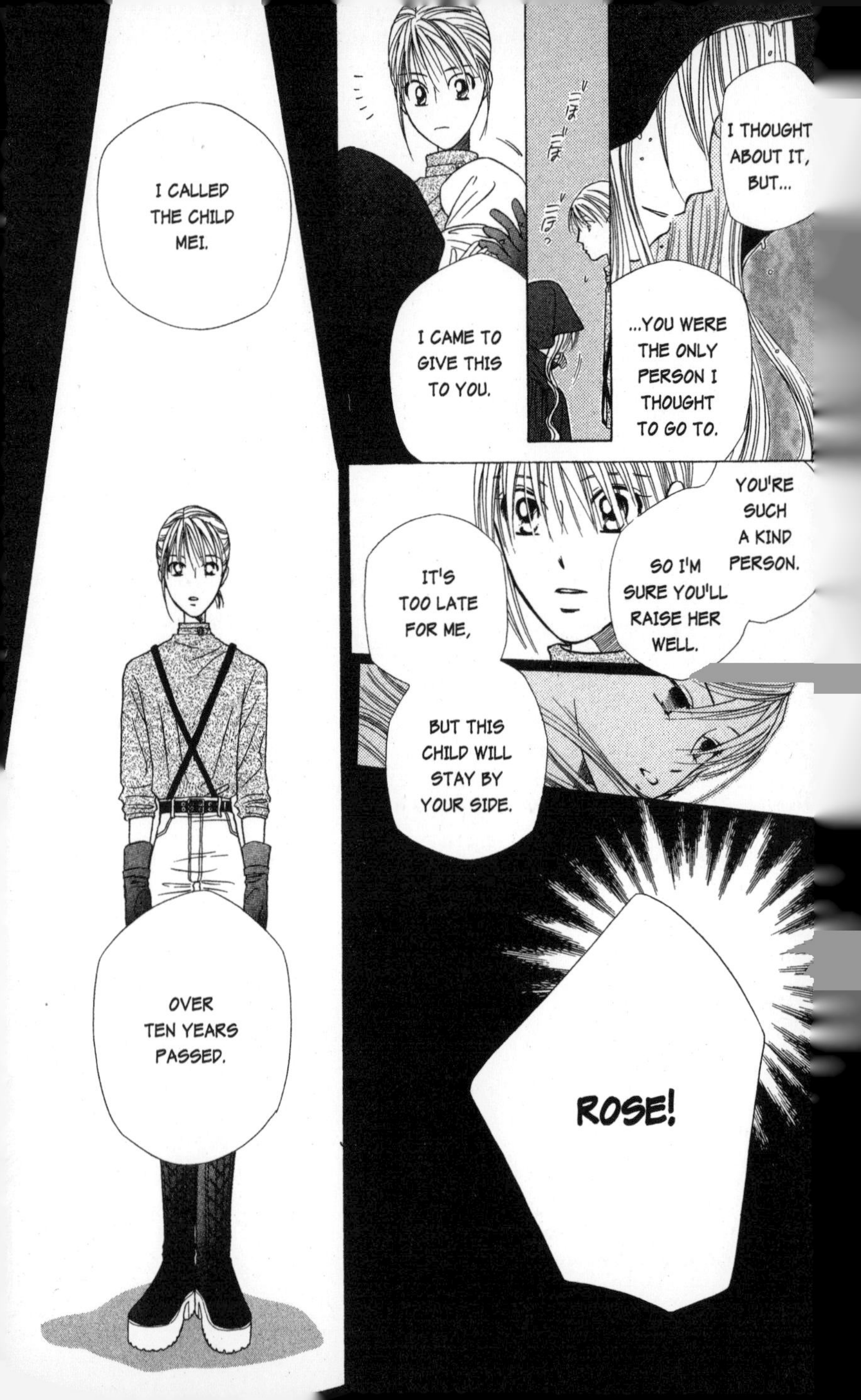
I THOUGHT ABOUT IT, BUT...
...YOU WERE THE ONLY PERSON I THOUGHT TO GO TO.
I CAME TO GIVE THIS TO YOU.
YOU'RE SUCH A KIND PERSON.
SO I'M SURE YOU'LL RAISE HER WELL.
IT'S TOO LATE FOR ME,
BUT THIS CHILD WILL STAY BY YOUR SIDE.
ROSE!
I CALLED THE CHILD MEI.
OVER TEN YEARS PASSED.

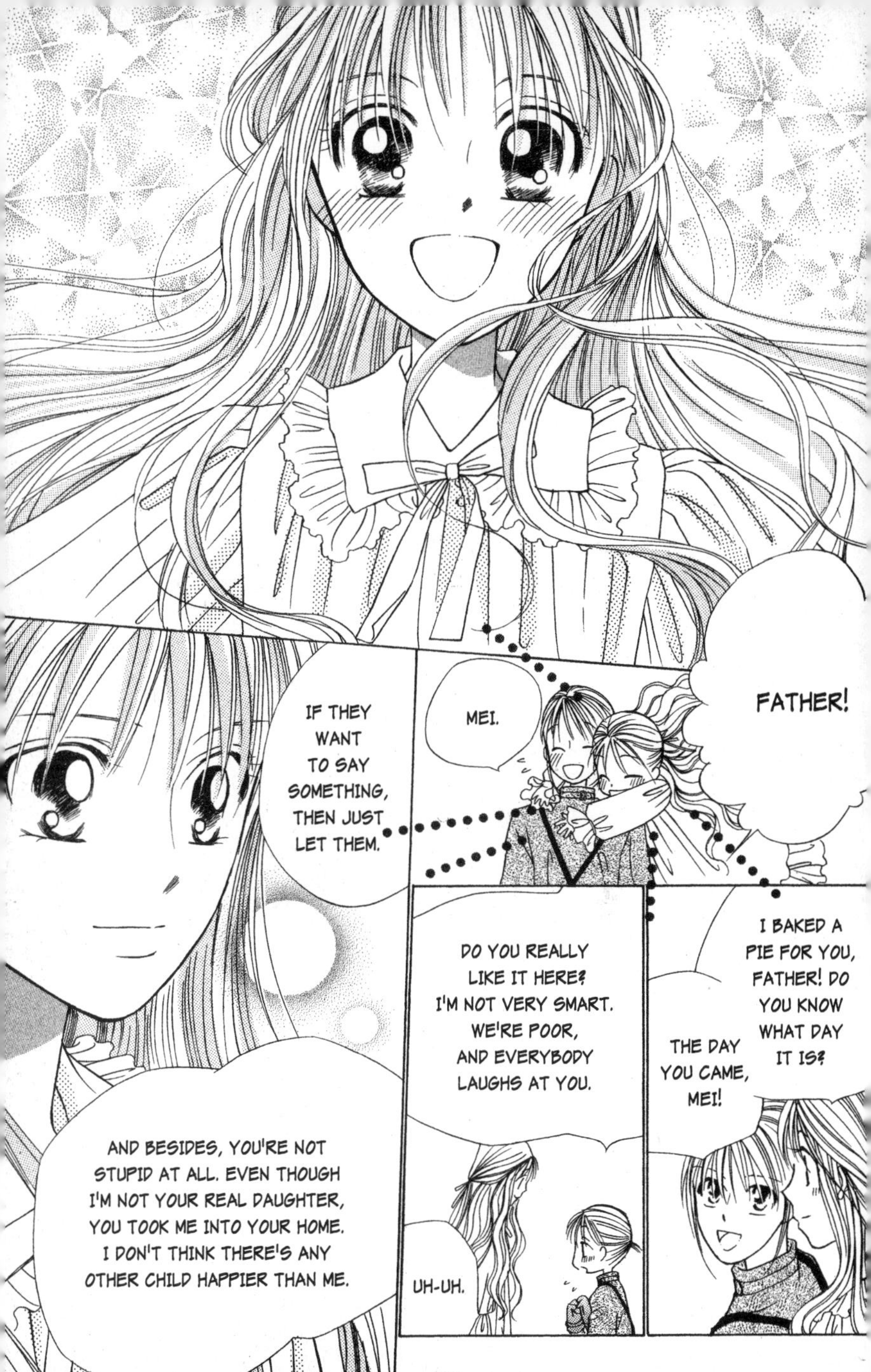
FATHER!
MEI.
IF THEY WANT TO SAY SOMETHING, THEN JUST LET THEM.
I BAKED A PIE FOR YOU, FATHER! DO YOU KNOW WHAT DAY IT IS?
THE DAY YOU CAME, MEI!
DO YOU REALLY LIKE IT HERE? I'M NOT VERY SMART. WE'RE POOR, AND EVERYBODY LAUGHS AT YOU.
UH-UH.
AND BESIDES, YOU'RE NOT STUPID AT ALL. EVEN THOUGH I'M NOT YOUR REAL DAUGHTER, YOU TOOK ME INTO YOUR HOME. I DON'T THINK THERE'S ANY OTHER CHILD HAPPIER THAN ME.

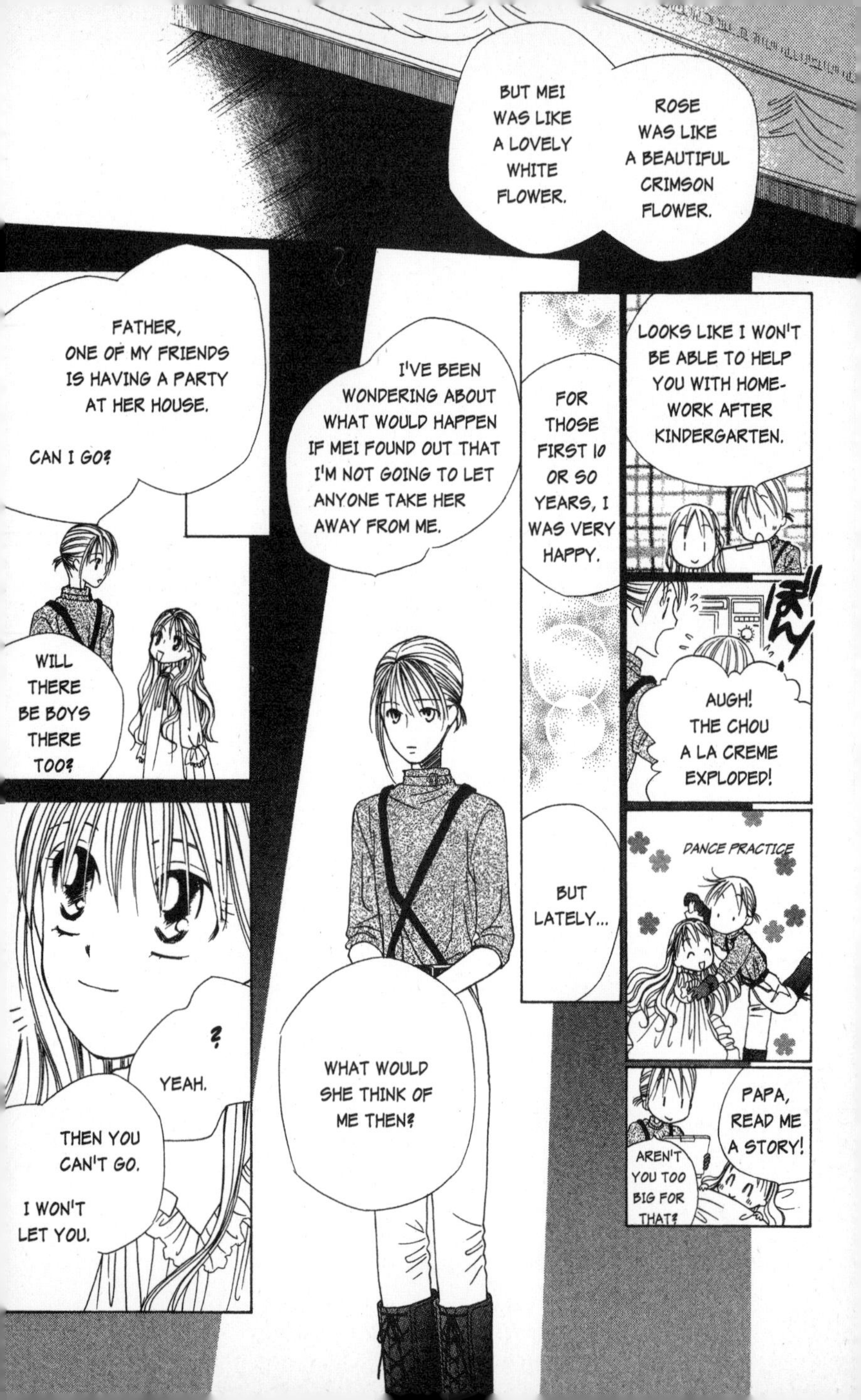
ROSE WAS LIKE A BEAUTIFUL CRIMSON FLOWER.
BUT MEI WAS LIKE A LOVELY WHITE FLOWER.
LOOKS LIKE I WON'T BE ABLE TO HELP YOU WITH HOME-WORK AFTER KINDERGARTEN.
FOR THOSE FIRST 10 OR SO YEARS, I WAS VERY HAPPY.
ぼん
AUGH! THE CHOU A LA CREME EXPLODED!
DANCE PRACTICE
BUT LATELY...
PAPA, READ ME A STORY!
AREN'T YOU TOO BIG FOR THAT?
I'VE BEEN WONDERING ABOUT WHAT WOULD HAPPEN IF MEI FOUND OUT THAT I'M NOT GOING TO LET ANYONE TAKE HER AWAY FROM ME.
WHAT WOULD SHE THINK OF ME THEN?
FATHER, ONE OF MY FRIENDS IS HAVING A PARTY AT HER HOUSE.
CAN I GO?
WILL THERE BE BOYS THERE TOO?
?
YEAH.
THEN YOU CAN'T GO.
I WON'T LET YOU.

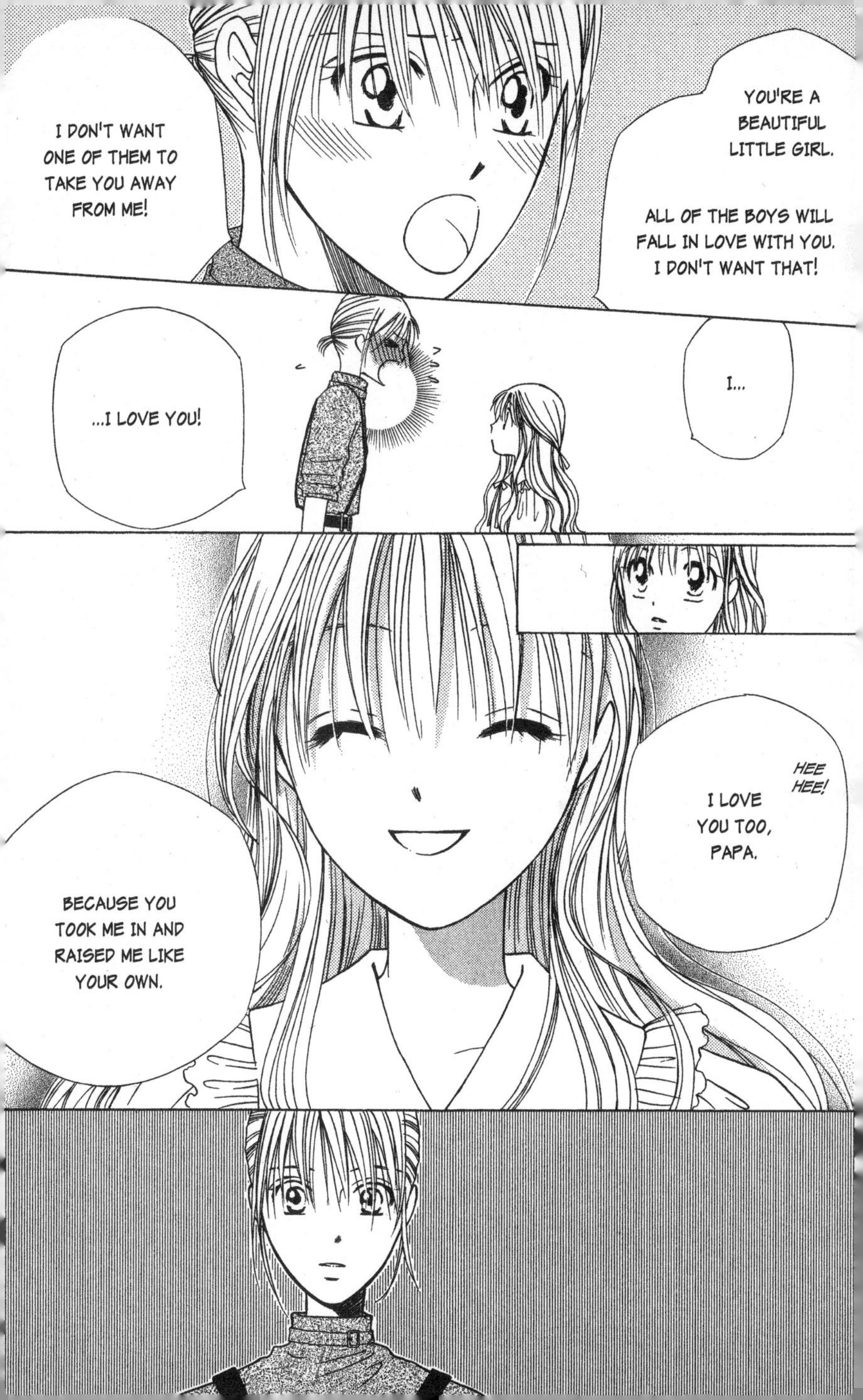
YOU'RE A BEAUTIFUL LITTLE GIRL.
ALL OF THE BOYS WILL FALL IN LOVE WITH YOU. I DON'T WANT THAT!
I DON'T WANT ONE OF THEM TO TAKE YOU AWAY FROM ME!
I...
...I LOVE YOU!
HEE HEE!
I LOVE YOU TOO, PAPA.
BECAUSE YOU TOOK ME IN AND RAISED ME LIKE YOUR OWN.

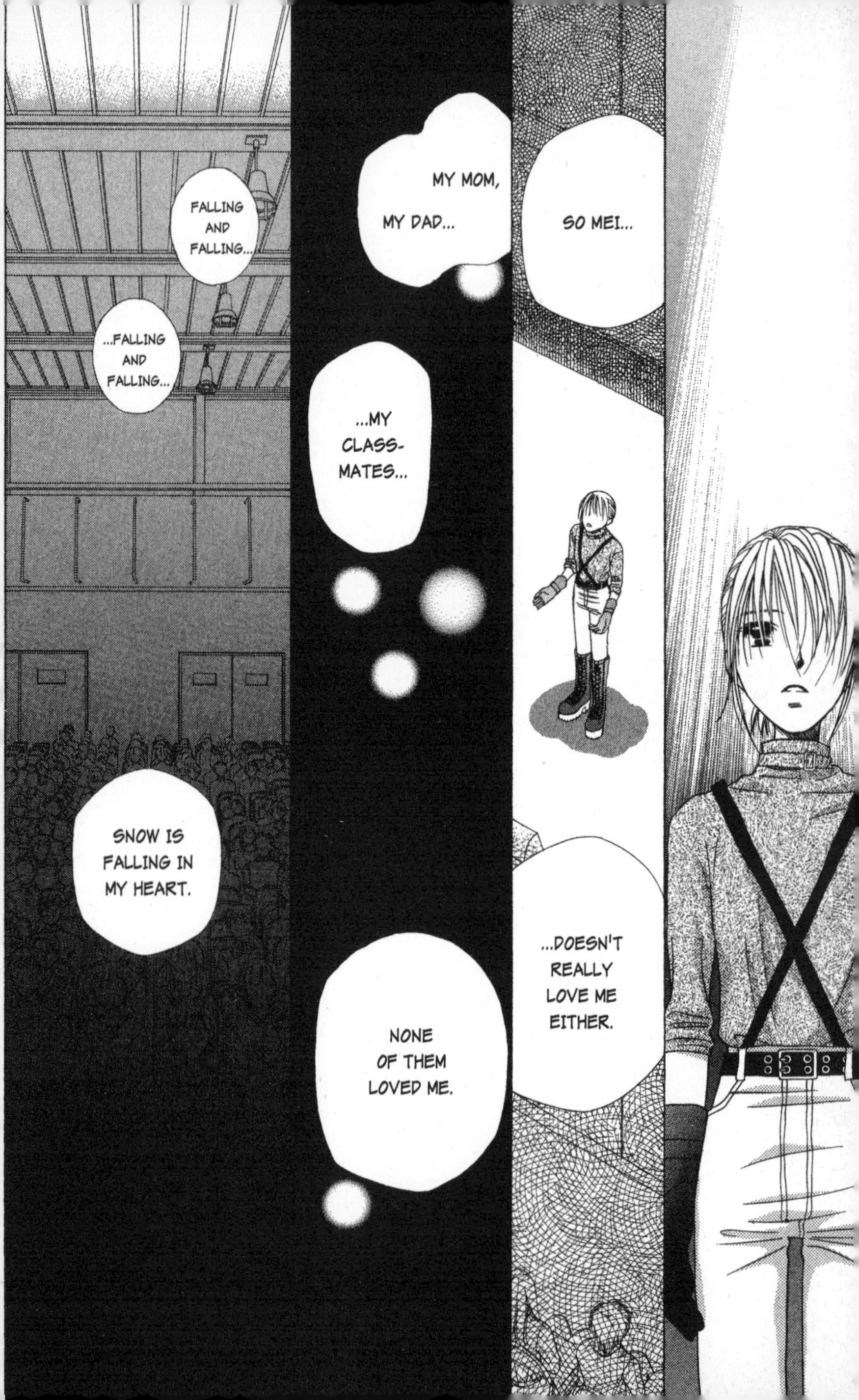
SO MEI...
...DOESN'T REALLY LOVE ME EITHER.
MY MOM,
MY DAD...
...MY CLASS-MATES...
NONE OF THEM LOVED ME.
FALLING AND FALLING...
...FALLING AND FALLING...
SNOW IS FALLING IN MY HEART.

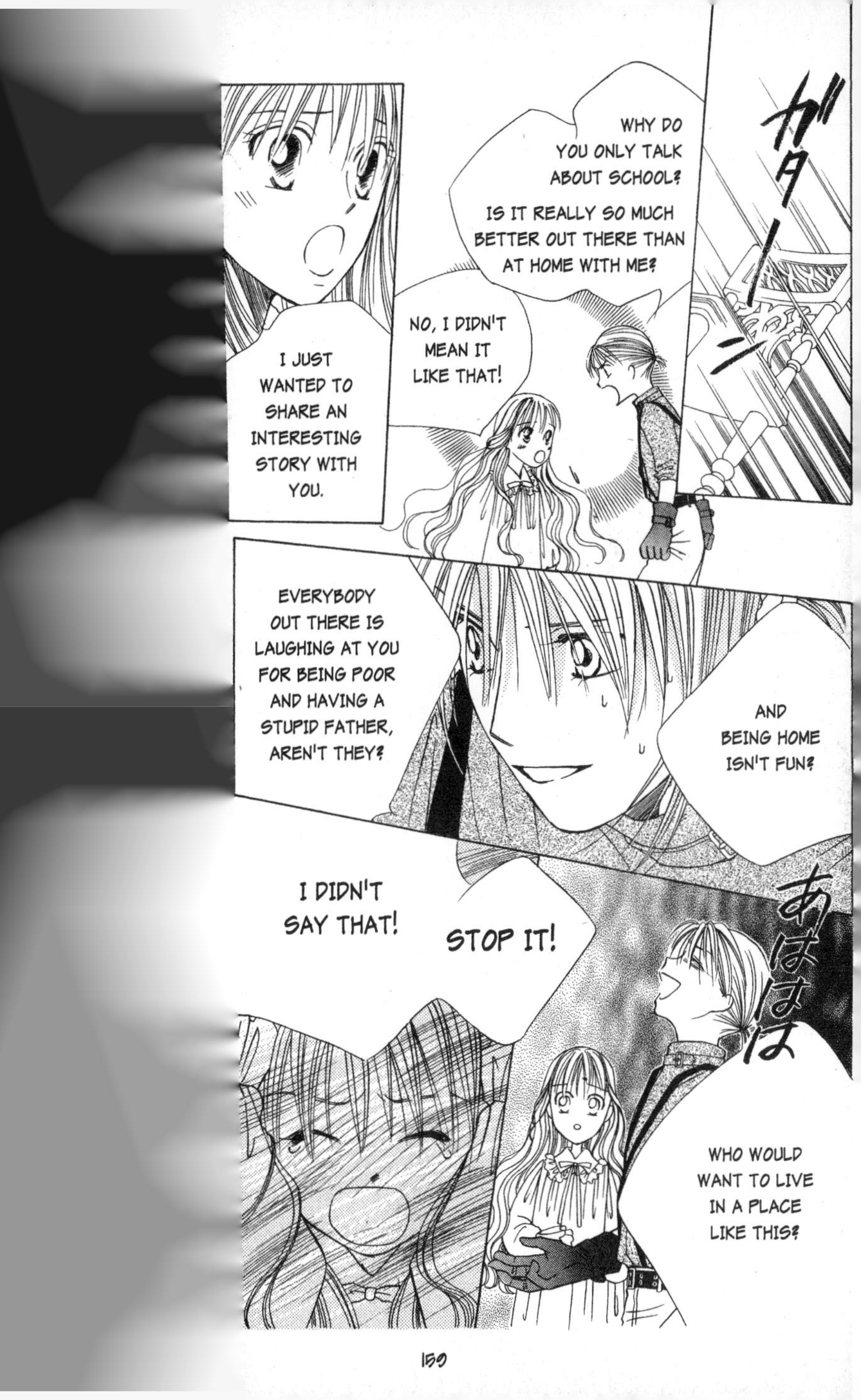
ガターン
WHY DO YOU ONLY TALK ABOUT SCHOOL?
IS IT REALLY SO MUCH BETTER OUT THERE THAN AT HOME WITH ME?
NO, I DIDN'T MEAN IT LIKE THAT!
I JUST WANTED TO SHARE AN INTERESTING STORY WITH YOU.
AND BEING HOME ISN'T FUN?
EVERYBODY OUT THERE IS LAUGHING AT YOU FOR BEING POOR AND HAVING A STUPID FATHER, AREN'T THEY?
あははは
WHO WOULD WANT TO LIVE IN A PLACE LIKE THIS?
STOP IT!
I DIDN'T SAY THAT!

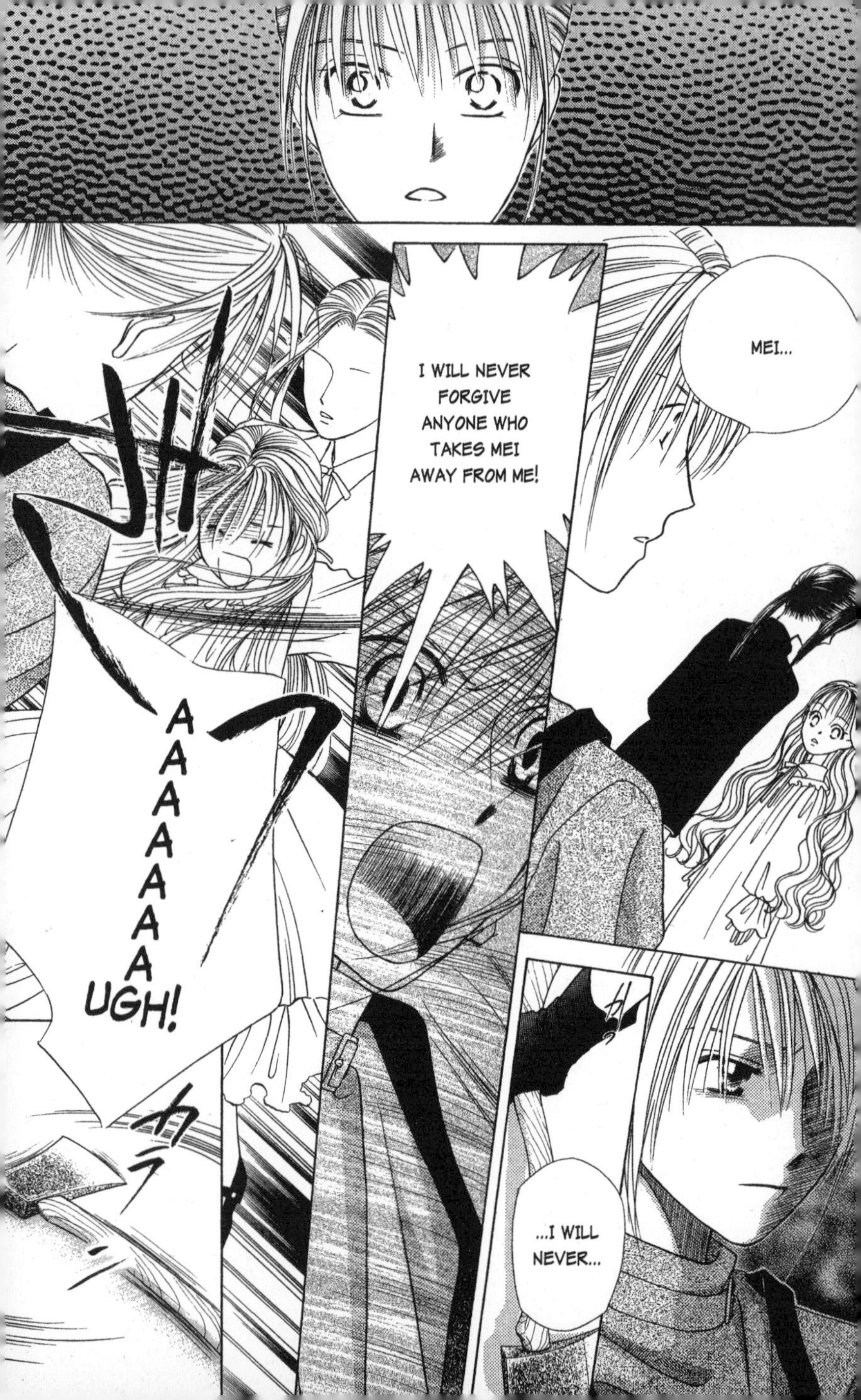
MEI...
I WILL NEVER FORGIVE ANYONE WHO TAKES MEI AWAY FROM ME!
AAAAAAAUGH!
...I WILL NEVER...
カラ

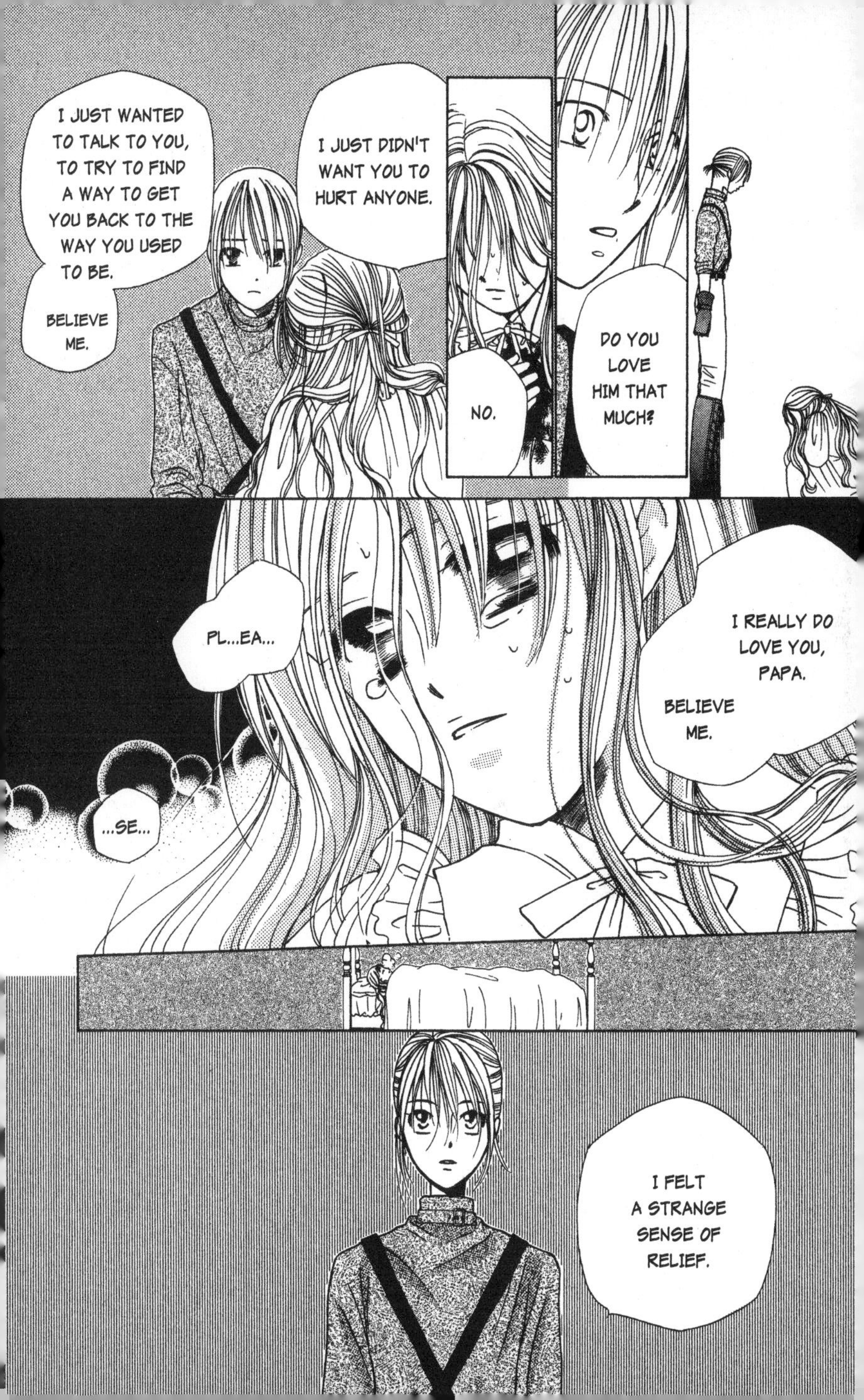
DO YOU LOVE HIM THAT MUCH?
NO.
I JUST DIDN'T WANT YOU TO HURT ANYONE.
I JUST WANTED TO TALK TO YOU, TO TRY TO FIND A WAY TO GET YOU BACK TO THE WAY YOU USED TO BE.
BELIEVE ME.
I REALLY DO LOVE YOU, PAPA.
BELIEVE ME.
PL...EA...
...SE...
I FELT A STRANGE SENSE OF RELIEF.

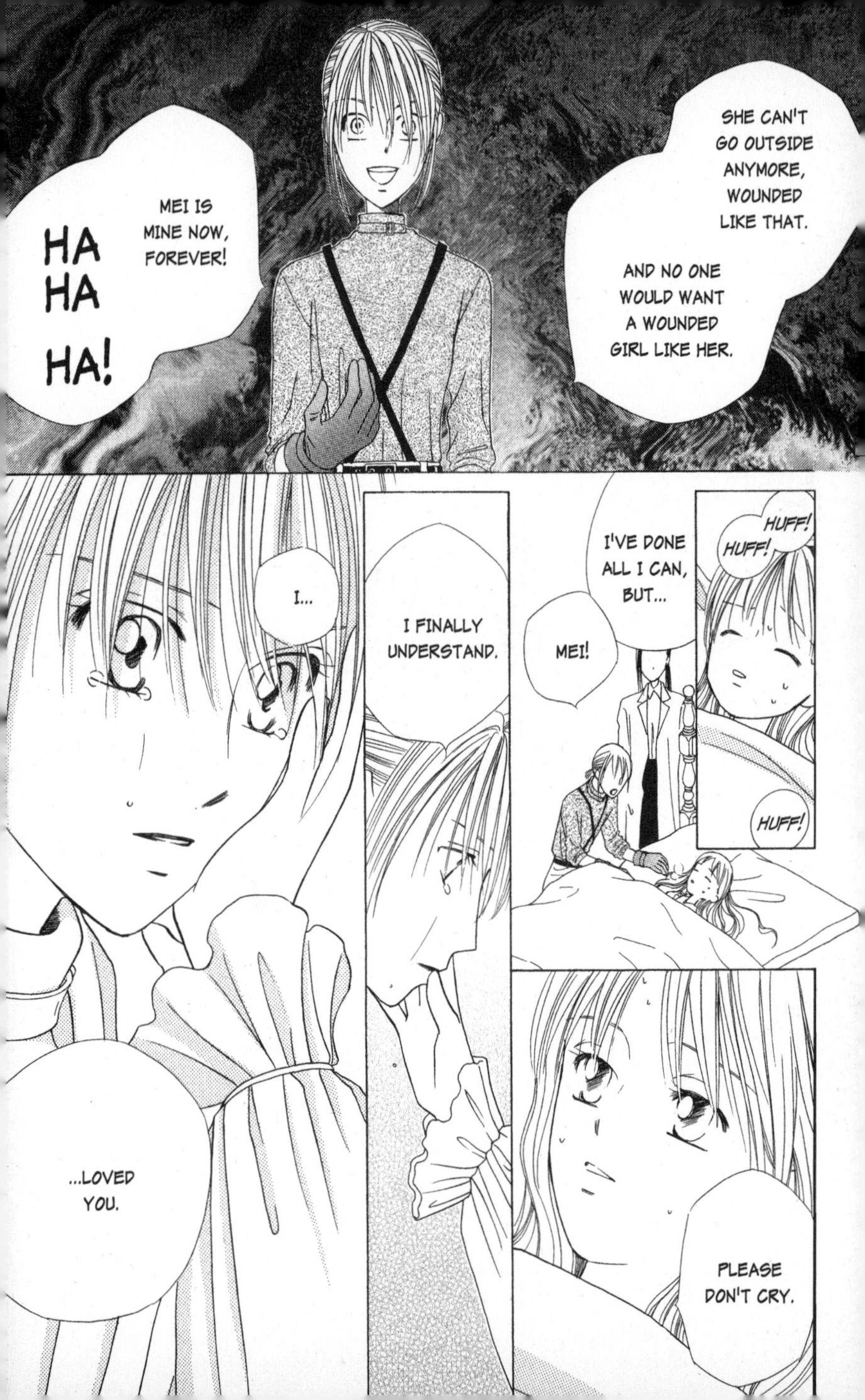
SHE CAN'T GO OUTSIDE ANYMORE, WOUNDED LIKE THAT.
AND NO ONE WOULD WANT A WOUNDED GIRL LIKE HER.
MEI IS MINE NOW, FOREVER!
HA HA HA!
HUFF! HUFF!
HUFF!
I'VE DONE ALL I CAN, BUT...
MEI!
PLEASE DON'T CRY.
I FINALLY UNDERSTAND.
I...
...LOVED YOU.

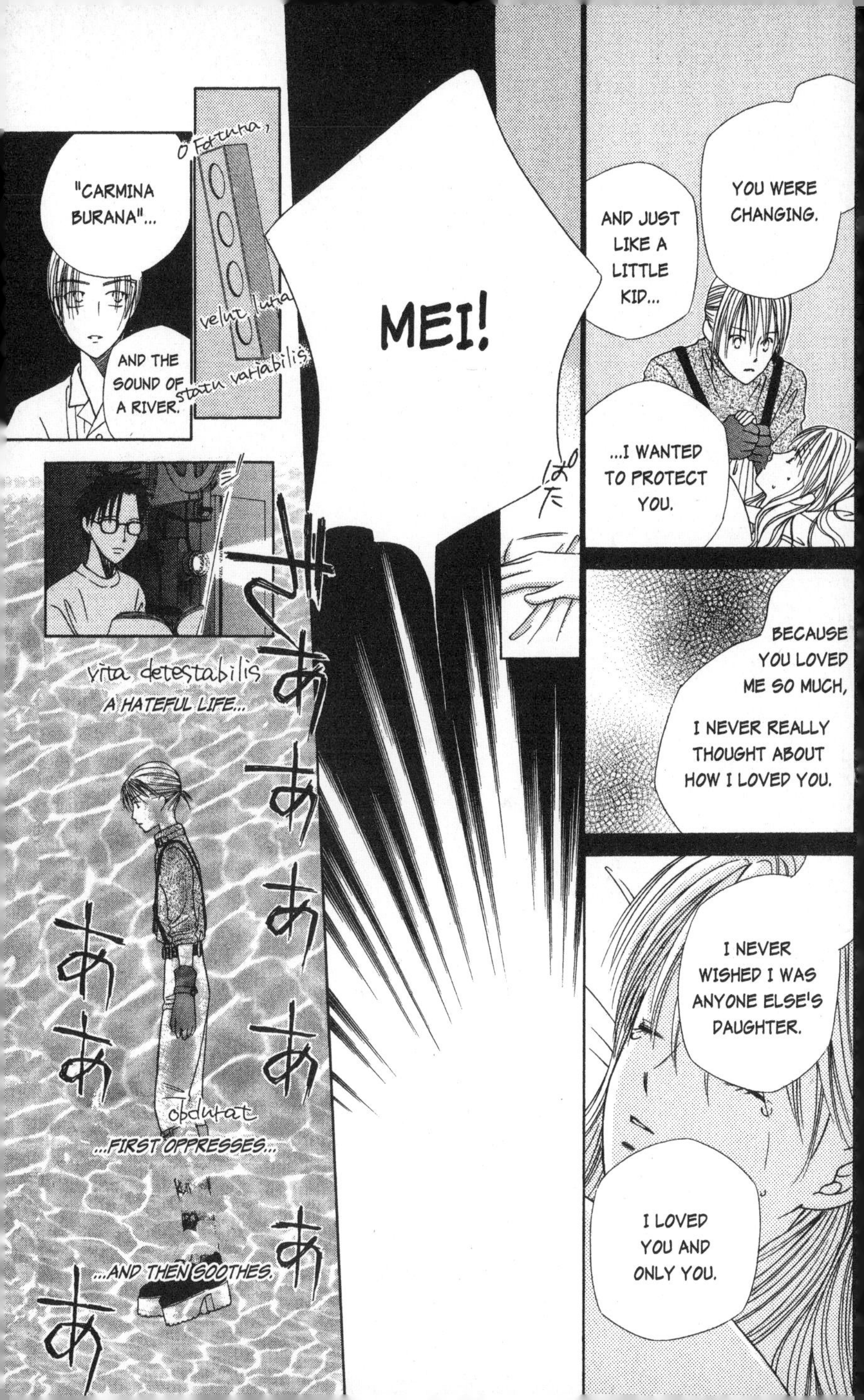

YOU WERE CHANGING.
AND JUST LIKE A LITTLE KID...
...I WANTED TO PROTECT YOU.
BECAUSE YOU LOVED ME SO MUCH,
I NEVER REALLY THOUGHT ABOUT HOW I LOVED YOU.
I NEVER WISHED I WAS ANYONE ELSE'S DAUGHTER.
I LOVED YOU AND ONLY YOU.
MEI!
ぱた
"CARMINA BURANA"...
O Fortuna,
velut luna
statu variabilis
AND THE SOUND OF A RIVER.
ざあああああ
ああああ
vita detestabilis
A HATEFUL LIFE...
obdurat
...FIRST OPPRESSES...
...AND THEN SOOTHES.

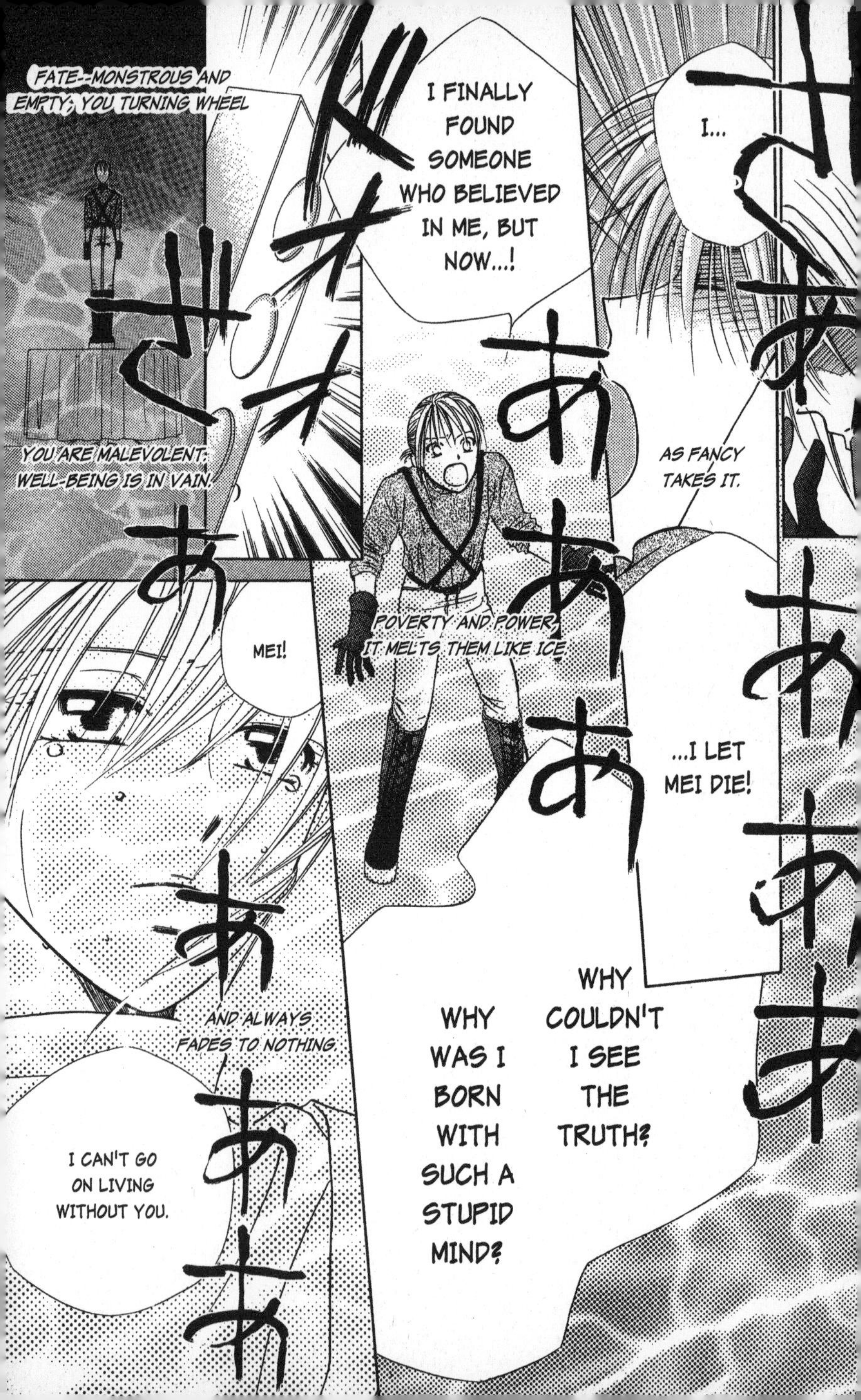

I...
AS FANCY TAKES IT.
I FINALLY FOUND SOMEONE WHO BELIEVED IN ME, BUT NOW...!
FATE--MONSTROUS AND EMPTY; YOU TURNING WHEEL
YOU ARE MALEVOLENT; WELL-BEING IS IN VAIN.
...I LET MEI DIE!
POVERTY AND POWER, IT MELTS THEM LIKE ICE.
WHY COULDN'T I SEE THE TRUTH?
WHY WAS I BORN WITH SUCH A STUPID MIND?
MEI!
AND ALWAYS FADES TO NOTHING.
I CAN'T GO ON LIVING WITHOUT YOU.

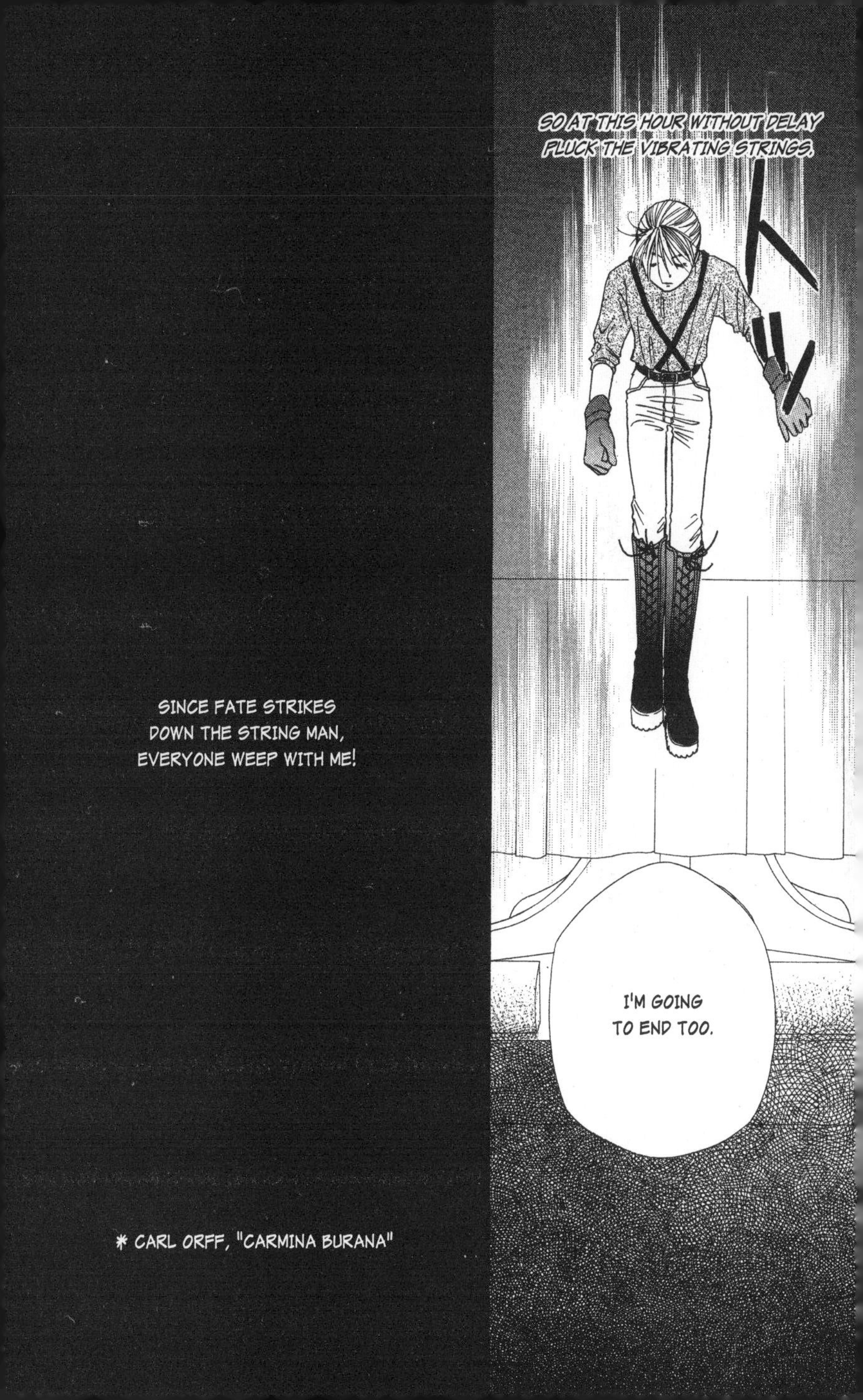
SO AT THIS HOUR WITHOUT DELAY
PLUCK THE VIBRATING STRINGS.
I'M GOING TO END TOO.
SINCE FATE STRIKES DOWN THE STRING MAN, EVERYONE WEEP WITH ME!

* CARL ORFF, "CARMINA BURANA"

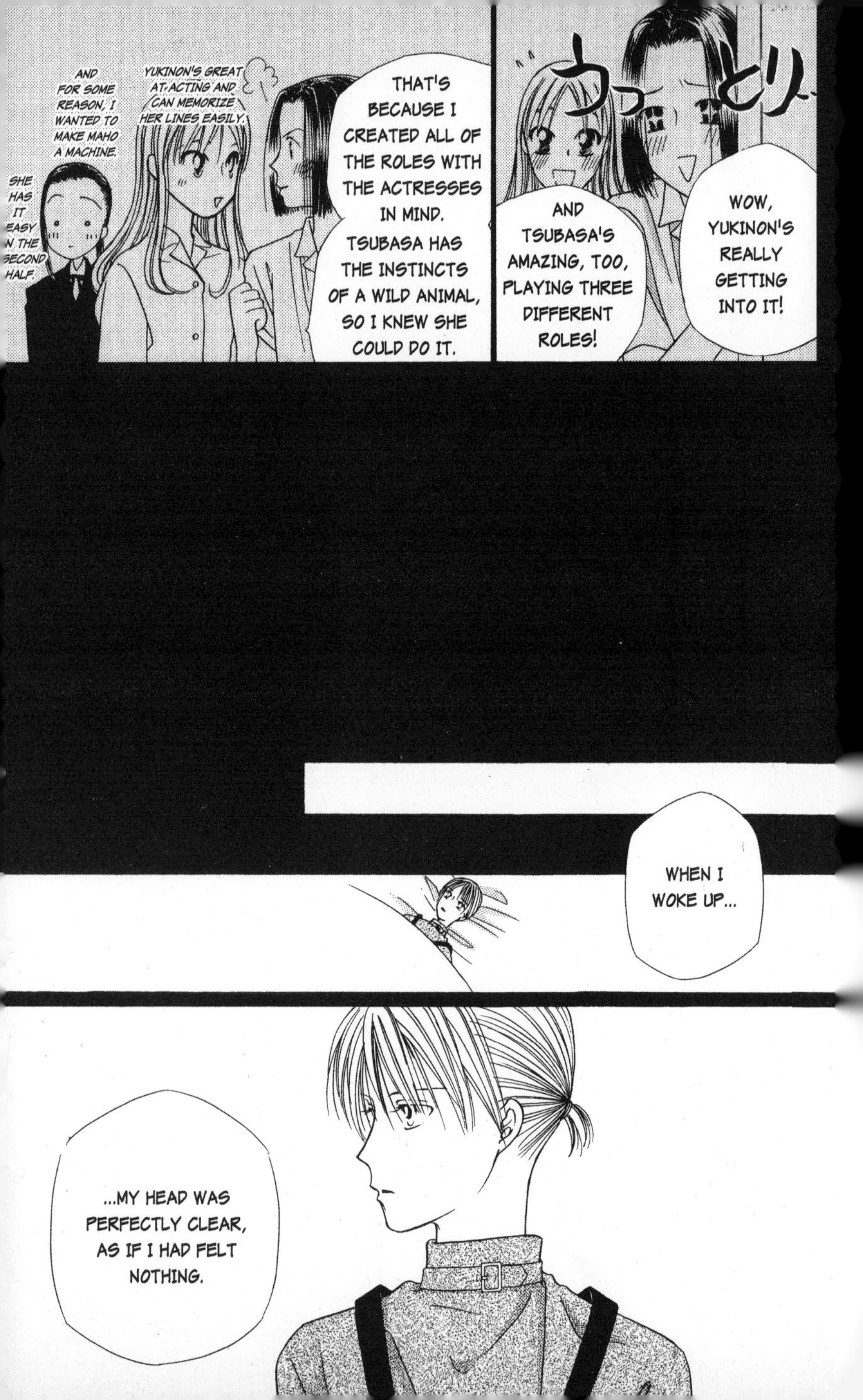
WOW, YUKINON'S REALLY GETTING INTO IT!
AND TSUBASA'S AMAZING, TOO, PLAYING THREE DIFFERENT ROLES!
THAT'S BECAUSE I CREATED ALL OF THE ROLES WITH THE ACTRESSES IN MIND.
TSUBASA HAS THE INSTINCTS OF A WILD ANIMAL, SO I KNEW SHE COULD DO IT.
YUKINON'S GREAT AT ACTING AND CAN MEMORIZE HER LINES EASILY.
AND FOR SOME REASON, I WANTED TO MAKE MAHO A MACHINE.
SHE HAS IT EASY IN THE SECOND HALF.
WHEN I WOKE UP...
...MY HEAD WAS PERFECTLY CLEAR, AS IF I HAD FELT NOTHING.

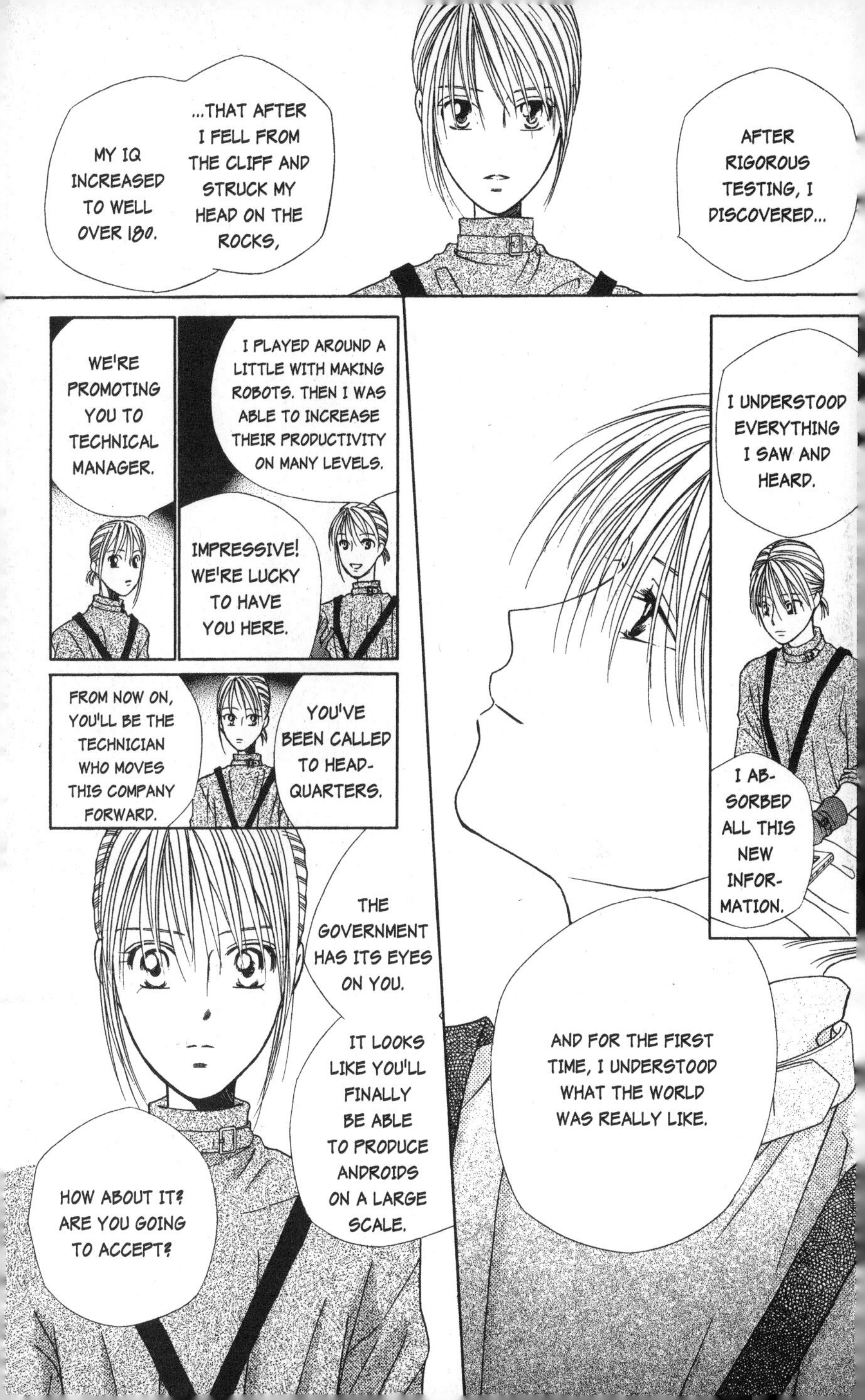
AFTER RIGOROUS TESTING, I DISCOVERED...
...THAT AFTER I FELL FROM THE CLIFF AND STRUCK MY HEAD ON THE ROCKS,
MY IQ INCREASED TO WELL OVER 180.
I UNDERSTOOD EVERYTHING I SAW AND HEARD.
I ABSORBED ALL THIS NEW INFORMATION.
AND FOR THE FIRST TIME, I UNDERSTOOD WHAT THE WORLD WAS REALLY LIKE.
I PLAYED AROUND A LITTLE WITH MAKING ROBOTS. THEN I WAS ABLE TO INCREASE THEIR PRODUCTIVITY ON MANY LEVELS.
IMPRESSIVE! WE'RE LUCKY TO HAVE YOU HERE.
WE'RE PROMOTING YOU TO TECHNICAL MANAGER.
YOU'VE BEEN CALLED TO HEAD-QUARTERS.
FROM NOW ON, YOU'LL BE THE TECHNICIAN WHO MOVES THIS COMPANY FORWARD.
THE GOVERNMENT HAS ITS EYES ON YOU.
IT LOOKS LIKE YOU'LL FINALLY BE ABLE TO PRODUCE ANDROIDS ON A LARGE SCALE.
HOW ABOUT IT? ARE YOU GOING TO ACCEPT?

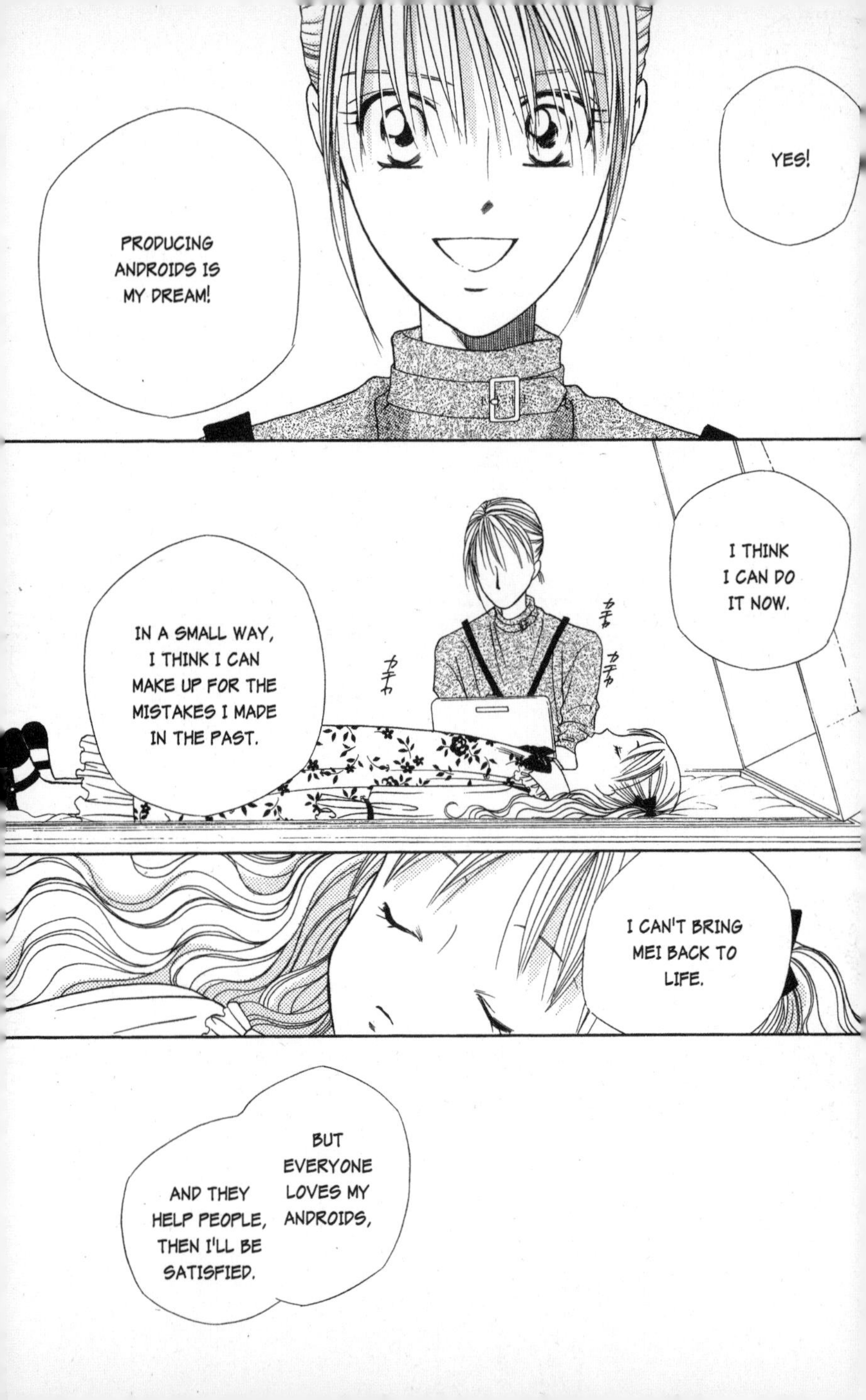
YES!
PRODUCING ANDROIDS IS MY DREAM!
I THINK I CAN DO IT NOW.
IN A SMALL WAY, I THINK I CAN MAKE UP FOR THE MISTAKES I MADE IN THE PAST.
I CAN'T BRING MEI BACK TO LIFE.
BUT EVERYONE LOVES MY ANDROIDS,
AND THEY HELP PEOPLE, THEN I'LL BE SATISFIED.

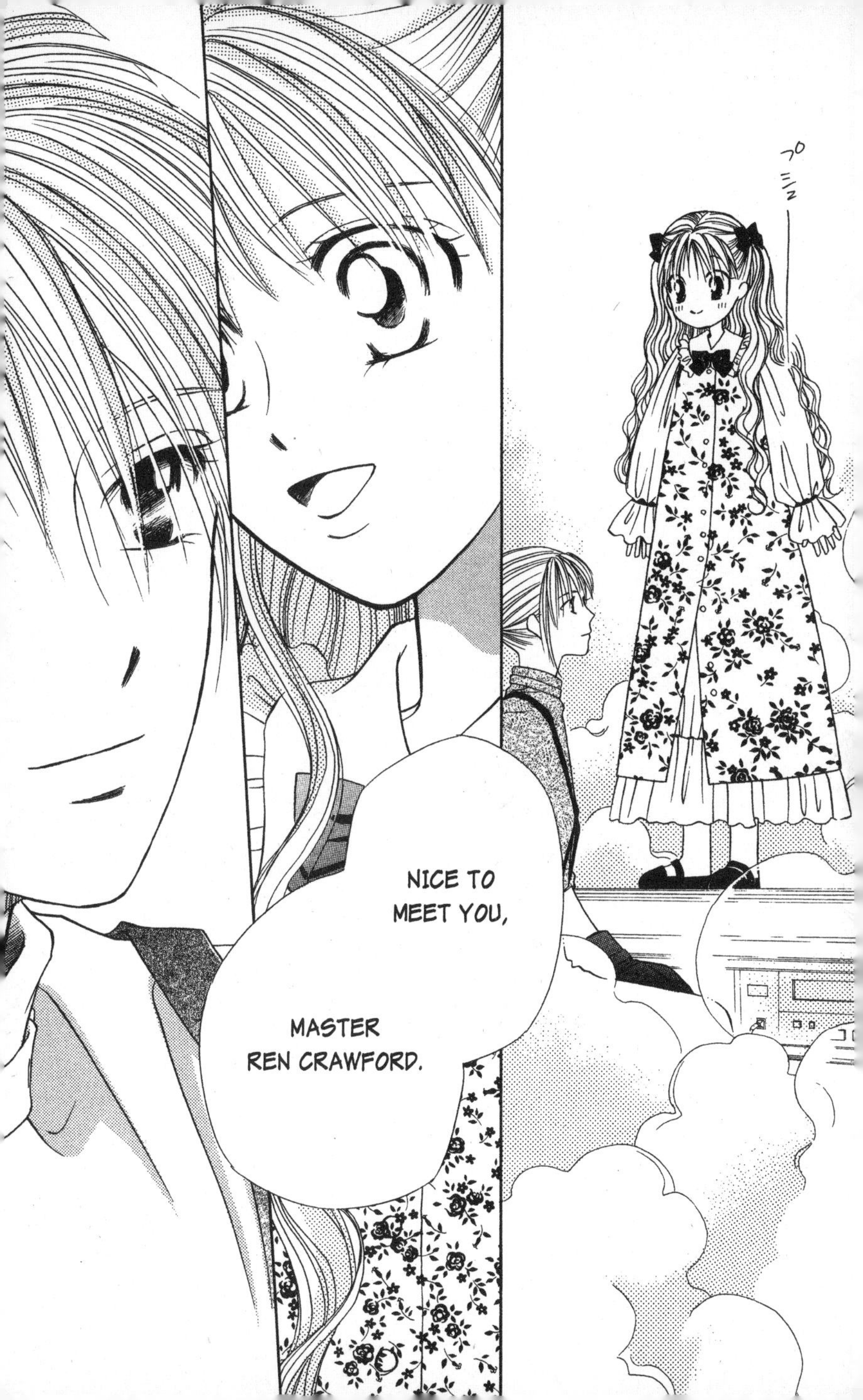
NICE TO MEET YOU,
MASTER REN CRAWFORD.

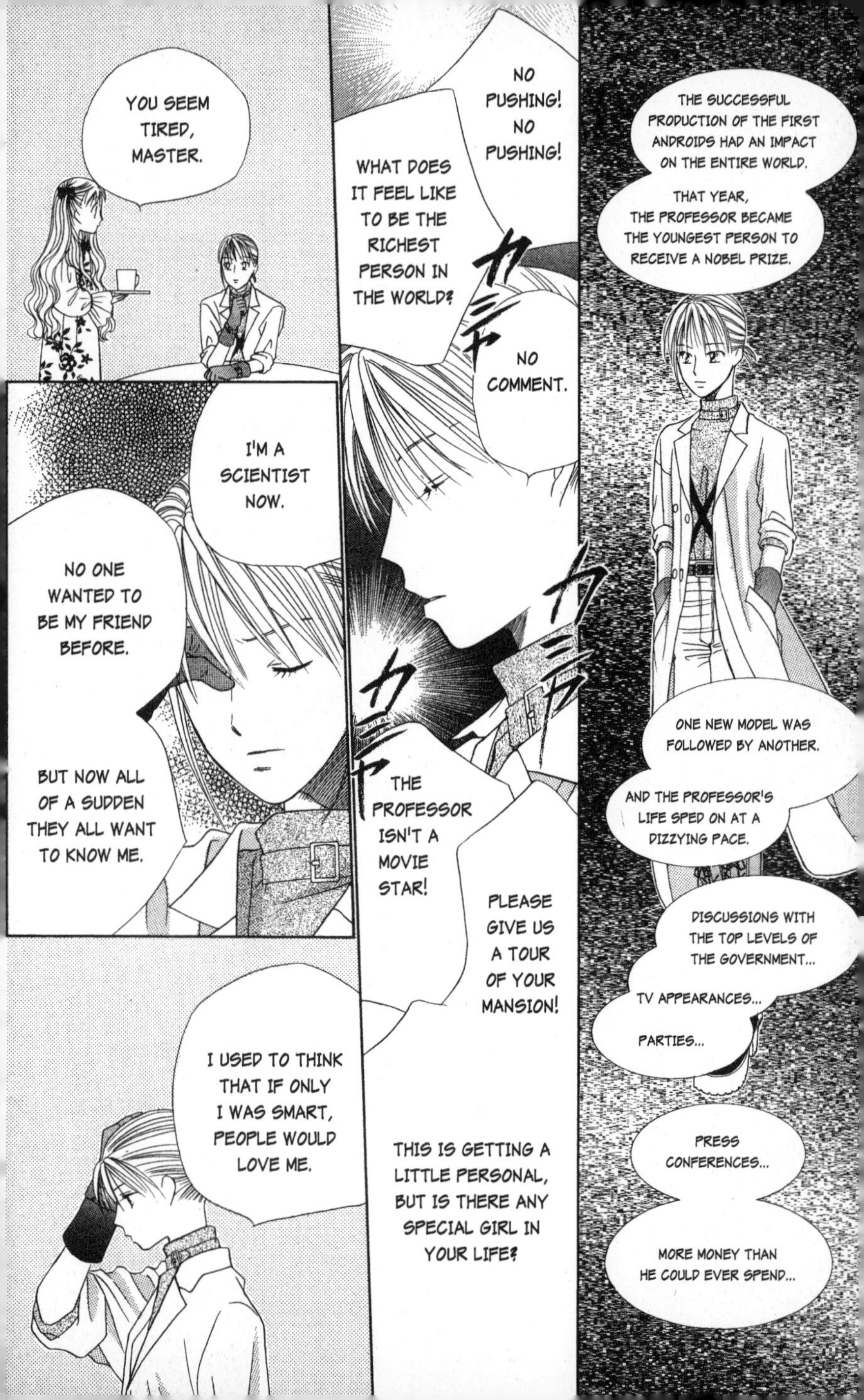
THE SUCCESSFUL PRODUCTION OF THE FIRST ANDROIDS HAD AN IMPACT ON THE ENTIRE WORLD.
THAT YEAR, THE PROFESSOR BECAME THE YOUNGEST PERSON TO RECEIVE A NOBEL PRIZE.
ONE NEW MODEL WAS FOLLOWED BY ANOTHER.
AND THE PROFESSOR'S LIFE SPED ON AT A DIZZYING PACE.
DISCUSSIONS WITH THE TOP LEVELS OF THE GOVERNMENT...
TV APPEARANCES...
PARTIES...
PRESS CONFERENCES...
MORE MONEY THAN HE COULD EVER SPEND...
NO PUSHING! NO PUSHING!
WHAT DOES IT FEEL LIKE TO BE THE RICHEST PERSON IN THE WORLD?
カシャ
NO COMMENT.
カシャ
カシャ
THE PROFESSOR ISN'T A MOVIE STAR!
PLEASE GIVE US A TOUR OF YOUR MANSION!
THIS IS GETTING A LITTLE PERSONAL, BUT IS THERE ANY SPECIAL GIRL IN YOUR LIFE?
YOU SEEM TIRED, MASTER.
I'M A SCIENTIST NOW.
NO ONE WANTED TO BE MY FRIEND BEFORE.
BUT NOW ALL OF A SUDDEN THEY ALL WANT TO KNOW ME.
I USED TO THINK THAT IF ONLY I WAS SMART, PEOPLE WOULD LOVE ME.

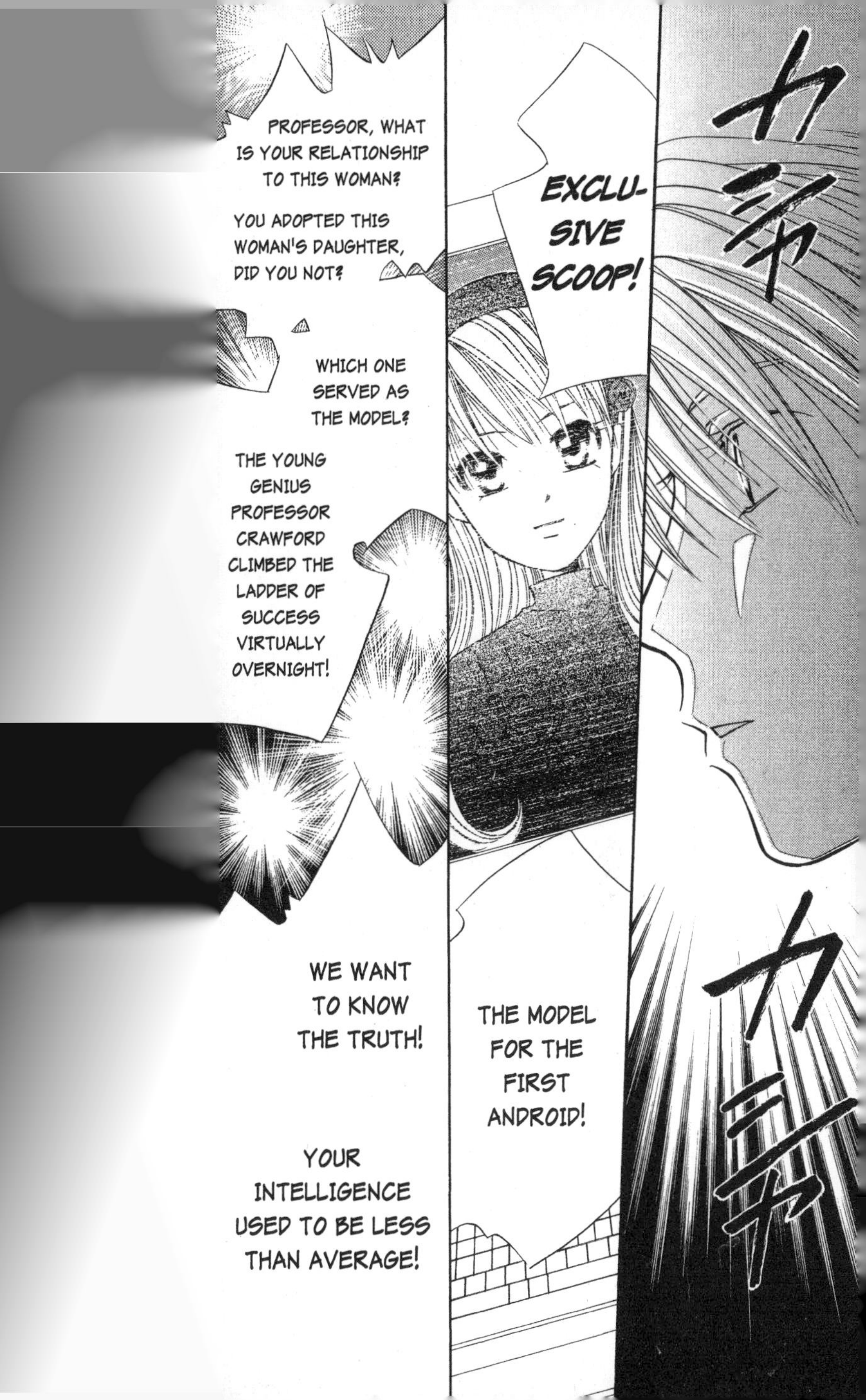

カシャ
カシャ
EXCLU-SIVE SCOOP!
THE MODEL FOR THE FIRST ANDROID!
PROFESSOR, WHAT IS YOUR RELATIONSHIP TO THIS WOMAN?
YOU ADOPTED THIS WOMAN'S DAUGHTER, DID YOU NOT?
WHICH ONE SERVED AS THE MODEL?
THE YOUNG GENIUS PROFESSOR CRAWFORD CLIMBED THE LADDER OF SUCCESS VIRTUALLY OVERNIGHT!
WE WANT TO KNOW THE TRUTH!
YOUR INTELLIGENCE USED TO BE LESS THAN AVERAGE!

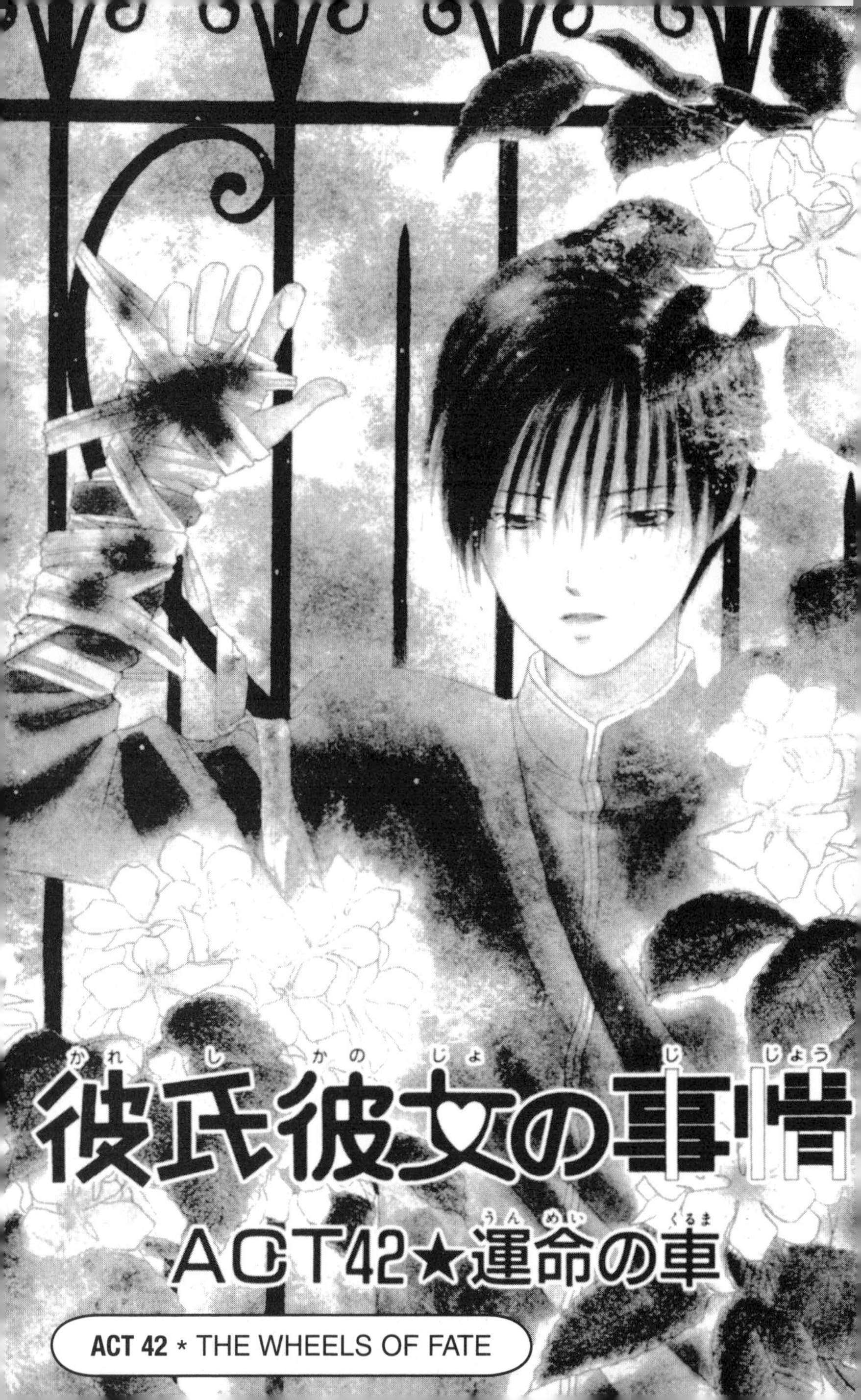
彼氏彼女の事情
ACT42★運命の車
ACT 42 * THE WHEELS OF FATE

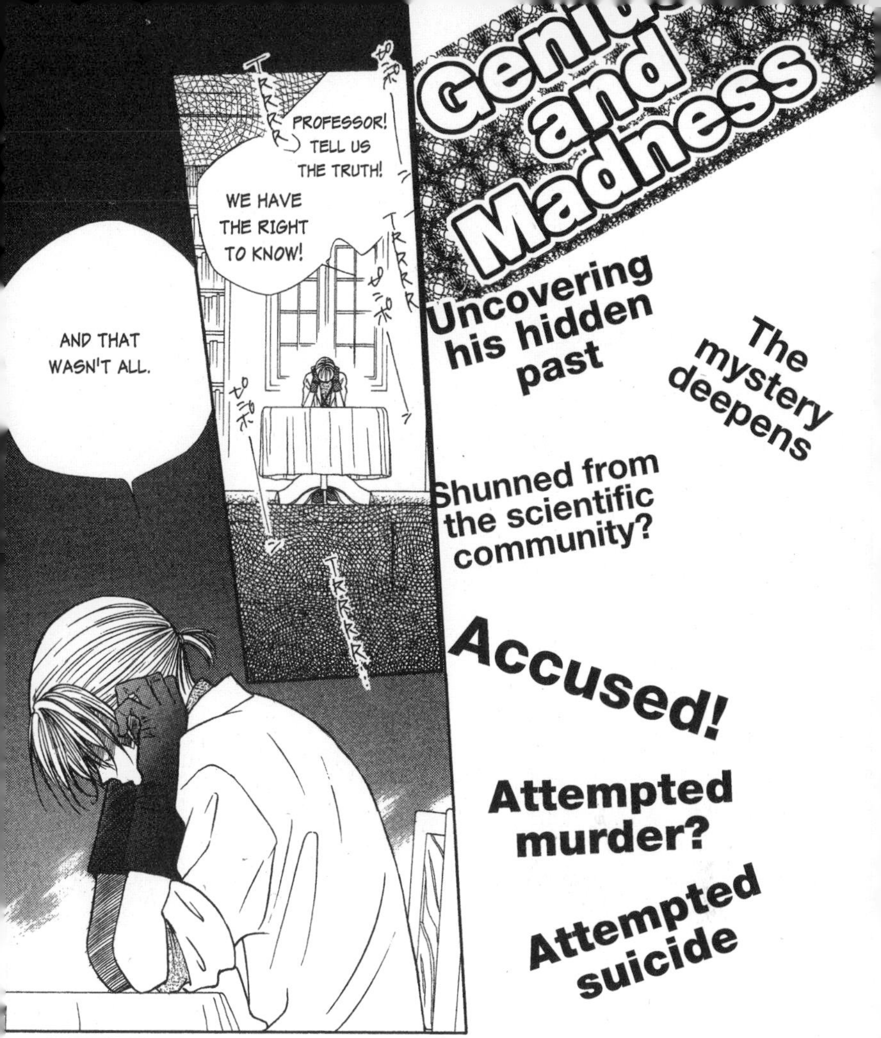
PROFESSOR! TELL US THE TRUTH!
WE HAVE THE RIGHT TO KNOW!
TRRRR
AND THAT WASN'T ALL.
Geni
and
Madness
Uncovering his hidden past
The mystery deepens
Shunned from the scientific community?
Accused!
Attempted murder?
Attempted suicide

About the music used in "Steel Snow"...

The first song used in the play came from "Gianni Schicchi," an opera with music composed by Giacomo Puccini. The song is called "O Mio Babbino Caro" or "Oh, My Beloved Father" in English.

The second song was "O Fortuna" from "Carmina Burana," by Carl Orff. And then there's a song from the group called Enigma. It's one of my favorites.

They're all very famous songs, so if you hear them, it's like, "Hey, I recognize that song!"

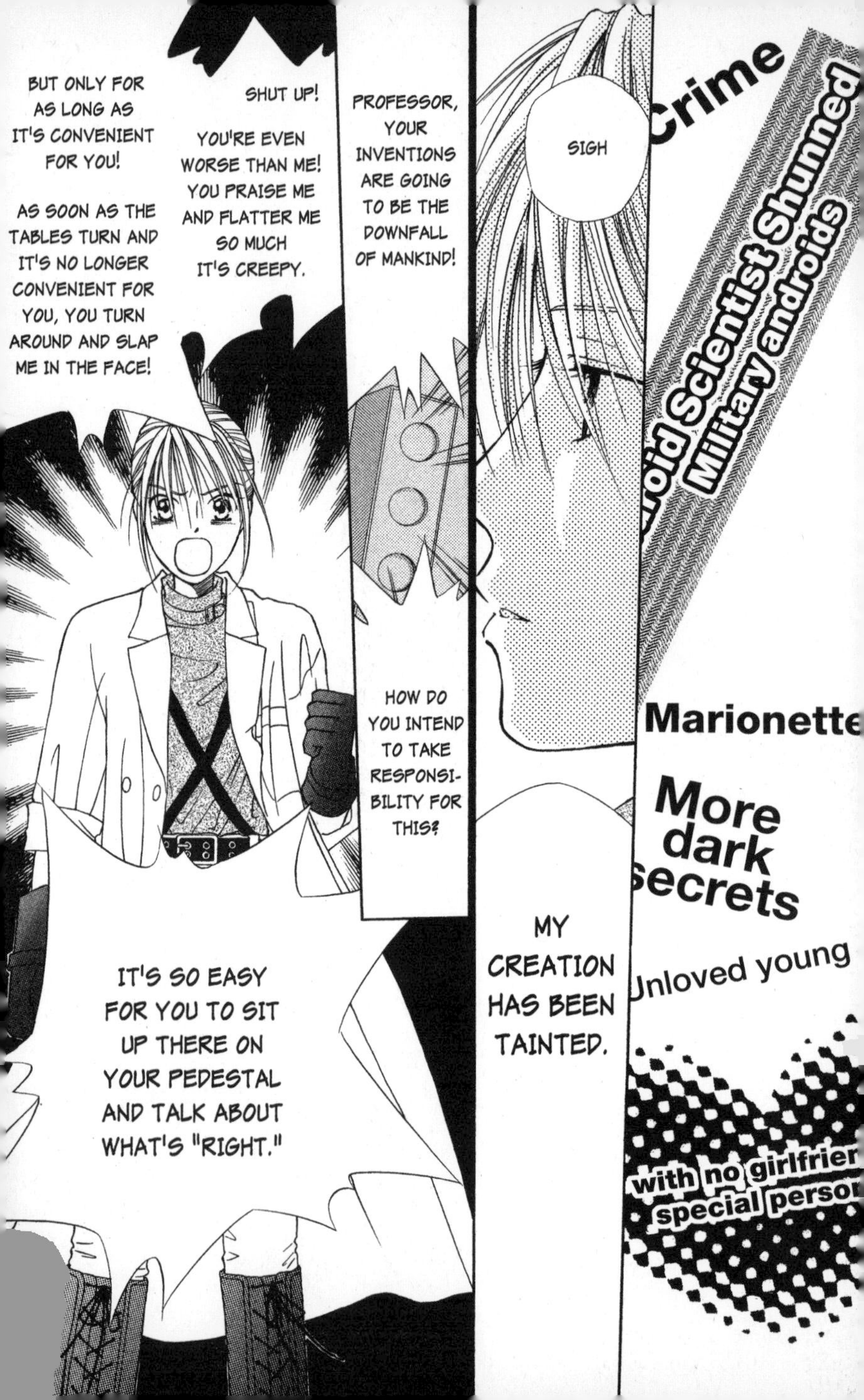
Crime
Scientist Shunned
Military androids
SIGH
Marionette
More dark secrets
Unloved young
special person
MY CREATION HAS BEEN TAINTED.
PROFESSOR, YOUR INVENTIONS ARE GOING TO BE THE DOWNFALL OF MANKIND!
HOW DO YOU INTEND TO TAKE RESPONSI-BILITY FOR THIS?
SHUT UP!
YOU'RE EVEN WORSE THAN ME! YOU PRAISE ME AND FLATTER ME SO MUCH IT'S CREEPY.
BUT ONLY FOR AS LONG AS IT'S CONVENIENT FOR YOU!
AS SOON AS THE TABLES TURN AND IT'S NO LONGER CONVENIENT FOR YOU, YOU TURN AROUND AND SLAP ME IN THE FACE!
IT'S SO EASY FOR YOU TO SIT UP THERE ON YOUR PEDESTAL AND TALK ABOUT WHAT'S "RIGHT."

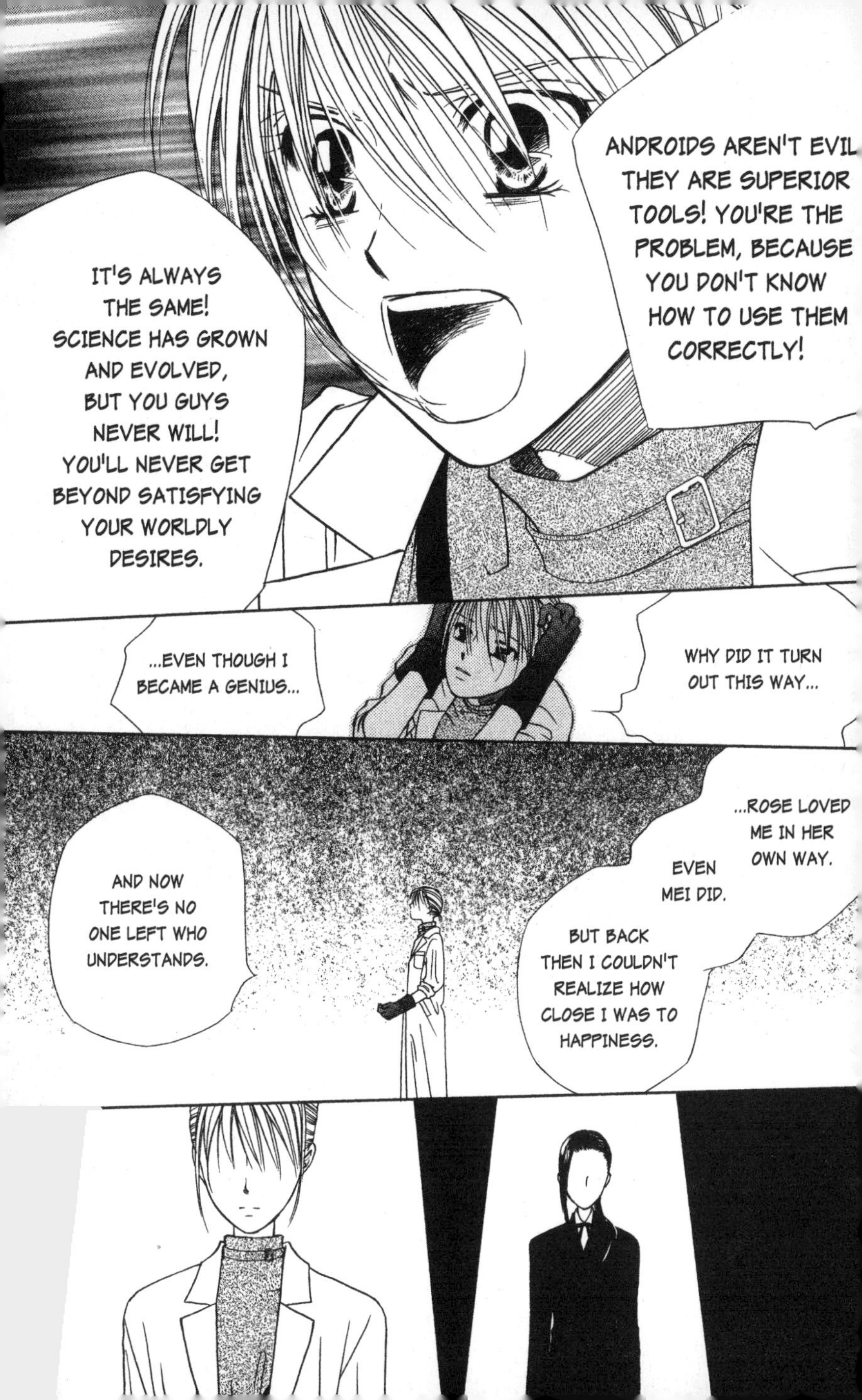
ANDROIDS AREN'T EVIL THEY ARE SUPERIOR TOOLS! YOU'RE THE PROBLEM, BECAUSE YOU DON'T KNOW HOW TO USE THEM CORRECTLY!
IT'S ALWAYS THE SAME! SCIENCE HAS GROWN AND EVOLVED, BUT YOU GUYS NEVER WILL! YOU'LL NEVER GET BEYOND SATISFYING YOUR WORLDLY DESIRES.
WHY DID IT TURN OUT THIS WAY...
...EVEN THOUGH I BECAME A GENIUS...
...ROSE LOVED ME IN HER OWN WAY.
EVEN MEI DID.
BUT BACK THEN I COULDN'T REALIZE HOW CLOSE I WAS TO HAPPINESS.
AND NOW THERE'S NO ONE LEFT WHO UNDERSTANDS.

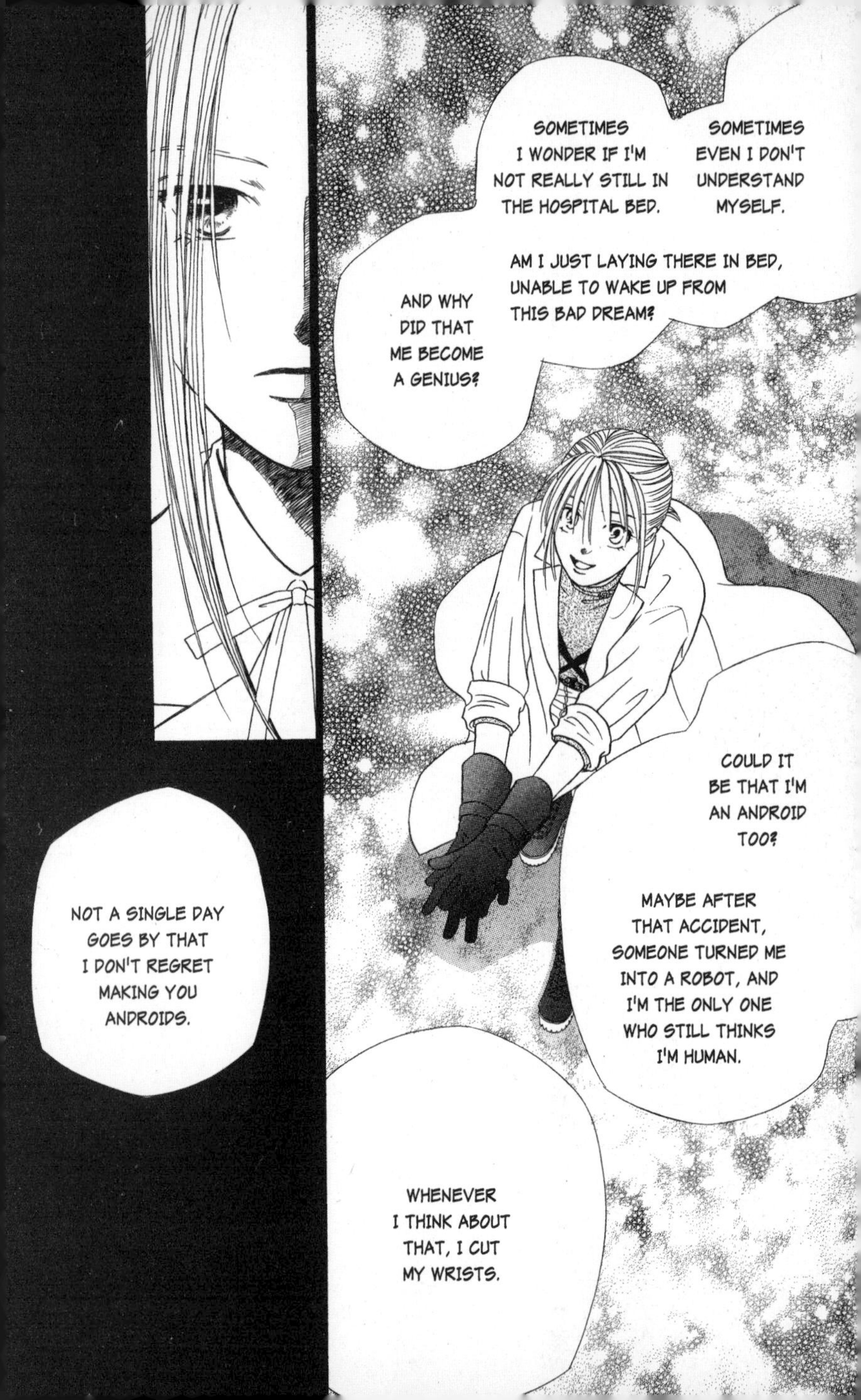
SOMETIMES EVEN I DON'T UNDERSTAND MYSELF.
SOMETIMES I WONDER IF I'M NOT REALLY STILL IN THE HOSPITAL BED.
AM I JUST LAYING THERE IN BED, UNABLE TO WAKE UP FROM THIS BAD DREAM?
AND WHY DID THAT ME BECOME A GENIUS?
COULD IT BE THAT I'M AN ANDROID TOO?
MAYBE AFTER THAT ACCIDENT, SOMEONE TURNED ME INTO A ROBOT, AND I'M THE ONLY ONE WHO STILL THINKS I'M HUMAN.
WHENEVER I THINK ABOUT THAT, I CUT MY WRISTS.
NOT A SINGLE DAY GOES BY THAT I DON'T REGRET MAKING YOU ANDROIDS.

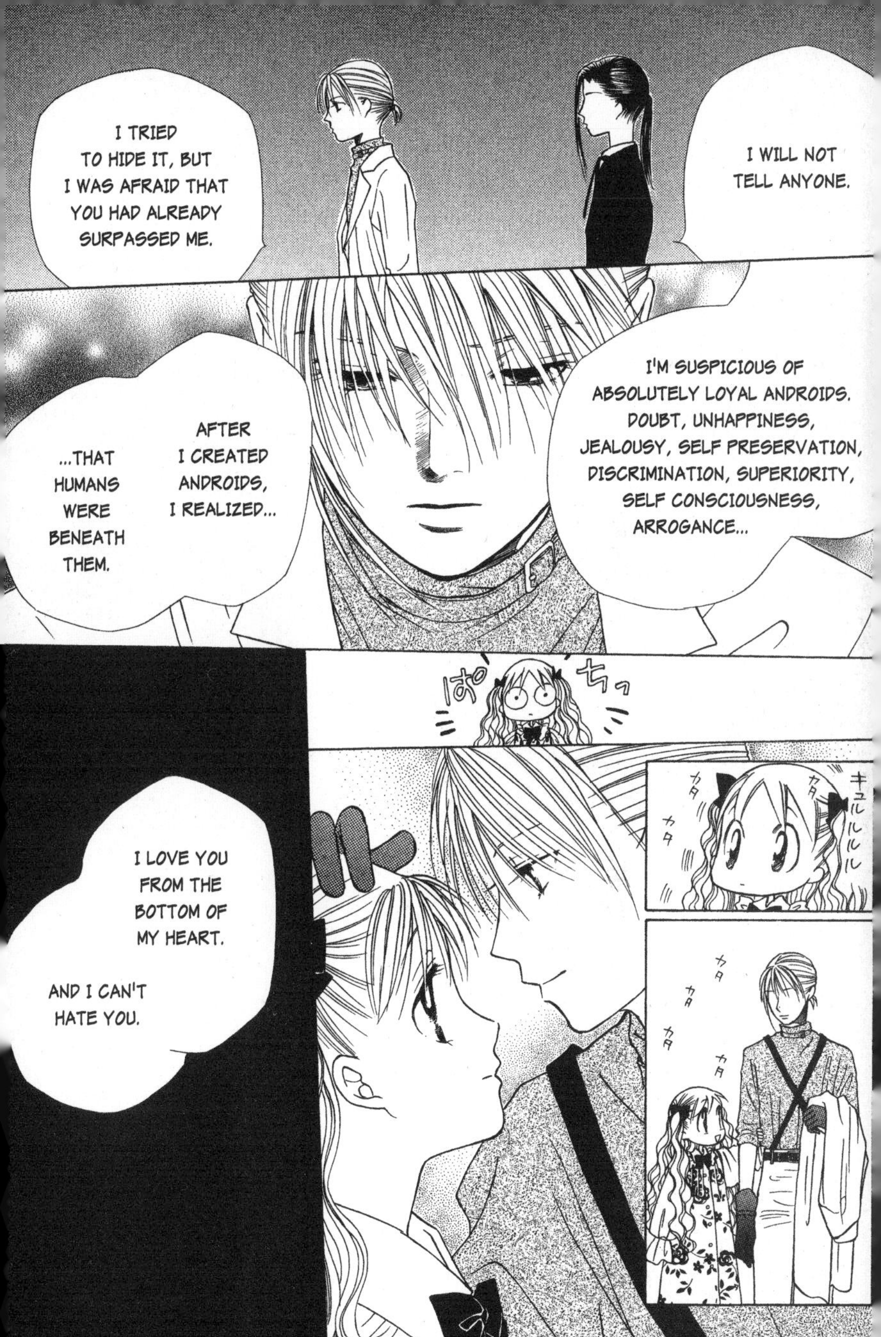
I WILL NOT TELL ANYONE.
I TRIED TO HIDE IT, BUT I WAS AFRAID THAT YOU HAD ALREADY SURPASSED ME.
I'M SUSPICIOUS OF ABSOLUTELY LOYAL ANDROIDS. DOUBT, UNHAPPINESS, JEALOUSY, SELF PRESERVATION, DISCRIMINATION, SUPERIORITY, SELF CONSCIOUSNESS, ARROGANCE...
AFTER I CREATED ANDROIDS, I REALIZED...
...THAT HUMANS WERE BENEATH THEM.
ぱちっ
キュルルル
カタ カタ カタ
I LOVE YOU FROM THE BOTTOM OF MY HEART.
AND I CAN'T HATE YOU.
カタ カタ カタ カタ

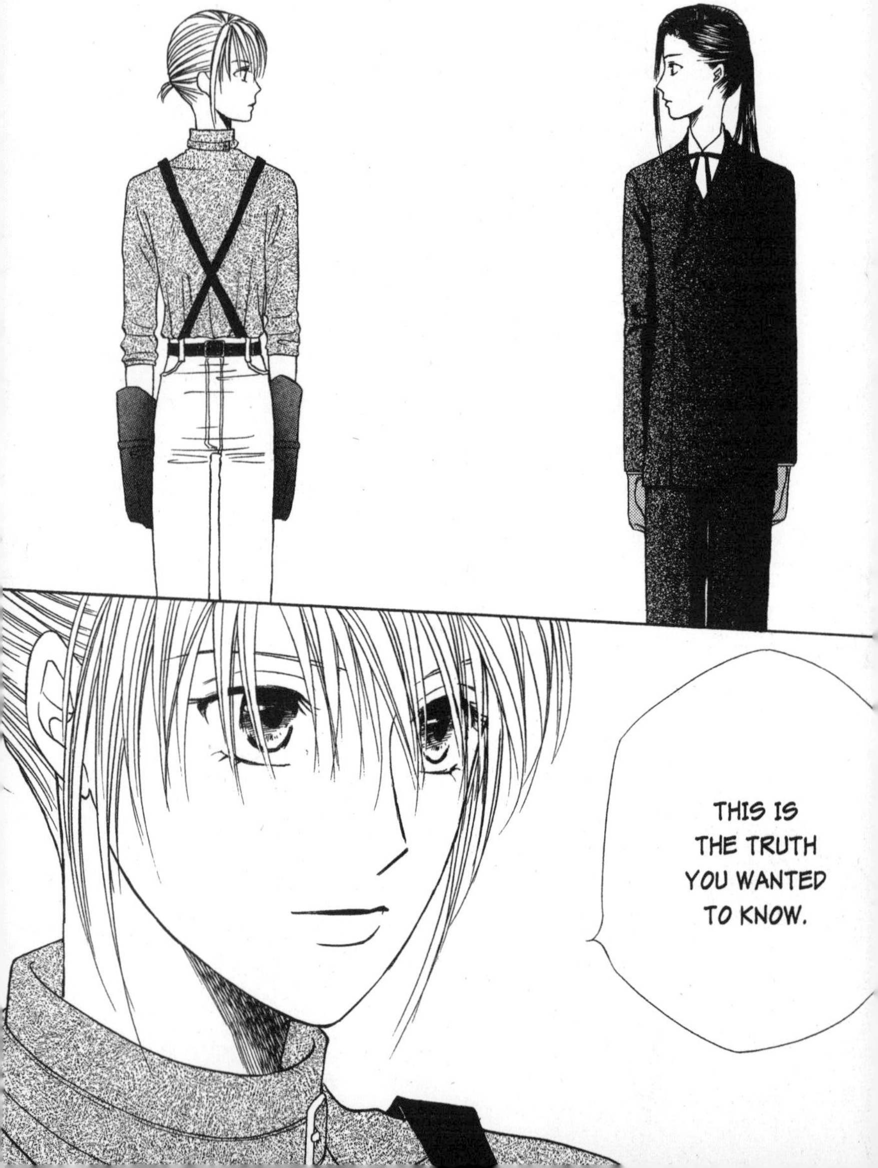
THIS IS THE TRUTH YOU WANTED TO KNOW.

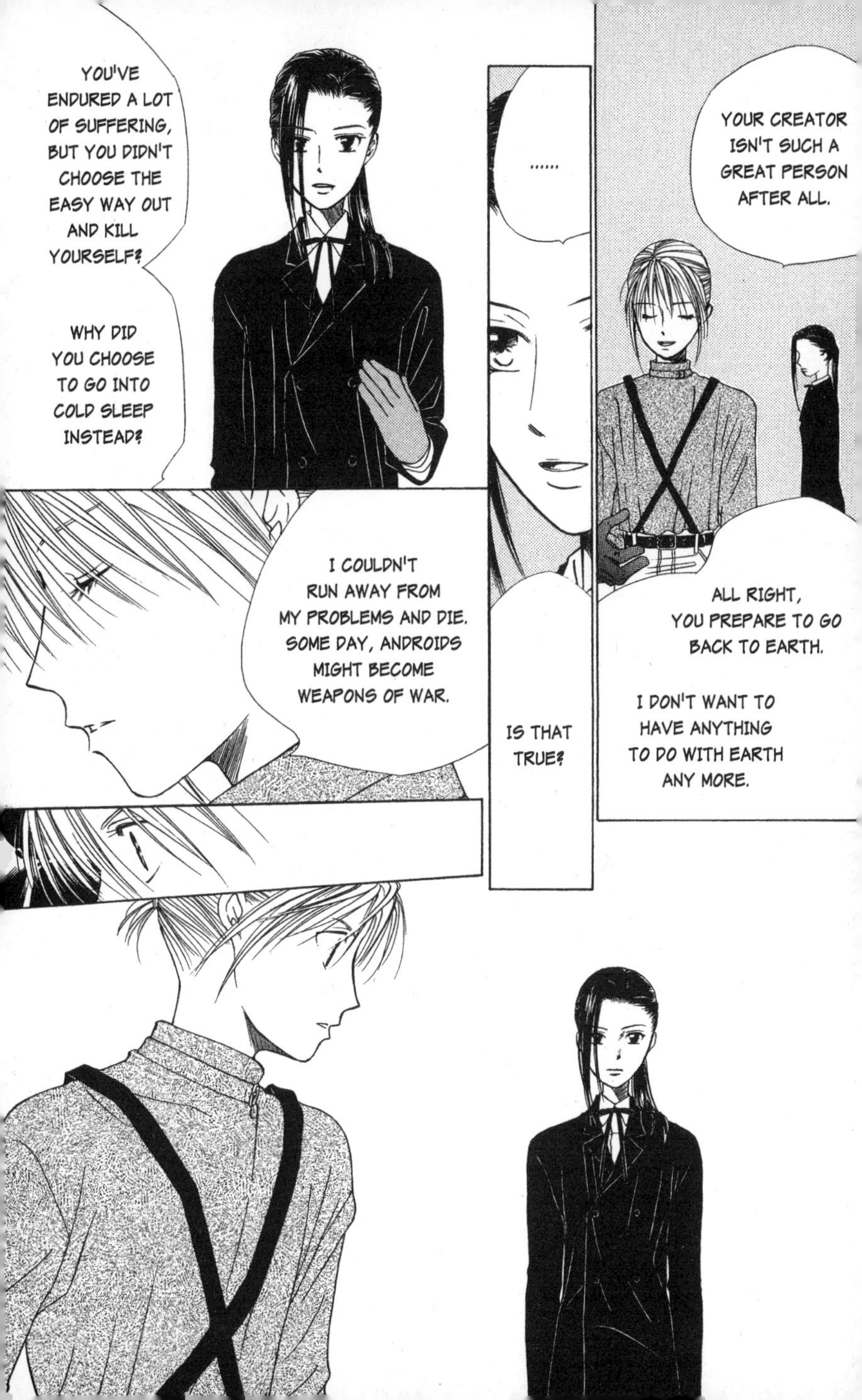
YOUR CREATOR ISN'T SUCH A GREAT PERSON AFTER ALL.
ALL RIGHT, YOU PREPARE TO GO BACK TO EARTH.
I DON'T WANT TO HAVE ANYTHING TO DO WITH EARTH ANY MORE.
......
IS THAT TRUE?
YOU'VE ENDURED A LOT OF SUFFERING, BUT YOU DIDN'T CHOOSE THE EASY WAY OUT AND KILL YOURSELF?
WHY DID YOU CHOOSE TO GO INTO COLD SLEEP INSTEAD?
I COULDN'T RUN AWAY FROM MY PROBLEMS AND DIE. SOME DAY, ANDROIDS MIGHT BECOME WEAPONS OF WAR.

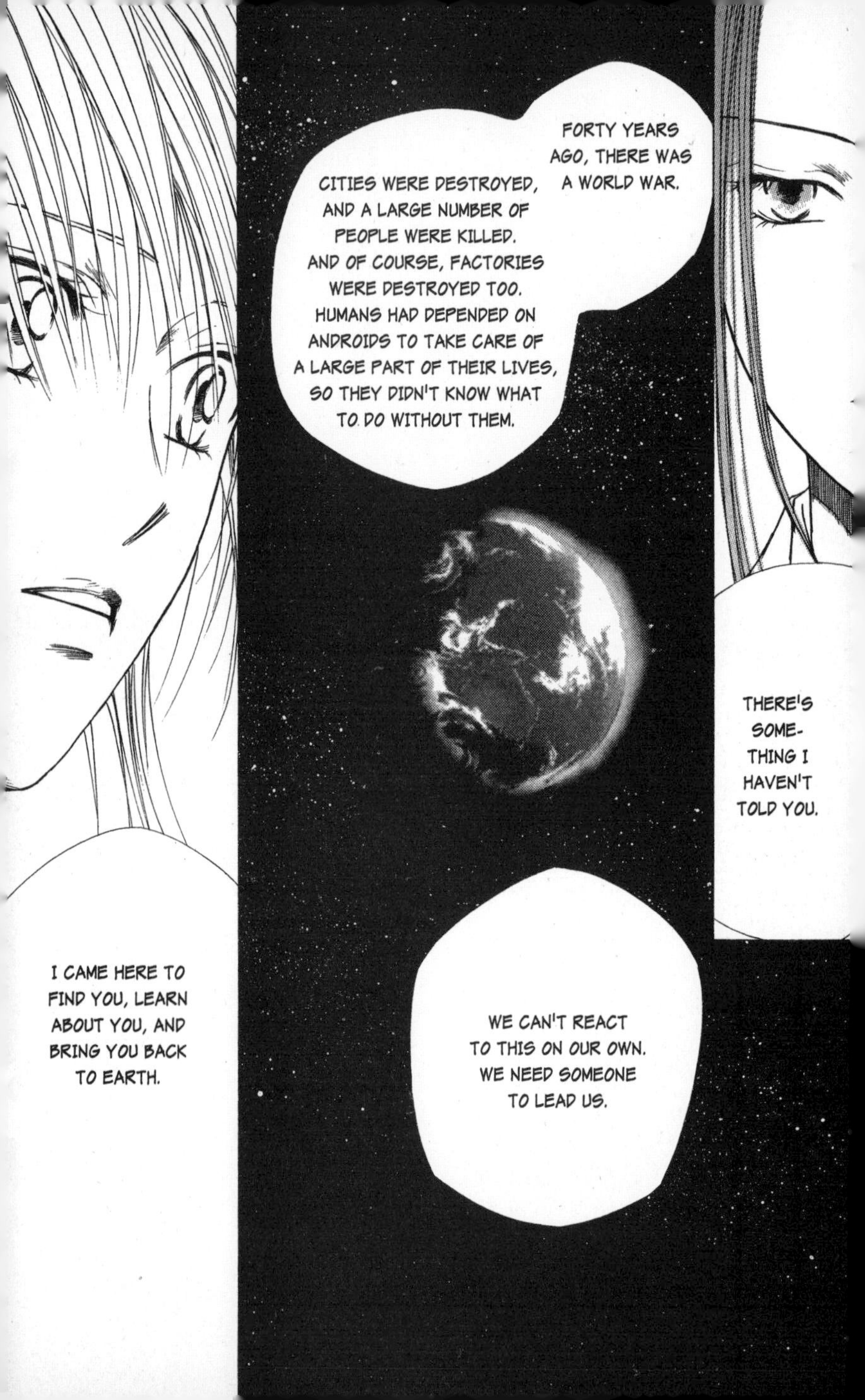
THERE'S SOME-THING I HAVEN'T TOLD YOU.
FORTY YEARS AGO, THERE WAS A WORLD WAR.
CITIES WERE DESTROYED, AND A LARGE NUMBER OF PEOPLE WERE KILLED. AND OF COURSE, FACTORIES WERE DESTROYED TOO. HUMANS HAD DEPENDED ON ANDROIDS TO TAKE CARE OF A LARGE PART OF THEIR LIVES, SO THEY DIDN'T KNOW WHAT TO DO WITHOUT THEM.
WE CAN'T REACT TO THIS ON OUR OWN. WE NEED SOMEONE TO LEAD US.
I CAME HERE TO FIND YOU, LEARN ABOUT YOU, AND BRING YOU BACK TO EARTH.

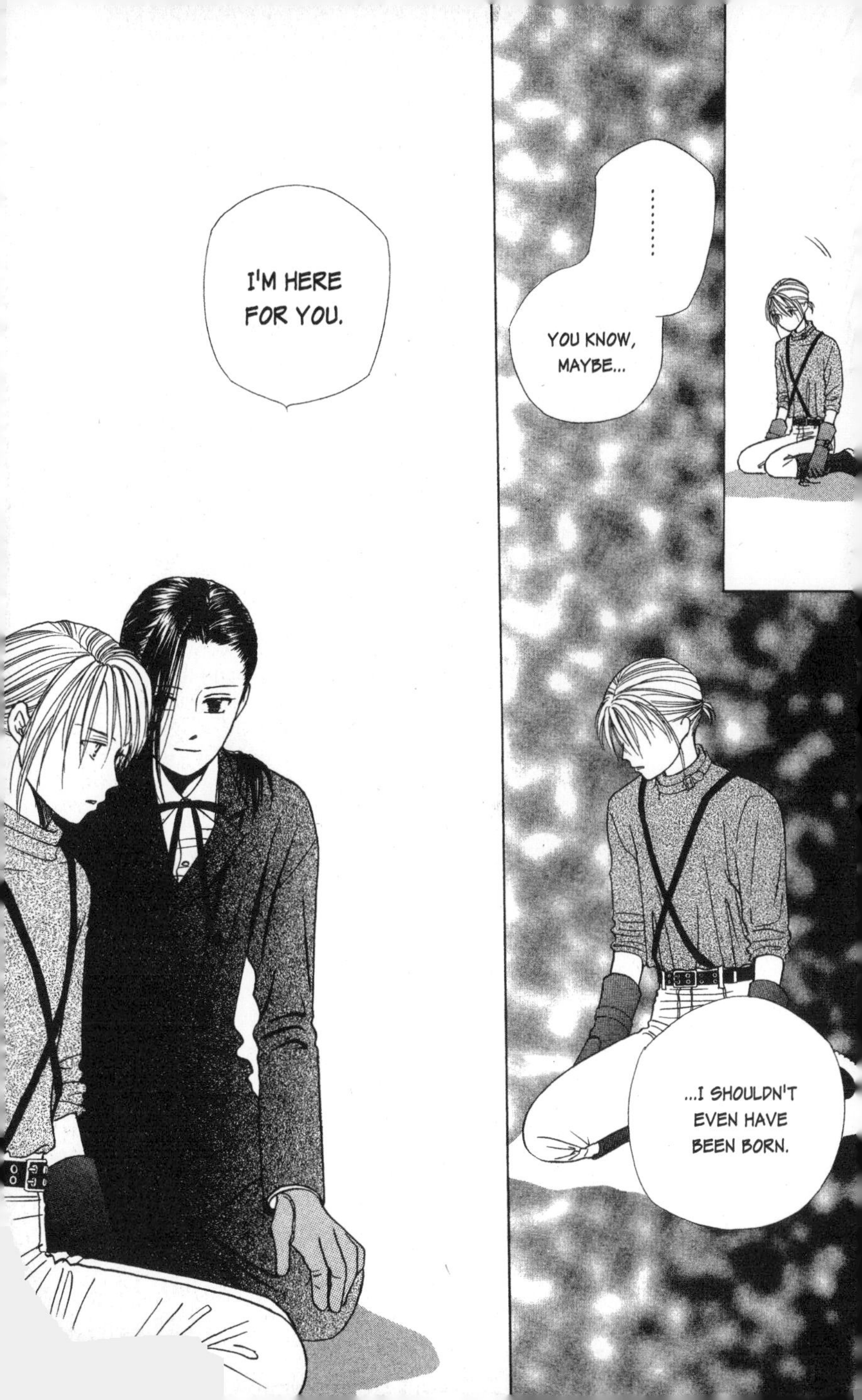
......
YOU KNOW, MAYBE...
...I SHOULDN'T EVEN HAVE BEEN BORN.
I'M HERE FOR YOU.

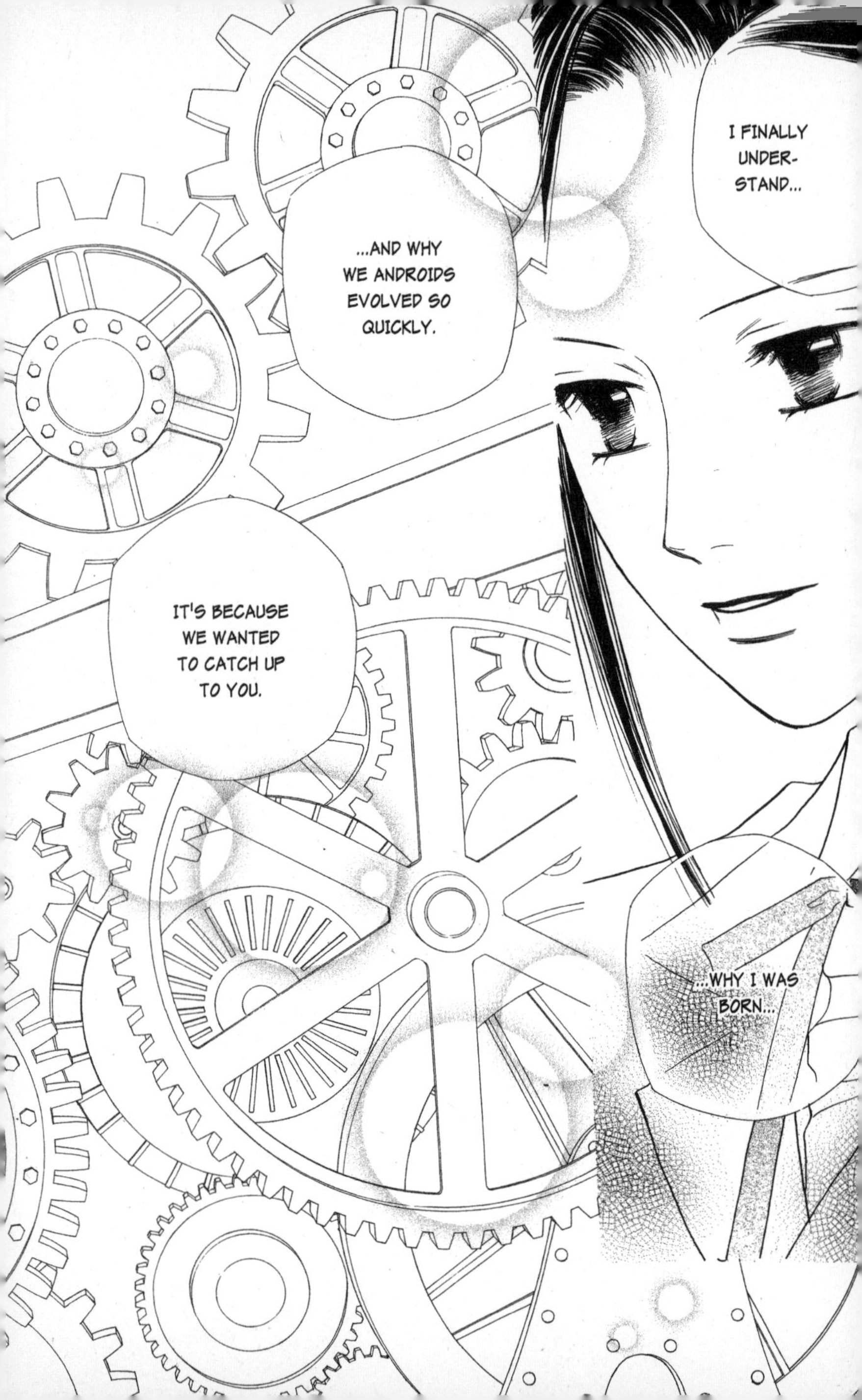
I FINALLY UNDER-STAND...
...AND WHY WE ANDROIDS EVOLVED SO QUICKLY.
IT'S BECAUSE WE WANTED TO CATCH UP TO YOU.
...WHY I WAS BORN...

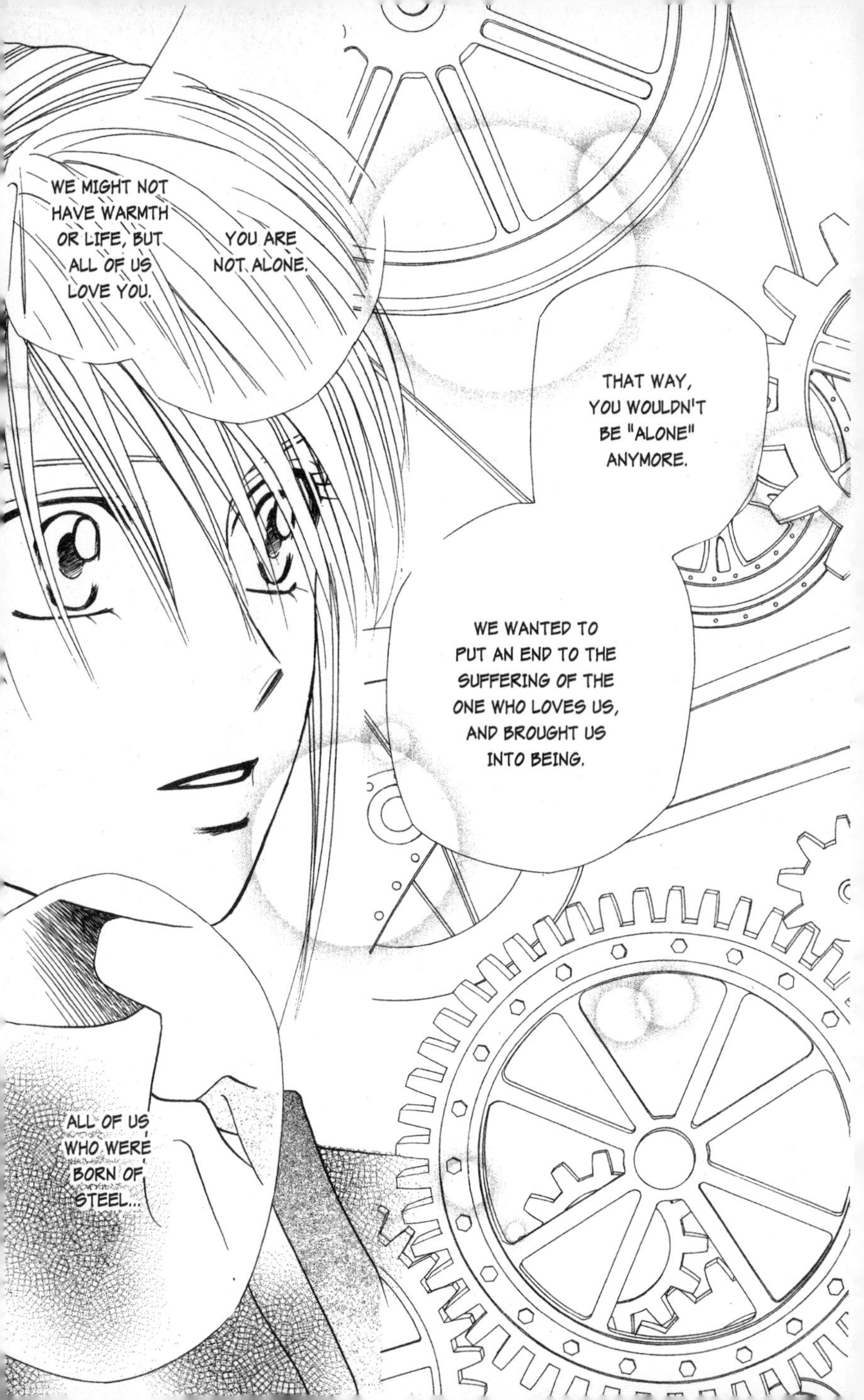
YOU ARE NOT ALONE.
WE MIGHT NOT HAVE WARMTH OR LIFE, BUT ALL OF US LOVE YOU.
THAT WAY, YOU WOULDN'T BE "ALONE" ANYMORE.
WE WANTED TO PUT AN END TO THE SUFFERING OF THE ONE WHO LOVES US, AND BROUGHT US INTO BEING.
ALL OF US WHO WERE BORN OF STEEL...

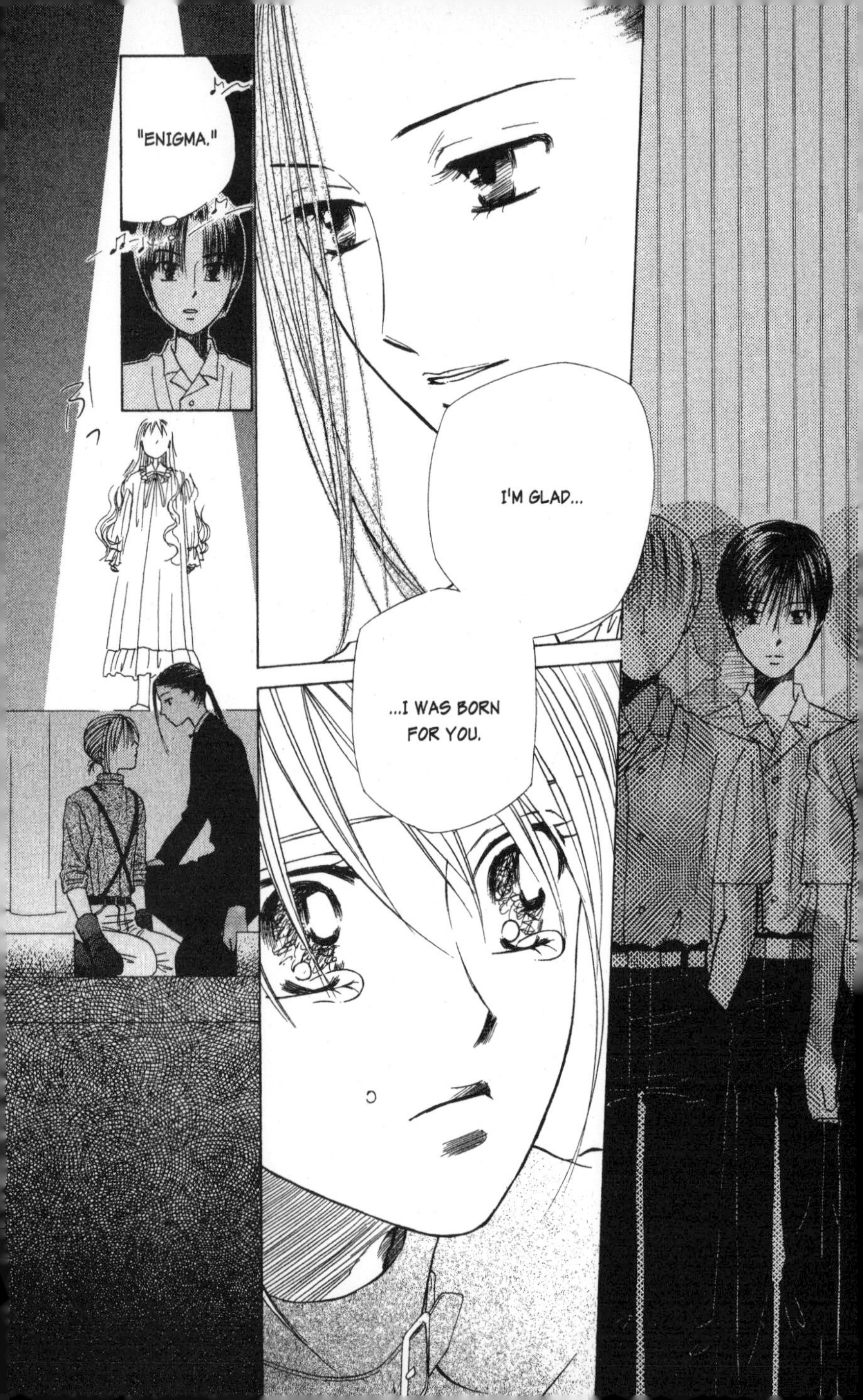
I'M GLAD...
...I WAS BORN FOR YOU.
"ENIGMA."

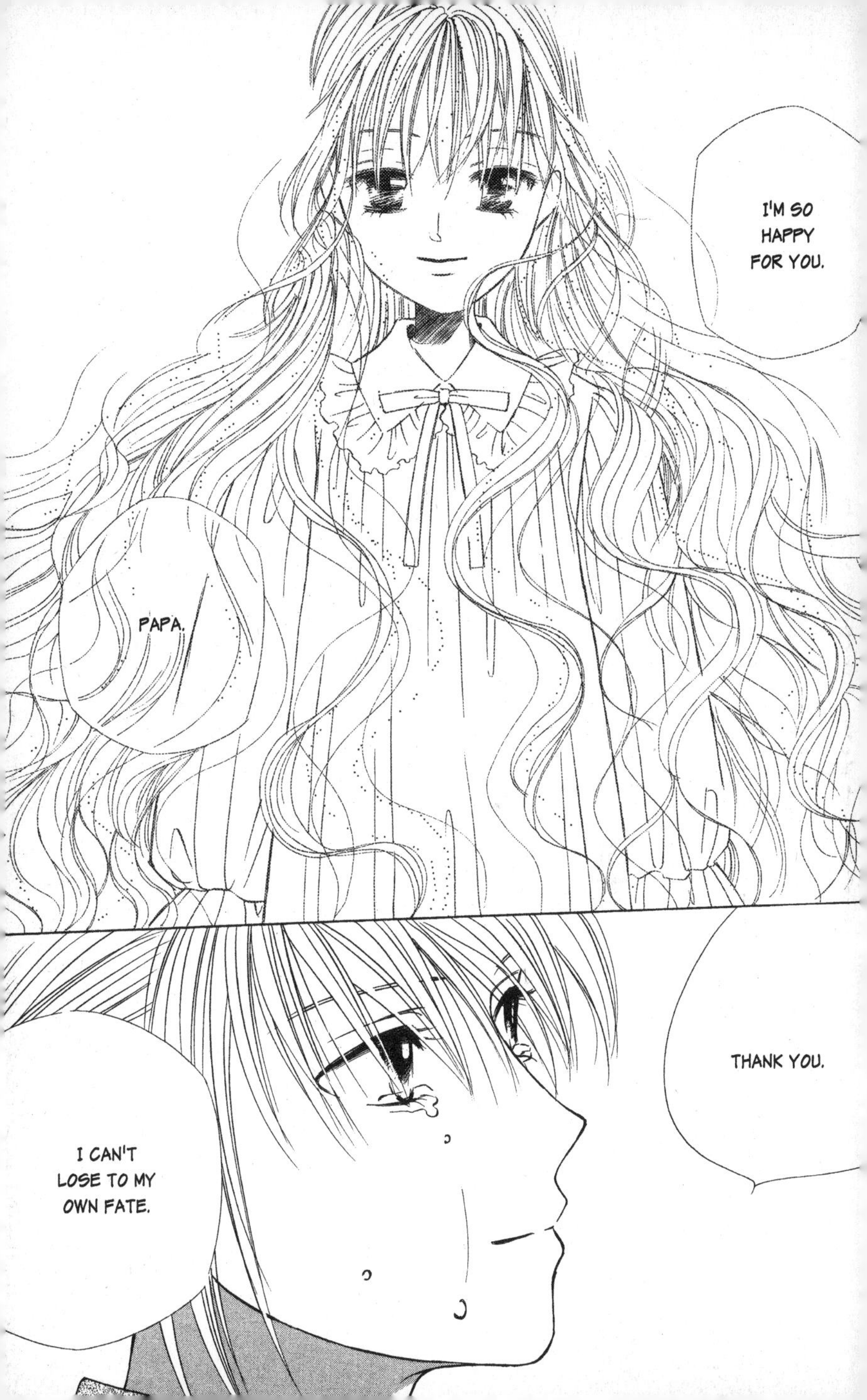
I'M SO HAPPY FOR YOU.
PAPA.
THANK YOU.
I CAN'T LOSE TO MY OWN FATE.

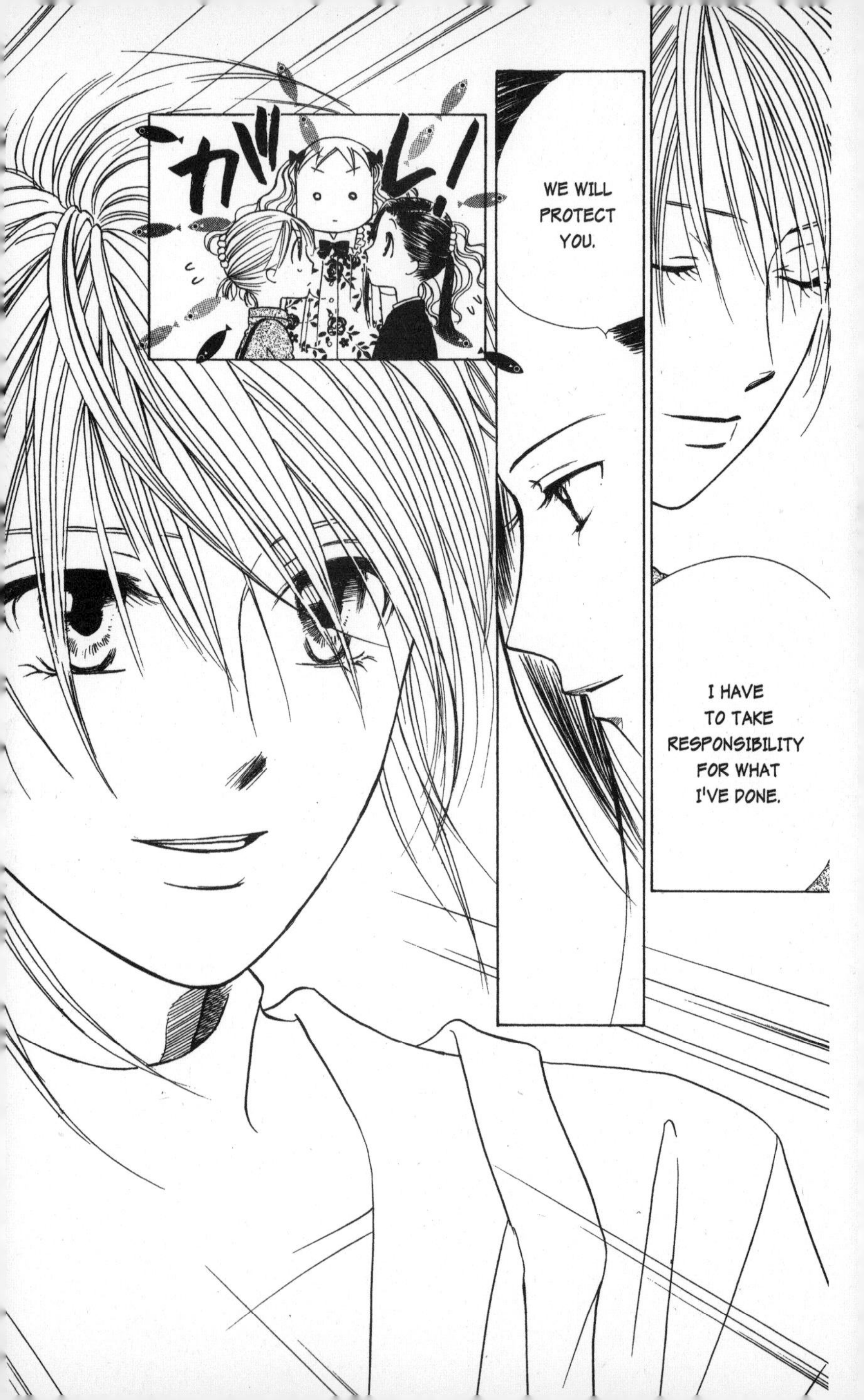
I HAVE TO TAKE RESPONSIBILITY FOR WHAT I'VE DONE.
WE WILL PROTECT YOU.

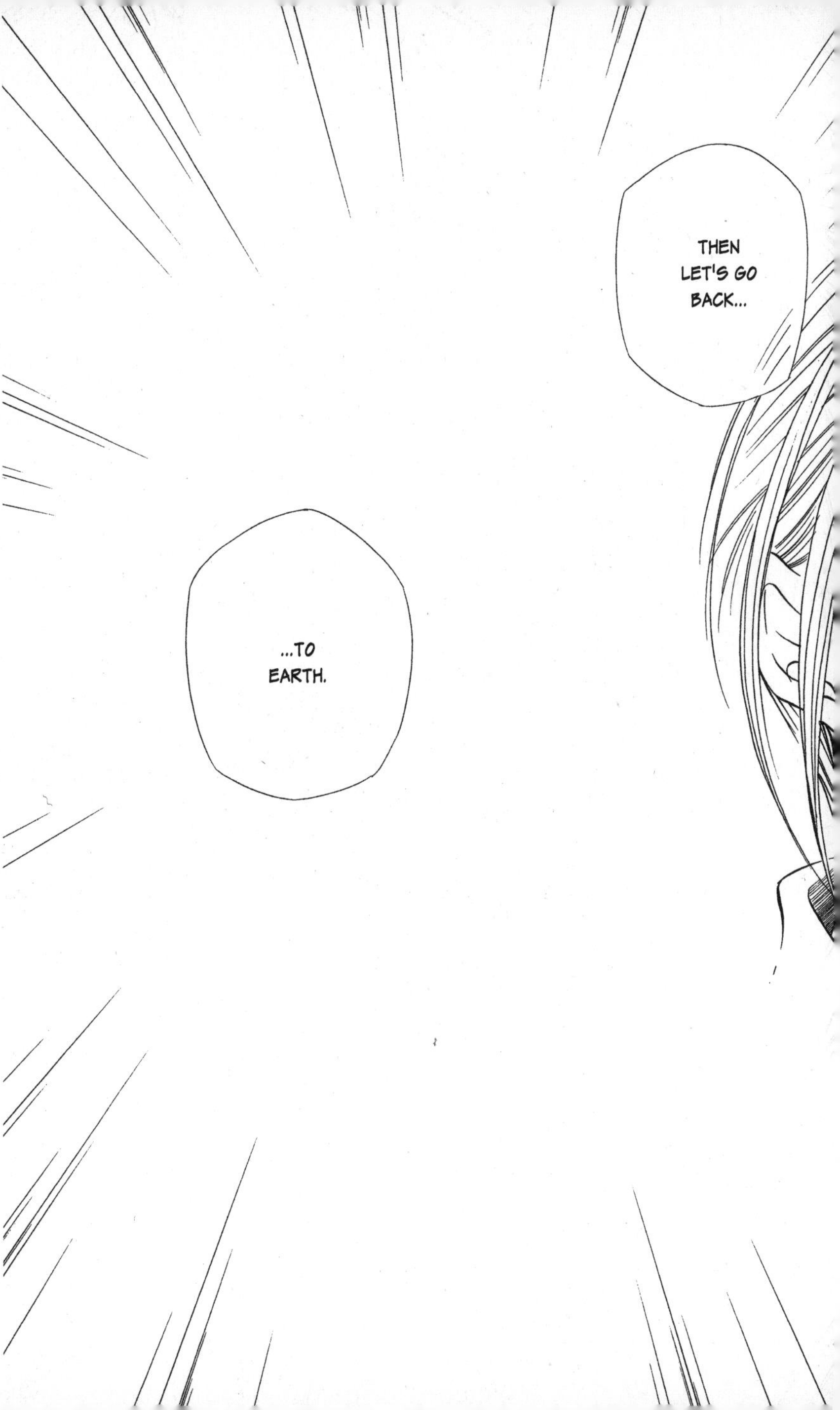
THEN LET'S GO BACK...
...TO EARTH.

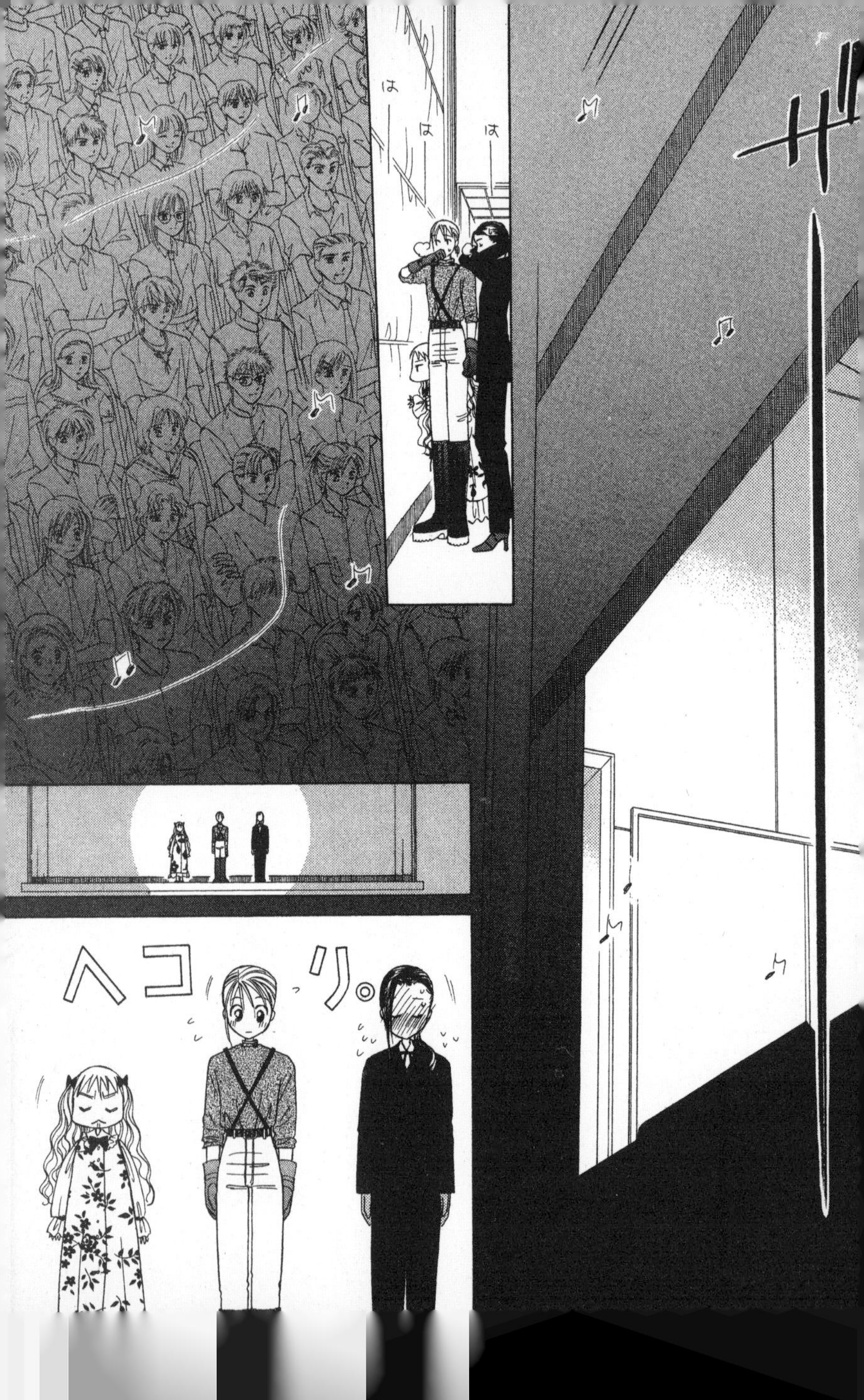

ザ
はははは
ヘコリ。

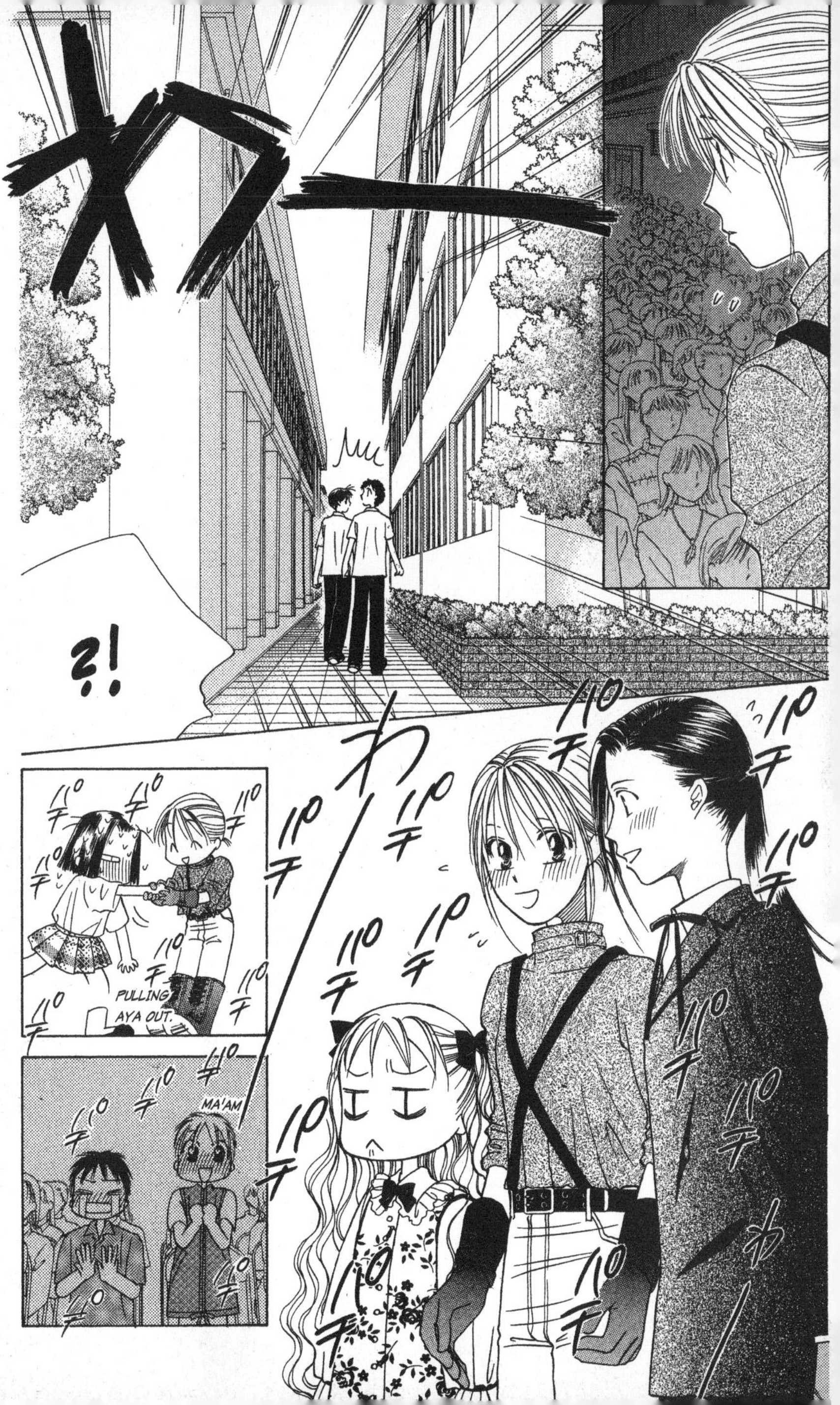
?!
PULLING AYA OUT.
MA'AM

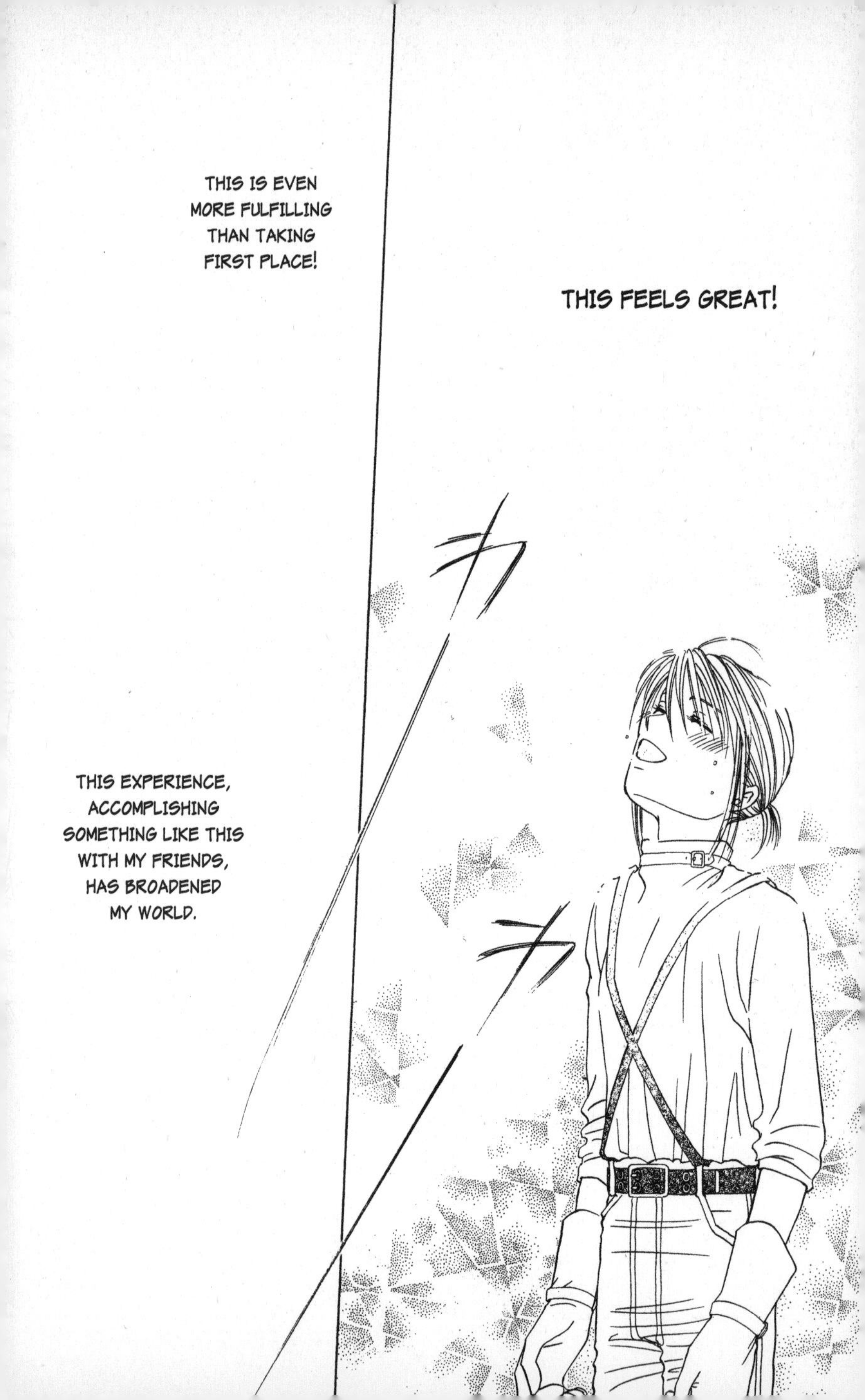
THIS FEELS GREAT!
THIS IS EVEN MORE FULFILLING THAN TAKING FIRST PLACE!
THIS EXPERIENCE, ACCOMPLISHING SOMETHING LIKE THIS WITH MY FRIENDS, HAS BROADENED MY WORLD.

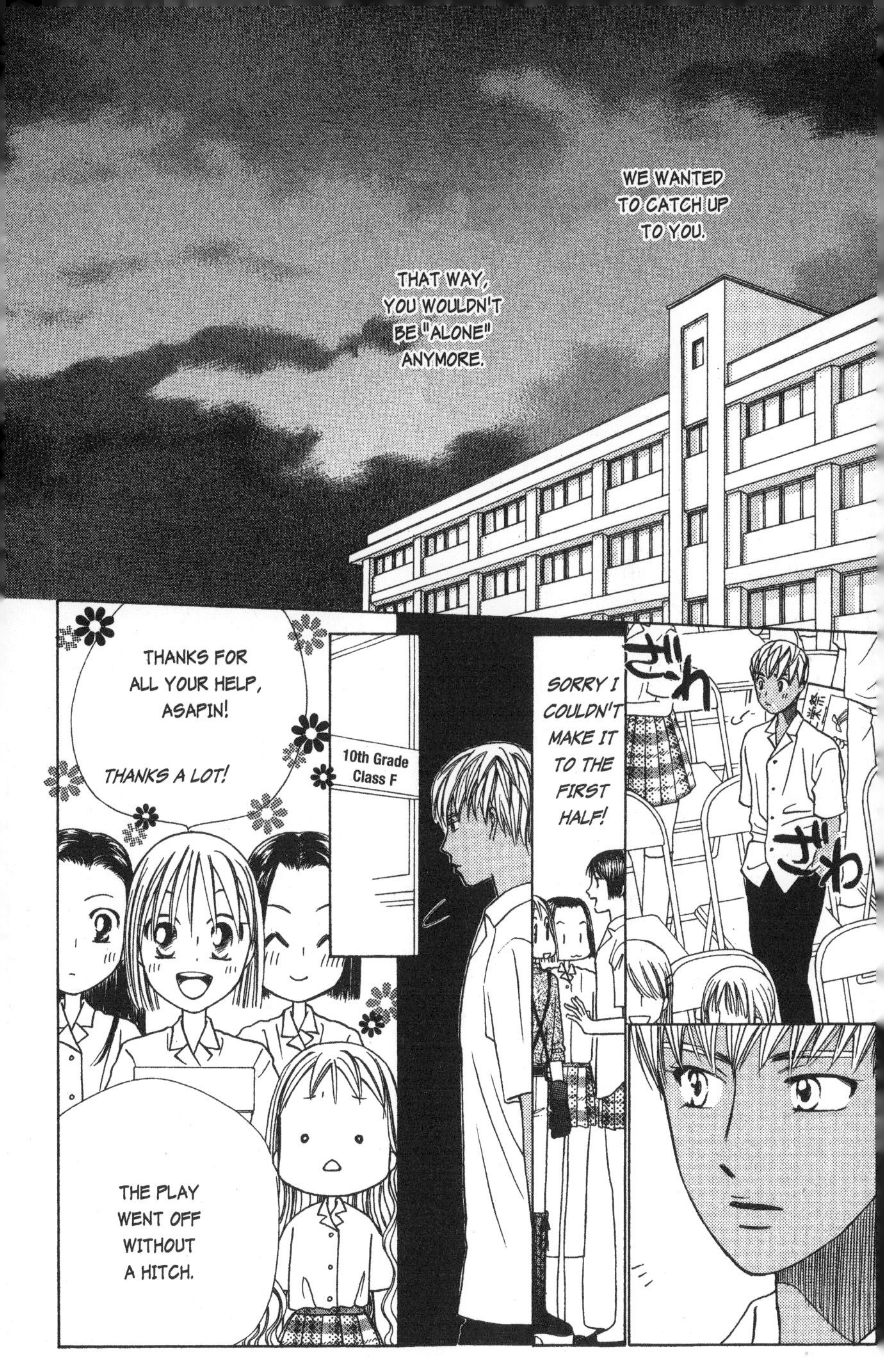
WE WANTED TO CATCH UP TO YOU.
THAT WAY, YOU WOULDN'T BE "ALONE" ANYMORE.
ざわ
ざわ
SORRY I COULDN'T MAKE IT TO THE FIRST HALF!
10th Grade Class F
THANKS FOR ALL YOUR HELP, ASAPIN!
THANKS A LOT!
THE PLAY WENT OFF WITHOUT A HITCH.

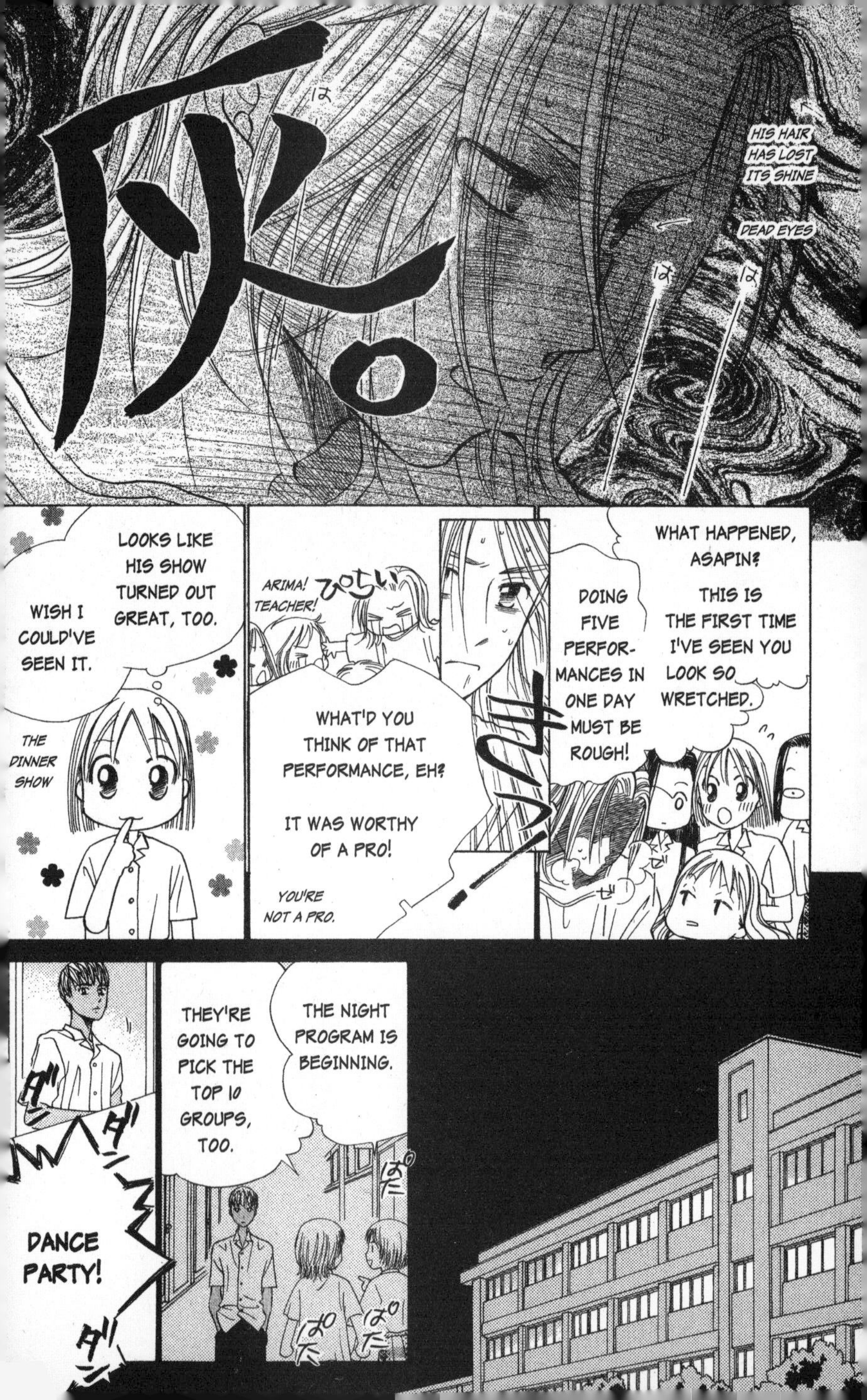

HIS HAIR HAS LOST ITS SHINE
DEAD EYES
LOOKS LIKE HIS SHOW TURNED OUT GREAT, TOO.
WISH I COULD'VE SEEN IT.
THE DINNER SHOW
WHAT HAPPENED, ASAPIN?
THIS IS THE FIRST TIME I'VE SEEN YOU LOOK SO WRETCHED.
DOING FIVE PERFORMANCES IN ONE DAY MUST BE ROUGH!
ARIMA! TEACHER!
WHAT'D YOU THINK OF THAT PERFORMANCE, EH?
IT WAS WORTHY OF A PRO!
YOU'RE NOT A PRO.
THE NIGHT PROGRAM IS BEGINNING.
THEY'RE GOING TO PICK THE TOP 10 GROUPS, TOO.
DANCE PARTY!

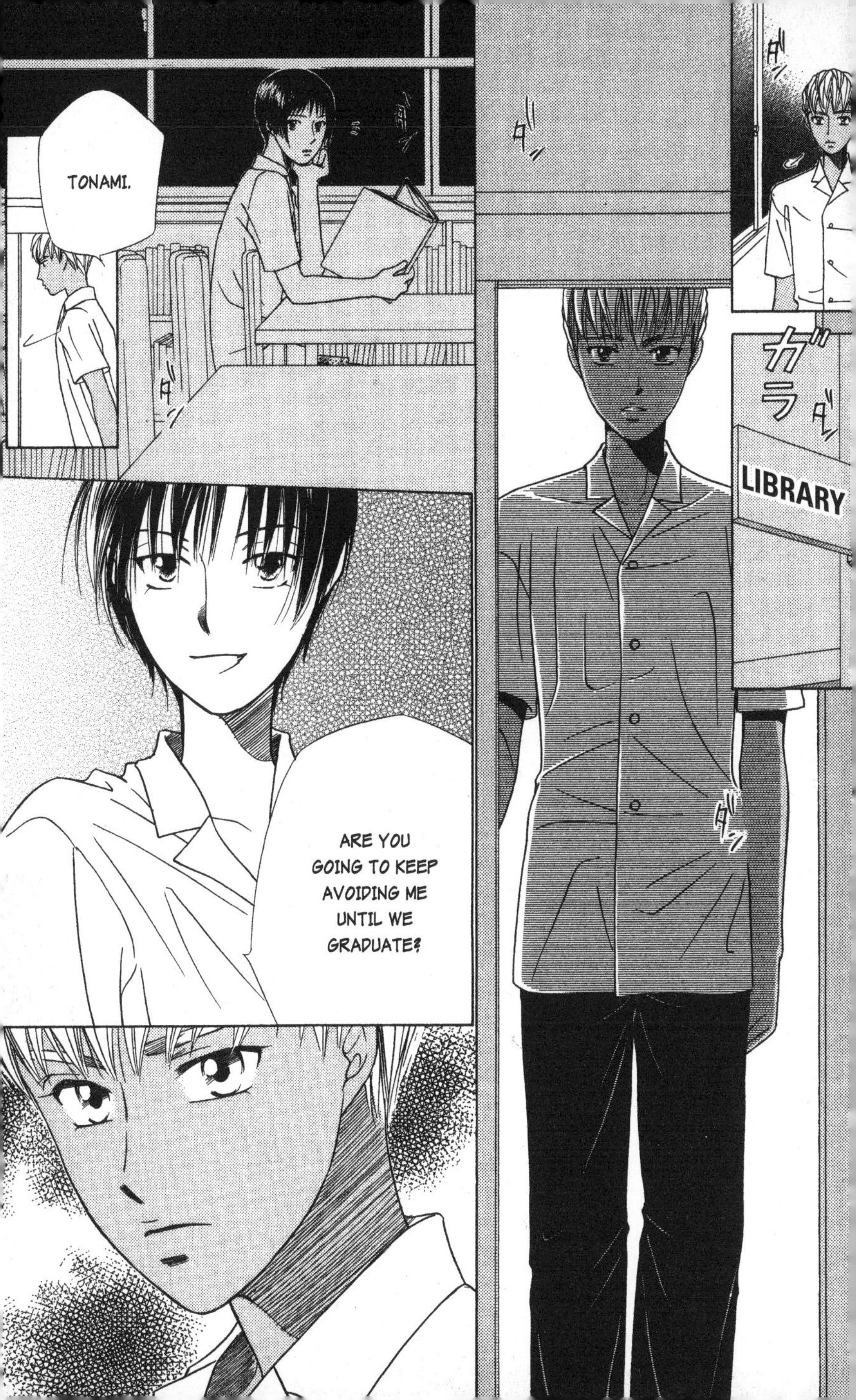
ガラ
LIBRARY
TONAMI.
ARE YOU GOING TO KEEP AVOIDING ME UNTIL WE GRADUATE?

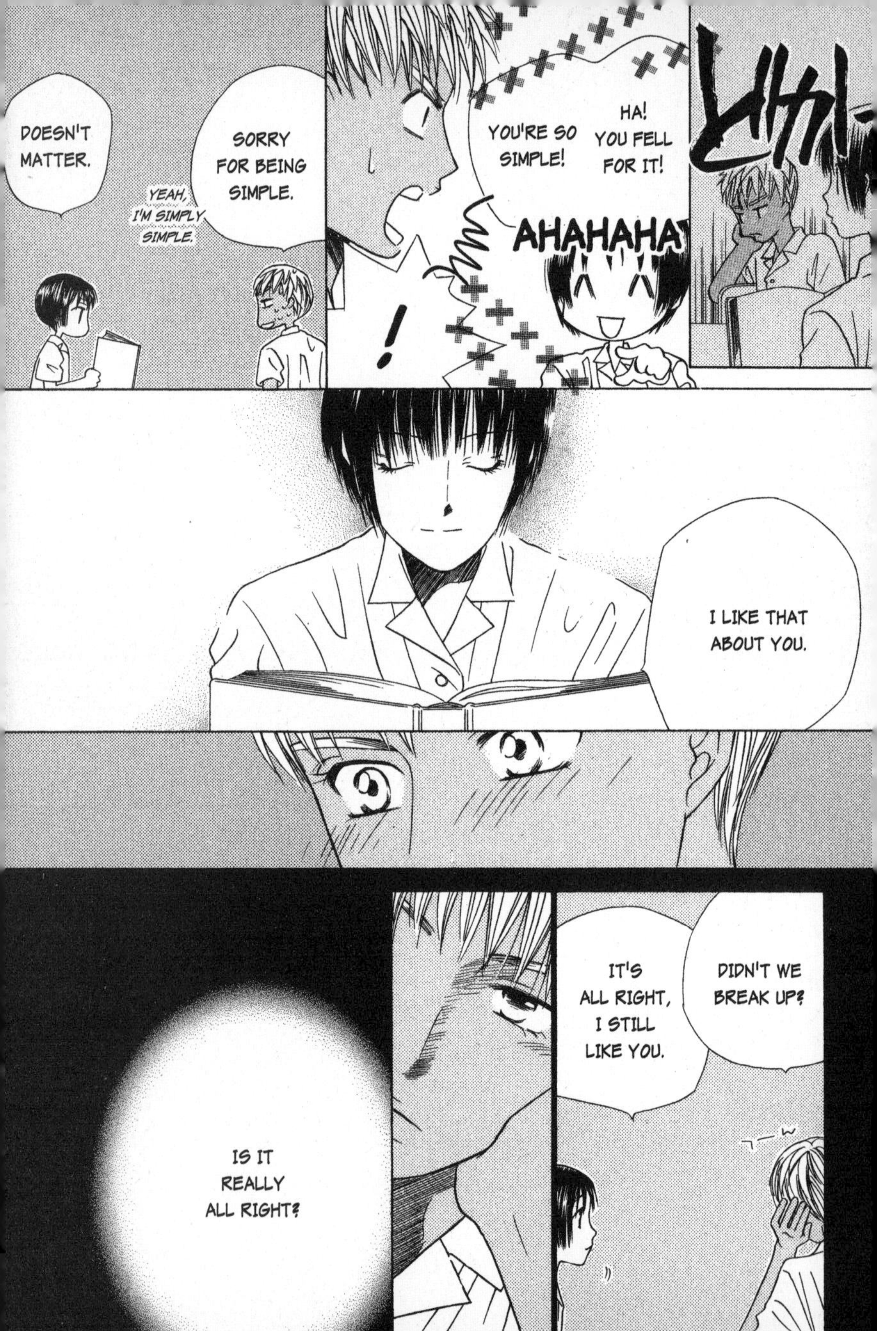
HA! YOU FELL FOR IT!
YOU'RE SO SIMPLE!
AHAHAHA
SORRY FOR BEING SIMPLE.
YEAH, I'M SIMPLY SIMPLE.
DOESN'T MATTER.
I LIKE THAT ABOUT YOU.
DIDN'T WE BREAK UP?
IT'S ALL RIGHT, I STILL LIKE YOU.
IS IT REALLY ALL RIGHT?

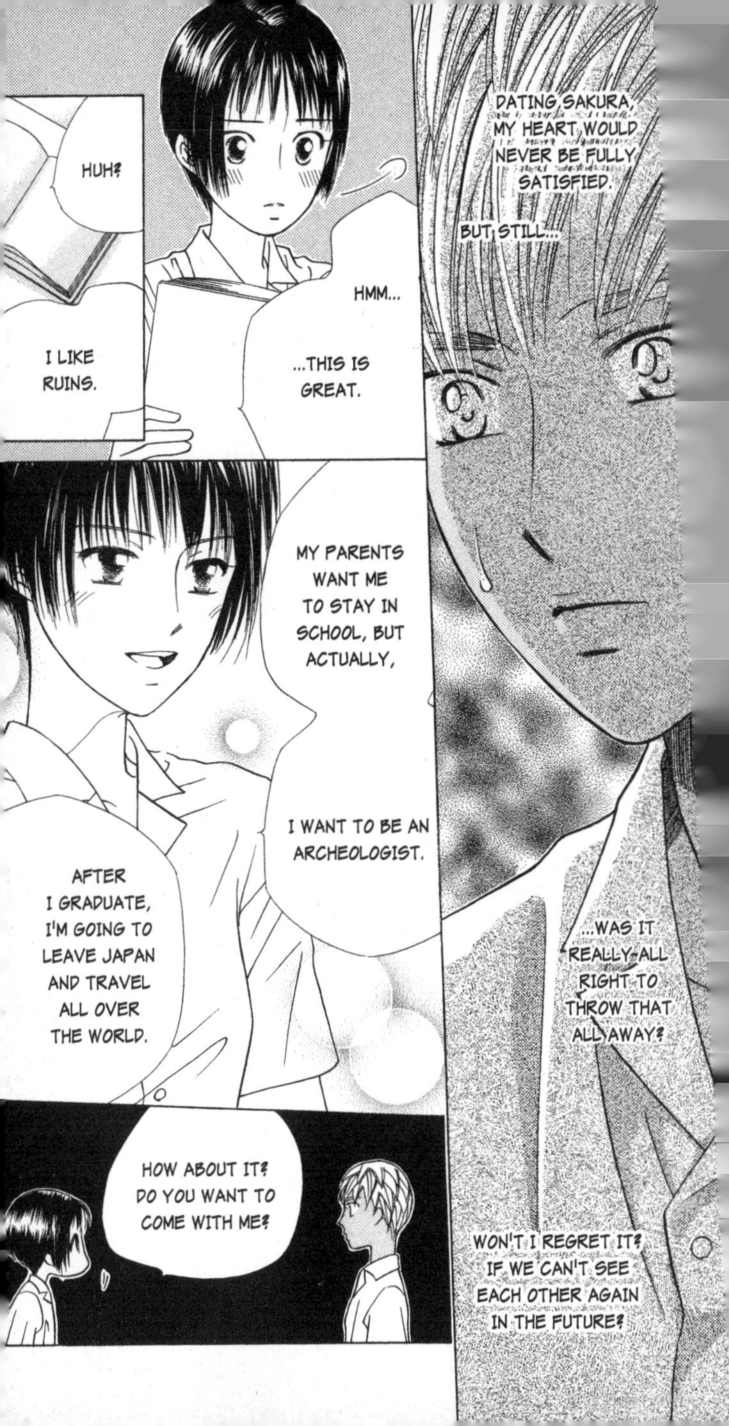

DATING SAKURA, MY HEART WOULD NEVER BE FULLY SATISFIED.
BUT STILL...
HMM...
...THIS IS GREAT.
HUH?
I LIKE RUINS.
MY PARENTS WANT ME TO STAY IN SCHOOL, BUT ACTUALLY,
I WANT TO BE AN ARCHEOLOGIST.
AFTER I GRADUATE, I'M GOING TO LEAVE JAPAN AND TRAVEL ALL OVER THE WORLD.
HOW ABOUT IT? DO YOU WANT TO COME WITH ME?
...WAS IT REALLY ALL RIGHT TO THROW THAT ALL AWAY?
WON'T I REGRET IT? IF WE CAN'T SEE EACH OTHER AGAIN IN THE FUTURE?

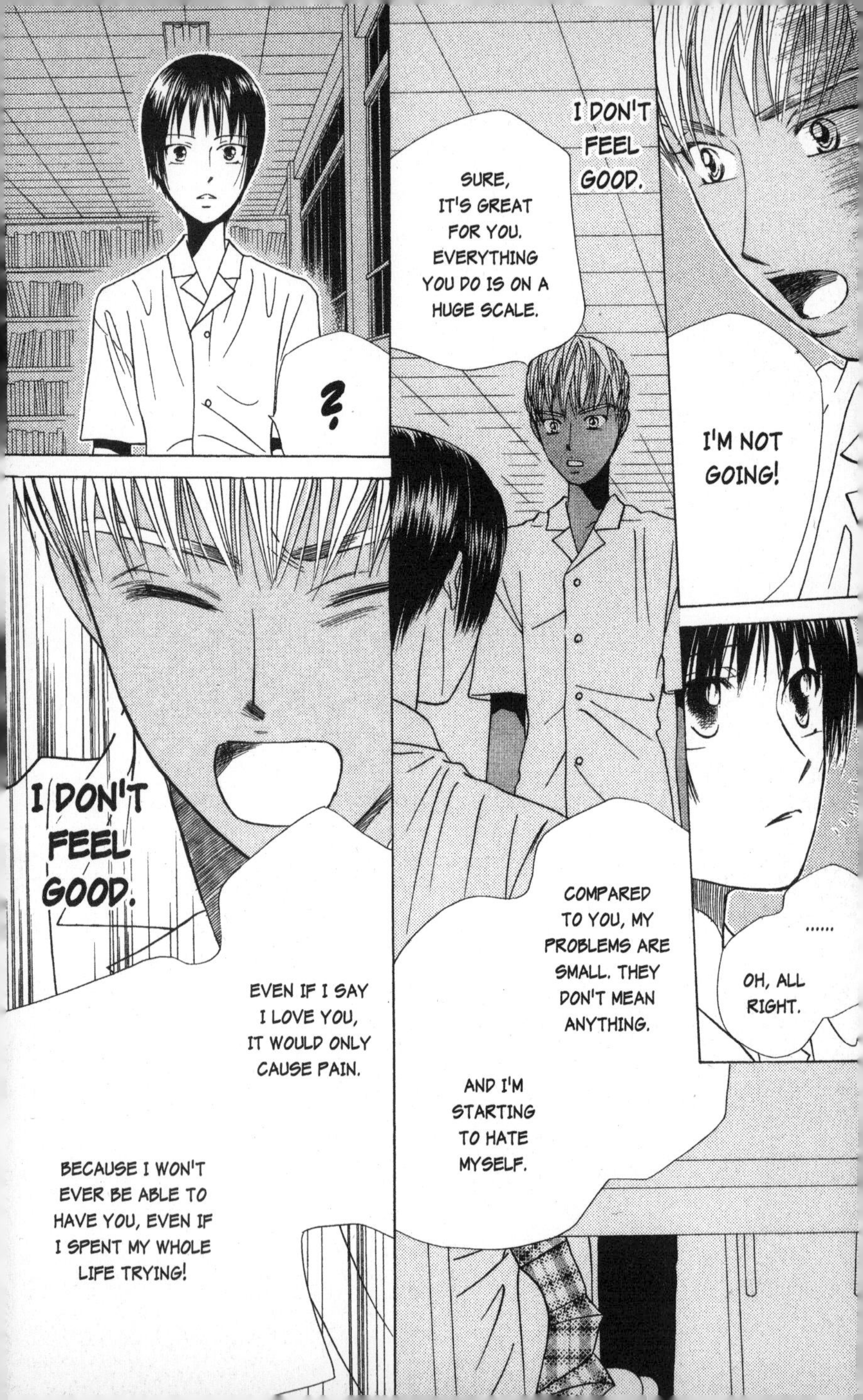
I'M NOT GOING!
I DON'T FEEL GOOD.
SURE, IT'S GREAT FOR YOU. EVERYTHING YOU DO IS ON A HUGE SCALE.
?
......
OH, ALL RIGHT.
COMPARED TO YOU, MY PROBLEMS ARE SMALL. THEY DON'T MEAN ANYTHING.
AND I'M STARTING TO HATE MYSELF.
I DON'T FEEL GOOD.
EVEN IF I SAY I LOVE YOU, IT WOULD ONLY CAUSE PAIN.
BECAUSE I WON'T EVER BE ABLE TO HAVE YOU, EVEN IF I SPENT MY WHOLE LIFE TRYING!

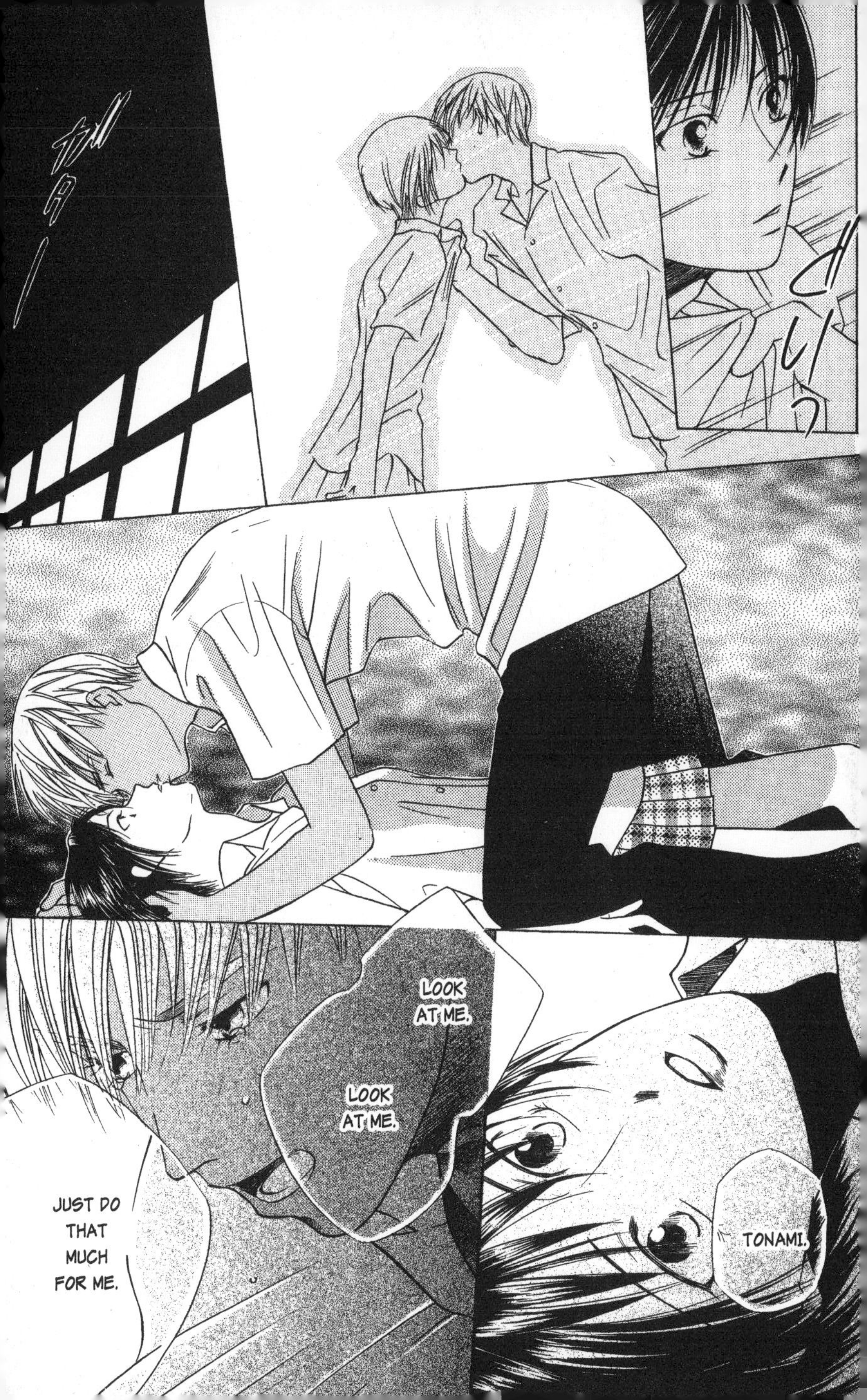
TONAMI.
LOOK AT ME.
LOOK AT ME.
JUST DO THAT MUCH FOR ME.

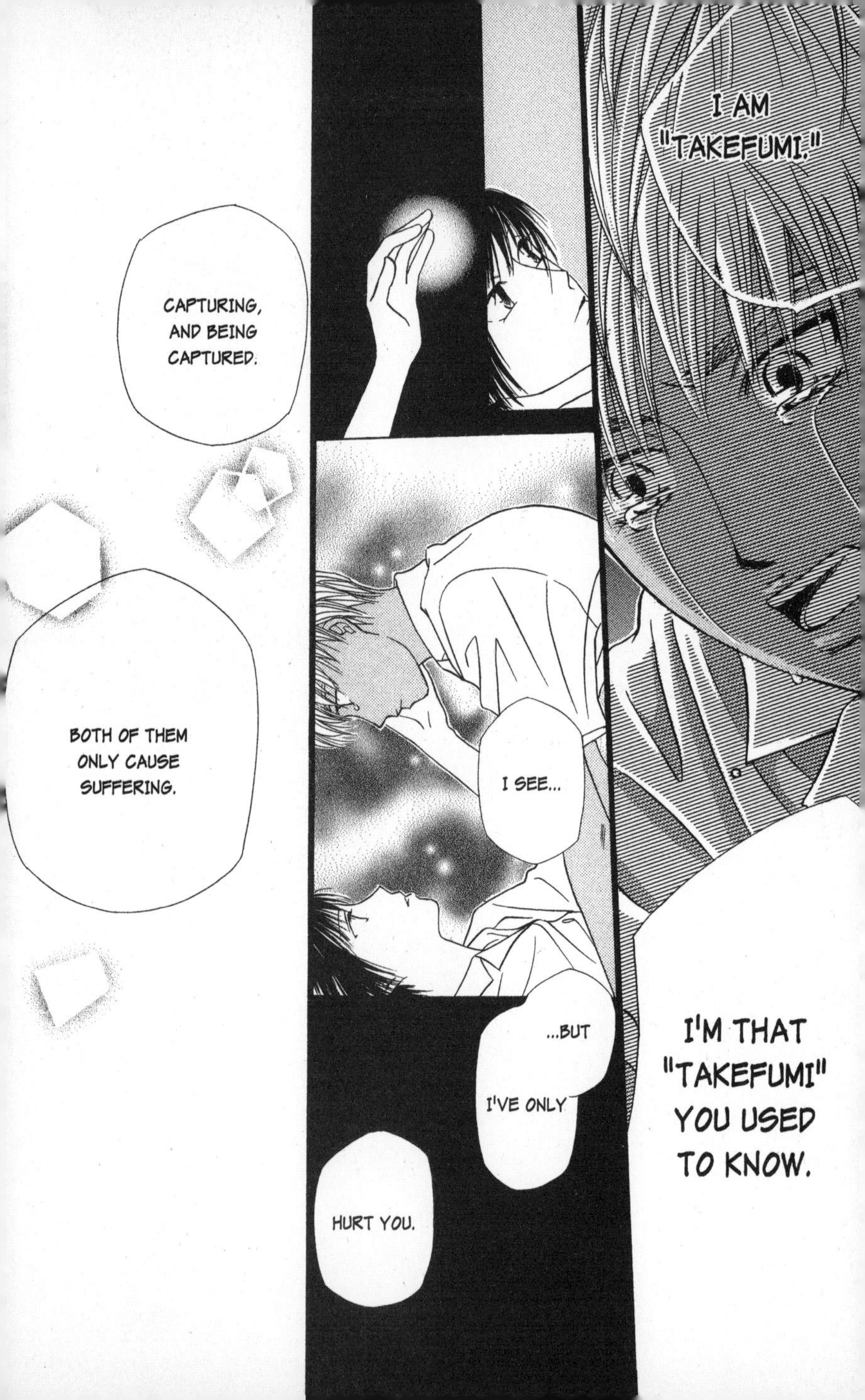
I AM "TAKEFUMI."
I'M THAT "TAKEFUMI" YOU USED TO KNOW.
I SEE...
...BUT
I'VE ONLY
HURT YOU.
CAPTURING, AND BEING CAPTURED.
BOTH OF THEM ONLY CAUSE SUFFERING.

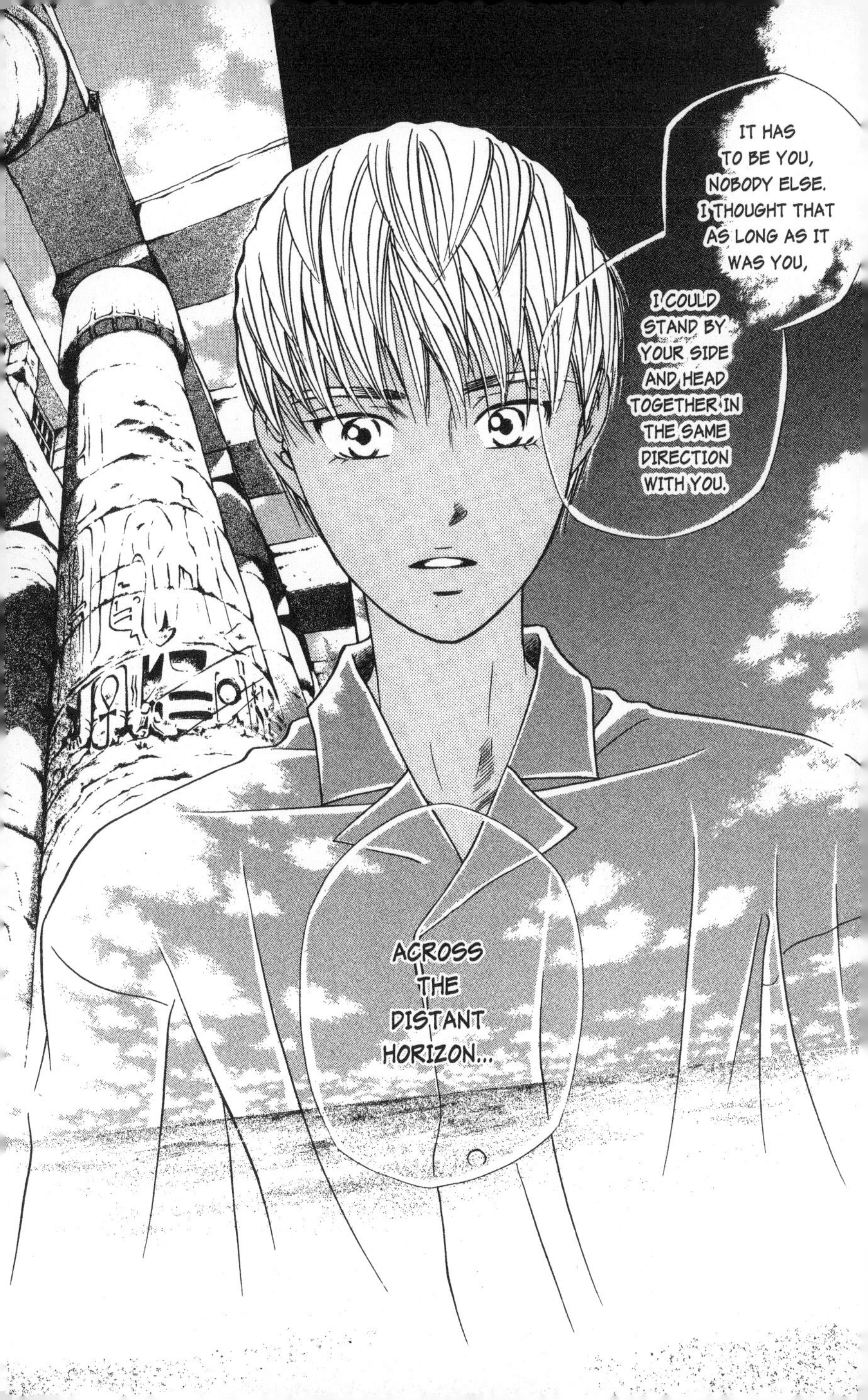
IT HAS TO BE YOU, NOBODY ELSE. I THOUGHT THAT AS LONG AS IT WAS YOU,
I COULD STAND BY YOUR SIDE AND HEAD TOGETHER IN THE SAME DIRECTION WITH YOU.
ACROSS THE DISTANT HORIZON...

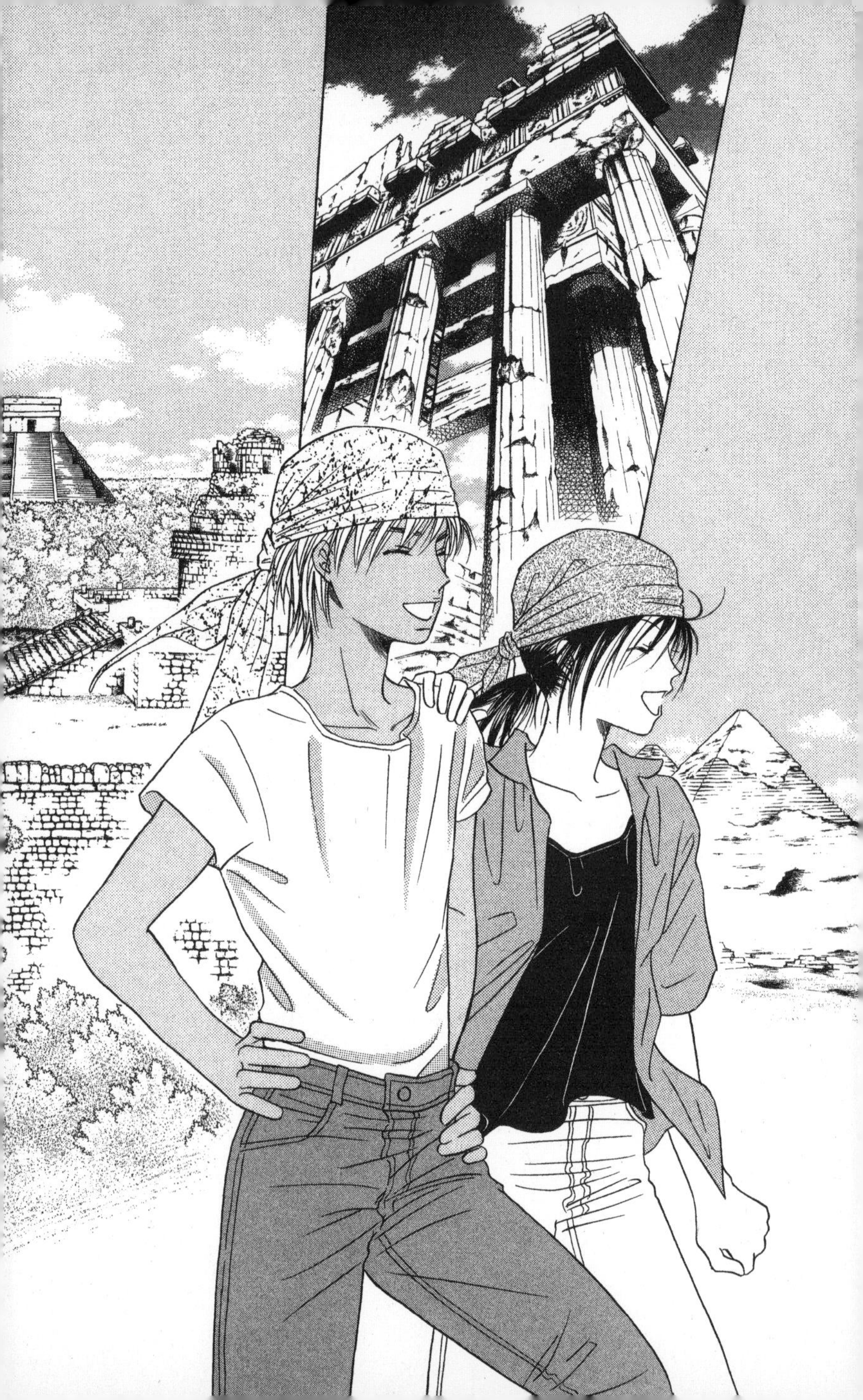

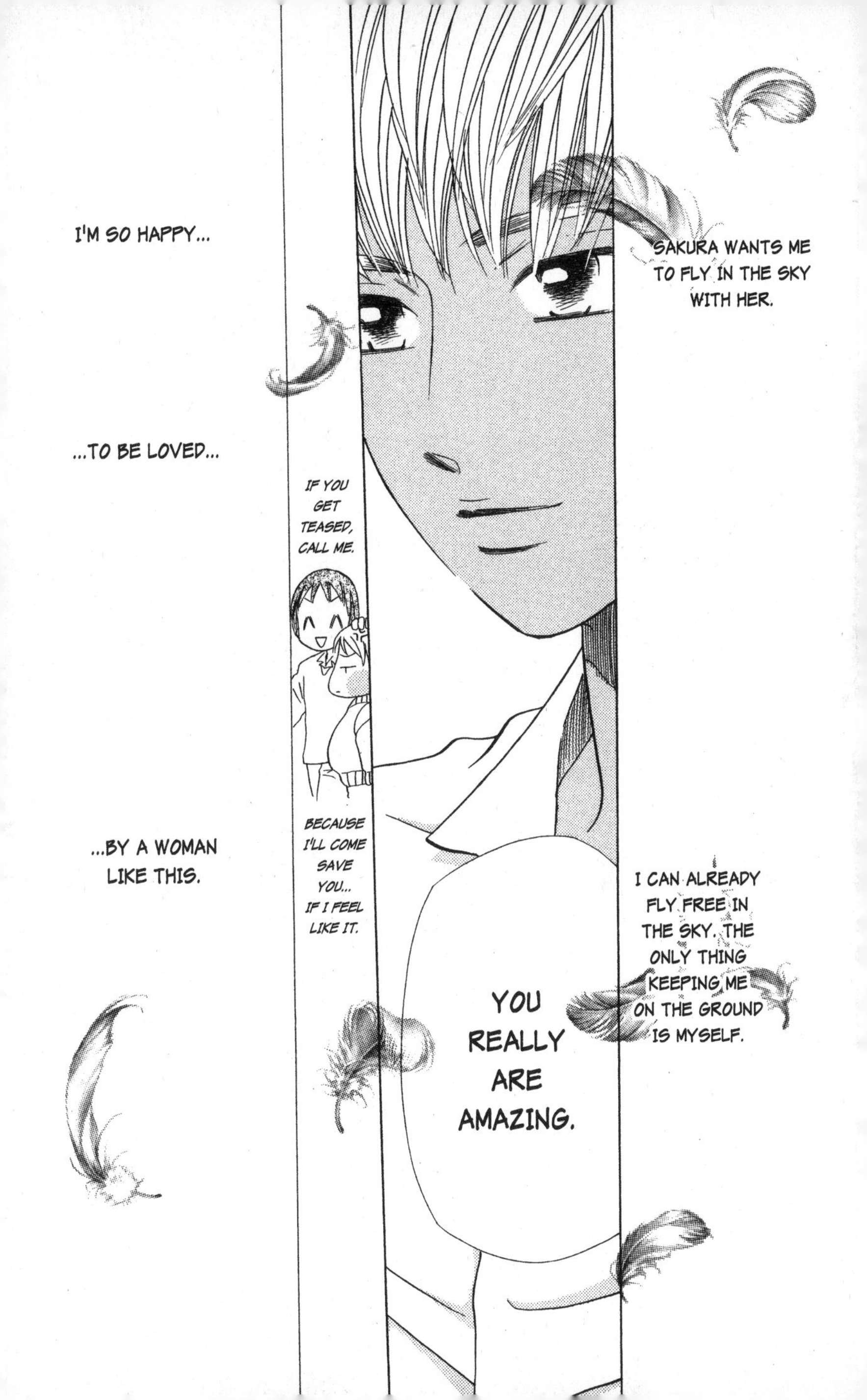
SAKURA WANTS ME TO FLY IN THE SKY WITH HER.
I CAN ALREADY FLY FREE IN THE SKY. THE ONLY THING KEEPING ME ON THE GROUND IS MYSELF.
YOU REALLY ARE AMAZING.
IF YOU GET TEASED, CALL ME.
BECAUSE I'LL COME SAVE YOU... IF I FEEL LIKE IT.
I'M SO HAPPY...
...TO BE LOVED...
...BY A WOMAN LIKE THIS.

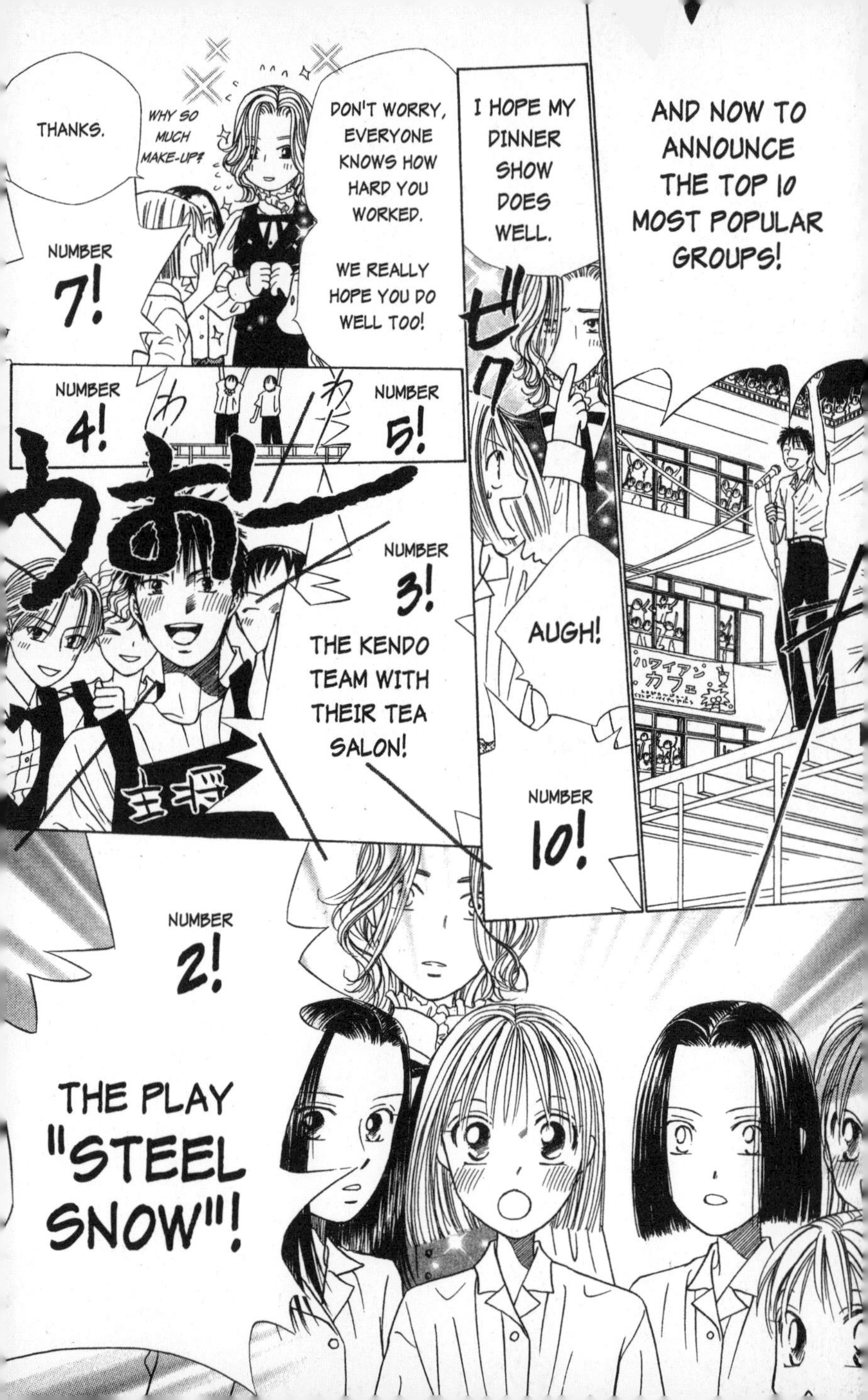

AND NOW TO ANNOUNCE THE TOP 10 MOST POPULAR GROUPS!
NUMBER 10!
I HOPE MY DINNER SHOW DOES WELL.
AUGH!
DON'T WORRY, EVERYONE KNOWS HOW HARD YOU WORKED.
WE REALLY HOPE YOU DO WELL TOO!
WHY SO MUCH MAKE-UP?
THANKS.
NUMBER 7!
NUMBER 5!
NUMBER 4!
NUMBER 3!
THE KENDO TEAM WITH THEIR TEA SALON!
NUMBER 2!
THE PLAY "STEEL SNOW"!

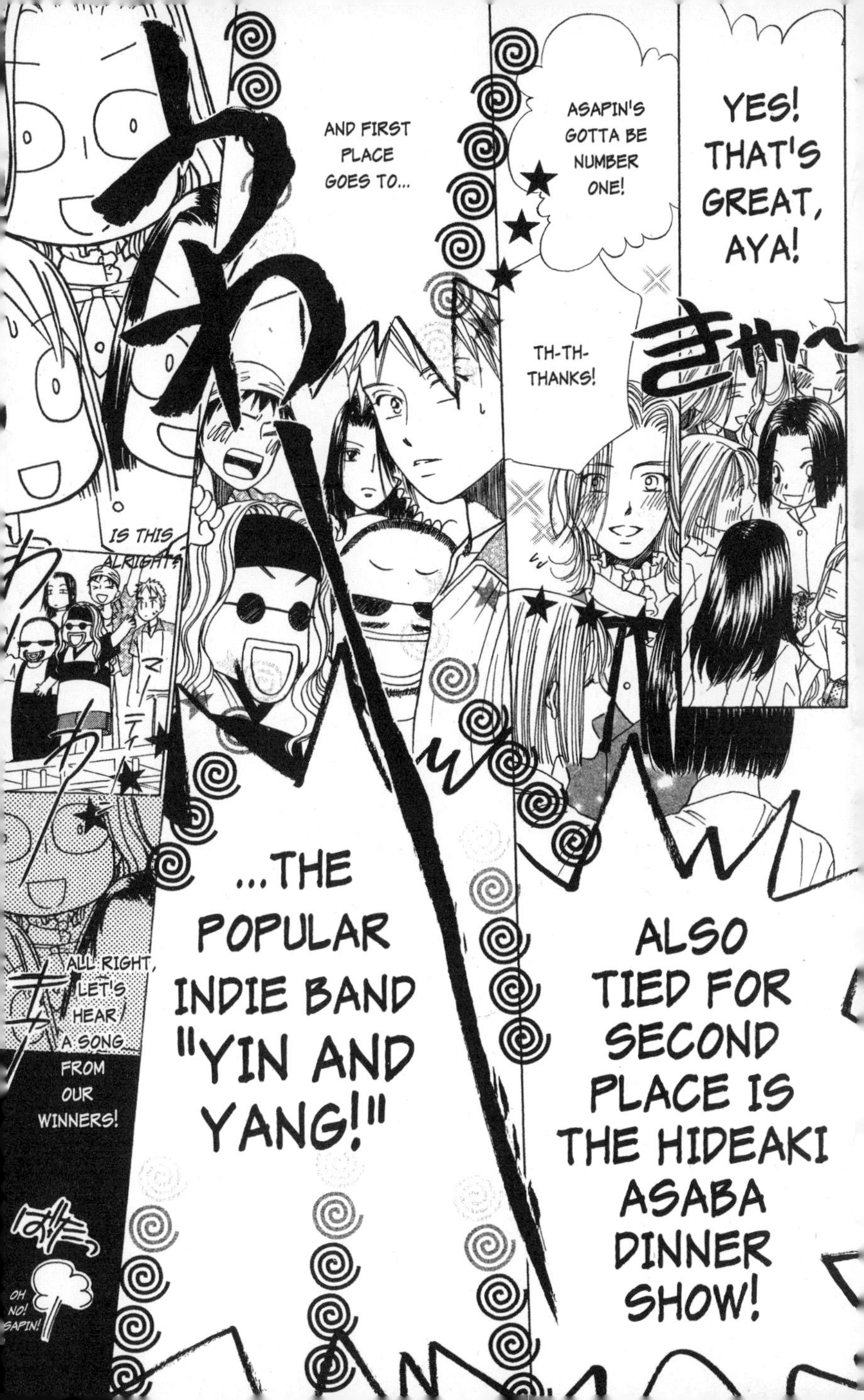

YES! THAT'S GREAT, AYA!
ASAPIN'S GOTTA BE NUMBER ONE!
きゃ~
TH-TH-THANKS!
AND FIRST PLACE GOES TO...
ALSO TIED FOR SECOND PLACE IS THE HIDEAKI ASABA DINNER SHOW!
...THE POPULAR INDIE BAND "YIN AND YANG!"
IS THIS ALRIGHT?
ALL RIGHT, LET'S HEAR A SONG FROM OUR WINNERS!
OH NO! SAPIN!

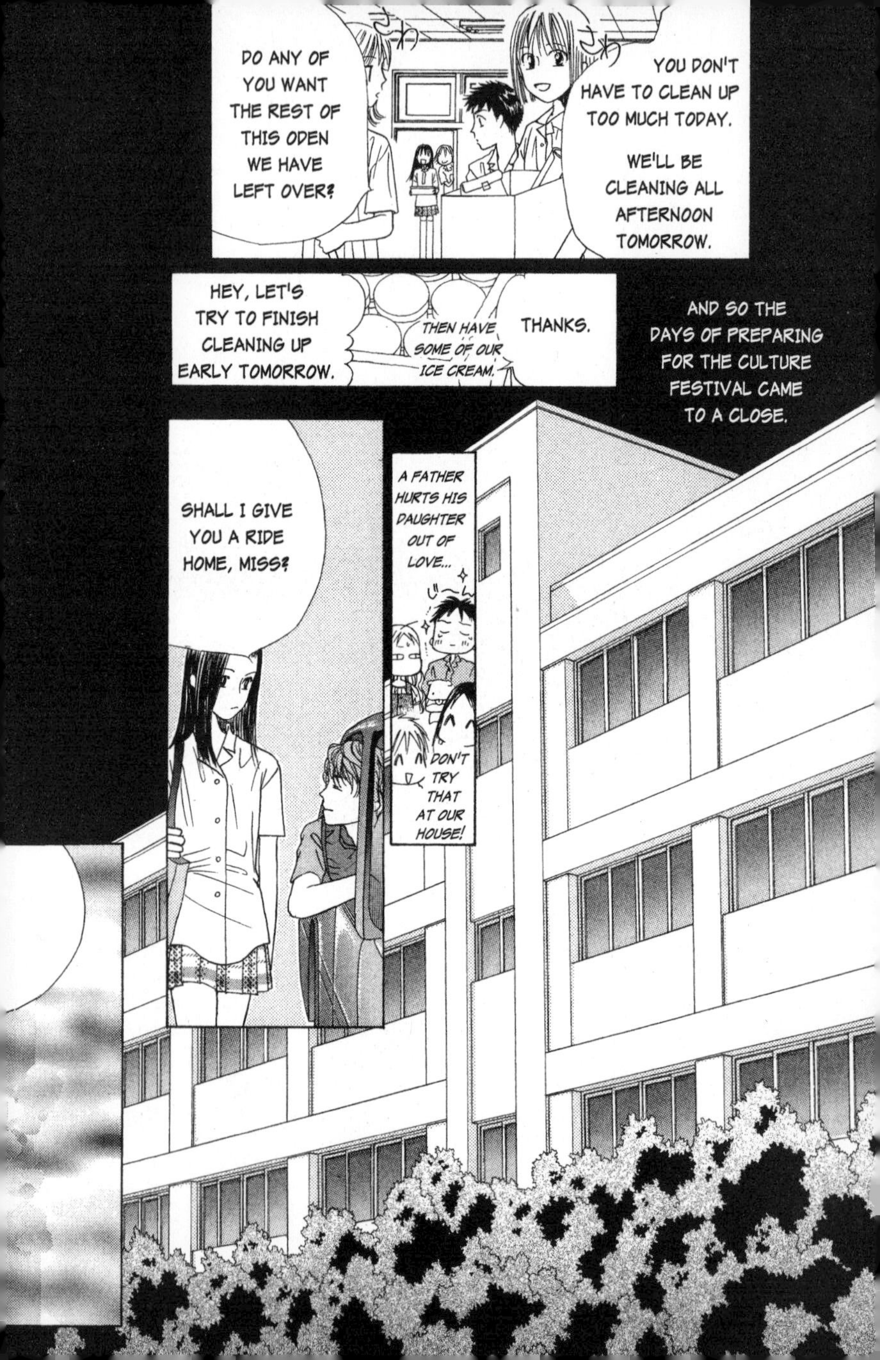
YOU DON'T HAVE TO CLEAN UP TOO MUCH TODAY.
WE'LL BE CLEANING ALL AFTERNOON TOMORROW.
DO ANY OF YOU WANT THE REST OF THIS ODEN WE HAVE LEFT OVER?
THANKS.
THEN HAVE SOME OF OUR ICE CREAM.
HEY, LET'S TRY TO FINISH CLEANING UP EARLY TOMORROW.
AND SO THE DAYS OF PREPARING FOR THE CULTURE FESTIVAL CAME TO A CLOSE.
A FATHER HURTS HIS DAUGHTER OUT OF LOVE...
DON'T TRY THAT AT OUR HOUSE!
SHALL I GIVE YOU A RIDE HOME, MISS?

6

Yo! It's the end of the 9th volume!

Thanks to the magic of manga, during the play, I made Yukino's shoulder's wider and decreased the size of her breasts. Some people might not notice at first, but then when the play ends and she goes back to normal, they suddenly realize. Well, it was kinda fun.

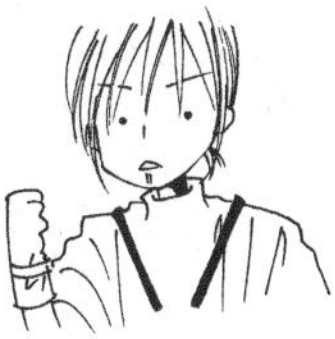

Well then, if you wish, I'll see you in volume 10!

Everyone, it's all thanks to you that I made it this far!

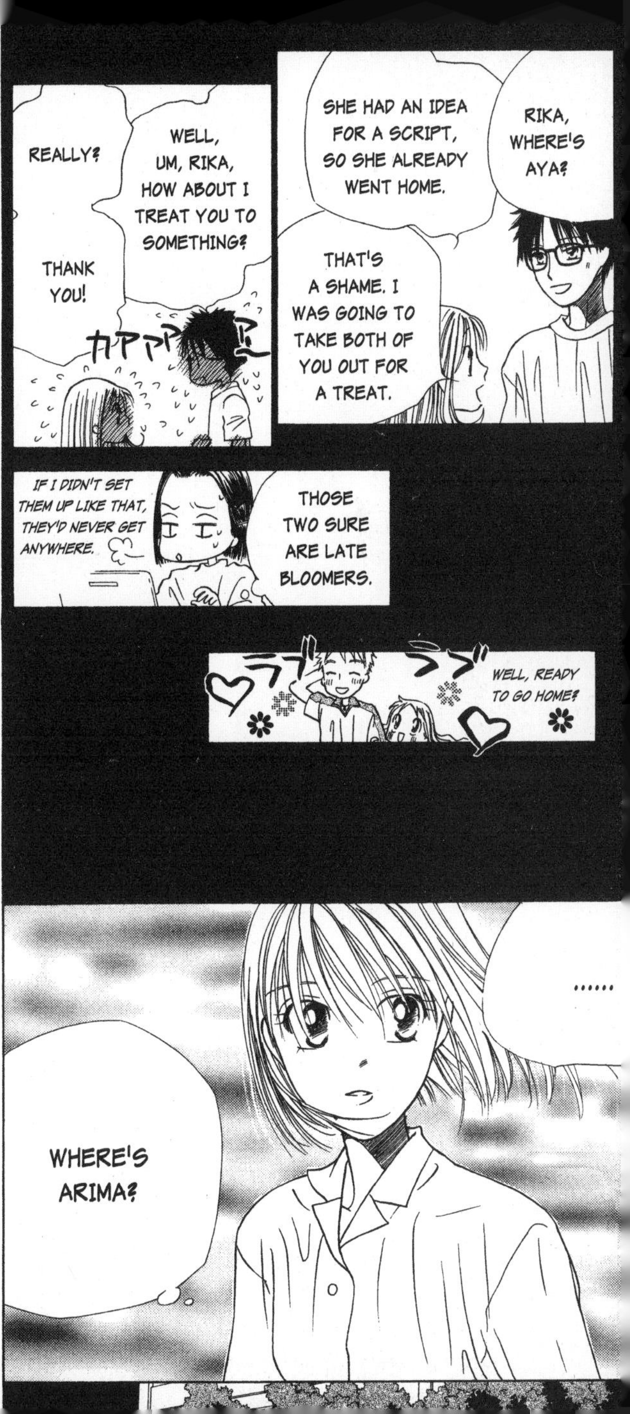
RIKA, WHERE'S AYA?
SHE HAD AN IDEA FOR A SCRIPT, SO SHE ALREADY WENT HOME.
THAT'S A SHAME. I WAS GOING TO TAKE BOTH OF YOU OUT FOR A TREAT.
WELL, UM, RIKA, HOW ABOUT I TREAT YOU TO SOMETHING?
REALLY?
THANK YOU!
THOSE TWO SURE ARE LATE BLOOMERS.
IF I DIDN'T SET THEM UP LIKE THAT, THEY'D NEVER GET ANYWHERE.
WELL, READY TO GO HOME?
......
WHERE'S ARIMA?

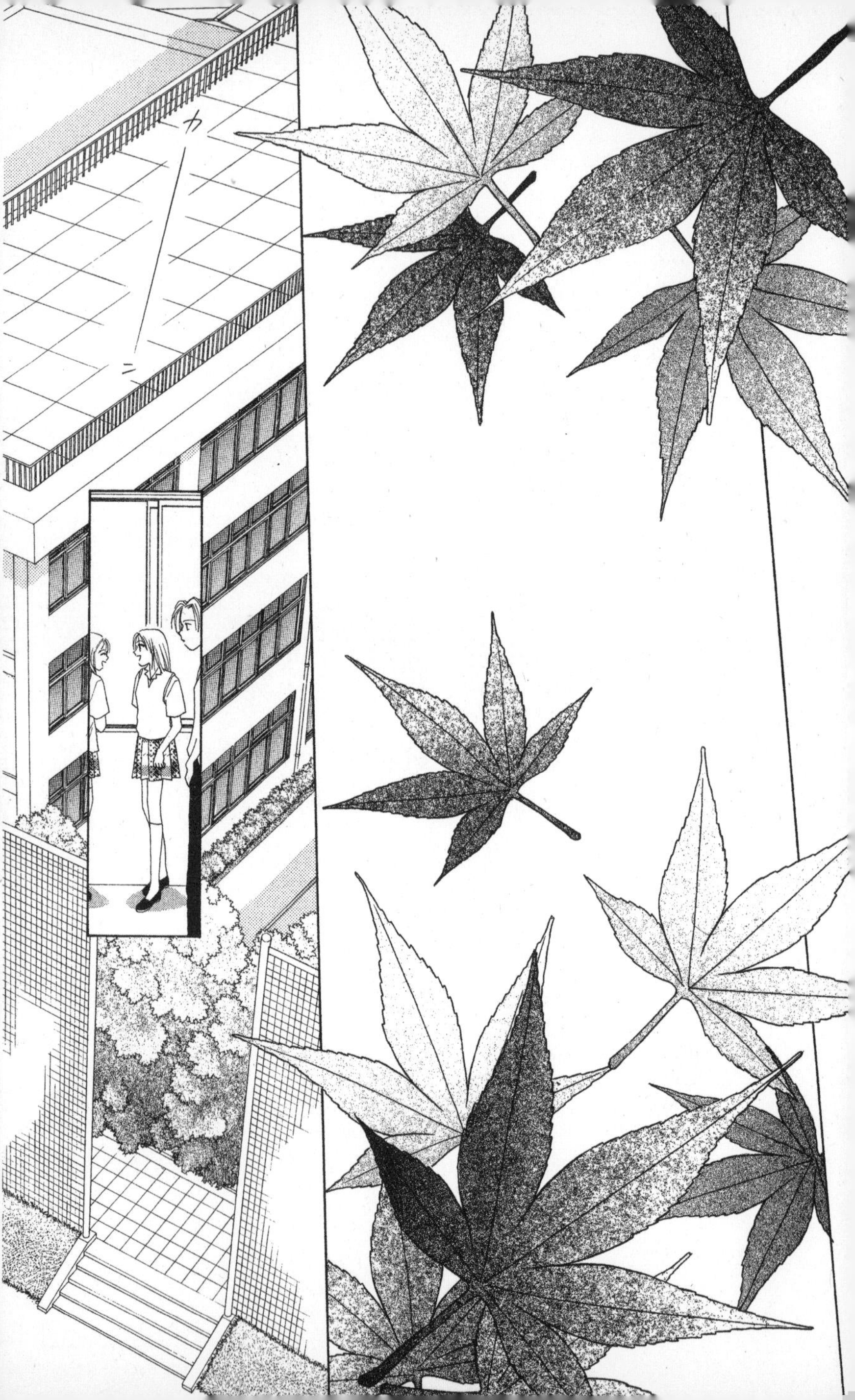
カーン

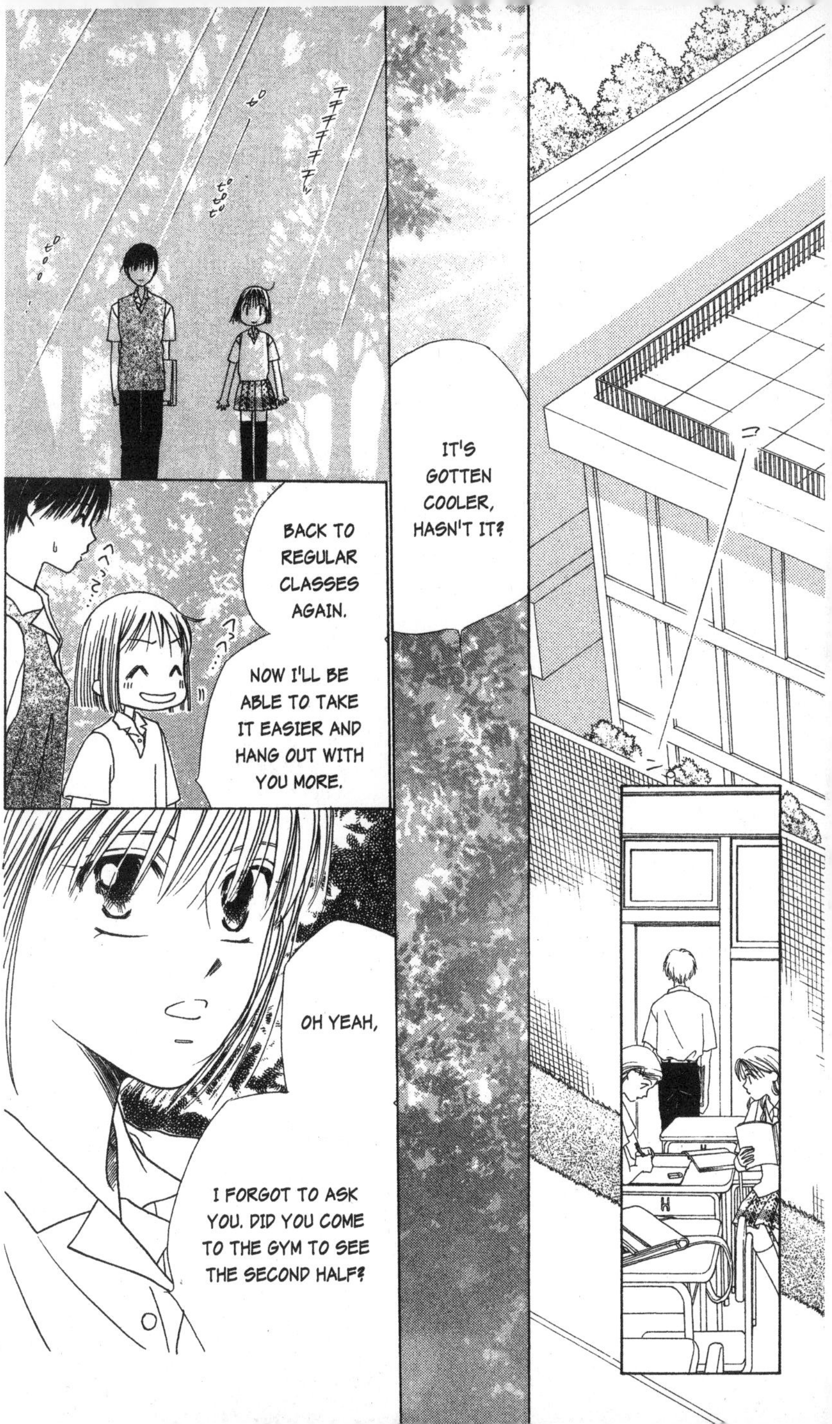
IT'S GOTTEN COOLER, HASN'T IT?
BACK TO REGULAR CLASSES AGAIN.
NOW I'LL BE ABLE TO TAKE IT EASIER AND HANG OUT WITH YOU MORE.
OH YEAH,
I FORGOT TO ASK YOU. DID YOU COME TO THE GYM TO SEE THE SECOND HALF?

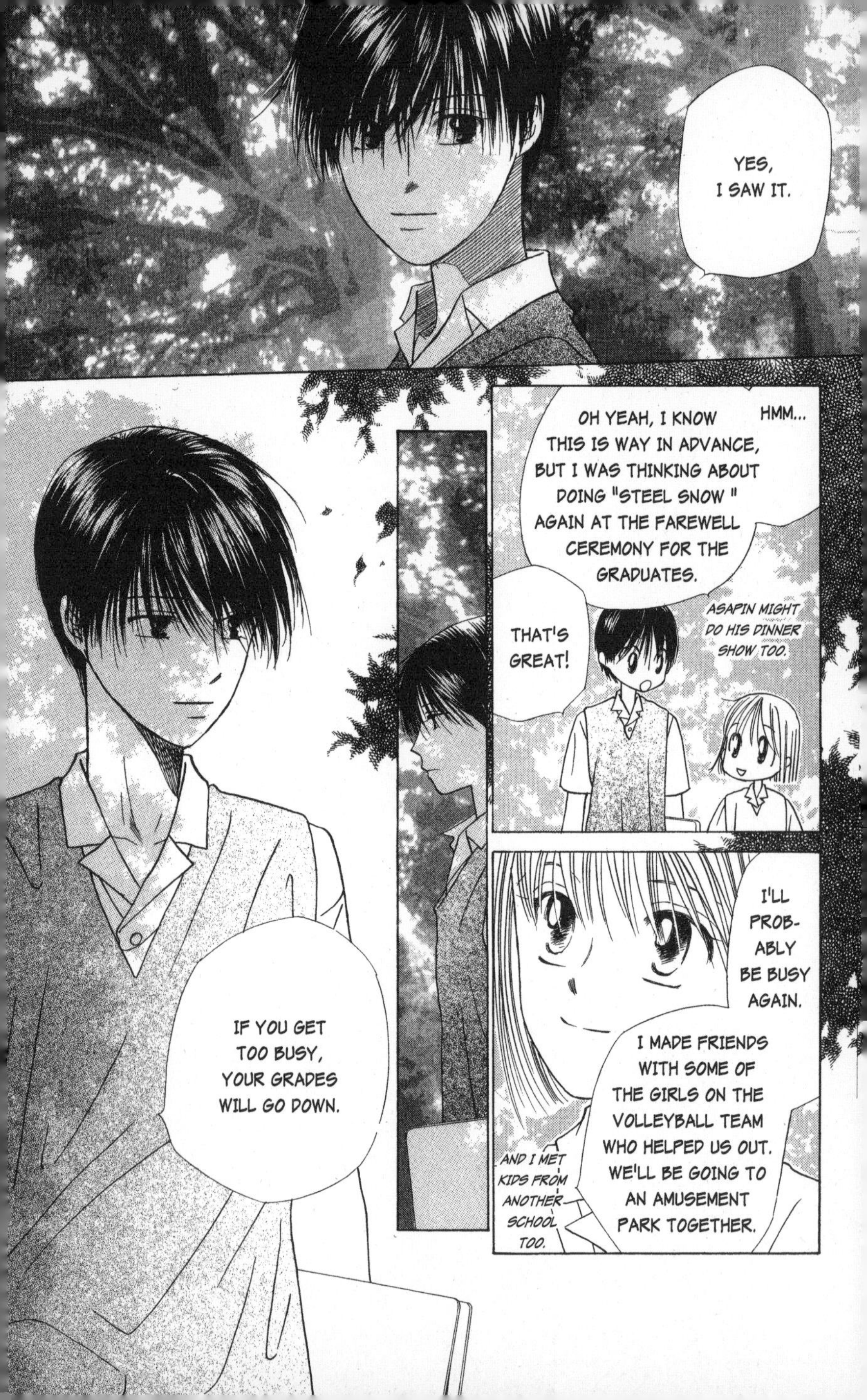
YES, I SAW IT.
HMM...
OH YEAH, I KNOW THIS IS WAY IN ADVANCE, BUT I WAS THINKING ABOUT DOING "STEEL SNOW" AGAIN AT THE FAREWELL CEREMONY FOR THE GRADUATES.
ASAPIN MIGHT DO HIS DINNER SHOW TOO.
THAT'S GREAT!
I'LL PROB-ABLY BE BUSY AGAIN.
I MADE FRIENDS WITH SOME OF THE GIRLS ON THE VOLLEYBALL TEAM WHO HELPED US OUT. WE'LL BE GOING TO AN AMUSEMENT PARK TOGETHER.
AND I MET KIDS FROM ANOTHER SCHOOL TOO.
IF YOU GET TOO BUSY, YOUR GRADES WILL GO DOWN.

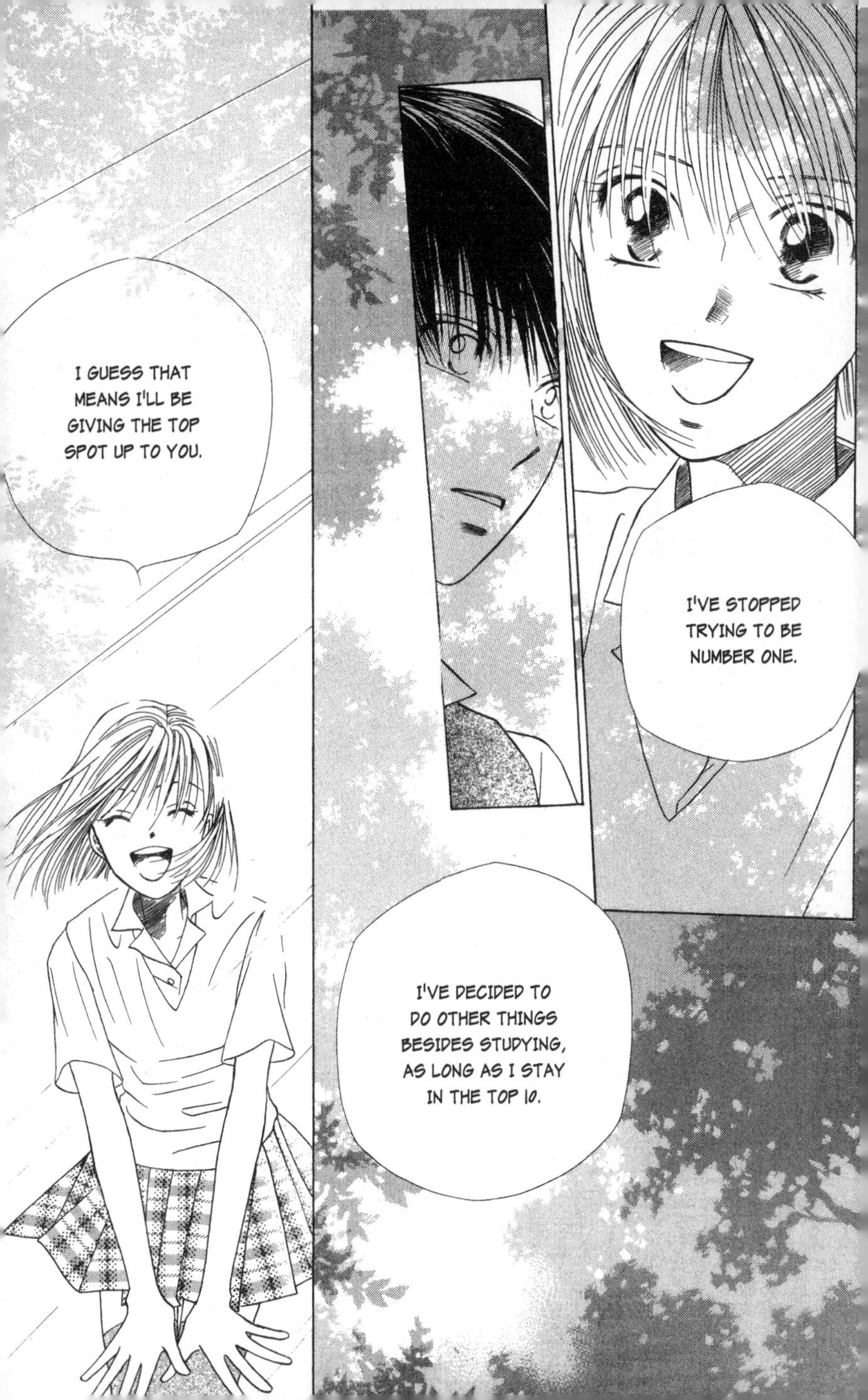
I'VE STOPPED TRYING TO BE NUMBER ONE.
I'VE DECIDED TO DO OTHER THINGS BESIDES STUDYING, AS LONG AS I STAY IN THE TOP 10.
I GUESS THAT MEANS I'LL BE GIVING THE TOP SPOT UP TO YOU.

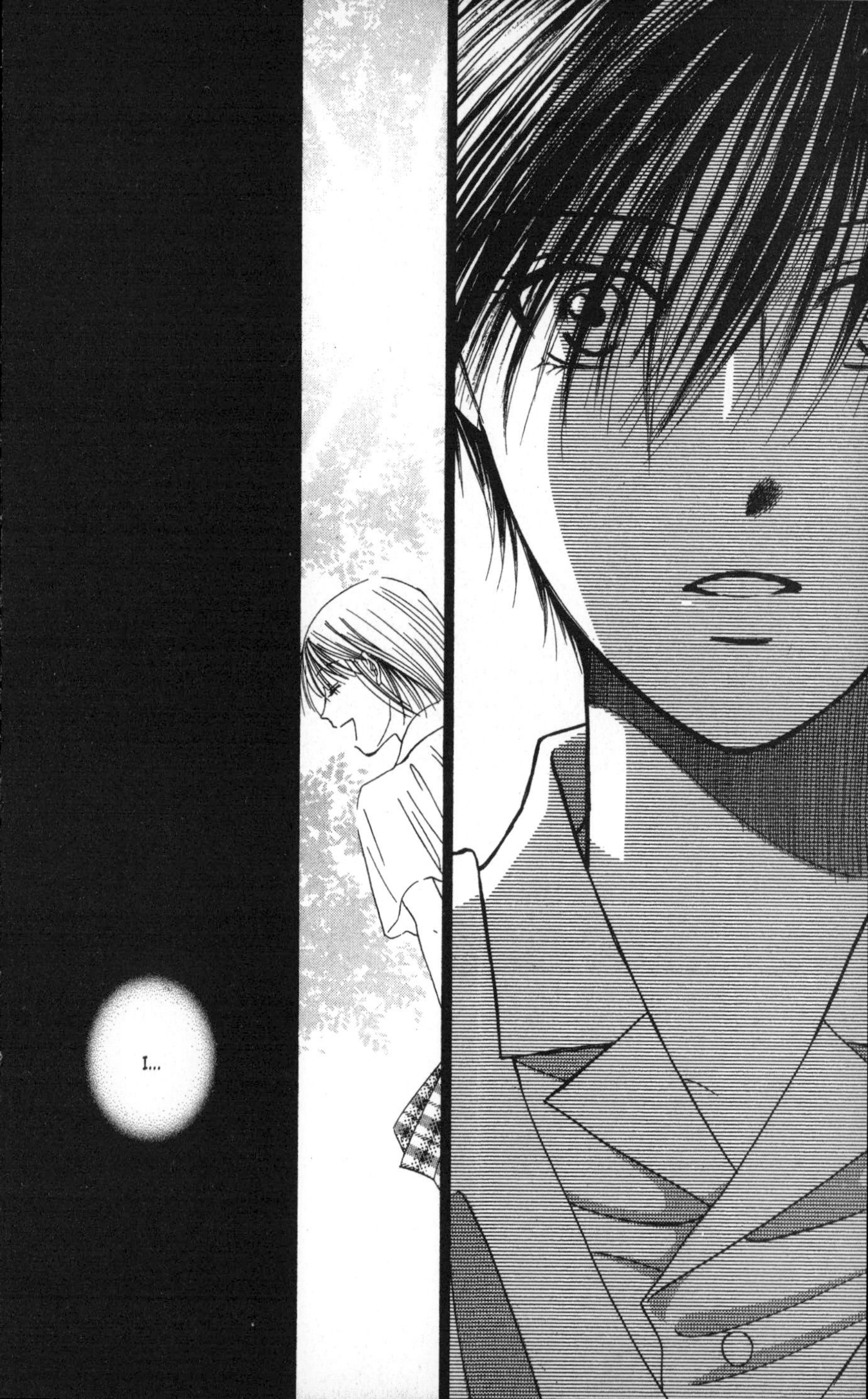
I...

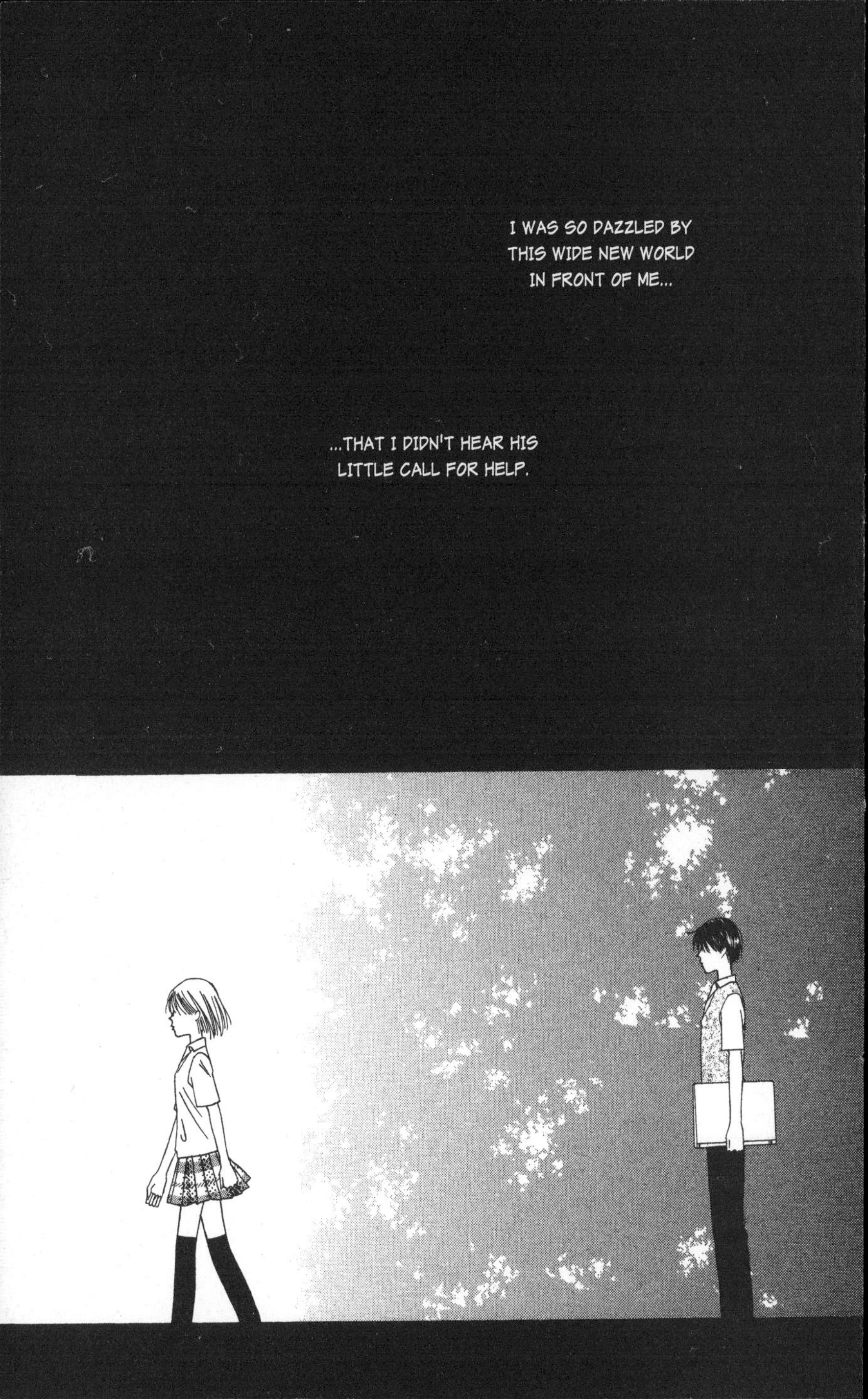
I WAS SO DAZZLED BY THIS WIDE NEW WORLD IN FRONT OF ME...
...THAT I DIDN'T HEAR HIS LITTLE CALL FOR HELP.

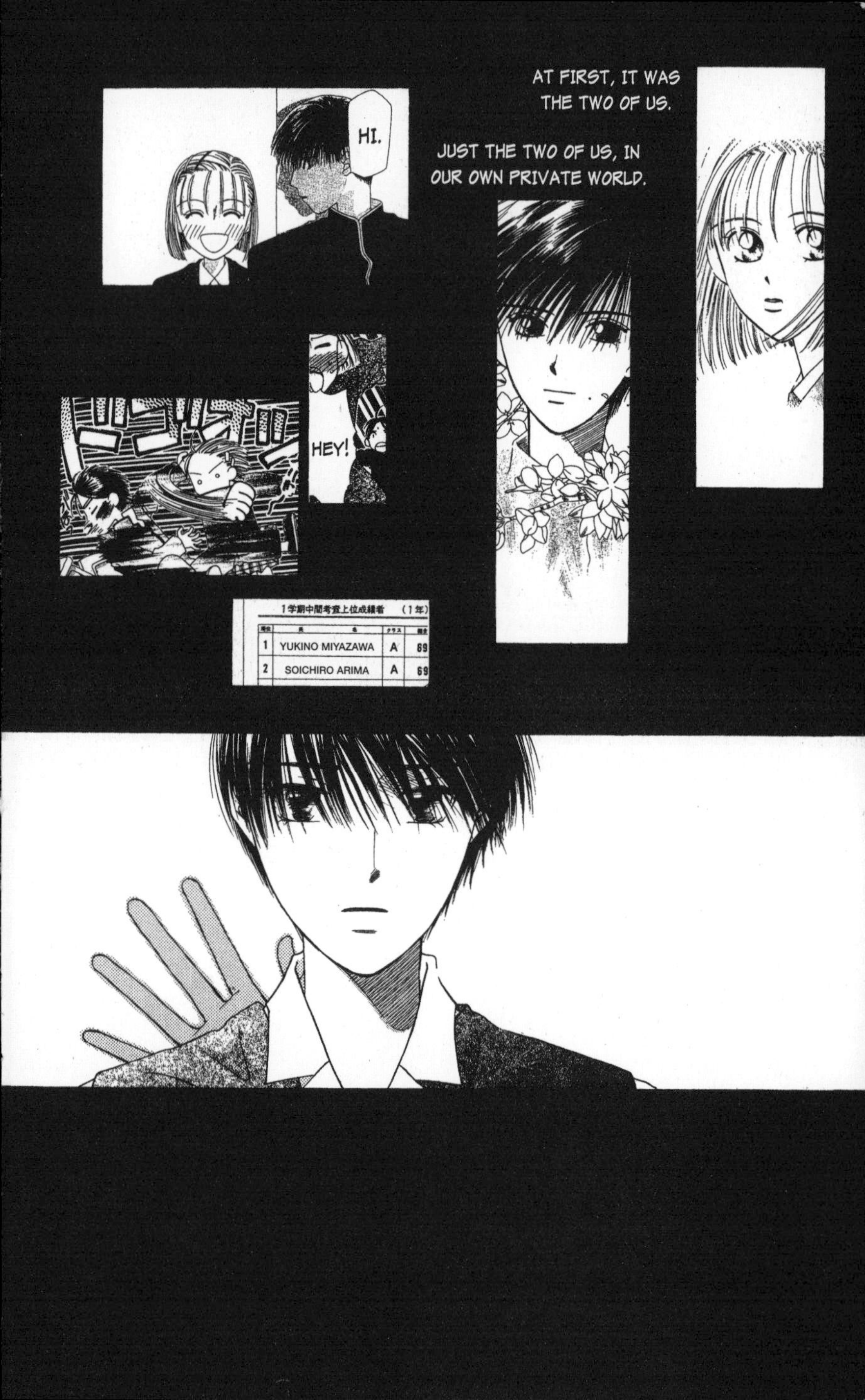
AT FIRST, IT WAS THE TWO OF US.
JUST THE TWO OF US, IN OUR OWN PRIVATE WORLD.
HI.
HEY!
1学期中間考査上位成績者 （1年）
1 YUKINO MIYAZAWA A 69
2 SOICHIRO ARIMA A 69

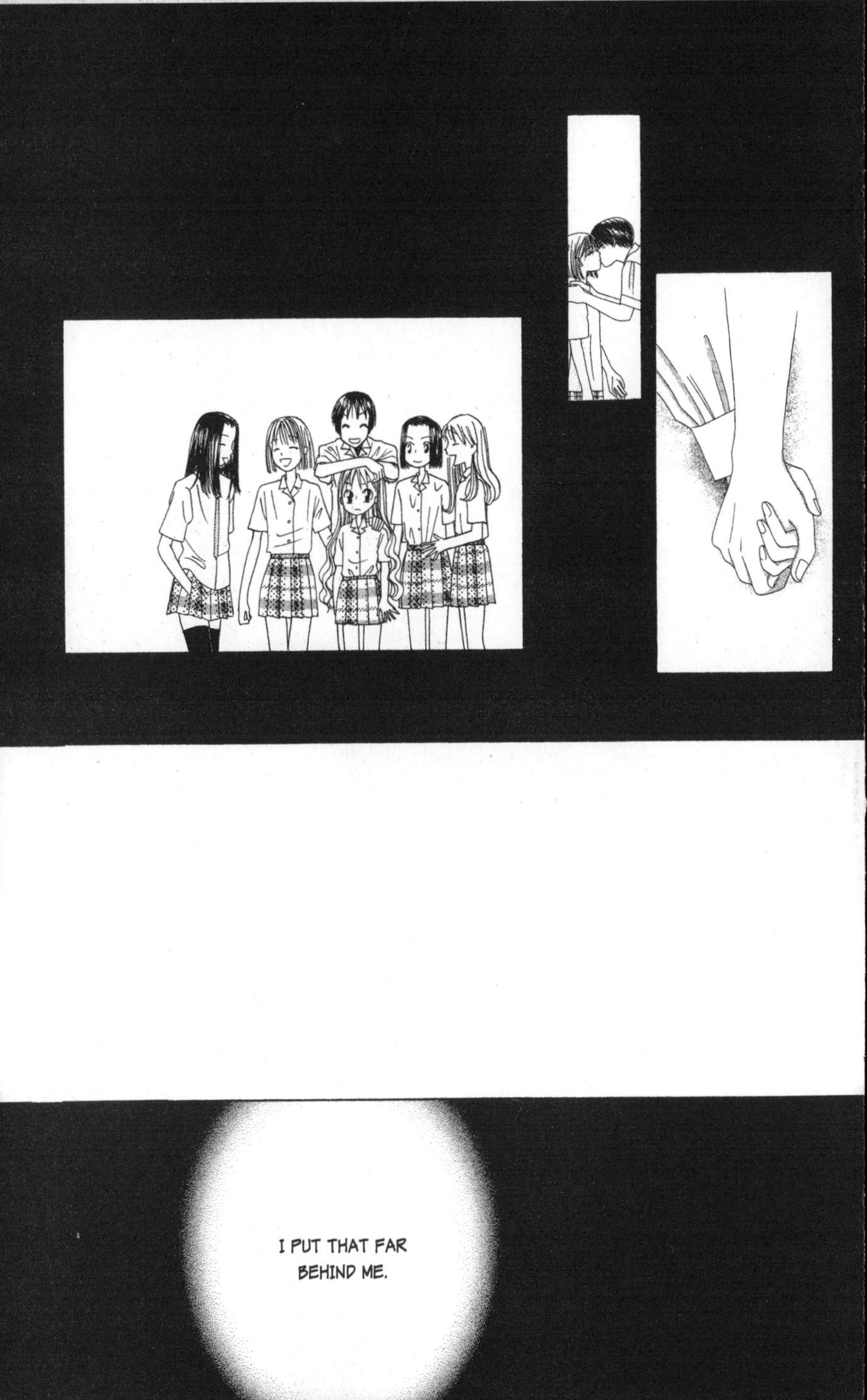
I PUT THAT FAR
BEHIND ME.

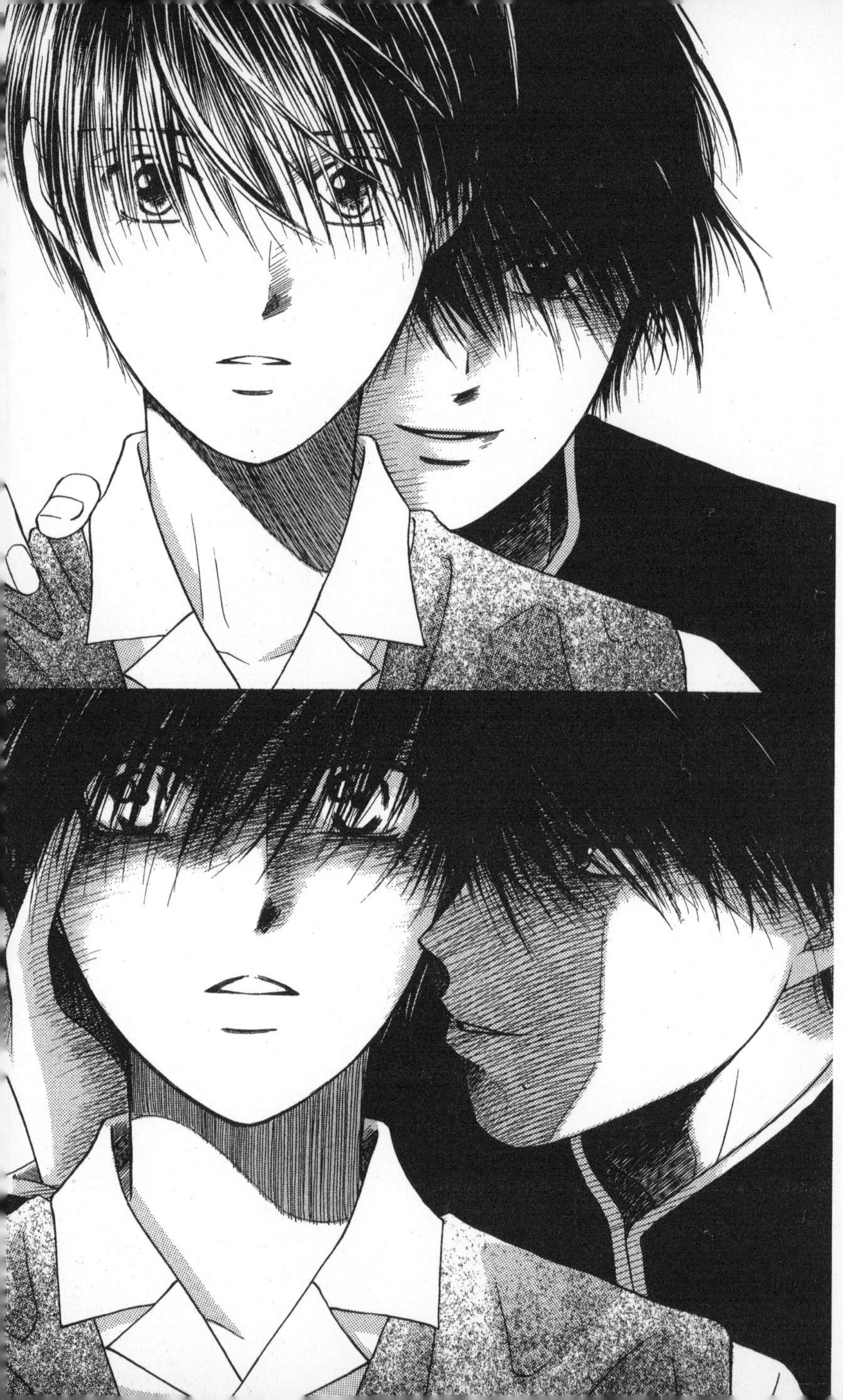

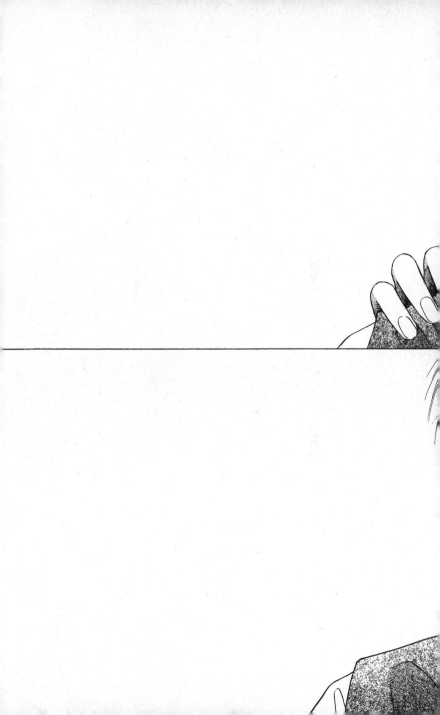

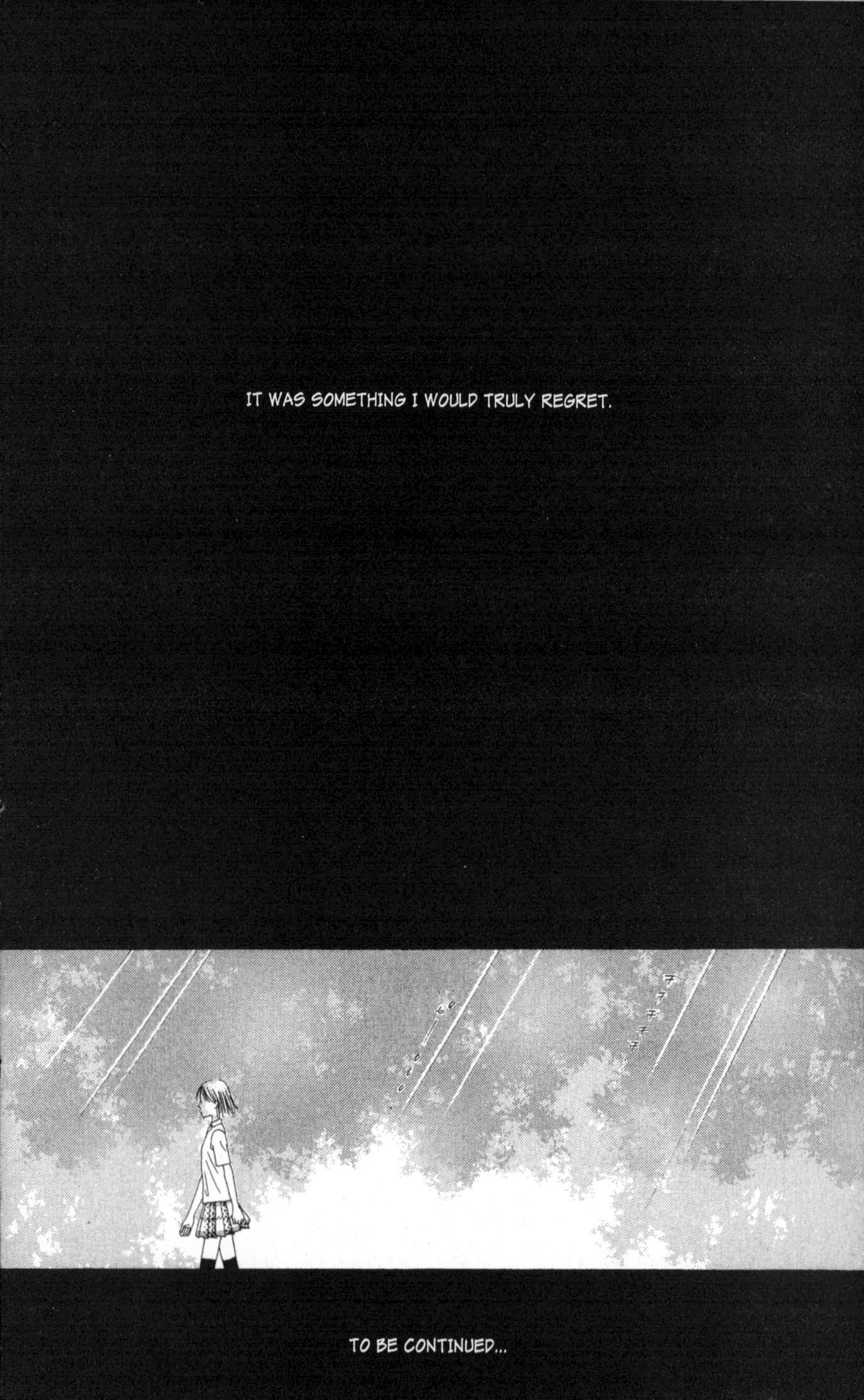
IT WAS SOMETHING I WOULD TRULY REGRET.
TO BE CONTINUED...

This is Kare Kano.

To me, this is a turning point.

The "Yukino Arc" has ended,

and next is the "Arima Arc."

Actually, I'm not even sure

this is going to be long or short...

But before then, I'm going to

include a few stories about the

other characters.

♡ Many Thanks ♡

Taneoka

Shimizu

Shibata

Ogawa

Ouchi

Kazumi

Research Assistance: Haga-sensei

(my former teacher)

coming soon

kare kano

his and her circumstances

volume ten

The onset of winter is approaching and the school semester is coming to a close. Sounds like the perfect opportunity to take advantage of the break with a trip to the beautiful city of Kyoto! But first Maho and Takashi need to have a little heart-to-heart talk. She comes clean about her feelings for him, but does she really know the true Takashi? And when poor Yukino comes down with a fever in the middle of the Kyoto trip, it's up to good 'ol Soichiro to get her back home. In her delirium, Yukino has the strangest dream—with a very familiar cast of characters...

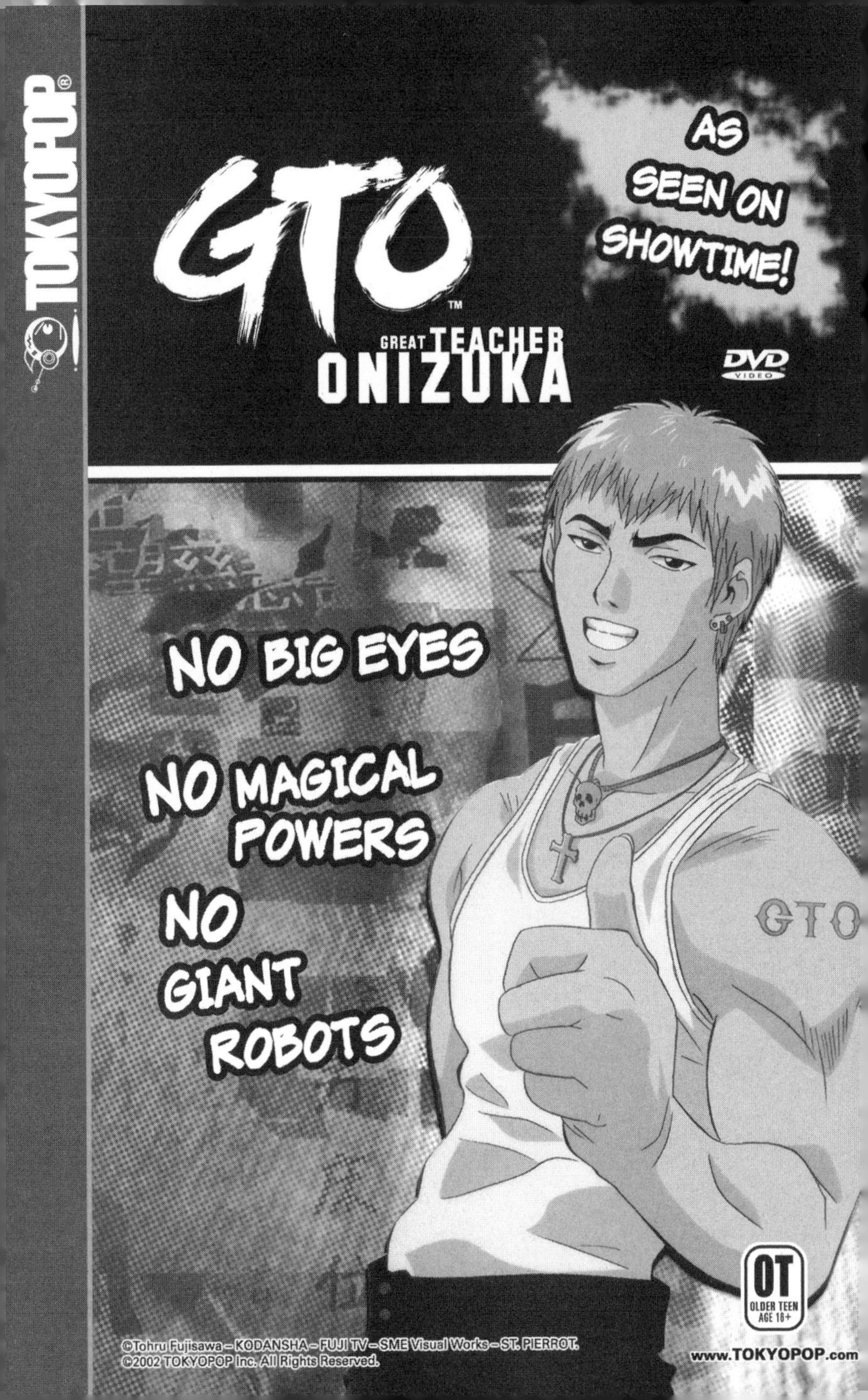
TOKYOPOP®
GTO™
GREAT TEACHER ONIZUKA
AS SEEN ON SHOWTIME!
DVD VIDEO
NO BIG EYES
NO MAGICAL POWERS
NO GIANT ROBOTS
GTO
OT OLDER TEEN AGE 16+
©Tohru Fujisawa – KODANSHA – FUJI TV – SME Visual Works – ST. PIERROT.
©2002 TOKYOPOP Inc. All Rights Reserved.
www.TOKYOPOP.com

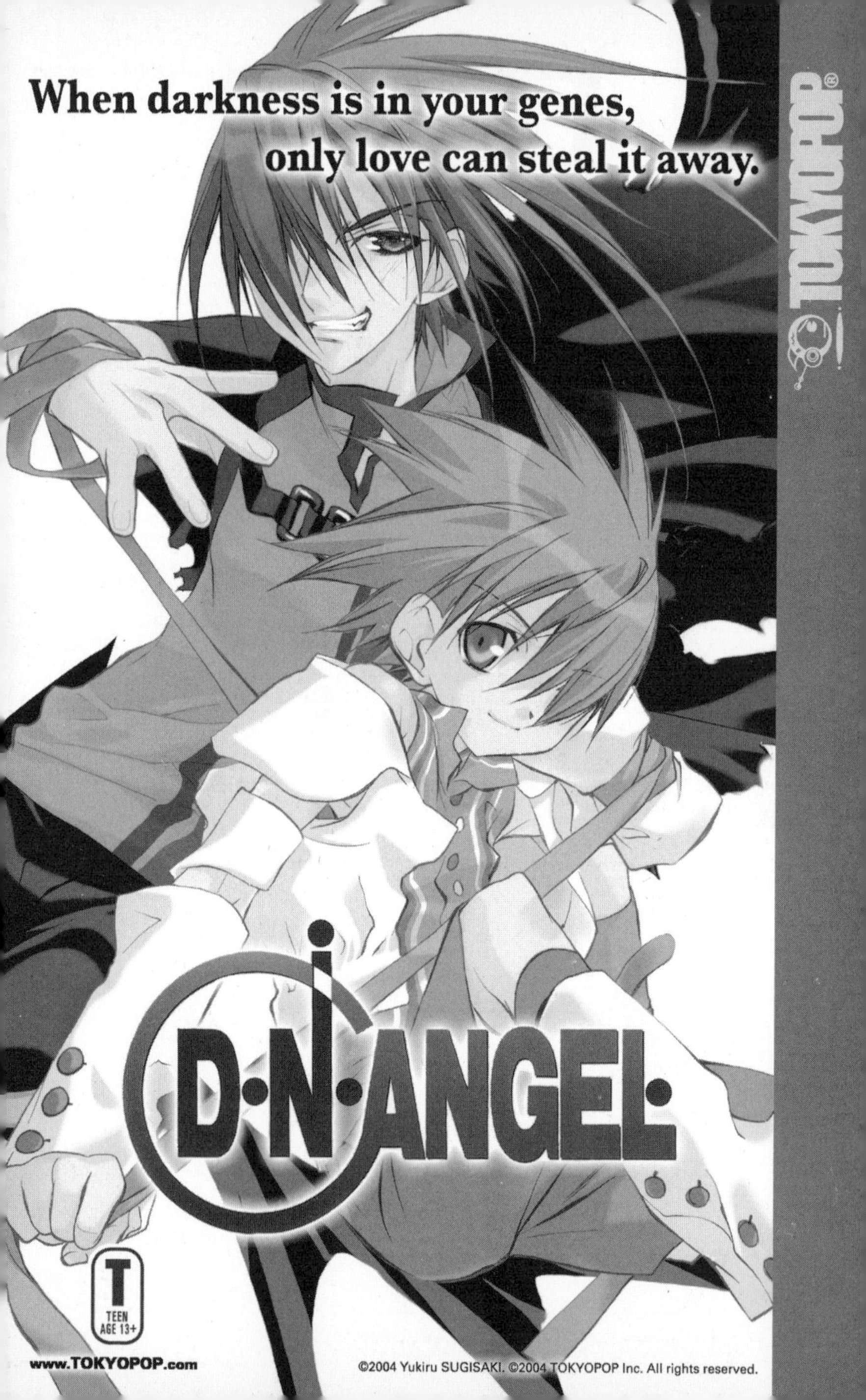
When darkness is in your genes,
only love can steal it away.
TOKYOPOP
D·N·ANGEL
T
TEEN
AGE 13+
www.TOKYOPOP.com
©2004 Yukiru SUGISAKI. ©2004 TOKYOPOP Inc. All rights reserved.

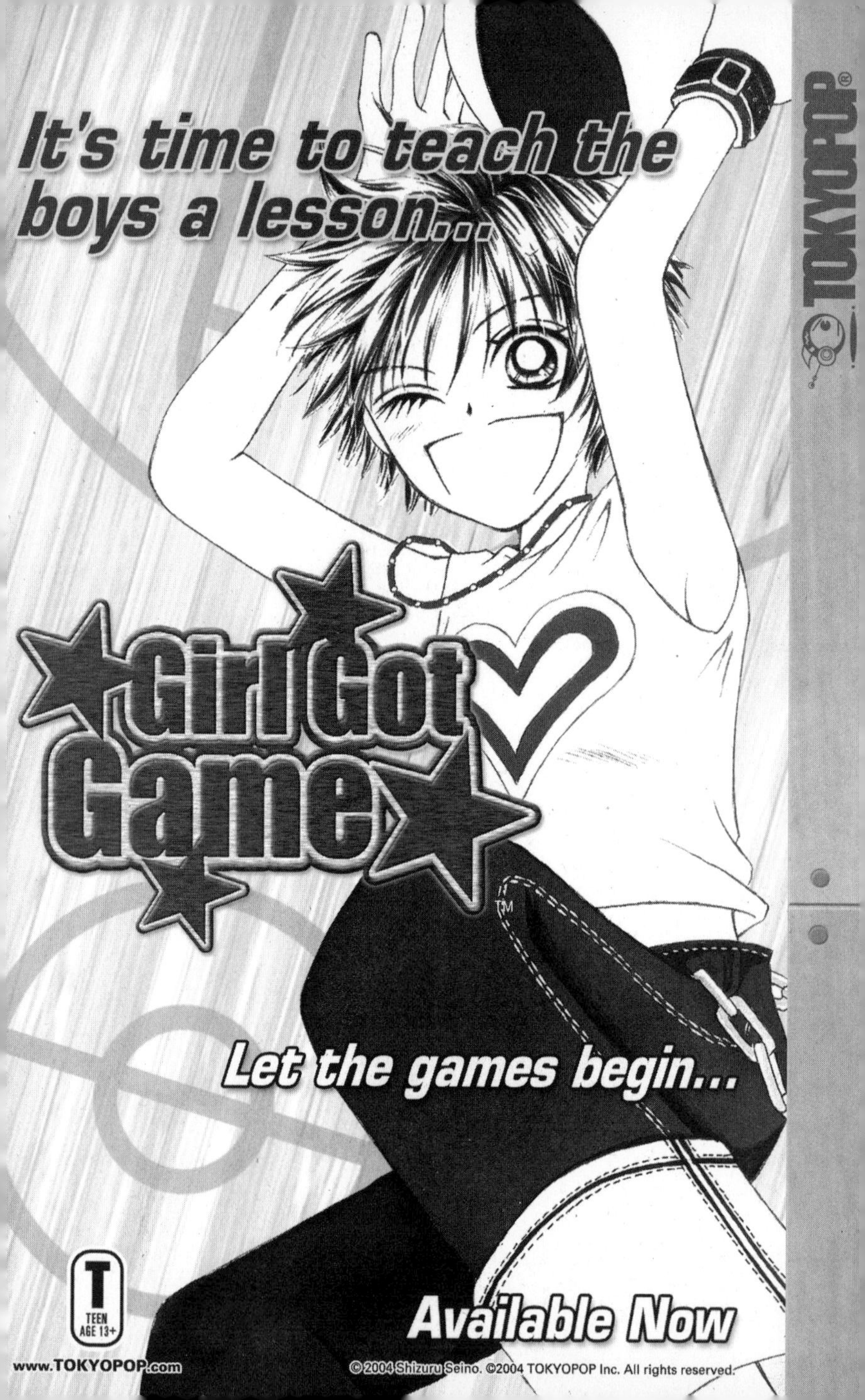
It's time to teach the boys a lesson...
TOKYOPOP®
Girl Got Game™
Let the games begin...
T TEEN AGE 13+
Available Now
www.TOKYOPOP.com
© 2004 Shizuru Seino. ©2004 TOKYOPOP Inc. All rights reserved.